the secrets of house music production

a reference manual from sample magic

credits

Written by Marc Adamo
Vocal chapter and additional content by David Felton
Interviews by Sharooz Raoofi
Edited by David Felton
Design concept and illustrations by Simon Marlow at KASH, www.kashcreative.com
Bonus CD artwork by Joseph Barker
Print by Newnorth Print Ltd, UK

Published by Sample Magic
145–157 St John Street
London, EC1V 4PA
www.samplemagic.com

First published in the UK December 2009.
Second Edition (revised) May 2010.
Third Edition (revised) April 2011.

ISBN: 978-0-9564460-0-8

Acknowledgements
The editor would like to acknowledge the content suppled by Mark Knight, Wolfgang Gartner, Sharooz, Way Out West and The Young Punx.

Printing
Sample Magic care about the world we live in. This book is printed on FSC-certified paper, using paper sourced from sustainably managed forests.

contents

Part 1 DRUMS 8
Kick drum 10
Snares and claps 14
Hi-hats 18
Cymbals and percussion 21
Synthetic percussion 22
Drum programming 24
Groove tricks 26
Drum programming grids 28
Pro tips: Wolfgang Gartner 30

Part 2 BASS 32
The bassics 34
Bass in the mix 36
The sub 38
Bassline programming grids 40
Pro tips: The Young Punx 46

Part 3 VOCALS 48
What kind of vocal? 50
The vocal session 52
Editing the vocals 56
Melodyne and beyond 59
Vocal production 62
Vocal FX 67
Pro tips: Way Out West 72

Part 4 THE MUSIC 74
Synth anatomy 76
Sounds: Classic piano and stabs 78
Sounds: Fat leads and arps 80
Sounds: Pads 82
Sounds: Soulful Rhodes 84
Working with loops 86
Rex, Apple Loops and more 88
FX 92

Part 5 STRUCTURE 98
Structure 100
Anatomy of a track: Electro-house 102
Anatomy of a track: Minimal & tech-house 104
Anatomy of a track: Vocal-led house 106

Part 6 EFFECTS 108
In detail: studio effects 110

Part 7 THE MIX 120
Mixing 122
Picture the mix diagram 125
Walkthrough: A mix in 32 stages 128
Mastering 132
Remixing 136

Part 8 OUTRO 138
Pro tips: Sharooz: A word on the money 140
Index 142

/welcome...

This book is about the techniques of dance music production. As far as we know it is the first of its kind dedicated purely to house music.

House producers learn their skills in a variety of ways: they watch producer friends and read blog posts; they adopt other production styles and use engineering guesswork guided by endless trial and error.

This book is written for the next generation of producers who want to hit the ground running armed with the essential techniques and skills it takes to produce cutting-edge dance music.

The tutorials cover Logic, Live, Cubase and Reason. But the techniques outlined are universal. It doesn't matter what kit you have: a banging kick drum is a banging kick drum however it was made, and the essential lessons in the tutorials remain the same, regardless of the soft and hardware you have at your disposal.

The truth is that classic house tracks are produced every day on cheap gear in bedroom setups – it's not just professionally trained engineers in expensive studios stacked with high-end equipment that are hitting the big time.

This book can be read from cover to cover or dipped into whenever you need specific guidance or inspiration. Use the index to quickly find what you're after.

Enjoy it. And never forget to bring the music back to the place where it all started: the dancefloor.

Marc Adamo

/all about house...

My introduction to dance music production was a baptism of fire. I shared my first studio with Dave Lee (Joey Negro) and I learned a vast amount of my production knowledge from Dave's then studio engineer Kevin Brooks. If I wasn't in the studio I would sit and watch him at work, learning everything from how to record brass sections to how to balance and comp backing vocals.

This was watching a producer in the true sense of the word – producer as project manager, who knew how to bring all the fundamental elements of a track together into a single unified whole.

Although I've diversified my sound through the years, moving through a wealth of sub-genres to stay ahead of the curve, the production values and techniques I learned back then – on kit far simpler than today's – have stayed the same.

Throughout my time in the industry the one thing that's never changed has been the thirst for house music. I started Toolroom Records with my brother Stuart back in 2004 in a tool shed outside my parents' house (hence the name). Initially it was just a label to release my own tracks. Six years on, and with a catalogue that spans over 150 releases, we are now a global brand and home to the biggest artists in dance.

Even with the demise of physical product and the massive problems we face with piracy, dance music has never been in such a great place. New producers hit the scene, new genres spill into the mainstream and, above all, great records continue to be made.

It's these records that are the future of the industry. Keep making them.

Mark Knight

/part one

drums

The beat is what puts the dance in dance music.

A solid rhythm is the most crucial element of a house track. It provides a foundation on which the rest of the mix is built and can take on a momentum all its own, whipping a dancefloor into whoops of ecstasy as each new, carefully honed sound emerges into the mix.

It starts with the kick: the solid punch of a 909, the subbed-out thump of an 808 or a tight snap from a disco kit.

Once the kick is rolling the groove builds above it. Shuffling hats, a dirty tom loop, crisp high-end claps: whatever it is, each new element should complement and support what's gone before in terms of how it works both rhythmically and as part of the overall sound.

A marriage of tone and rhythm: that's what the best beats are about.

Get the drums right and the rest will follow.

/the kick drum

in house, the kick is king. how do you get it right?

In terms of defining characteristics, in house music the kick drum is king. It is the single most important part of the rhythm section, on which everything else is built. Get the kick right and the rest will follow. Get it wrong and your track stands little chance of being played in a club, let alone being bought by discerning DJs.

With thousands of kicks to choose from, what are the factors you need to consider when choosing – or building – your kick?

Depth, length and vibe

The depth and length of a kick should be directly related to the bassline, as the pair work hand-in-hand to power the track. They also overlap in their respective frequencies, so it's vital that they produce the maximum amount of energy together and not fight for space.

They say opposites attract, and that's definitely true when mixing kick and bass. Picture the two as you choose them, thinking about where each sits in the frequency spectrum. If they sit in the same sonic place they will rub against each other uncomfortably. Neither will shine and you'll struggle to make them gel. As a general rule, a higher, short kick (a classic disco kick) will work well with a booming, deep bassline, while a higher bassline will sit nicely alongside a longer, deep kick drum (like the Roland TR-808 kick). As the relationship between the two will probably alter during the mixing process, be prepared to make minor adjustments to each as you go to ensure that they continue to work well together.

Tip / If you use a kick from a drum machine / sampler you can easily tune it to the key of the track and adjust the amp envelope to get the right length.

Getting the right sound

Each house sub-genre makes use of kicks with distinct character traits. Because of various seminal recordings certain types of kick have become associated with different styles. Selecting the kind of kick popular in the genre you're producing in is a good starting point when writing as it sets a basic vibe that can help focus subsequent production decisions.

Classic / funky / deep house

Classic, deep and funky house producers use 909-style kicks that are often layered with samples from disco tracks. This pairing gives the beat the best of both worlds – the power of the 909 and the live party vibe of a disco beat. If you get the disco kick from an old record then you'll end up with layered hi-hats in the mix, along with some vinyl-infused vintage reverb. This all adds top-end clarity and spatiality to the kick, helping it cut through the mix.

Electro and jackin' house

The kinds of kicks used in electro tracks vary. Some take inspiration from the 80s, with chunky E-mu Drumulator or LinnDrum-style kicks laced with sub reinforcement to power the low end. Others take a more minimal-tech tip, using analogue 808-style kicks topped with a disco or electronic high-hat for definition. A third variant – that has found fans in the nu-rave and nu-disco arena – is to use rough and ready live kick samples from funk or even rock records. Tracks from the 70s and 80s offer a wealth of possibilities. The emphasis throughout is on the slightly dirty warmth that only vinyl gives. Whatever direction you choose, there are plenty of excellent samples to choose from.

Minimal house

Minimal is all about simplicity and producers tend to lean towards analogue and synthetic generated kicks. The quintessential minimal kick is based on the Roland TR-808 bass drum, but thanks to the flexibility of software such as Logic's Ultrabeat and Waldorf's Attack drum synthesiser, you can create more interesting variations than the 808 ever could (see **Creating an analogue kick**, right).

Progressive / tech-house

Prog and tech-house producers make use of a range of kicks, including 909 styles as well as analogue variants and kicks from more esoteric drum machines.

The closer prog house gets to trance, the more reliance there is on the 909 which, more than 20 years on, remains the quintessential trance drum machine.

/overview
tricks for kicks

1 A club track fails or succeeds on the basis of its low-end energy. The two inhabitants of this area of the frequency spectrum are the kick drum and bassline.

2 The key to a great dance track is getting these two elements to work together. A booming sub-bass kick will clash with a similarly subby bassline.

3 The classic Roland TR-909 kick drum is a great place to start. It has enjoyed so central a place in house music precisely because it works so well in dance tracks.

/walkthrough

creating an analogue kick in ultrabeat

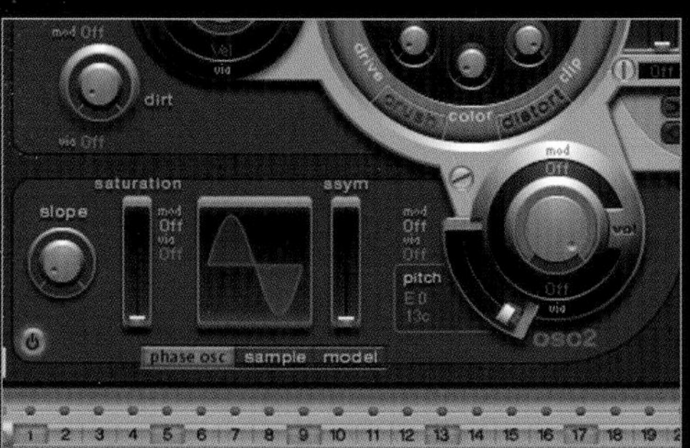

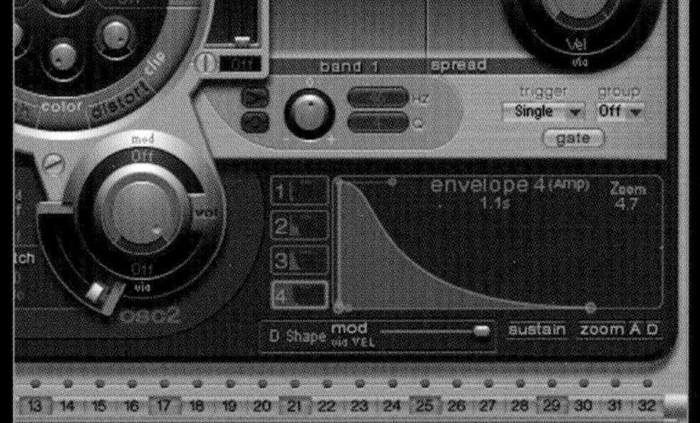

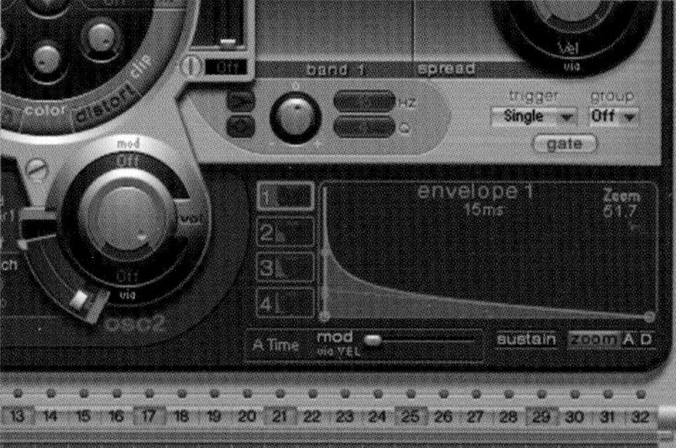

1 Select a standard sine wave and tune it to the root or key note of the track. If you're not sure of the key use a standard one like A, G, E or C to start with. You can easily re-tune the kick later. A sine wave is ideal because it is the cleanest, most neutral tone, producing a lot of power without additional harmonics.

2 Edit the amp envelopes. Set the attack to 0 to give the kick a nice punch. Set decay to medium for a smooth downwards slope. Set sustain to 30% and release to about the same so the sound doesn't cut off too abruptly. Drum machines like Ultrabeat usually trigger the whole envelope, regardless of the length of the Midi note.

3 Assign an envelope to modulate the pitch. This will allow you to bend the pitch of the sine wave so that it sweeps from high to low. Increase the modulation depth so the pitch sweeps down quickly. The envelope can be varied around this basic shape to produce many usable kicks. A curvaceous envelope usually produces the most musical results.

4 Use the modulation envelope to shape the pitch of the kick so that it sounds like an 808. Set attack to minimum and decay between 10–35%: the ideal setting will depend on the shape of the envelope curves. To reduce the amount of click at the start increase the amp envelope attack parameter.

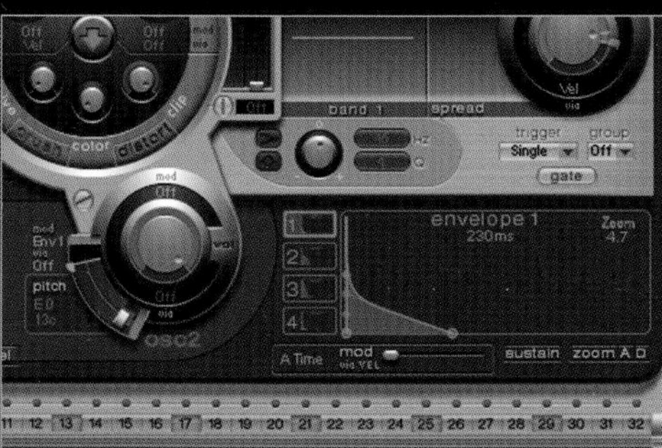

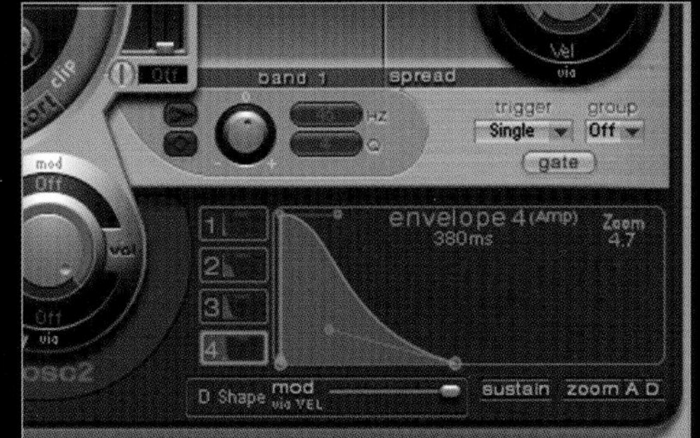

5 It only takes a little adjustment to change the kick from a smooth 808 to a thumping 909. The secret is in the shape of the decay hump. Take the decay time and extend it. Small changes here make a big difference. Make the hump a bit more linear, like in the grab above, to get more 'knock' from the kick.

6 For the final touch, adjust the amp envelope decay to get the right note length. If the attack sounds too harsh, increase it a little to soften it. To make the sweep stronger increase the modulation depth. To make it more subtle decrease it. Experiment for a range of different kicks.

7 For more definition and tone at the start of the kick introduce another oscillator. Use a square wave because it has lots of harmonic tone and tune it to either the same note as the sine or a 5th above. This will supply additional bite and tone.

8 This second oscillator only needs to sound at the start, so set the attack envelope to 0 and the decay to drop away fast. Sustain and release should be 0 too. This will give a little blip at the start of the sound. Mix this blip kick with the deeper kick to taste. Finally, layer up a hi-hat for additional bite and presence.

Dynamite compression

The compressor comes into play when it's time to work the kick into the mix. Compression changes the punch and clarity of a kick by affecting its volume level and transients. Compression allows you to tighten the kick and increase its perceived loudness so that it sounds bigger on a club system.

It is good practice to insert the compressor after any EQ. This combination means only the desired frequencies are compressed, rather than frequencies you'd rather cut.

The ratio and threshold controls of a compressor determine how strong the effect will be and the amount of signal processed, while the attack and release settings decide how fast the compressor reacts, influencing the shape of the resulting sound.

When using a compressor make gradual adjustments and listen to the changes by bypassing the compressor and comparing the original and processed sounds. It's worth auditioning changes at both low and high volumes as they are some of the most important decisions you'll make during the production of a track.

Fast attack / medium release

This will tame the transients, reducing the clicky part at the start of the waveform and reducing its relative volume. Good for smoother kicks in deep and minimal styles.

Medium attack and release

Medium settings retain a kick's initial punch by letting the first part of the sound go through before reacting to it. The compressor will also suck in the kick's body, making it tighter and thicker. This setting is good for sorting out a baggy kick and is useful for electro styles.

Signs of excess

If the attack is too fast you will end up flattening a kick and removing all of its bite / click. Equally, if the release is too fast you risk turning a firm kick into a muddy bass mess.

Transient shaper

Plugins of choice:
SPL Transient Designer, Logic Enveloper, Sonnox Transient Modulator

The transient shaper does exactly what it says on the tin – shaping a sound's transients – offering a powerful means of changing a sample's attack and release values in a similar way to a synth's amp envelope.

A good time to use a shaper is when your kick needs a little more definition to cut through the mix but you don't want to boost the volume in case the overall kick gets too loud. In this situation add the shaper after the compressor and increase the gain of the attack to provide a little spike at the start of the kick. Then adjust the time parameter to determine how long the boost should last. If a kick has too much bite at its start you can reduce it by lowering the attack gain.

Be careful when using a transient shaper as it can quickly ruin a decent original sound. Subtle changes are what you're after, and in general it is best to view it as a problem solver, to be used only when needed.

EQ

The kick drum can be split into three distinct frequency areas, each of which may need your attention. It's a good idea to think about your kick in this way as it will help you make quick decisions on how it's working in the mix and where to cut and boost frequencies.

The **high end** provides a kick's detail and clarity. The zone ranges from around 1–18kHz. For extra edge and bite boost around 2–4kHz and for extra clarity in the high-hat zone boost above 4kHz. Use a wide parametric Q for gentle results. If you need a more mellow kick, roll off higher frequencies with a shelving EQ.

The **mid-range** contains the knock, thump and banging qualities of a kick. These sit in the 120Hz–1kHz zone. If a kick needs to cut though the mix, add mid-range knock by boosting between 200–800Hz. To identify the best point, boost using a medium parametric Q and sweep up and down until you find a frequency that pushes the kick through the mix. When you find it ease back on the boost. Don't overdo it: 3dB worth of gain is usually more than enough and it can become fatiguing to hear an overcooked kick at high volumes. Also consider the relationship between kick and bass. The bassline needs to share some of the kick's mid-range space, so you may need to reduce a few dBs in the bass at around 200Hz–400Hz to reduce overlap.

The **low end** contains the power and depth of the kick. It's the frequency range that needs the most care: definition here will make waves on big club speakers. The EQ range here runs from around 20–120Hz. For added weight and warmth boost a couple of dBs in the 60–80hz region. Be wary of boosting lower than this – not only will you need a good set of monitors and listening environment, but it is often unnecessary: the truth is that most of the bass action happens in the 50–90Hz zone. Finally, if you know the pitch of the kick you can use a note-to-frequency chart (**page 127**) to boost its fundamental frequency. A

/flashback
the mighty 909

The early house music pioneers of Detroit were looking for synthetic sounding drum sounds to complement their futuristic electronic music and the Roland TR-909 fitted the bill perfectly. It was wholly unrealistic but packed a massive punch in club settings. Part of the reason the 909 kick works so well is its combination of low-frequency energy and mid-frequency noise. This enables it to fill out the low end without clashing with the bassline, giving each its own space in the mix.

kick tuned to E2 resonates around 82.41Hz. A gentle notch boost here (with a simultaneous cut in the bassline) can sound nice, bringing additional resonant bite to the kick.

Tip / If you have small speakers and/or your acoustics are not ideal, use a frequency analyser to see the spectrum content of a kick. This can reveal aspects of the sound that your speakers might not, or that your acoustics colour, especially in the bass and sub-bass regions.

Tip / As a rule keep a high-pass EQ set to 25hz/30hz on the kick track to roll off unnecessary sub energy that will unnecessarily consume headroom. Depending on the character of the bassline you may need to roll away slightly higher to make more space for the bass.

Tip / On-beat hats bring clarity to a dull kick. Layer subtly for additional definition.

Tip / Some kick samples have nice hats mixed into them, but dodgy bass ends. Use a high-pass filter to take out the bass end and layer the remaining hat with a different kick that has a solid bottom.

Layered kicks

If you can't find the right kick for a track then do what the pros do and layer up two or three to create a new hybrid. The aim here is to use bass drum samples that gel well together when combined.

Producers approach drum layering in one of two ways. Either they take an **EQ-based approach**, looking for one kick to supply the low-end, one the lower-mid knock and one the upper-mid crack. Or they take a **transient-based approach**, combining one kick that has a biting attack with a second featuring a solid decay. Play to each kick drum's strength and use EQ to remove overlapping frequencies (you only want one sound providing the lowest frequencies, so roll the lows off the others). Feed all kicks to the same bus so that the resulting single kick can be compressed as a unified whole. (Or better, bounce down the new kick and use that, adding it to your sample pool at the same time.)

Tip / When layering kicks, is the resulting one quieter than the original? If so, chances are there is some degree of phase cancellation going on. This can arise when similar waveforms cycle at 180 degrees to each other. In some situations it can be corrected by reversing the phase of one of the samples. Alternatively, try altering the tuning of one of the kicks or moving its sample start point forwards or backwards by a few ms.

/beware
tuning clashes

Kick drums – like bongos and congas – are tuned instruments, and you should ensure that the kick and bassline are tuned so that they complement each other (do this in your sampler by changing the semitone and, if necessary, the fine tuning dials). The low-end will sound wrong if the kick drum is tuned to a note that clashes with the bassline. If you find this is a problem then try changing the pitch of the kick drum, and if this is still a problem, changing the kick drum sample itself. Ultimately, let your ears be the guide.

/walkthrough
layered kicks in battery

1 Load up two kick drum samples – one deep, one tight and bright – into separate cells of Battery and switch on the amplifier envelopes. Draw in a regular four-to-the-floor kick pattern ensuring the Midi note length is long enough to trigger the full samples. Adjust the relative volumes of each to get the best qualities from both.

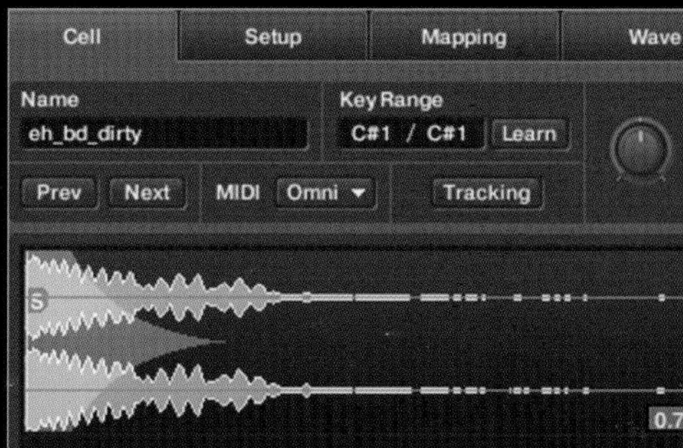

2 Adjust the amp envelope of the top, bright kick sample. We only want the first part of it, so set attack to 0 (immediate) and the decay to tight. The rest of this higher kick is unimportant so set sustain/release to 0. If the sampler has AHD envelopes, take full advantage of the hold stage for maximum shaping options.

3 The next parameter to change is the tuning / pitch of each sample. Higher tunings give a tighter, brighter sound, while lower tunings add more biting frequencies in the mid-range. Both kicks will need to be tuned independently to ensure that they work together. See **Tuning clashes**, left.

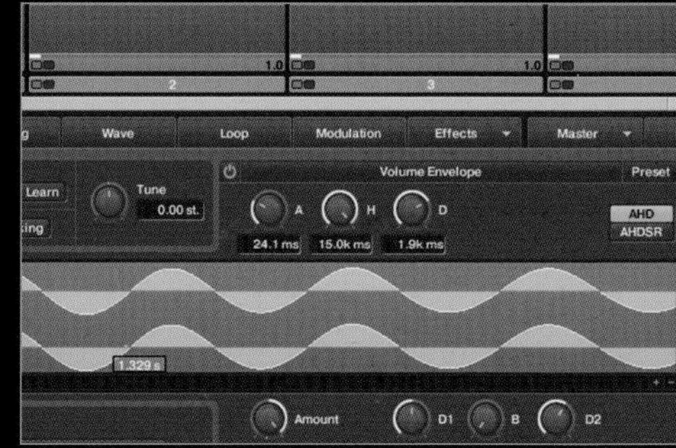

4 Now turn your attention to the decay of the lower kick. Balance mix functionality with getting a sound you like. Quick decay settings add definition, while longer decay settings allow more of the 'knock' to cut through. You may need to make a last adjustment to the attack of the deeper kick to smooth it out a little.

/snares and claps

the second weapon in the beat armoury is a snappy companion to the kick.

After the kick, the next element in a house groove is the snare drum. Its main function is to provide a counterpoint to the steady pound of the kick, typically sounding on the second and fourth beats of the bar. It's not essential for a house track to have a snare: a clap is occasionally used instead. What follows applies to both.

The snare sits in the mid-range of the frequency spectrum. It is commonly blended with other percussive sounds, including claps, sticks, clicks, hi-hats and other percussion to create the requisite snap, crackle and pop.

Many snare sounds in house are derived from drum machines and synthesisers, which are then processed with effects including distortion, compression, bit-crusher and reverb. Sampled acoustic snares are often layered with them for added character.

Sonically, synthesised snares have two tonal elements. The first is a sharp attack transient that contains high and mid-range frequencies usually made from white or pink noise. The second, which forms the body of the sound, is a low-pitched sine or triangle wave with a recognisable pitch and a longer sustain. This can be doubled with another oscillator an octave or so above for a more complex body knock.

This combined noise / sine oscillator model was used to create the snare sounds on analogue drum machines including the Roland TR-808 (thwat) and TR-909 (cluck).

Choosing the right sound

Thanks to the diversity of influences permeating house music there's no right or wrong choice for the raw snare sound.

Classic choices include drum machines, especially the snappy 909 and deep-tuned LinnDrum. The latter is a favourite with electro-house producers looking to add a wonky layer of synthetic bite to the mix.

Bassline, electro and nu-rave producers look to old rave records and classic hip-hop breaks for snare samples. These are fed through overdrive units, bit-crushers and compressors for added grit and filth.

Funky, deep, tribal and Latin house tracks feature more organic snares and claps from disco and rare-groove records, or targeted sample collections. Such samples often feature hi-hats, which add to their character.

Newer choices, in minimal and progressive house, include tight DSP-derived sounds and white-noise generated hits.

/overview
who snares wins

1 The snare supplies the rhythm section's snap, crackle and pop. Choose one that complements the kick.

2 Drum machines provide solid sample choices, but layer them with other samples for bigger, more unique sounds.

3 Snares are ripe for all kinds of processing treatments, from compression to bit-crushing. Delay layered samples for great stereo sounds.

4 In progressive and minimal styles snares are often mixed so low that they become almost inaudible – their role simply to supply a little extra bite to kicks two and four.

Snares are frequently layered for a thicker sound. The timing between hits can be loosened by triggering each layer a little before or after the beat. This gives the groove a more relaxed feel (**see page 17**).

Sometimes clap samples come with lead-in noise to give them a sucking quality. Don't cut this noise: just trigger the sample a little before the main hit so that the noise anticipates the snare like in the funk records of old.

As with kicks, the secret to a successful layered snare is choosing sounds that complement each other rather than fight. An example of a successful combo might be a fat LinnDrum snare filling out the bottom end, a live disco hit with low-end removed supplying the highs, and a stereo clap that anticipates the beat to add a sheen of mid-range polish and depth.

Tip / If your sampler offers a loop stage, like Battery, it can be used to add extra crack to a clap. The impact stage of a clap features a series of impulses before the main body of sound hits. Set the sampler loop points around the impact portion and restrict the count to around three cycles. If there is a loop tuning parameter, experiment with this too.

Compression for snares

A compressor can be applied to snares in two key ways. Turn a wimpy snare into a fat, chunky beast by using a medium attack (between 5 and 20ms) and a fast release. This retains the snare's initial snap and thickens its body. If a snare is too clicky and you want a softer, deeper sound, smash the life out the transients by using a fast (0ms) attack.

When combining claps and snares, even them out by grouping them and sending

Increasing snare width

Figure 1: Take two identical snare drum samples and pan them hard left and hard right. Insert an EQ on each. Choose one frequency on the left snare and boost it by a couple of dBs. Select a different frequency on the right and cut it by the same number of dBs. Aim for a mid to high range frequency for a subtle effect. Somewhere in the 400Hz–2kHz range is a good starting point.

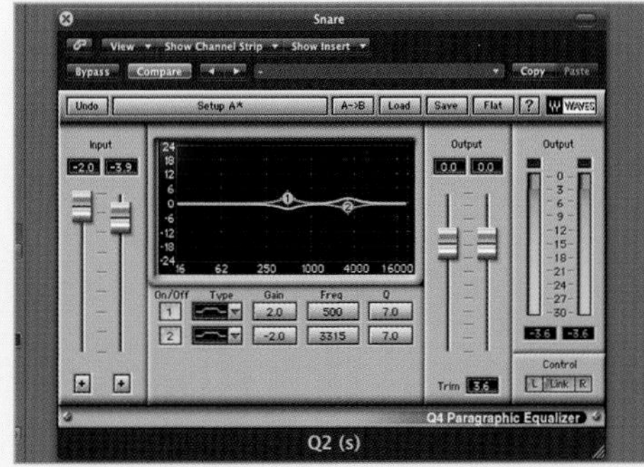

Figure 2: The difference in the EQ curve on each channel expands the stereo width of the sound. When you find the desired width bounce it to a new stereo audio file. Some stereo EQs such as Waves Parametric offer independent control of the left and right channels. This allows you to achieve the same stereo feel from one audio file. Adjust the input and output gains to avoid clipping.

Figure 3: Here's a second way to increase width that introduces tiny amounts of delay between the left and right channels to radically increase stereo separation in a mix. Choose two snare or clap samples and layer them together. Route each to its own mixer channel and insert a stereo sample delay plugin on each. On the first channel set left delay to 0 clicks, ms or samples and right to 1,000. Do the opposite on the second sample, with left delay at 1,000 and right to 0. The settings will mean both samples hit the centre at the same time, while reaching the left and right sides a fraction later. Lowering the sample delay time brings everything towards the centre of the stereo image. Increasing it spreads everything wider.

them to the same bus, where compression can be applied to the group to even out variations in volume. Use a medium to fast attack (5–20ms) and slower release (100ms) to preserve the transient-to-sustain ratio.

Snares and reverbs

Turn a weak snare into a thunderous crack by sending it to a big hall reverb. On the other hand, If you're looking to increase the width and depth of a snare to help it gel in the mix use a shorter hall or a room setting; start with 1s decay and 10% mix.

Tip / To add width and a sense of space without compromising the up-front quality of a snare, choose a reverb that has parameters for **early reflections (see page 114)**. Bypass the tail part of the effect and just use the early reflections. Sometimes this is all that's needed to add sparkle to a flat sound.

Tip / A huge chamber / hall reverb with a long modulating decay can be used for impact FX hits. The Black Hole reverb setting on Eventide units is well renowned for its depth and space. Look for **impulse responses** on the net, or try an algorithmic reverb with modulation parameters.

Tip / Re-sampling is the best way to get maximum control over reverb tails and precision gated effects. (See **The gated Snare walkthrough, page 16**.)

Tip / If you're making deep or more organic house try sending the snare to the same bus as the kick to compress them together. This helps gel the two – particularly when the compressor is pushed hard. If you need to retain the kick on its own channel then use **parallel compression** (**page 111**) and divert some of its signal to a shared drum bus.

/walkthrough carving snare space

Making the kick and snare work together isn't simply a question of tuning and picking complementary sounds.

1 To keep the snare from interfering with the kick open a high-pass filter and roll off everything below 150–250Hz to remove rumble. Above that the frequency you cut at is a matter of taste, but generally the higher the frequency, the more delicate and crisp the resulting snare will be.

2 Mid and high frequencies supply the body and crack qualities of a snare. The body sits between 200–400Hz and the crack from 1kHz upwards. Use a parametric EQ to sweep through the sound until you locate a sweet spot that has the best of both. Avoid boosting narrow bands.

3 Most of the time a little cut and boost with EQ will be all that's needed to help the snare sit comfortably in the mix, but in some situations it can be worth experimenting with a transient shaper to emphasise or reduce the attack or decay. Try boosting whatever the kick's missing: so if the kick has a biting attack don't push the snare in the same way, and increase its release instead. Solo the kick and snare together for this kind of work.

4 In old-school drum machines like the Roland 808 and 909, the Linn Drum and E-mu Drumulator, the kick and snare were designed to work together straight out of the proverbial box. If you need drums that sit tight, use these as a foundation for ready-rolled beats and then layer with your own samples.

/walkthrough the gated snare

1 Route the snare to its own audio channel in the mixer. Insert a reverb plugin and set up a long reverb tail that decays over the course of around a bar. Start with a decay time of three seconds and set the diffusion high so that the reverb tail sounds thick and comes in with a lot of impact.

2 Add a noise gate after the reverb and set the threshold to 0dB – the maximum level. The snare will only pass through when it reaches the threshold so chances are you'll no longer be able to hear it. Lower the threshold until the initial impact of the snare can be heard. Change the gate hold and release settings to get exact reverb lengths.

3 You can get the same sound with more control by using Midi note length to control the reverb tail. To do this bypass the noise gate and bounce the snare with reverb and load it into a drum machine or sampler. Switch on the volume envelope. Set the ADSR with 0 attack, 100% decay and sustain, and 0 release. Draw in the Midi note to set reverb length.

4 With release set to 0 the reverb tail cuts off abruptly. Increase this value for a smoother tail. You can also reduce the amount of reverb on a sample. To do this dial in a long decay and low sustain value, then gradually reduce decay until only the original snare sound is heard. A little compression can be added to restore the thickness.

/walkthrough creating an analogue snare

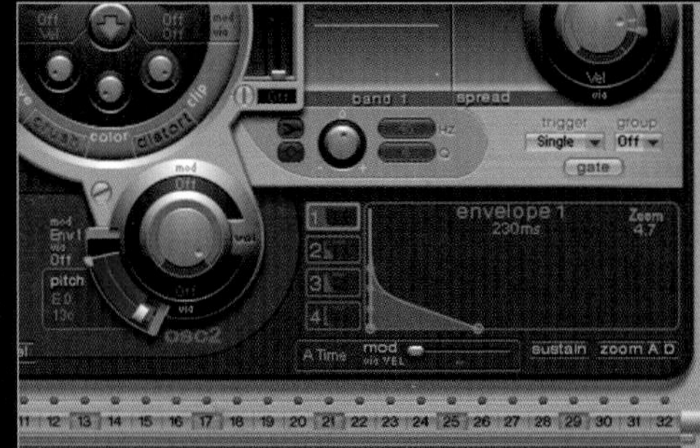

1 For the initial 'tuned' sound layer select a synth with a sine or triangle wave oscillator to create the body of the snare. Tune it to the key of the track and place it in the second or third octave range. Use an amp envelope with a tight attack and fast decay. Sustain and release can be set to 0.

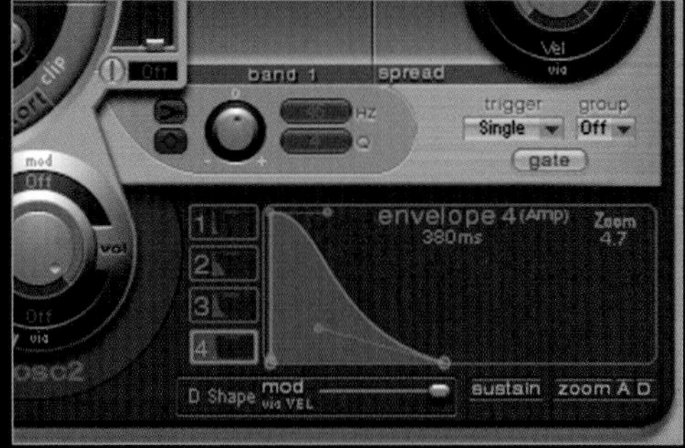

2 For the second, 'snappy' layer, use a white noise oscillator. Route it through a high-pass filter with cutoff in the region of 400–500Hz. Dial up a similar amp setting and adjust the decay and release for a range of tones. Longer release times simulate the splash of reverb.

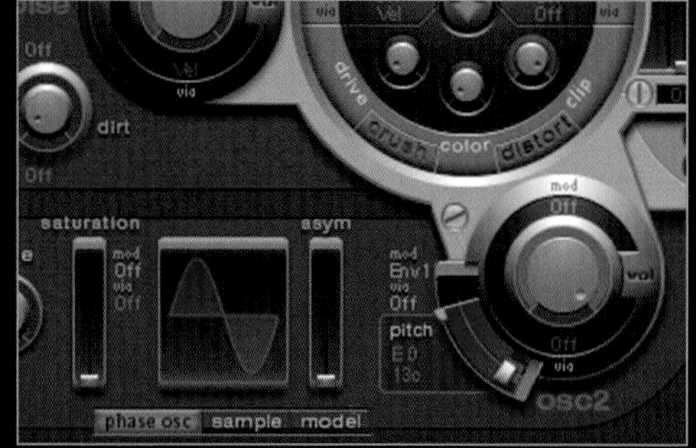

3 For a more complex 'knock' in the body of the snare, add an additional sine or triangle wave oscillator and tune it 11 semitones higher than the first. The slight atonal tuning is what produces the extra knock. If the oscillators were exactly one octave apart the snare would sound more tonal, like an acoustic piccolo drum.

4 Shape the sound with EQ. Use a high-pass filter to cut the lower end and a wide band parametric to boost the body of the tone (the sweet spot is usually around 400–800Hz). If the sound needs more definition take another parametric and hone in on the crack in the upper mid-range. Finish with some compression to control the dynamics.

/walkthrough
layered clap and snare

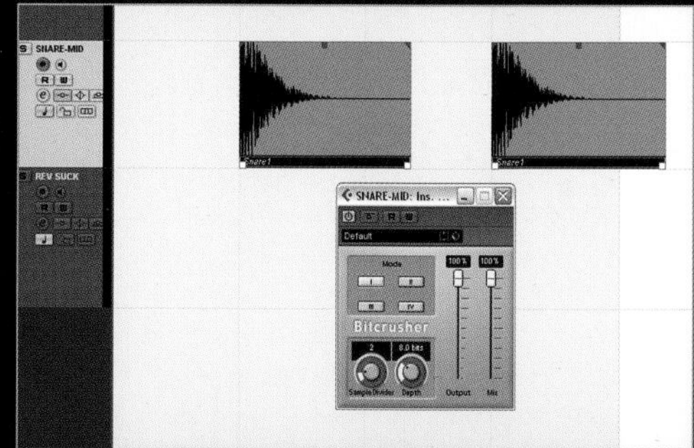

1 To create one big snare/clap combo that sucks in all the right ways you need to get layering. In this example we're using three separate layers: one for the centre thud, one for the stereo crack and one for the initial suck. For the centre thud use a mono LinnDrum or 808 snare. Give it balls with a bit-crusher using 12 or 8-bit downsampling.

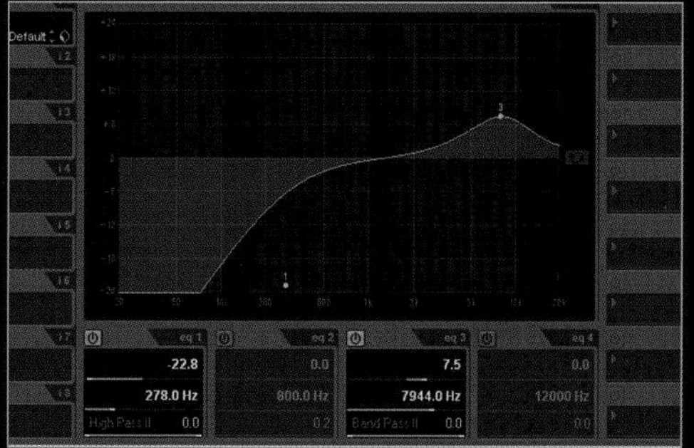

2 Some of the high frequencies get lost when you use a bit-crusher. Restore the air by boosting around 8kHz and up. Add a high-pass filter at around 150Hz to clean out any subs and separate the snare from the kick.

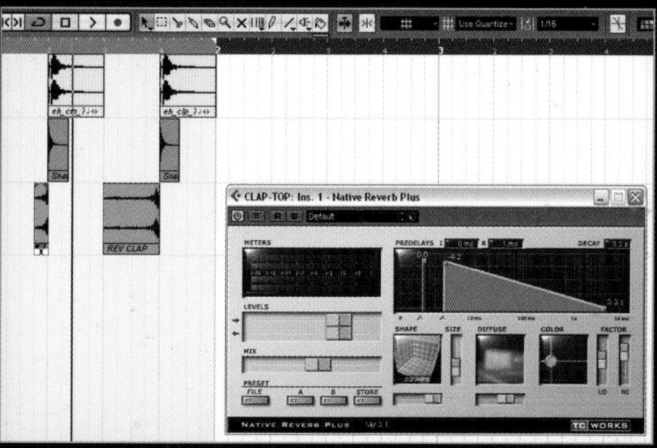

3 Now the suck. Place a clap on beats 2 and 4 on a new audio channel. Send it through a reverb with a long, thick tail and bounce it down (in yellow). Place this bounced clap on a third audio channel and reverse it so that the reversed reverb (in pink) sucks into the clap. Line up the end of the sample with the start of the main snare/clap.

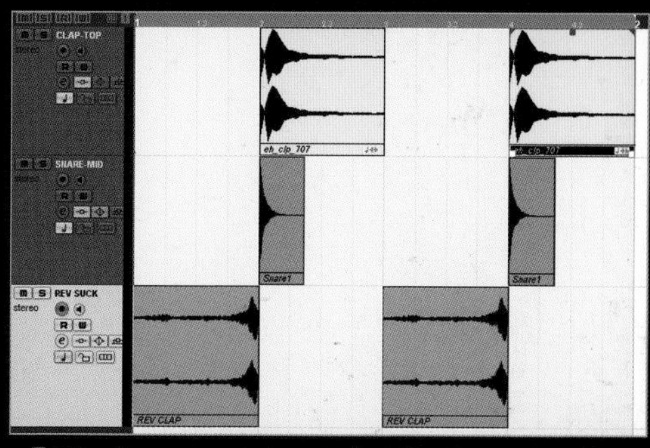

4 Trim the reverse clap so that the dry part of the original sample doesn't play and all you're left with is reversed reverb. Nudge it forward on the grid a little so that the suck eases into the snare.

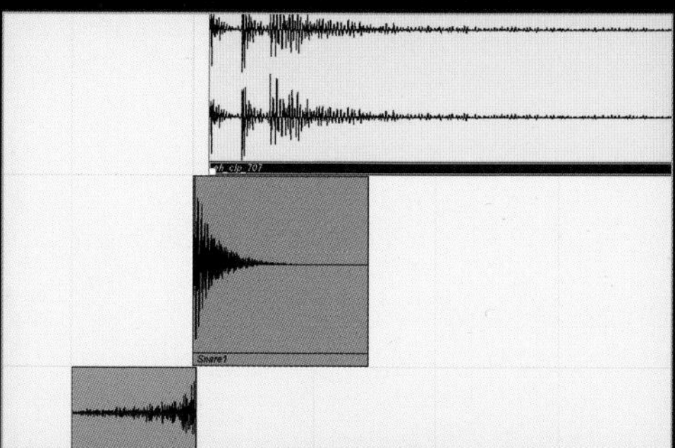

5 Return to the clap sample you introduced in step 3 (the one in yellow). Switch off the reverb and shift the clap so that it plays a little before or after the beat. This moves it off the kick to create a nice loose vibe to the groove.

6 Turn the reverb back on and add a noise gate after it. Keep the threshold high – high enough that the clap only triggers it for a moment. Program between 20–80ms of release to hear the extra sparkle of the reverb tail. Introduce a sample delay plugin and adjust either the left or right side anywhere up to 1500 samples for a stereo feel.

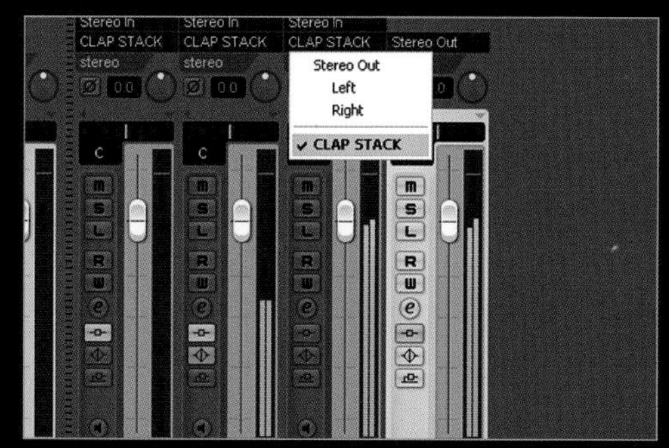

7 The three elements should all now have their own distinct identities in the mix. To help pull them together route all three channels to the same group or bus channel. On the bus add a compressor. This will merge the three sounds into one big hit.

8 Set the compressor attack to around 5ms. This will allow through some of the initial hit. Dial in a quick release using a VCA-style compressor. 15ms should be enough. Set the ratio to 2:1 and lower the threshold to reduce 2–4dBs of gain. To add more weight and crunch to the snare combo insert a bit-crusher before or after the compressor.

/hi-hats

the cracking, sizzling, slurping, body-rocking hi-hat is the third sound in the beatmaker trilogy.

Hi-hats are the third essential component for building the groove. They can be used to reinforce any element of the rhythm and are the primary tool for increasing the pace and excitement of your rhythm track.

Most drum machines have two types of hi-hat – open and closed (OH and CH). The terms refers to the two different ways an acoustic drummer strikes the hi-hat cymbals in their kit. Closed hats are short and tight because the drummer closes the hats with their foot pedal, while open hats are played with the foot pedal released and have a longer sustain. They are often played on the off-beat, earning them the nickname 'disco slurpers' for the sucking sound they make.

Mute groups

Because a drummer only has one hi-hat set in their kit, a closed and open hat can't be played at the same time. Instead, when an open hat is playing and the drummer puts their foot back on the hi-hat pedal, the open hat is ended, the sustain 'choked' as the two cymbals return together. This 'choking' style was emulated by early drum machine sequencers, which restricted open and closed hi-hats to one note polyphony so that only one or the other could be triggered at any one time. This shaped the sequenced sounds of the TR-808 and 909 rhythm boxes, adding a sense of realism to their beats.

Software samplers and drum machines like Battery use 'mute groups' to determine how many notes can be triggered simultaneously. To emulate the classic choking style, assign all hi-hats to their own mute group and restrict polyphony to one. (See **Mute groups**).

Top hats for style

The style of house you're making will influence your choice of hi-hat sound. Classic and retro choices come from the vintage E-mu, Linn and Roland (particularly 909) drum machines. In main-room and deep house these are often layered with hats sampled from disco records. The same sampled hats find their way into funky and Latin productions too.

Away from sampled vinyl and classic drum machines, hats can be created using synthesis. Of increasing popularity are entirely synthesised white-noise hats favoured by minimal and techno producers.

These white-noise hats are easy to make using most soft synths. All you need is a white noise oscillator as the source (FM synthesis works just as well). The amp envelope is all important in shaping the dynamics and requires at least two different settings to re-produce open and closed versions. Since white noise occupies the full frequency spectrum, it is essential to use a combination of filters (both high and low-pass) to shave off high and low frequencies to help the hats sit in the mix (**See White-noise hats walkthrough, page 20**).

Electro-house and bassline/fidget producers use a range of sources, from drum machine hits to sampled hats from rock and even old rave classics. Their inherent filth comes from liberal doses of distortion, compression and reverb-created space. Look for impulse responses on the net, or try an algorithmic reverb with modulation parameters to really mess with the sound. (**See Chunkier hi-hats walkthrough, right**).

/overview
mute groups

1 In Logic's EXS24 sampler route all hi-hat sounds (closed, open, pedal) to a single 'Group'. The Group pull-down menu offers the ability to create new named groups. For the hats group set the number of voices to one. The same technique can be used for percussion instruments like bongos.

2 To recreate the choking effect using a sampler such as Battery or Guru locate the polyphony parameter and reduce it to one note. If your sampler is used for other drum sounds as well, allocate the hi-hats to one group and restrict that group's polyphony.

3 Another way to achieve the same result is to switch sample triggering from 'one-shot' to 'envelope' mode. Then set the release to 0 and draw in Midi note lengths so that there are no overlapping notes. Most DAWs have a 'Force note legato' function to do this automatically.

Sculpting hi-hats

Hi-hats are supporting rhythmic instruments that must work effectively alongside – and not overshadow – the kick and snare. After selecting the right sound the important part is shaping the hat so it works in, and fits with, the groove. Attention to detail here is paramount, and beat programmers use a mix of sampler amp settings, compressors and transient shapers to shape their hats in the same way a sculptor would stone: cutting and chiselling the sound until it sits perfectly in the groove.

Sampler shaping

When shaping hats start with the sampler amp envelope settings, changing the attack from hard to soft for minimal shaker-style patterns, or tightening the decay to make a closed hat from an open one. It's worth re-iterating that the overriding requirement here is that the hat works with the groove. Although soloing for short times is never a bad idea, most of the sculpting work at this stage should be done with the kick and snare rolling.

In the mix – transient shapers

The dynamics of a hi-hat can be further refined using a transient shaper or envelope plugin. When the attack is increased, the front 'edge' becomes harder and more defined – great for adding definition to a groove. If the sound is too biting ease back on the attack. The tail can also be manipulated for shorter or longer tails. A long, compressed-to-the-max sucking tail can be great in lo-fi electro beats.

In the mix – de-essing

When pressing vinyl it is essential to ensure sibilant hi-hat frequencies don't distort at the cutting stage. Hi-hat sibilance (that nassty sss sssound) occurs in the upper mid-range, around the 5–6kHz region and beyond. An effective way to tame it is to use a de-esser to dynamically lower the volume of problem frequency bands.

Tip / An echo or delay effect on a hi-hat can increase the pace of a track and introduce an extra element of rhythm. Use a 1/16 note setting for speed or 1/8 note triplet setting for dub rhythms. Ping-pong delays are also nice. Roll away the high end of any returns.

Tip / Flangers and phasers introduce movement into linear hi-hat patterns by sweeping through the frequency range. For subtle changes keep the mix value low and sweep the LFO across an 8 or 16-bar cycle. Automate the wet mix level and bring it up slowly when the track needs more intensity.

Tip / Lock the frequency of a phaser so it resonates at a fixed pitch. Tune the resonant frequency to the key of the track, choosing either the route note or one that's in harmony.

Tip / If you're after ultra-wide hats send them through a frequency shifter. Look for the offset parameter: this is the key to stereo width enhancement. Keep the frequency range below 1–10Hz for sublime panning. At settings below 1Hz the sweeping motion of the frequency shifting becomes more noticeable.

/pro tips
panning hats

A classic old-school hi-hat trick is to pan identical closed hats hard left and right and then create a 16th note sequence that alternatively triggers the left and right hats for fizzing rhythmic width. Put an open hat in the centre to anchor the top-line energy.

Tip / Hats and shakers occupy the same high frequency area. When using both in a track be careful that they don't clash. You can do this using programming to ensure one supports the other rhythmically, rather than playing the same line. Separate them further by using a mix of panning, EQ (cut one and boost the other in the same area) and reverb (pushing one further back in the mix by using a little more reverb on it).

Tip / For a heavily compressed nu-rave / electro-style disco slurp, sidechain a long, dirty open hat with the kick drum so that it gives nice syncopated off-beat breaths. Use a very slow release so that you never hear the start of the hat. Get even dirtier by adding bit-crusher or distortion. Long white noise hats are great candidates for this too.

Tip / It's always tempting to reach for an exciter to add high-end to hats. But beware: excited hats can sound brutal on a club system. If you use one, be subtle.

/walkthrough
chunkier hi-hats

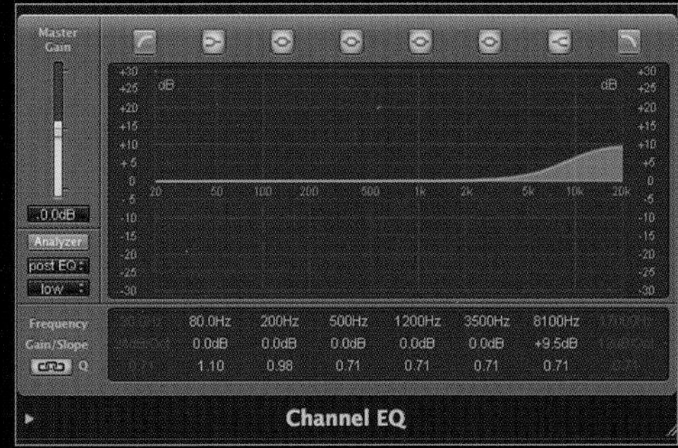

1 A quick way to add chunk to a hi-hat is to route it through a bit-crusher. Reducing the sample rate by one or two steps using a bit-crusher makes the hat thicker in the mid-range. A by-product is that the high-end content is diminished. Boost the airy high frequencies before sending the signal to the crusher. Increase above 8kHz using shelving EQ.

2 If a hi-hat needs to cut through a busy arrangement try lowering the bit-rate. 8 and 12-bit settings are ideal for the old-school beatbox sound (the MPC-60 had an 8-bit chip). Going lower increases the snap but will introduce digital hiss into the signal. As the sound decays, it will begin to break up.

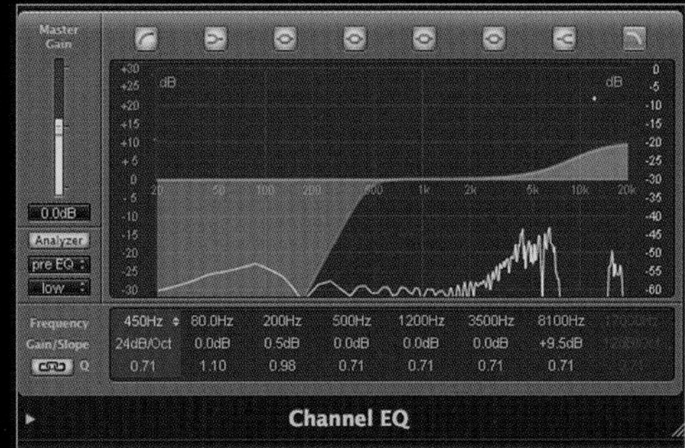

3 In both cases, check out the bit-crushed sound through a spectrum analyser. Bit-crushing often introduces unwanted sub-bass frequencies. If you can see them (or hear them) use a high-pass EQ to filter them out or a parametric to hone in on specific rogue frequencies and dip them.

4 Another way to increase the high frequency content of brittle or dull hi-hats is with distortion and filtering. Use a saturator or clip-distortion plugin and adjust the tone/frequency parameters to hone in on the portion of the spectrum you want to increase and then boost to taste.

/walkthrough white noise hi-hats

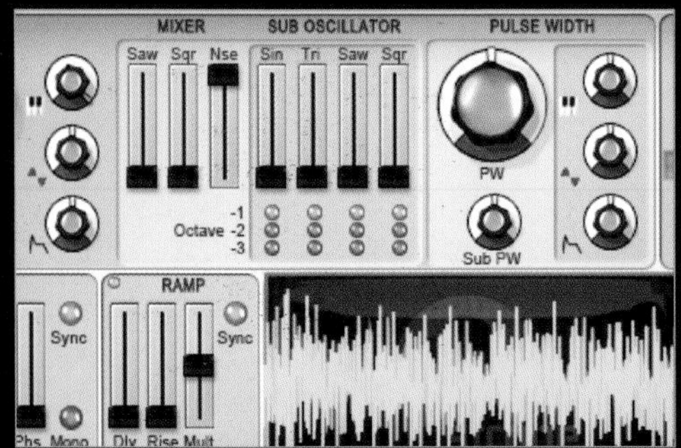

1 Select the noise oscillator on the synth. No other waveforms are needed. Turn up the volume and set the amp to respond to Midi velocity. The amp only needs a liitle sensitivity – try 25%. Select a high-pass filter, either a two or four pole type. For a dry, brushy sound keep resonance to a minimum. For a more tonal sound increase resonance to taste.

2 Set the amp envelope with fast attack, medium decay, a tiny amount of sustain and medium release. This gives a tight sound. Even with this basic setting, extra expression can be created by programming both short and longer note lengths in the Midi sequence.

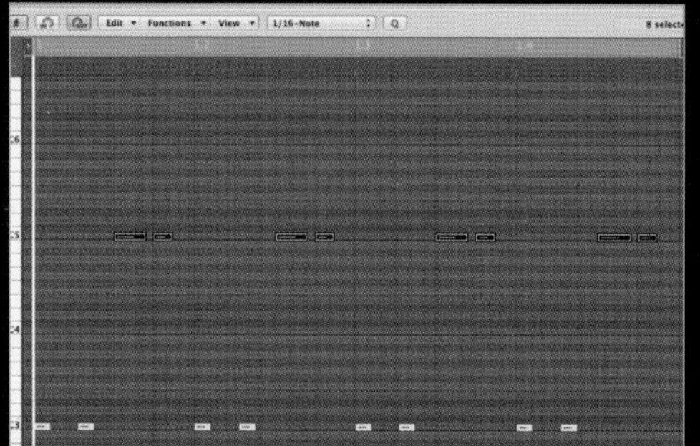

3 Program a 16th note pattern split between two different notes. Alternate these notes so that the first two are at one octave and the second two play three octaves above. This enables you to use Midi note position to modulate the filter with key-tracking. Make the off-beat note slightly longer in length to accent it.

4 On some synths, Midi note value modulation route is hard wired as 'key-tracking'. Route the note pitch to filter cutoff in the modulation panel. This makes the filter respond to different Midi note values. Open modulation depth to around 50%. Positive and negative values can both work well, opening and closing the filter to different velocities.

5 Slowly change the filter cutoff point until you hear it changing with the note sequence. To make the modulation more extreme either increase the modulation depth or change the note positions in the sequence.

6 Introduce another range of expression by routing note-velocity to amp attack and decay values. By programming different velocity values for the notes in the pattern you can alter the dynamics of each hit, from soft brushed to tight tacked. You can create highly expressive and evolving rhythmic patterns using this method.

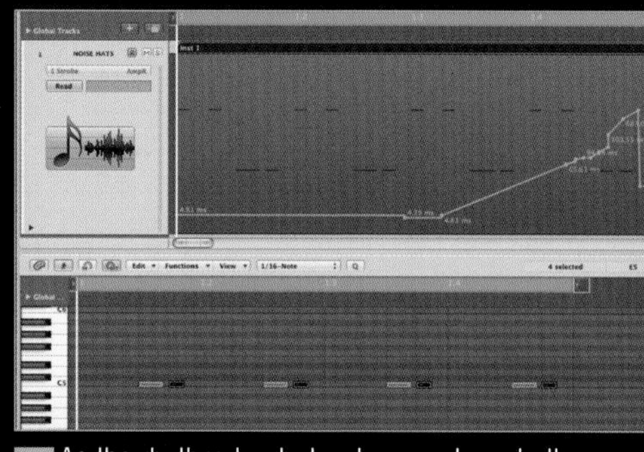

7 As the rhythm track develops, automate the amp release parameter for fills and other moments where the hi-hats can be more intense. Increasing the release value makes the hats sustain longer and sound thicker. Automation is key to making credible detailed minimal beats – allowing complex detail and glitchy fills.

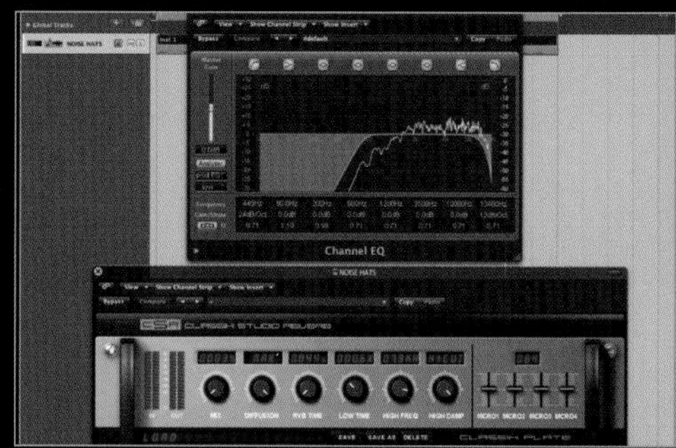

8 White noise hats tend to sound harsh on their own, so they will need EQing and some subtle reverb to smooth them into the mix. Add an EQ with a 24dB high-pass filter to scoop out the low end. Start at 400Hz and sweep up. At the other end, use a 12dB low-pass filter to roll off the high end. Finally, add a touch of short room reverb.

/cymbals and percussion

the spice of the rhythmic snack: cymbals and percussion bring flavour to the groove.

Crash

Crash cymbals are used like sonic energy bursts to emphasise key points in a track, or to soften transitions into new sections of a song, like the breakdown or chorus.

Crashes can be live samples or synthesised. They contain mostly high-end frequencies and are therefore easily produced on a synth with a white noise oscillator and high-pass filter. Crashes usually sit on the first beat of a new bar and can be repeated every 16, 32 or 64 bars when new parts come in and out. The classic crash trick is to reverse the sound so that it creeps in slowly. Position it so the suck finishes just as the first beat of the next bar drops (See **Crash FX, page 95**). Crashes sound great in wide stereo. Use a stereo widener with delays and reverb to give them additional depth and character.

Ride

The acoustic ride cymbal has two distinctive tones depending on where it is hit. Striking the edge gives a smooth, jazzy sound with a long decay, while tapping the central bell produces a shorter, defined pitch in the form of a metallic 'klang'. The controls for the ride on an analogue beat box are designed to produce one or other of these tones. When programming, ride patterns can take the part usually assigned to the closed hat (1/8ths or 1/16ths), or they can cut across the groove like cowbells. Melodic deep house and jazzy house make use of loosely-programmed ride lines to give a relaxed, lazy feel to the beat. A long, sustained ride sound with a simple 8th note downbeat pattern is also prime material for pairing with heavy sidechain compression for classic sucking effects.

Percussion

Don't underestimate the power of the less significant percussive sounds. When used right, they can become the focus of a groove. In some styles they are essential.

Every drum machine has its variation of toms, usually offered at high, medium and low pitches. These are based on a deep, warm sample that can be tuned to the key of the track. If they are tuned low enough, synthetic toms can be programmed to play the bassline. This type of programming is common in both minimal and deep house.

The sounds of Brazil and Africa are both excellent sources for drum and percussion loops, especially hand drums like congas and bongos. Latin and disco house often feature conga and bongo loops, bringing an irresistible live, funky feel to the beat, while full-on traditional rhythms have enjoyed a recent resurgence among tribal producers.

Original percussive patterns can be analysed and re-created using Midi programming. Note that when bongos and congas are played by percussionists the sounds vary according to the type of hit made by the palm, generating a variety of open, slapped and muted hits. Load up the different sound variants into a sampler and use velocity changes and **mute groups** for a more realistic feel. When programming percussive parts it can also be useful to tap them in live (see **How to humanise your beat walkthrough, page 25**).

Easier than generating an authentic loop with Midi is using a live percussion loop. These can be sourced from any number of sample collections or old records. The important thing when using a loop in this way is to maintain as much control over it as you can to ensure it sits comfortably in the groove you've got rolling. You can do this in a number of ways.

The first method is the 'old-school' way, cutting up different hits using scissors in the arrange page and then nudging the cut samples back and forth until they are in time with the groove. It's tedious but can be very effective. A second method is to leave the loop as a single Wav and then re-groove it using realtime tools such as Logic's Grooveshifter.

The third – and most powerful – option is to use tools that intelligently chop a loop into its constituent parts and then map these parts to different sampler zones. This allows you to totally change a loop's construction and alter its groove to fit the track. Rex files are ideal for this. The methods used are covered in detail in **Working with loops, pages 86–92**.

/overview
what is...?

Conga: Tall, narrow Cuban drum with African origins, typically played in sets of two. Each drum can be played with five different strokes – including open, slap and touch.

Bongos: Pair of single-headed, open-ended drums attached to each other, played by striking drumheads with fingers and palms. Produce relatively high-pitched sounds.

Cowbell: Hand-held percussive instrument. Brings definition when struck along with snare. Popular in Latin house.

Claves: Pair of short, traditionally wooden, sticks that produce a bright clicking noise. Used in Afro-Cuban music.

Tom (or tom-tom): Tunable drum commonly used in Western music, most frequently during drum fills. Modern drum kits typically feature three different toms.

/synthetic percussion

zaps, clicks and glitches are the bongos of the tech age, and an essential beat element in minimal and electro.

Synthetic percussion has been steadily rising in popularity to the point where it has become a staple ingredient of minimal and electro grooves. Synth-derived hits are used to spice up the rhythm in place of traditional acoustic and ethnic percussion with zaps, clicks and glitches taking the place of congas, bongos and shakers, introducing detail and rhythm to the groove.

When choosing percussive synth sounds, it can be helpful to think in terms of the tonal qualities (in terms of size, shape and frequency) of traditional percussive instruments and use similar sounds for similar purposes. Clicky, high frequency metallic noises, for example, are ideal substitutes for hi-hats; thick, chunky, snappy noises are good snare replacements; and hits with a recognisable pitch can be used instead of toms, bongos and congas.

The most obvious synthetic percussion is that offered on drum machines like the 808 and 909, where the drum sounds are synthesised versions of their real-life cousins, each sound offering a tonal and frequency approximation of the acoustic original. These machines are tweakable, with many of the sounds editable using front panel controls. Toms can be tuned and hat decay times altered, giving producers the tools to fit individual sounds into the mix. This tweakability accounts for the multiple variations of percussive sounds in vintage beatbox sample collections.

Old-school percussion remains popular today. But house producers have widened their sonic palette to make use of many other sounds – often used sparsely and picked solely for the way they work in the groove.

Sound sources

The beauty of synthetic percussion is that the source material can be almost anything, from a vinyl click to a sampled burst of digital feedback.

Sample CDs are a great source of ready-made noises (often in percussive 'hits' folders). Once loaded into a sampler these hits can be sculpted to fit the track's beat using filters, envelopes and any number of effects.

Synthetic percussion is also easy to create from scratch. Any analogue synth can be used as a source. For more complex textures such as atonal or metallic sounds, use frequency modulation (FM synthesis), ring modulation, cross modulation or phase distortion techniques. These techniques sound good when used with basic sine waves as the sound source. For subtle sounds spread the tuning between the two oscillators by a few semitones. For more extreme effects, detune the two by several octaves. Swapping the carrier and modulator modulators around will change the tone dramatically. Digital FM and wavetable synthesis can also create unusual textures.

For more sophisticated sounds try drum synthesisers such as the Waldorf Attack, Elektron Machinedrum and Logic Ultrabeat. These offer a number of drum models specifically designed to create kicks, snares and cymbals. They also have advanced programming functions.

/focus
glitched fx

Some effects are perfect for processing glitch percussion. These include bit-crushers, ring modulators, frequency-shifters, multi-band distortion and FFT-based ('Fast Fourier Transform') filter effects.

With bit-crushers, changing the sample-rate value will introduce atonal harmonics to the sound, while lowering the bit-depth will make it more chunky and abrupt.

DestroyFX make an essential series of freeware plugins including Buffer Overide, while Audio Damage have the reasonably priced Replicant, Automaton and Big-Seq. These can transform a tiny splinter of sound into something wildly different.

Tip / White noise can be used on its own or as an extra layer of a percussive sound. Use high and low-pass filters to shave off unnecessary frequencies around the sound.

Tip / Use reverb to position a sound in the groove. Keep it up-front and snappy with early-reflections. Use a long reverb tail for occasional dramatic hits.

Tip / Distortion transforms thin, weak hits into thick strikes laden with character.

Tip / Any short, simple sine wave blip can be mutated into a lo-fi computerised percussion noise with the help of a bit-crusher. Lower the sampling frequency to introduce tonality. Reduce the bit length to add noise.

Tip / Up the expression by automating a few parameters in a percussive line over time. Try changing a sound's amp attack/decay, filter cutoff and oscillator pitch.

Tip / Create a hooky, highly personalised beat by introducing a distinctive hit or sound effect into a straight rhythmic pattern. Use the hit sparingly – once in eight bars is often enough.

/walkthrough zap percussion

1 The 'lazer zap' sound can be short and tight like a hi-hat or longer and thicker like a snare. The key is to use an envelope sweep to create the sharp, downwards motion of the sound. There are two ways to do this. The first uses any oscillator waveform (from sine to square) as the source. Assign the mod envelope to the oscillator pitch and set depth between 75% and 100%.

2 Set the envelope so that attack, sustain, release and decay are all 0. Now gradually open the decay until it starts clicking. As the decay increases, the zap becomes more audible. Try adjusting the pitch of the oscillator manually to help position it in the correct frequency range.

3 Select a 12 or 24dB high-pass filter to progressively take out the bass and mid-range until the lazer sound is as thick as you want it. You don't need to use resonance but it can add a little extra zoomph.

4 A second way to get the zap is to use the white noise oscillator and a low-pass filter with resonance set to maximum so it self-oscillates and produces a pitched sound. Assign the mod envelope to filter cutoff and set the depth between 75% and 100%. Dial in the same settings for the mod envelope as in step 2 with a cutoff of 0. Now open the decay slowly to morph the click into a zap.

/walkthrough click and glitch percussion

1 To generate the high frequency content for glitch sounds, use a synth with FM or PM (phase or pitch modulation) capabilities. Program a 16th note sequence to trigger the synth. Programme notes that are in tune with the track. The random element is introduced through the use of modulation sources, so start with basic harmonic tuning.

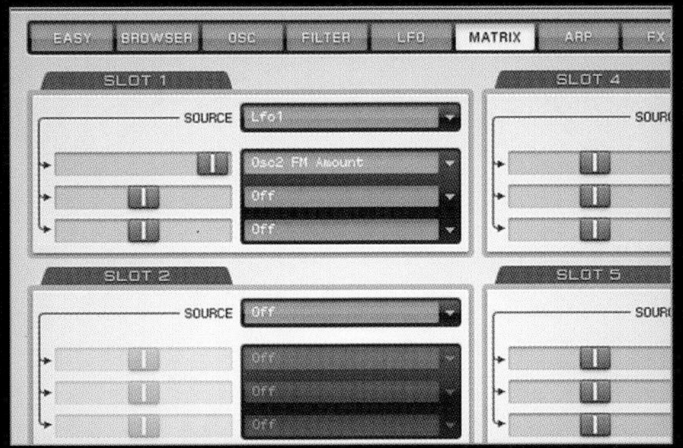

2 To allow glitching, adjustments need to be made to the synth's modulation matrix. The pitch of osc 1 needs to be modulated. Patch this in the mod matrix so that osc 1's FM modulation depth is controlled by an LFO. Set the LFO's waveform to random or Sample & Hold and set the speed and tempo-sync to 16th note intervals

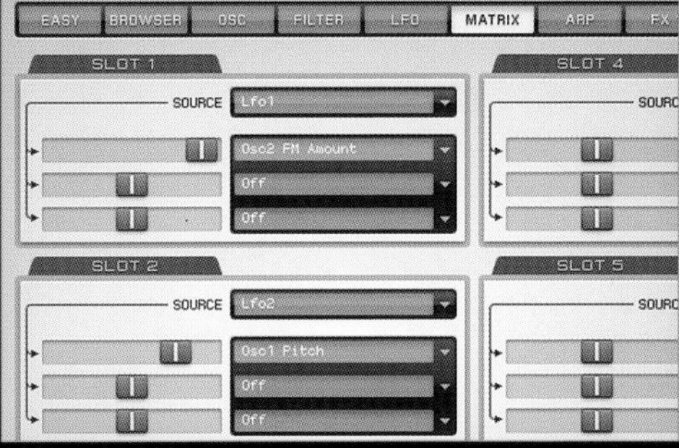

3 Select a new LFO, with a random waveform, and route it to modulate osc 1's pitch. For extreme randomness experiment with higher modulation depths for the pitch and FM amount. If you want to hone in on a particular sonic quality reduce the modulation depths, tune the oscillators and experiment with the LFO speeds.

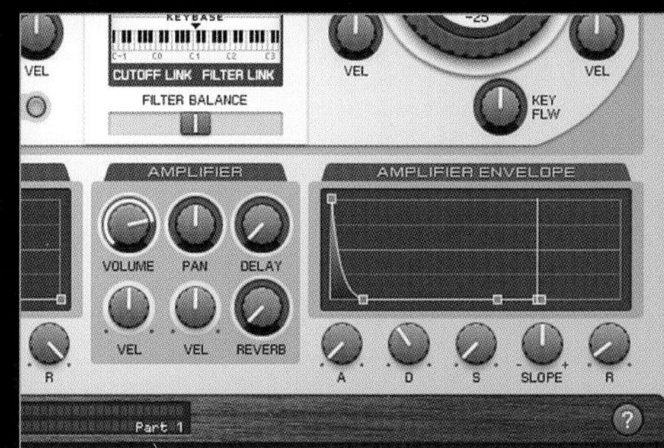

4 The difference between tight clicks and solid klangs lies in the amp envelope values. Set the ADSR to fast attack, immediate decay and 0 sustain and release for clicks. If the decay and sustain levels are higher then the sound becomes more distinctive and tonal. Use a high-pass filter for delicate sounds and a low-pass one for heavier hits.

/drum programming

the key to great beats is the right sounds in the right order – plus a little processing magic.

There are three main ways to program beats – using step-sequencing, Midi sequencing or audio editing.

Step sequencing

The oldest beat-programming method is step sequencing, born in the era of the classic drum machines. A step sequencer divides a four bar beat into a grid, usually of 16 notes or 'steps'. Drum sounds can be triggered on any of the steps. Machines like Roland's TR-808 and 909, and the classic Akai MPC-60 (**right**) use this kind of method. In the last few years this intuitive approach of sequencing has been adopted by the major software companies to form the backbone of drum sequencers like Reason's ReDrum, Logic's Ultrabeat, Guru from FXpansion and Native Instruments' Maschine. Although step sequencing was originally limited to just triggering a sound, with Ultrabeat, Maschine, and the Elektron Machinedrum the step sequencer also makes it possible to program parameter changes for each step, which adds a powerful extra dimension to beats.

Midi sequencing

Midi sequencing came along next, offering a more detailed way of programming. It remains popular to this day. Midi sequences are most frequently input via a piano roll or 'matrix'-style editor window in the DAW. The major advantage of this form of sequencing is the ability to control a host of parameters beyond the standard on/off triggers. Using different Midi values programmers can control the velocity and length of each hit. There is also much more control over the placement of hits, with users able to drag sounds forwards or backwards on the grid in very small units. The real power comes when combining Midi programming with a high quality drum machine or VST instrument.

It's easy to program a given sound to respond to Midi messages. Usually the default is to map velocity to volume, but that's just the start. Try mapping other Midi CC (control change) parameters to pitch, sample start, filter cutoff, loop points and more for greater expression and control of a rhythm part.

Audio programming

Audio programming is the newest method of creating beats, made possible by the ubiquity of computer-based studios. It involves laying samples onto different tracks in the DAW's arrange window. Many producers like making beats this way as it is visual, offers huge amounts of processing control and can sidestep potential problems introduced by Midi timing. The usual approach is to use one audio track per drum sound, so for a simple beat using kick, snare, clap and hi-hat, you would use four audio tracks. Audio programming is ideal if you're working with loops or if you've decided on specific drum sounds – especially if you use a lot of individual effects on each drum sound. But it can be frustrating if you want to manipulate tuning or lengths of individual hits, or change a specific drum sound late in the mix.

/flashback
the mpc

The Akai MPC sampler has become legendary in house (and hip hop) circles for the feel of its swing quantise. If you don't have one handy you can get the flavour by using one of the groove templates that come with the preset library in Reason and Ableton. Logic users can track down the MPC templates from the web (search for 'MPC Groove templates' and import them using Groove > Import Groove Template).

Quantise and swing

What is quantise?

Quantising is the process of aligning notes and triggers onto a defined grid so that the beat plays tight and in sync. This grid can be divided into a range of time divisions, from bars to single beats and fractions up to 1/128th of a beat, sometimes beyond. The typical setting for dance music is a 1/16th grid and a 4/4 rhythm, with kicks on steps 1, 5, 9 and 13.

Quantising – like step sequencing – started life on drum machines as a mechanical way of correcting timing mistakes introduced when users punched the rhythm in using the pads. The in-built quantise would nudge loose hits to the closest regular interval, tightening the beat and giving it an almost mechanically perfect feel – the trademark sound of many 80s hits. Quantising is used in Midi sequencing, drum machines and audio editing, and can be turned on and off so that elements snap to the pre-selected grid as they are introduced during the programming process.

Swing, shuffle and triplets

Although quantising helps ensure a tight beat, with all elements pulled neatly together, it can also make the beat sound robotic, unnatural and lifeless. This is not always a bad thing – think back to those big 80s tunes – but lots of house music relies on a bouncier, more human feel in the groove, which can be introduced by using **swing settings** in quantise menus or by applying a **groove template**.

Swing – also known as **shuffle** – was introduced by the hardware and software companies to return the shuffly funk to the beat that their quantise functions had ironed away. The feature replicates the pulling/dragging way a human drummer plays parts of the groove, giving the beat a particular feel. House producers took to this new shuffle feel. House producers took to this new shuffle sound – specifically the classic MPC swing – like ducks to water. All styles of house music, from old-school New York to cutting-edge minimal, have used swing rhythms of various intensities at some point or another.

When applying swing quantise some notes get shifted off grid, while others stay rooted in place. Typically in a 16th note shuffle pattern, every second note gets dragged a little later in time. Swing can be applied incrementally, meaning a groove can have any amount of swing, from light to heavy.

Triplet patterns occur when a bar is divided into three instead of the usual four. Triplets can be useful when programming syncopated percussion grooves, and can introduce a Latin or African influence to a track. They also sound great for dub-style echo effects. Some producers program deep-house grooves using a 24/4 quantise grid pattern to easily see where the triplets should fall.

Swing in practice

When starting a track, or if you're relatively new to making beats, it's worth applying the same swing value to all rhythmic elements – including basslines and melodic parts that serve a rhythmic purpose, like guitars or synth arps. However, there are also times when one or more elements sound out of place with the same swing value. If so, try increasing or decreasing the swing amount for that part in gradual steps, paying attention to the way the part interacts with the wider groove.

In styles where the beat rules supreme – particularly minimal and deep house – the use and frequent abuse of swing to bring wonky rhythms into the mix has become something of a fine art. Rules are there to be broken, and you can get some awesome rhythms by using contrasting swing settings on different parts.

Finally, remember that all swing settings do is shift notes in time. If a particular note sounds wrong, manually correct it by moving it forwards or backwards from its current position using the DAW's note or matrix editor.

Tip / At very high swing settings, a 16th shuffle begins to feel similar to an 8th shuffle giving the heavily syncopated 'jacking' sound used in deep and fidget house.

Tip / Logic users can add swing and accent to audio files with the specialist Grooveshifter plugin. Set the grid to 8th or 16th divisions depending on the track, and increase the swing parameter to adjust the timing. Use the accent slider to alter dynamics.

Tip / Switch from 16th or 8th quantise divisions to triplets in fills. This will increase the energy momentarily before releasing back to the regular 16th/8th groove.

Tip / Even echo and delay plugins have built-in groove features. Look for the swing control on Logic's Delay Designer. The EchoBoy from SoundToys also has extensive groove controls.

Advanced programming

Tip / Gating or cutting the decay time of a kick drum or snare can keep a groove tight, improving the rhythmic flow, particularly at faster tempos.

Tip / Try looping percussive sequences at odd numbered bars. Instead of looping every four, try the third or seventh bar, for interesting, ever-evolving percussion lines.

Tip / When building towards a drop, you can create intensity without any extra programming by inserting a ping-pong delay into the chain. Increase the feedback to build a wall of sound before cutting back again.

Tip / Some drum machines have humanising features and performance variations. Most of these are designed to emulate acoustic drum strokes like flams, rolls and so on, but they can be abused in many creative ways.

Tip / In samplers such as Battery use the loop tool with a short setting to create stuttering, glitchy percussion from standard samples. Experiment by modulating the pitch with an envelope or LFO and filter the result.

Tip / For a unique one-bar fill, simply change the swing template of all rhythm parts so that the beat suddenly goes wonky, throwing the listener off track, before resolving back to normal in the next bar.

Tip / Program beats live for a looser human feel, a trick employed regularly in nu-rave and electro tracks. (See **Humanise the beat**).

Tip / Use samples for inspiration. If you've got a loop you like try overlaying it with your own sounds and then dropping it from the mix when you've built a better version.

/how to... humanise the beat

Electro-house and nu-rave producers are starting to do what their deep and disco counterparts have been doing for years: humanising their beats. Here are a few ideas how:

1 Program beats live. This is easy with drum pads but it's just as simple using a Midi keyboard. Simply loop up a four-bar kick drum pattern, press record and then manually tap new sounds over the top. Keep all quantise settings off. You'll need to do a bit of editing afterwards to correct the more noticeable errors, but you should end with a nice human-feeling beat, with velocity differences and the subtle imperfections of a drummer. This technique works well with percussion too.

2 If you prefer to program using a note or matrix editor you can introduce timing imperfections by dragging notes a little before or after the bar/division, or by running a sequence through a humanising algorithm like that found in Logic's Transform window.

3 Learn how a drummer plays. Physical and kit limitations mean that only certain sounds can play at certain times, so, for example, a closed and open hat can't hit at once, nor can a snare, crash, closed hat and tom. Until the three-armed drummer is born these limitations provide useful pointers on how to program realistic parts.

4 Choose your sounds carefully. If you want live sounding drums, pick samples from real kits. Layer them with machine-derived one-shots for the best of both worlds.

/walkthrough groove templates in logic

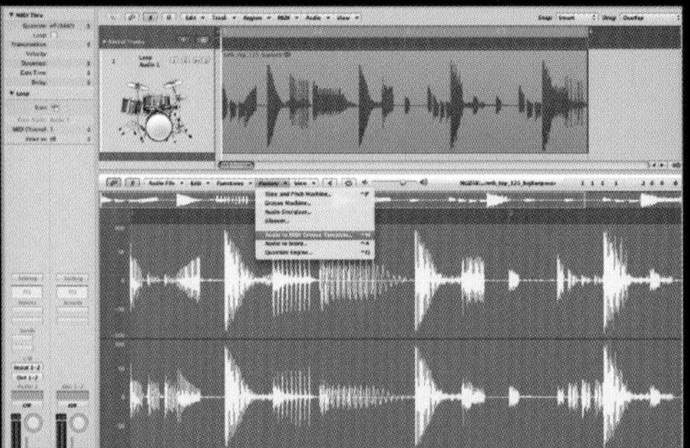

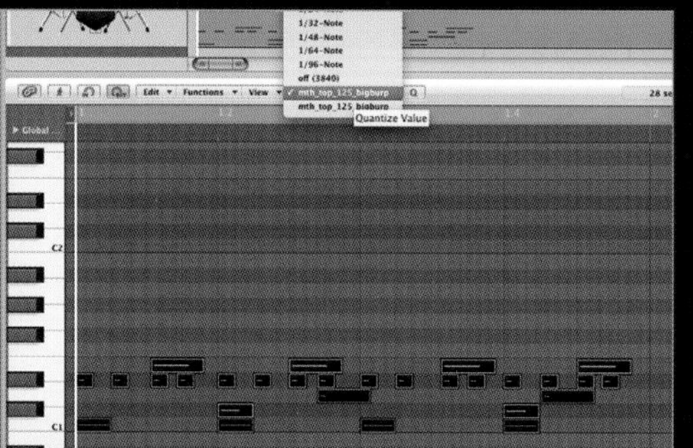

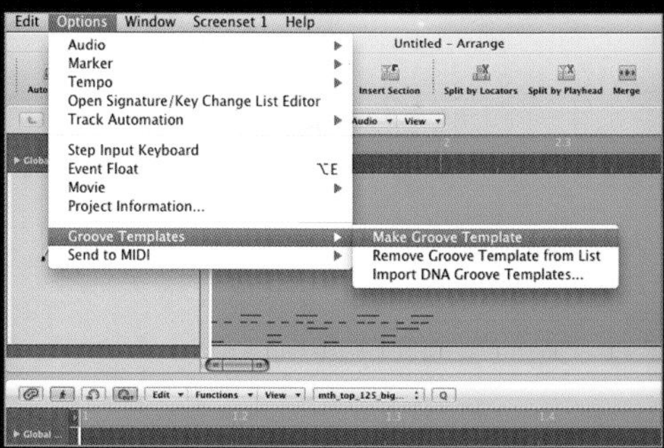

1 Open the loop you want to use to create a new groove template. In the Transport bar set global bpm to the same tempo as the loop and open the audio file in the sample editor. The start and end of the loop should perfectly align with the start and end markers. In the 'Factory' tab choose 'Audio to MIDI Groove Template' from the drop-down menu.

2 A new window opens showing several parameters that analyse the audio file and extract the groove. A quantise grid also appears below the audio file showing the hit points of the groove. To make more hit points, lower the granulation and velocity threshold parameters until the hit points match the loop events. Click Use.

3 Program in a Midi pattern for a new drumbeat (pick a beat template from the next pages if you're short of ideas). Then select the new quantise template from the quantise drop-down. It will have the same name as the audio file. If you want to keep this template as part of Logic's default set then you will need to save them into the Autoload template.

4 To do this, save the Midi pattern out (File > Export > Selection as Midi File). Now load the Autoload template. Import the Midi pattern. Choose 'Make Groove Template' from the Options menu, and your new quantise template will appear in the quantise menu. Mute the pattern, put it on an unused track and choose 'Hide current track' from the View menu. Click save.

/walkthrough swing and groove in ableton live

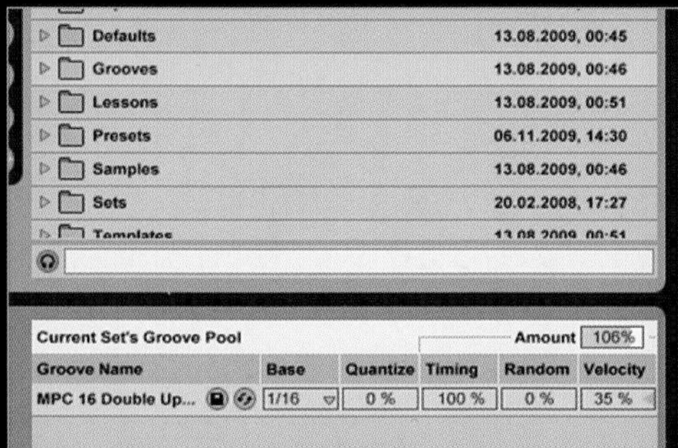

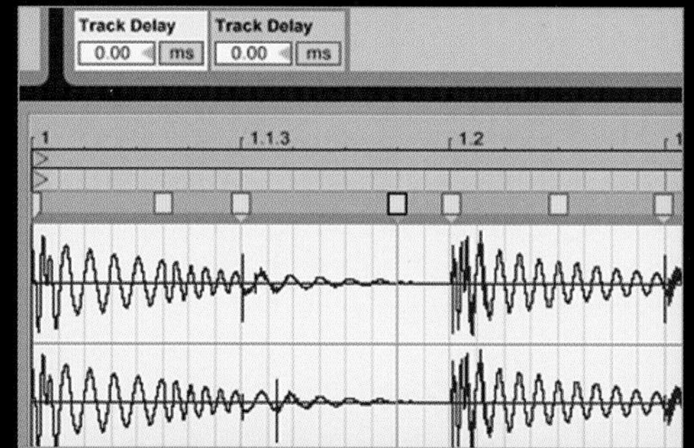

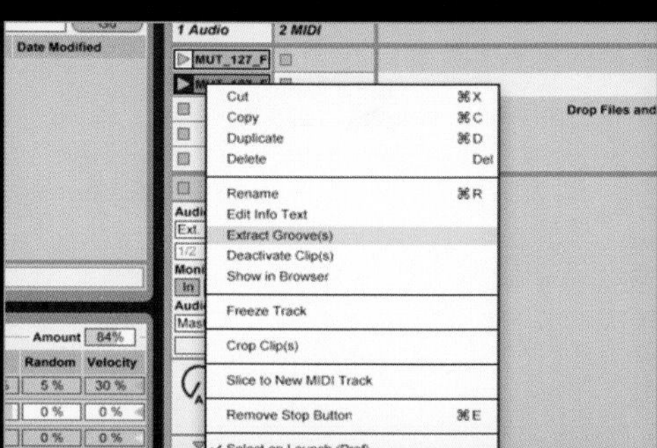

1 To access the swing presets open the Ableton library and locate the folder entitled Grooves. Double-click it or drag it into the Groove Pool. Open the Groove Pool by clicking on the wavy icon in the sidebar. Load a 16th note preset to get you started. You can drag and drop clips straight into the Groove Pool: Ableton will extract their groove automatically.

2 To dial the right amount of swing, set the Timing parameter to 100% for that groove, and then increase the global amount until you get the kind of feel that fits your song. There are two more parameters that introduce randomness and dynamic volume changes based on the original pattern.

3 When you're done tweaking, fix the swing to the audio file using the Commit button. This sets the warp markers (the yellow blocks) to new positions on the file. If there were any changes in volume introduced by the velocity parameter, these are drawn onto the clip volume envelope.

4 To take a groove template from another audio or Midi file right-click the clip and select 'Extract groove from clip'. Ableton analyses the clip and exports it to the Groove Pool where it can be applied to any other clip.

/walkthrough
groove tricks in reason

1 Open the ReGroove Mixer panel by clicking the icon at the bottom right of the Transport bar. The mixer has a Global Shuffle dial on the left. This sets the overall amount of swing for the track. It works alongside the shuffle buttons on ReDrum, RPG-8 and Matrix. Switch shuffle on for each to vary the amounts of swing on each part.

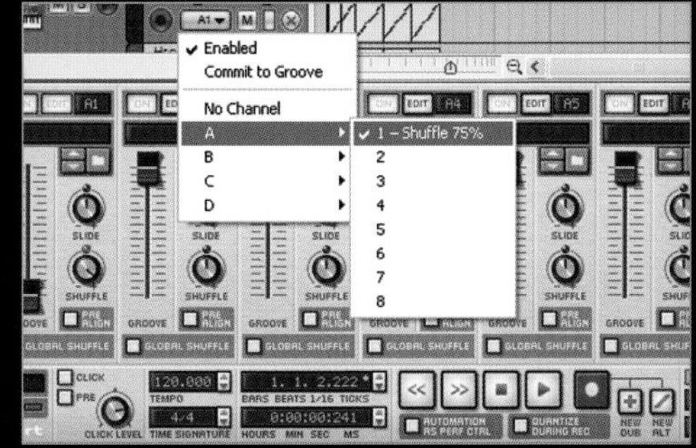

2 To apply a different shuffle or groove to an individual Midi pattern assign it to one of the channels in the ReGroove mixer. There are eight lanes and four banks, from A to D, totalling 32 possible grooves. Allocate a groove channel by selecting it from the drop-down menu on the device lane.

3 The dial for shuffle works the same way as the global one. 50% yields a straight feel while 66% gives bouncy triplets. The second dial is Slide. This shifts notes forwards or backwards in time, giving a more urgent or relaxed feel. Switch back to Global Shuffle by clicking the button under the slider.

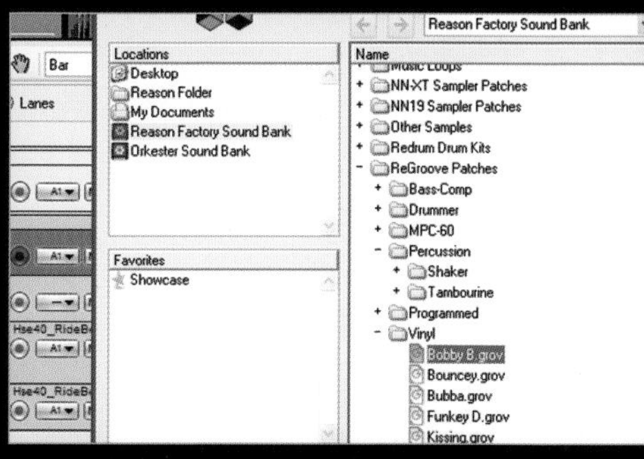

4 Another way of injecting feel into a stiff pattern is by using the quantise templates – or 'Groove Patches'. There are lots of presets but they can also be extracted from audio files and Midi patterns. The lanes on the mixer can each load one Groove Patch. To get started, browse or load a patch from the channel menu.

5 Use the slider to increase the amount the groove affects the pattern. If the groove doesn't sound regular enough, engage the 'Pre-Align' button below the Shuffle dial. This will quantise the incoming pattern before the groove is applied and make the results more uniform.

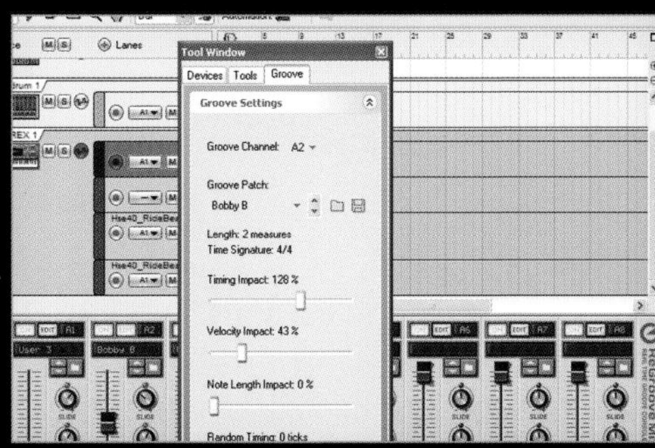

6 Refine the groove by hitting the Edit button at the top of the mixer channel. This opens the floating Tool window, which offers four parameters with sliders. When Timing and Velocity Impact are at 100% the groove will be applied to the pattern with the same feel as the patch. You can vary each one separately to affect either timing or volume.

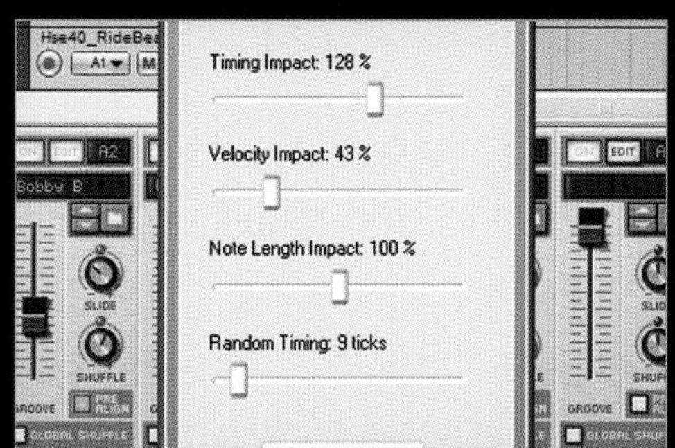

7 You can impose the phrasing from the groove patch onto a pattern by adjusting the Note Length parameter. The last parameter is Random. Use this to add subtle timing changes similar to those made by a human drummer. Higher amounts start to make the beat sound sloppy.

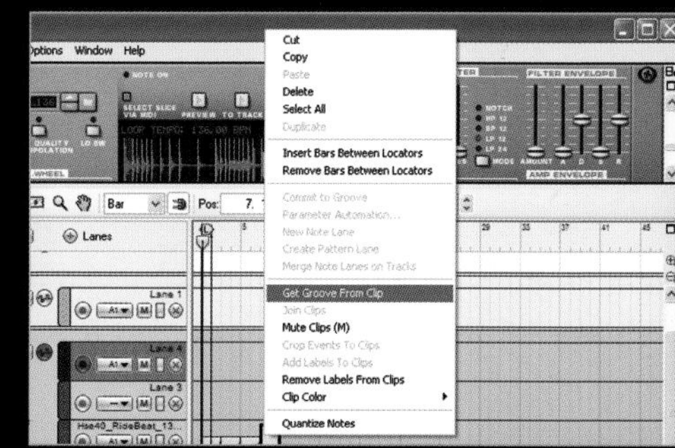

8 A ReGroove patch can be extracted from a pattern, sequence or Dr:Rex file. Select a channel on the mixer, right-click on a pattern then select 'Get groove from clip'. Make sure the Tool window is open and save it as a new patch.

/walkthrough drum programming grids

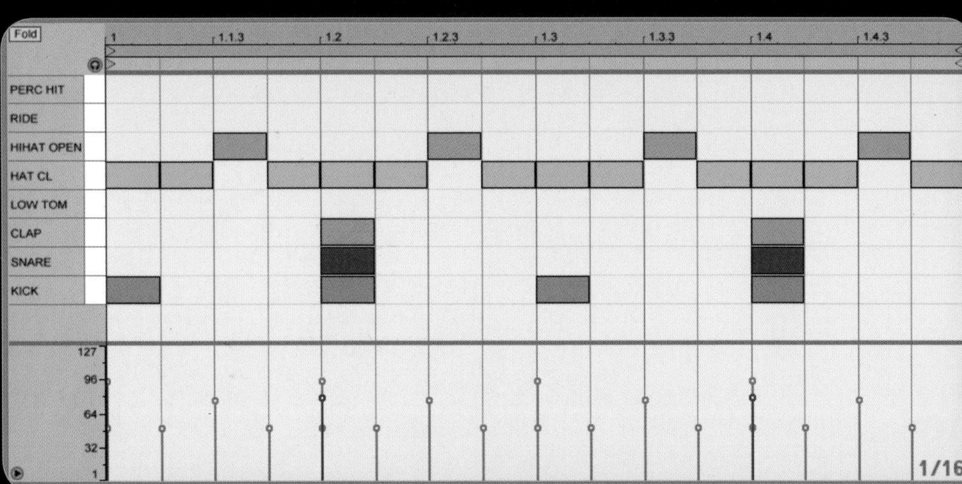

1. HOUSE BASICS: The archetypal house rhythm. It may look simple, but get the sounds right and it can keep the dancefloor moving all night. Place a kick at the start of each beat for the classic 'four-on-the-floor' loop. Next, layer up a snare and clap on beats two and four. Add an open or pedal hat on the off-beat between each kick. To finish, add a closed hat on every 16th measure, except where the open hat is placed.

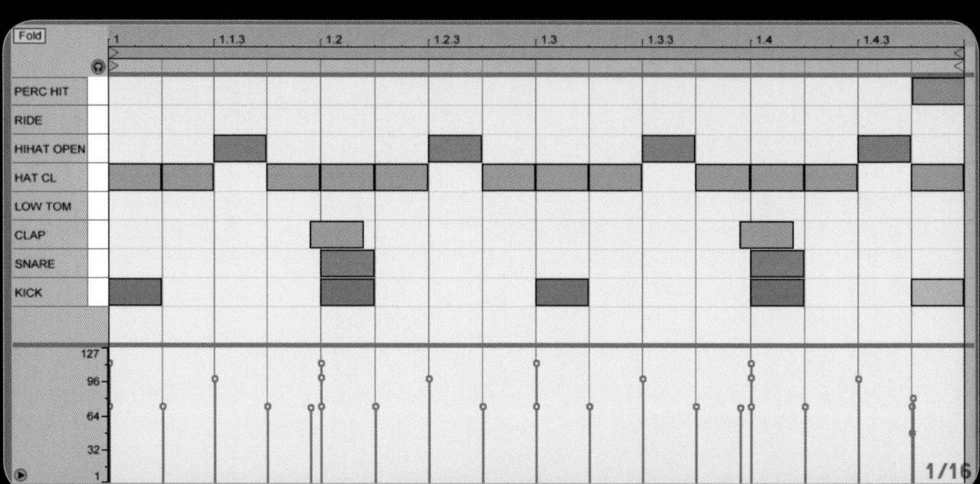

2. HOUSE IMPROVEMENTS: This pattern builds on the basics by adding an extra kick at the end of the beat. This can be reinforced with an extra percussive noise. It doesn't matter what sound is used as long as it works with the beat. A second change involves nudging the clap a little forward so that it sounds a few ms before the snare. This provides extra snap. Use a medium to heavy swing setting to assure the funk.

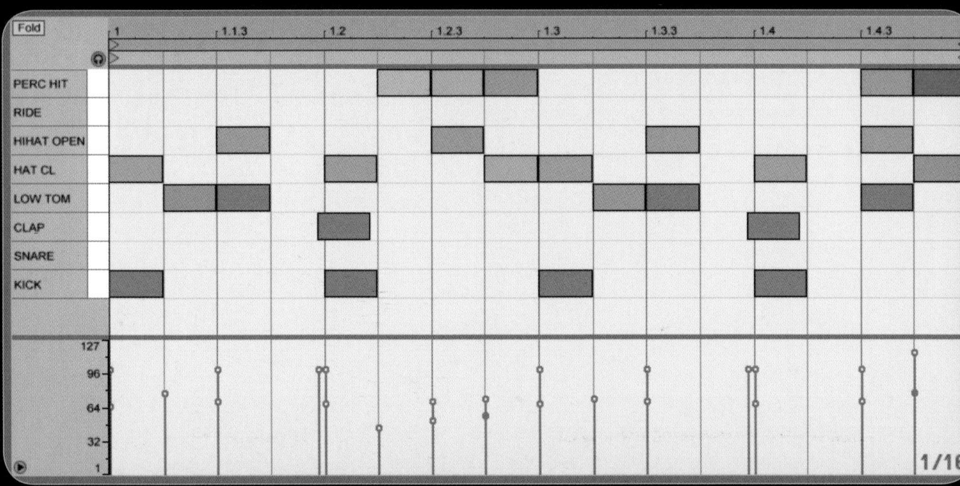

3. PROGRESSIVE BEAT: This beat uses low toms on the first and third quarters to introduce momentum. An extra percussive pattern on the second and fourth quarters acts as a response to the tom. This pattern can be played by a synthetic click, clave, stick or even a high tom depending on the kind of sound you're aiming for. Straight, medium and high swing settings all sound good with this pattern.

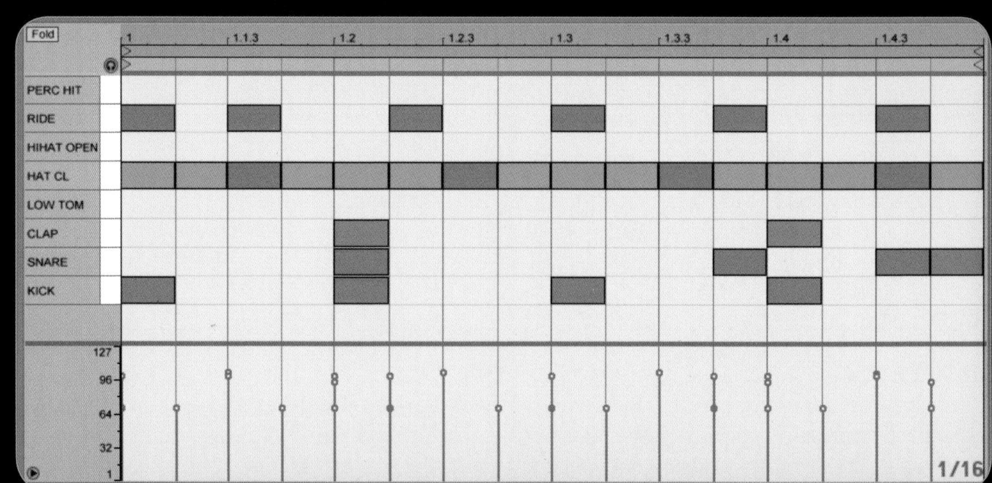

4. TECH-HOUSE: This beat is influenced by old-school house and techno. The ride hits that fall on the first and third beats give a downbeat vibe, while the syncopated hits on measures 6 and 14 convey the funk. Note the snare pattern, which is a little more complicated than the straight clap pattern, and works alongside the ride in the second half of the beat. Straight, medium or high swing settings work well here.

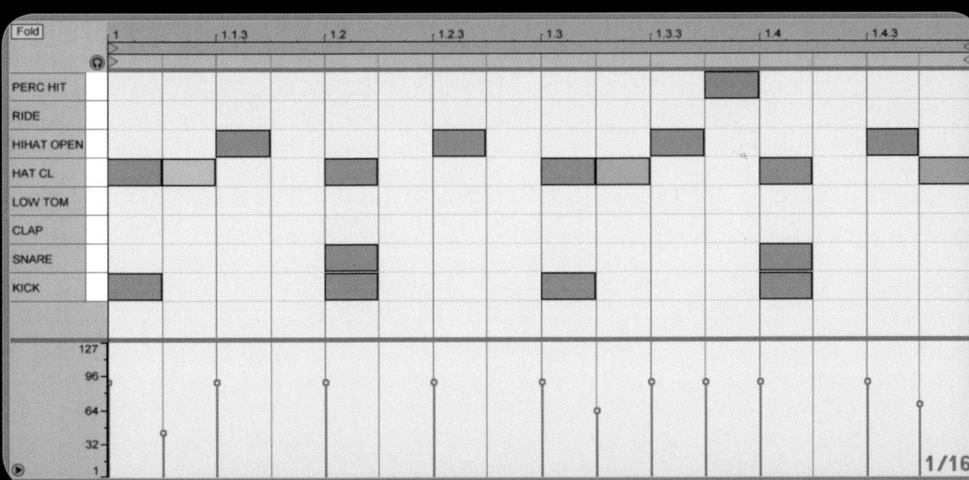

5. ELECTRO-HOUSE: The simplicity of this beat leaves plenty of room for the characteristic up-front bass riffs that drive electro-house tracks. The hi-hat interplay is the main element that defines the rhythm. Note the use of lower velocities on hits 2, 10 and 16 (the lighter shade of red). Finally, the single percussion hit introduces a variant groove. The beat works well straight and with varying amounts of swing.

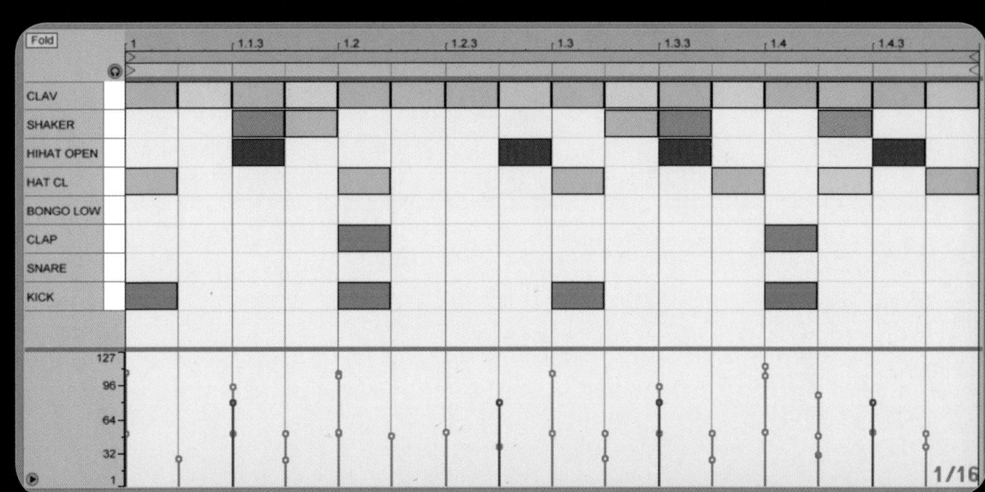

6. MINIMAL: The kick and clap (or snare) form the backbone of this beat. The hi-hat pattern is syncopated on the third beat, introducing an element of subtle funk. The shaker reinforces the hi-hats, with individual volume levels changing so the off-beats play a little louder. Swing is an essential feature of the groove and is most easily heard in the clave pattern, which plays a 16th note rhythm with accents on select beats.

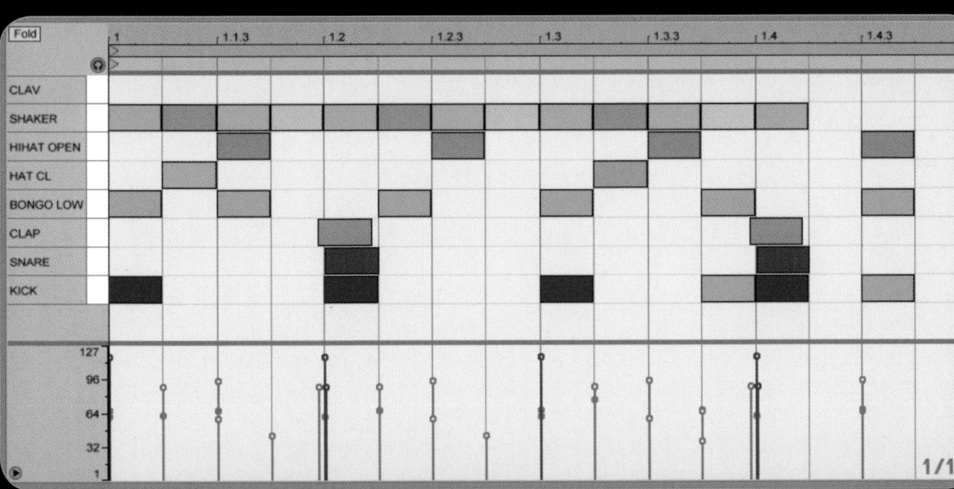

7. FUNKY HOUSE: The bounce in this groove comes from the syncopated kick pattern, which adds extra hits either side of the fourth beat. Work their volume levels so they don't overpower the on-beat kick. Both the alternating hi-hat pattern and shaker drop-out on beat four help to accent the final kick. Experiment with a combination of bongo samples for the bongo pattern. Add medium swing.

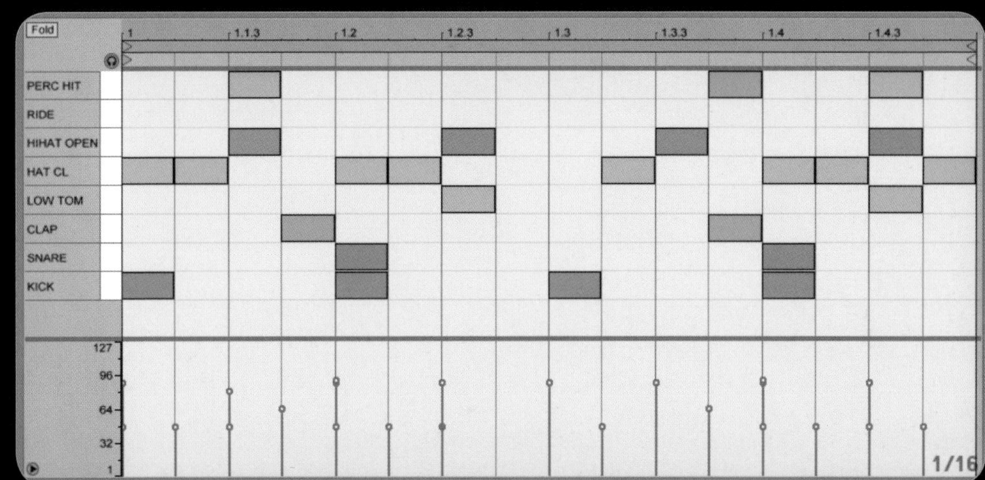

8. JACKIN' / FIDGET: This beat draws inspiration from old-school jackin' house. The key ingredient is the clap that hits before the snare. The heavier the swing quantise, the closer the clap gets pushed towards the snare's position, and the funkier the beat will be. The percussion elements offset the groove and work with the tom in a highly syncopated way. The hi-hat should be up-front and loud to maximise jackin' potential.

/pro tips

wolfgang gartner

His name is one of the biggest in dance music. We talk to the electro-house master about 'wtf sounds', when to abandon a mix and the importance of hard work.

How do you see the dance music industry developing over the next two to three years?
I see it developing in a big way! It already is. You look at people like David Guetta doing collaborations with Akon and such, and you see more and more people embracing dance music. It's really on the rise here in America too, which is exciting because it had a pretty bad lull here in the early 2000s. Some people think mass consumption of dance music is a bad thing. I feel the other way. The more people who get into it, the more people will start producing, and it just leads to more talent, more music and more of what we love.

When mixing, what do you find the hardest thing to get sounding right?
The low end: the way the kick and bass sit together – always has been, always will be. The solution for me ends up being a mix of sidechaining and multi-band compression, but I still haven't found any magic settings or combination of plugins. It's always hard to get it right, and the process is different every time.

Which sounds do you struggle to make most?
Those 'what the fuck' sounds. By that I mean sounds that you can't identify or say: "that's a saw or a square wave" and you can't pin down how they were made when you hear them. I use these kinds of sounds as leads or hooks in a track.

Just a melody played with one or two oscillators on a synth isn't enough for me. I'm not satisfied with using a vanilla preset or saw wave; it's too simple, too predictable. I like to try and create a sound the synth wasn't supposed to make. I usually end up using a lot of modulation and automation to tweak different parameters and morph the sound into something unique.

Any advice on monitoring? Quiet? Loud? Do you prefer flat and boring speakers, headphones or big, chunky monitors?
I've been using the same pair of Tannoy Reveal monitors since 1997, powered by a rare model Nikko amp that was made in about 1979. It's a completely coloured monitoring system, and probably very inaccurate, but it sounds great! The old amp can drive the monitors really hard, and I push it as hard as it will go when I'm working.

I've battled on and off with getting some high-end powered monitors and ditching this setup but every time I go into somebody's studio and hear what flat, accurate monitors sound like, I'm turned off. Maybe they're good for mixing and getting levels right, but the sound seems so sterile. When I'm trying to write a bassline, or jamming on one of my synths, I need a deep bass and a crispy treble with the sound in my face. I do have another set of smaller monitors in the studio on a parallel wall as an A/B system, but they are pretty coloured and inaccurate too. I guess it works for me because my ears know the speakers. I always test out the finished tracks on other systems in the house and in the car and my mixes end up sounding OK.

What is your biggest self-criticism?
Not knowing when an approach or attempt at a certain sound is working in the studio, and spending too much time trying to nail something that just isn't going to work. Sometimes you need to know when to move on, and I have a tendency to be too persistent. This can play both ways, but a lot of the time it's more of a flaw than an asset.

How important do you think it is to have your music mastered commercially? Can you do it yourself as effectively and what tools would you recommend?
It's extremely important to have a good mastering job, but how you choose to do it is down to personal taste. I decided to start mastering my own stuff recently and invested in some nice hardware to help do the job. My main tools now are a Crane Song STC-8 compressor and an SPL Tube Vitalizer, in addition to a pair of Empirical Labs Distressors.

What do you believe is the secret to your success as a producer?
First and foremost, it's that making dance music is the only thing I ever wanted to do since I was a kid. I had absolutely no interest in anything else that could materialise into a job. Girls, food, making music – that's pretty much what I was interested in. If there had been something else that had interested me I probably would have pursued it a long time ago and quit music during one of the hard periods where I wasn't successful. But there's just nothing else out there for me besides this.

Another thing is that I'm extremely antisocial and reclusive, so I pretty much don't go out, don't socialise and don't do anything except sit at home and make music. That means I get a lot done. And I seem to have a personality trait that makes me persistent when I want something. Once I've decided what it is that I want I'm willing to do almost anything to get it.

It's not easy for me to make good music; it doesn't just flow out of me like water. It's something that takes a lot of effort and hard work with every track I make, but I want it so bad that I'm willing to sit in all weekend and try and write a bassline for 15 hours until something finally comes out. Yes, it really does take me that long.

And finally... Have you any advice for aspiring young producers out there?
Keep at it. I know everybody says it, but that's because it's true. I had been sending demo tapes to record labels for seven years before I got my first record deal.

"Keep at it: I'd been sending demo tapes to labels for seven years before I got my first record deal."

/part two

bass

The kick's working its magic, a subtle 808 hat picks up the pace, a raucous snare gets hands in the air and then – wham – in comes the bassline.

Whether it's a disco-inspired workout, an off-beat progressive rhythm-rocker or the full-on rudeness of an electro cone-melter, the bassline works with the beat and melody to propel the track forward to get feet moving and heads nodding.

The bass is both the sonic glue that binds the melody and rhythm, and the bedrock on which subsequent instrumentation sits. In electro and nu-rave productions it is increasingly taking the lead in its own right.

Pros often say the hardest thing to get right is the bass. Not only does it require programming mastery, it also needs firm production knowledge and a little bit of luck.

But when it sits right it can tear up the dancefloor.

/the bassics

supplying low-end energy, rhythmic balls and occasionally cracking melodies, the bass can make or break a track.

The most important relationship in dance music is between the kick drum and the bassline – the king and queen mix elements that have the power to drive a dancefloor wild and the sonic foundations upon which the rest of the production is built. Get it right and you're halfway to a hit.

The key to getting the two working together is picking a kick and bass that complement each other, rather than fighting each other for frequency space and impact.

As a general rule of thumb, if the kick is high in low-mid energy (the kind of cracking kicks used in nu-rave, electro or disco), the bass should sit below it, while if the kick is laden with low-end energy (like minimal 808 subs that boom at 60Hz) the bass should weave its magic in the lower mids. For those that insist on fat bass and a deep kick, sidechain compression can help keep the two apart – ducking bass volume when the kick drum hits.

Basslines inhabit two distinct frequency ranges. **Regular bass** extends from around 90Hz to 300hz (higher for harmonic overtones), while **sub bass** peaks at around 90Hz and extends as far down as 20Hz. For a full sounding house track you need to tickle both the regular and sub-bass frequencies in a precise, controlled way.

Sub bass frequencies are relatively new in recorded music. Acoustic instruments struggle to get anywhere as low as 90Hz – with only the biggest church pipe organs coming close – meaning that sub frequencies are absent from most orchestral and early pop recordings. Indeed sub bass generation was only made accessible to sound designers thanks to developments in electronics, with synths and more recently computers able to create and control the 'below bass' frequencies their acoustic forebears couldn't.

Ignoring sub bass frequencies in dance music will leave your track sounding flat and weak, particularly on club systems. But the sub should never dominate, and getting the balance between sub and regular bass frequencies right requires a good listening environment – or frequency monitoring plugin – and some careful production.

The easiest way of thinking about sub frequencies is in terms of very low notes. These lower-than-low sounds are created by triggering notes in the C1–A1 zone (and a few notes either side). To fill out this zone using a synth all you need to do is introduce an oscillator that covers this range. If you're using a live bass sample you'll need to layer up a synth to bulk it up, or use a specific sub bass plug-in to generate lower sub harmonics.

Styles

Basslines can be split into three broad personality types.

The rhythm bassline

The simplest is the **rhythm bassline**, which underpins the groove with simple melodic content. It sees the bass take on a rhythmic rather than melodic role, working alongside the kick to drive the groove and anchor the beat. This kind of bassline can be programmed using just one note, which follows the key of the song. The most basic example is an off-beat pattern where the bass plays between each kick in a 4/4 groove – a favourite among progressive house producers.

Simple as it is, this kind of bassline can be devastatingly effective on the dancefloor. Stick it in the right frequency range and the regular pulse will provide a rhythmic backbone without drawing unnecessary attention to itself. Where the main interest of a track is a euphoric synth riff or complex percussive workout, the rhythm bassline will sit in the background, freeing up space for other mix elements to shine.

In some cases this simple off-beat bassline is all that's needed in a track. In others it can be used to track the groove in the sub area while a second bass plays a busier sequence an octave above.

The bass riff

The **bass riff** tends to be more complex and memorable, with a melodic element and hooky quality that does more for the track than simply augment the rhythm section. It is a bassline that can stand loud and proud alone, but which works equally well below an often complex musical arrangement. Inspired by old disco and funk lines, it is the kind of bass favoured by disco, deep, latin and funky house producers. It shines in tracks like Daft Punk's **Around the World.**

Getting a great bass riff is as much about experimentation as musicality. Jamming and recording to a backing track then editing later may yield good results, as will programming directly into a note editor. Programming should take inspiration from live bass playing, with short notes and subtle use of pitch-bend to replicate live finger-plucks and slides. Keep velocities changing: certain hits should be short and loud for added emphasis.

For a truly live sounding bassline, introduce some samples. A mix of programmed and live bass can sound great: hits and hard-to-reproduce slides are particularly useful for adding authenticity.

The bass riff should generally be quantised with the same amount of swing, and to the same groove template, as the beat. This helps all the key elements lock together. If it feels too forced, reduce the amount of swing.

Bassline as lead

In both the rhythm line and bass riff the bass provides backing and support for a track's lead lines. But there's a third type of bassline popular in the electro and fidget scenes: **bassline as lead**. Here the bass is the most dominant melodic force in the track. It doesn't just hold down the rhythm: it plays the lead riff and is mixed up-front and loud, occupying the frequency space normally occupied by both bass and synth top-line.

The sound source for this kind of bass is usually a synth with several oscillators and flexible enough filter and modulation sources to produce unique tones. Because this kind of bass takes the place of the lead extra oscillators should be stacked into upper octaves to increase its harmonic quality and extend it up into lead territory.

The lead bassline needs to maintain interest throughout the track. This requires more complex programming than other kinds of basslines. Producers use a straight version of it early on and then mess with it using a series of programming and effects tricks to alter both the sound and the sequence as the track progresses.

Tip / For a punky, cut-and-paste style fidget bassline, program a 'raw' version of the lead bass and bounce it down. Then loop it and tweak the filter, envelope and LFO settings live while the backing track plays, bouncing down the tweaks. Listen to the tweaked version in the context of the track. Save sections that work and use them for edits and fills. Fire up a new set of effects and do the same again until you have a collection of glitched edits that you can call on as you continue building the track. This kind of technique produces a lot of rubbish, but it occasionally gives birth to real gems. The results are also often wildly different to what you'd get by using a mouse to program fills and tweaks manually.

Tip / Electro basslines are prime candidates for 'call and response' programming. Play the lead riff using the main bass sound then mute it and play the riff on a second channel using the same synth with contrasting settings (or a different synth). Program the riff so it switches between the two sounds at regular intervals, like every two beats in the bar.

Back to the source

Synths

The synthesiser is the major source of house bass sounds. Both analogue and digital types are used, and a strong, effective bass can be programmed on the most basic synth. There are some long-time favourites though, including the MiniMoog, Yamaha DX7 and mighty single-oscillator Roland TB-303.

Most basslines are monophonic – with only one note playing at any one time. You can use any combination of oscillators and waveforms to produce the raw tone. In most cases, it's best to start simple, with a single oscillator supplying the weight, then add additional oscillators to enrich the tone. For depth, add a sine sub an octave below the initial oscillator. Introduce a third, either a saw or triangle, an octave above. Detune upper oscillators to thicken the sound.

Tip / If a bassline lacks presence double it with a different sound sent through a high-pass filter to add fullness in the mid and upper frequencies. Send the original and upper bass to the same bus for joint treatment.

Live bass

The use of live bass – from sessions or sample collections – is less prominent than it was in the days when disco, latin and funky house ruled. But there are producers still using it, and the latest wave of Parisian nu-rave producers have been mixing the best of both worlds, splicing heavily compressed and overdriven single bass hits with synths to create hybrid basslines oozing with attitude.

Playing disco and funk-style bass requires a bundle of niche talent. Fortunately there are a wealth of sample collections featuring great bass players. Don't just look for collections aimed at house producers: funk and disco products are often goldmines too.

If you've got the cash to pay for clearance (or rock-hard balls) then basslines are some of the easiest parts of classic records to incorporate into a track: just find a great line, edit it into time and then roll off the top end of the sample using EQ. Double the sampled bassline with a synth playing the same notes an octave above to augment the high end.

Finally, remember that live basslines will not have enough sub bass frequencies to shake a club system so will invariably need to be either doubled with a synth playing an octave below, or fed through a sub-bass plugin.

big bottom bass boxes

Some synths have been providing floor-shaking basslines for decades. The Minimoog (**below**) is renowned for its power and girth. The Yamaha DX7 has an uncanny ability to cut through the densest of mixes. And the king of all – single-handedly responsible for the acid-house revolution and some of the most memorable riffs in music history – is the Roland TB-303.

Despite having just one oscillator, the 303 has a flavour all its own, enhanced by the unique character of its internal step sequencer with its 'accent' and 'slide' steps. Clever programming, and the liberal use of overdrive alongside real-time cutoff and resonance tweaks give the 303 the rare ability to rock a party all night long.

The 303 has many clones, but possibly the most convincing is the DIY X0Xbox kit from Ladyada. As well as sounding and behaving almost exactly as the original, it is also has an easy-to-program sequencer and a USB connection for backups.

Also worth a mention is Propellerheads' classic ReBirth, the first great-sounding software clone, which is now available as a free download from the Propellerheads website.

/bass in the mix

eq, compression, overdrive and sidechaining all help the bassline throb.

Bass EQ

When it comes to mixing, the secret to a punchy bassline is often as much to do with what is cut out as what is left in. Not only does the bass have to work closely with the kick drum, it also needs to fit into the wider mix, not intruding too far into frequency areas inhabited by lead sounds (unless you're using the 'bass as lead' technique), and not eating too much headroom at the lower end. To carve the sound down to size a bass usually needs to be cut at both its upper and lower ends. However, cuts needs to be done carefully: getting it wrong can seriously damage a mix.

Low-pass filters cut high frequency harmonics, creating more room for lead sounds while leaving the low end intact. When deciding the filter cutoff point, aim to balance the fundamental weight of the bass – where its real pressure is felt – with the upper harmonics that fill out the frequency spectrum for a solid, rounded sound.

Here a bit of technical explanation is useful. A bassline playing E2 generates a fundamental frequency of 82.41Hz (**see page 127**). Frequencies above that are harmonic overtones of the original note. When EQing this note, you'd want to balance the fundamental 82.41Hz frequency, where the bass has its power, with its upper harmonics.

In practice most basslines contain more than one note, and the presence of a kick and other mix elements means that EQ decisions are as much about fitting the bass into its surroundings as bringing out fundamental frequencies. That said, your aim should still be to find the EQ 'sweet spot' that captures both the deep frequencies and the sweet upper harmonics. With basslines that move a lot, filter key-tracking can be used to maintain this key relationship between fundamental frequencies and upper harmonics, helping bulk up higher notes that might otherwise lose pressure.

High-pass filters play a different role, cutting often inaudible low end frequencies that eat headroom. To add punch to a weak bassline roll off some of the very low end (below 50–60Hz) before it hits the compressor. Next use a shelving or high-pass filter to carve out some of the subs to make more room for the critical frequencies in the 50–120hz range. An additional EQ can be inserted after the compressor to boost and cut other frequencies to help it sit right. Cutting a notch at the main frequency the kick occupies may also help separate the two of them.

Tip / EQ can be used as an effect to create sonic tension in builds and breakdowns. Strap a high-pass filter across the bass and slowly raise the frequency during the breakdown so the bass gradually loses its impact in the mix. Then, as the drop comes, bypass the EQ so that the full bass returns to cause maximum dancefloor mayhem. Experiment with resonance too, for added scream-factor, but avoid big boosts when sweeping the lower frequencies as you'll quickly end up with unpleasant volume spikes.

Compression

Compression is used to tighten up a flabby bassline, increasing its thickness and presence in the mix. It can also be used when volume spikes and transients are eating too much headroom to make the volume more consistent. To increase body use a soft setting with medium attack and release to shave between 3 and 5dBs off the signal. To calm volume spikes, use a fast attack and release to catch the front of the sound so that the volume remains stable. Use the make-up gain to bring the volume up to the same level as the original and compare the difference in tone by A/Bing with the uneffected version.

Some engineers use **parallel compression** on a bassline, either by bussing the bass to another track with stonewall compression (see **page 111**), or by using a compressor with a wet/dry mix control. The trick is to slam the compressor hard, and mix it back into the original signal to add extra body and texture.

Sidechaining the bass

Sidechain compression on the bassline acts as both a technical problem solver and a creative tool. Whichever way you use it, the method is the same.

Sidechaining involves routing the signal from one channel on the mixing desk to control another. When used on a bassline it is almost always the kick drum that drives the compressor's sidechain to control the volume of the bass. The four-to-the-floor kick ducks the bass volume in perfect sync against the kick so that it breathes with the groove.

This compression can be used subtly to prevent headroom space battles. On medium settings the rhythm becomes more noticeable and the bassline will start to audibly pump. On more extreme settings, the whole bassline ducks and sucks back up in volume, creating the classic fidget sound. Experiment with the compressor's attack and release settings to change the shape of the sucks and help the bass lock to the groove.

Tip / It is good practice to trigger the sidechain from a muted track that has a kick on each beat so that even when the main kick isn't playing the bassline still pumps. This technique has other advantages. Sometimes the track's main kick will have too much sustain or too many sub frequencies, throwing the compressor so that it doesn't give a good bounce-back. In these cases use a shorter kick or adjust the muted kick sample's envelope for greater timing control.

/walkthrough
sidechaining the bass

1 Set up the kick track and route it to a bus. Create a one bar kick loop that plays on the beat for the four-to-the-floor sound. Mute the output of both the bus and trigger track. This means the kick will still be playing, but not be audible in the mix. (Sidechaining from a silent kick means you can keep the bassline pumping even when the main kick drops out.)

2 Insert a compressor on the bassline track. Turn on the sidechain input and select the bus that the trigger kick has been assigned to.

3 Reduce the threshold and slowly increase the ratio to increase the intensity of the effect. The threshold parameter sets the minimum volume level the bass will drop to when the kick hits. Use the ratio parameter to control the intensity of the pump.

4 Work the groove by adjusting the attack and release controls. These shape the way the compressor pumps and sucks. To get bouncing, set the attack to minimum and slowly reduce the release control from the maximum position. All compressors react differently. Experiment with different types to see what works best with the track.

5 If there is a slight click at the front of the bass it can usually be eliminated by increasing the attack.

6 In some situations a long, subby kick can cause the trigger to stay open for too long because the compressor doesn't have time to suck back. Using

7 Another way to resolve potential trigger length problems is by tweaking the decay and sustain lengths of the kick driving the sidechain by altering

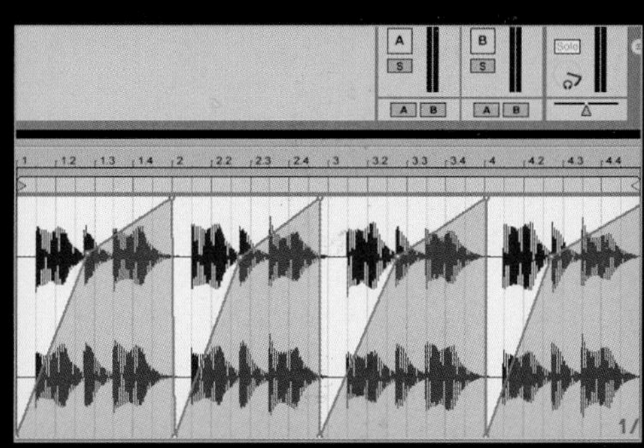

8 Some DAWS, including Cubase and Ableton Live, let you draw a pumping volume curve directly onto an audio file. This can be a quick and

/the sub

the heart-pounding energy of the sub is what makes dancefloors rock – but don't go too low.

Where the main bassline is heard in the mix, the sub is felt. The extra throb of the sub locks down the bass end, providing the additional depth needed to balance a banging kick.

As noted earlier, the sub is a relatively recent addition to recorded music, made possible by advances in sound generation technology. It sits one or two octaves below the main bassline. Exactly where will depend on the key of the song, the notes used for the bass riff and another important factor – the limitations of club speakers.

Like studio speakers, club systems only go so low. Although some reproduce sounds as low as 30Hz, the vast majority start to drop away above that. This has clear implications when programming the sub bass – as there's no point creating a bassline that a club system won't play. On a keyboard, C2 lies at 65.41Hz and C0 at 16.35Hz. C1 reproduces at around 32.7Hz – a frequency that will play on only the best club systems. To be safe, it's a good rule of thumb to make the lowest sub bass note E1 (41.20Hz), a frequency that will reproduce well on all but the very worst club rigs. (See **Note-to-frequency table, page 127**)

There's a second consideration too. The ability to hear bass and sub bass in a track will be limited by the size of your monitors and the acoustic response of your studio. The classic studio reference speakers, the Yamaha NS-10s, for example fall off sharply below 90Hz and disappear at 60Hz, making them less than ideal for checking low-end sub bass.

Check the frequency range of your studio monitors. If they don't extend far down it can be more efficient to plot basslines within the limitations of what you can hear. And even if you do have great speakers, it is still good practice to check sub energy visually using a frequency analyser plugin. The more knowledge you have about the all-important low end, the better your final mix will be.

Creating sub bass

For a simple, supporting sub bass that lies below the main bassline, use a single sine wave as it doesn't have any harmonics to interfere with the tone of the main bass.

If you want the same sine wave to provide the main bass sound as well, then you'll need to increase its harmonic content to give it more balls in the mix. To do this send part of the signal via a send to an overdrive or distortion unit. This is a quick, but highly effective way of introducing additional harmonics. Software effects such as the PSP VintageWarmer, Crysonic nXtasy and even Logic's clip distortion all help heat the sub.

Sometimes triangle, saw or square waves are used for the sub, but if they are to be mixed in with the main bass, it's important to consider the impact of their extra harmonics.

Tip / Because sub bass sits so low in the mix it can be hard to hear potential tuning errors. Open up a score editor to see if any notes look out of place, or briefly transpose the sequence up a couple of octaves to see whether it works there.

> **/pro tips**
>
> ## lower than low
>
> Sound waves below 20Hz are classified as 'Infrasound' and are beyond the scope of almost every sound system and PA to reproduce.
>
> In fact, most club sound system engineers tend to roll off bass around 30–45Hz to provide extra headroom for the P.A to sound louder and fatter in the more critical sub-bass frequency range of 50–90Hz.

A note on headroom

It is important to find the right balance between the sub and main bassline volumes. If the sub supports the main bassline, first balance the volume between the main bass and the kick, then slowly bring in the sub until it is just audible. If it's a deep sub you should only be able to feel it, adding extra weight to the bassline but not audible in the mix.

The trick is to make the sub loud enough to supply valuable sonic energy, but not so loud that it starts to dominate the mix.

If you max out the amount of volume available on a channel there will be no 'headroom' for other sounds in the mix (**see page 122–123**). Ironically, adding too much sub results in a mix that doesn't sound as loud and punchy as it would if it had less. When producing on small speakers (cones of six inches or less) it's common to overdo the sub.

Sub EQ

There are several tried and tested methods of maximising sub bass pressure in the mix. Start with a high-pass filter and set it to roll off below 40Hz with a medium slope. Even better: roll off frequencies below the lowest note of the bassline. So if A1 is the lowest, roll off at around 55Hz. Going higher will soften the deepest notes and preserve headroom. The opposite trick works too. Use a low-pass filter and roll off frequencies above the highest note to open the top end of the mix.

Sub compression

To prevent the kick drum colliding with the sub and producing muddy thuds that eat mix space, break out a compressor and sidechain the sub to the kick drum. Sub bass responds well to the ducking treatment. When ducked, you'll have created space in the mix for a fat kick *and* a deep bassline.

Sub bass plugins

You can generate sub bass frequencies from a bassline that doesn't have any – like one played using a bass guitar – by either doubling it with a sine wave, or by using a dedicated sub bass plugin. These plugins track the frequency of the bassline and generate a sine wave in the sub frequencies to add clout. Be careful with sub bass plugins though, especially if your speakers don't reproduce sub frequencies well. It's easy to overdo the bottom end when you can't hear it properly.

Stereo floor-shakers

To get those massively wide, bendy bass tones, you are going to need to expand the stereo width of the sound with the help of modulation effects such as chorus, ensemble, flange or stereo width tools.

It is important to note that when creating wider bass, it's not the sub bass that is widened. The sub-frequency energy of a bass tone always works best in mono. There are two key reasons for this: firstly our ears are less sensitive to the direction of low frequencies compared to mids and highs, which is why most audio monitoring systems only use a single sub bass unit. The second reason is punch. Mono is tighter and packs more punch, so it hits harder and tighter than an ultra-wide stereo bassline.

Wide bass comes from a happy medium of mono sub and stereo upper bass. The trick involves splitting the signal into upper and lower frequencies (much like the crossover on a sound-system) and applying the effects to the upper portion only (see **Wider bass walkthrough, right**).

This technique works best on bass sounds that have a decent amount of harmonic content, like rich multi-oscillator square and sawtooth basslines favoured by electro-house and fidget producers.

Tip / Phase cancellation causes parts of the mix to disappear when played back on a mono sound system. This can happen when effects that manipulate the phase of a signal are used. The list includes chorus, phasers, frequency shifters and anything that inverts the phase of a mono signal by 180 degrees. Check the mix in mono and listen for any signs of phase cancellation, including drum, bass and vocal drop-outs. If anything does, then go back to that element and reduce the amount of stereo effect or phase displacement and check in mono again.

Tip / Stereo bass can be bad news when cutting to vinyl, resulting in problems at both the cutting stage and when playing back pressings. In extreme cases it becomes impossible to cut a record that the needle can properly track. Keep the very low end in mono to avoid these problems.

Tip / Sometimes more definitely is more, and so is the case with synth **unison** controls. Unison bestows instant fatness in a single control. It works by adding extra voices to a sound and then detuning them by varying amounts. The result is a thicker, wider version of the original tone. Many classic sounds, including the beloved hard-house 'hoover', are built using this technique. Most digital synths have a unison-style effect built in.

/walkthrough wider bass

1 Set up an aux send on the bass channel. On the associated bus insert a high-pass filter. Next in line add a stereo modulation effect. A chorus, modulation delay, ensemble, flanger or spread effect will do the job perfectly. Set the wet/dry mix level to 100% wet and increase the amount going through the send until your bass feels supremely stereo.

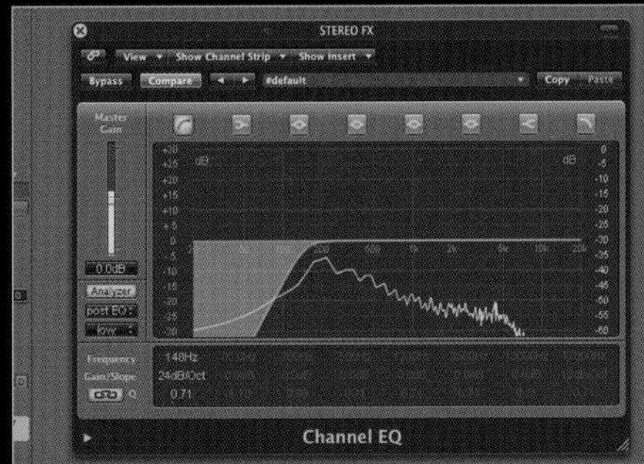

2 Stereo effects on low frequencies can cause mix (and stylus) mayhem. Remove them by slowly raising the cutoff frequency on the aux bus using a high-pass filter to around 100–200Hz. The high end will remain wide, but the low end on the origina channel will get gradually tighter until it sits centrally in the mix.

3 For greater control of the stereo effect, split the bass into two channels and process each independently. Use two aux sends on the bass track in pre-fader mode, with the volume to 0. Set up the first aux send as per steps 1 and 2. This will control the high end of the bass. The second aux is for the lower frequencies. It should be set to mono.

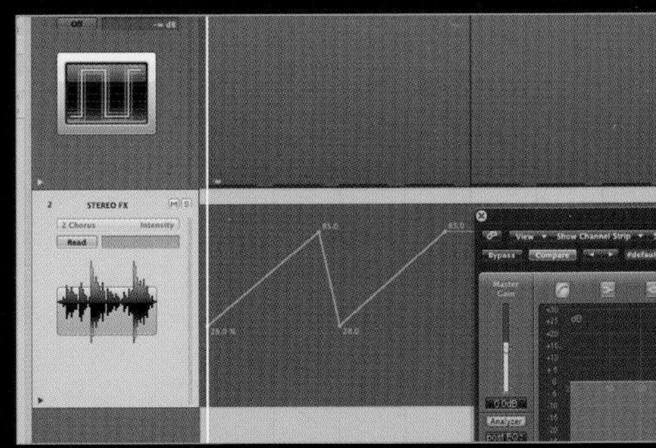

4 Roll off the high-end of the lower mono bass – start at around 300–400Hz. You will now be abl to alter the wider upper frequencies independently to the lower body, keeping the essential low frequencies tight while everything above is given the stereo treatment. Automate cutoff point and chorus depth fo all kinds of stereo trickery.

/walkthrough minimal basslines

When composing minimal basslines less is often more. This applies as much to the complexity of the rhythm as to the harmonic quality of the synth tone. A sine wave sub is ideal. It is deep and occupies only the fundamental frequency in the spectrum. It sucks the listener in and it leaves space in the mid-range to build the often busy upper mix.

Rhythmically the bass pattern should complement the drum loop. The two should move together, providing a solid foundation to the track. A regular tool in the minimal producer's arsenal is portamento. It allows you to create a hypnotic sound that slides between notes. Check the portamento settings on your bass synth to see if there is a choice between 'always on' and 'legato'. Choose legato for the best slides. You may also need to reduce polyphony to one for a purely monophonic bassline. To program a legato slide, overlap two notes in the Midi editor. Choosing which notes to program is a matter of experimentation. Adjust the speed of the glide to taste.

The hypnotic 1/8th note pattern on the right builds from a simple off-beat bassline in two ways. Firstly, it adds four notes on the up-beat. Secondly, it moves them an octave apart. It's the overlapping of notes that creates the portamento glides. A more advanced trick is to automate the speed of the glide during parts of the riff for added rhythm and style.

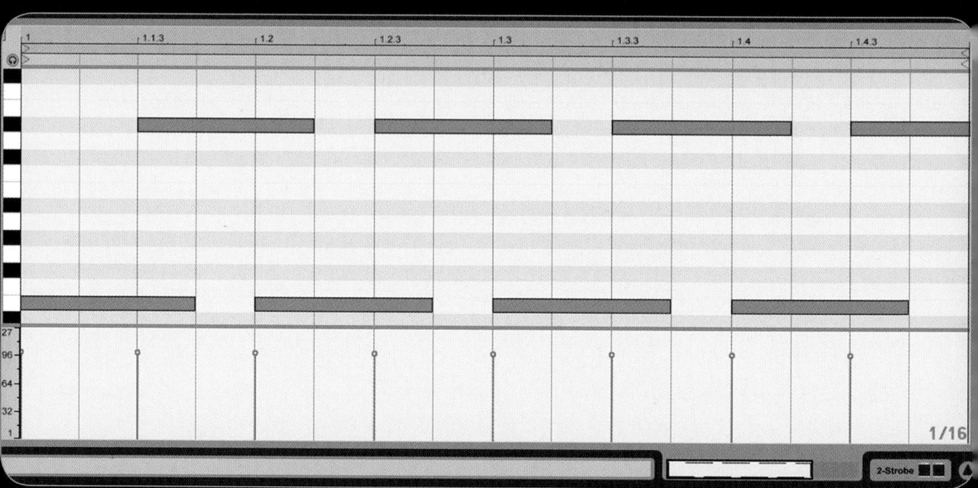

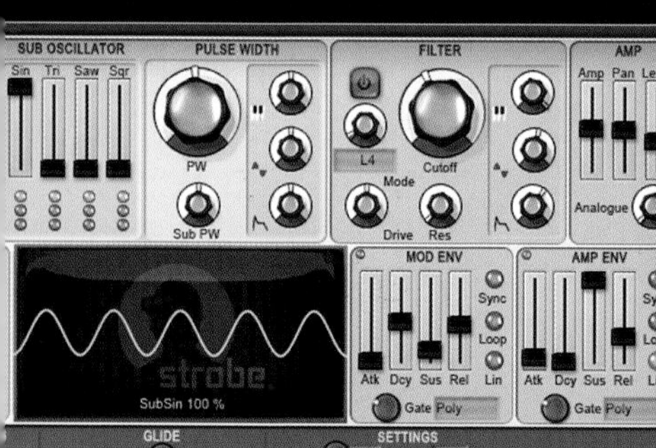

1 Start with a single sine wave sub oscillator. Set the amp envelope's attack, decay and release to minimum, and sustain to 100%. If the sound is too clicky open the attack and release a little. For a more pronounced bump to the note open the decay very slightly and lower the sustain. No filter is required.

2 The portamento speed or glide rate is the most important parameter for shaping the sound. Switch it on and adjust the speed of the glide. On lower settings the glide will be very fast. Open it slowly to find a speed that works with the groove. An advanced trick is to automate the speed on selected notes.

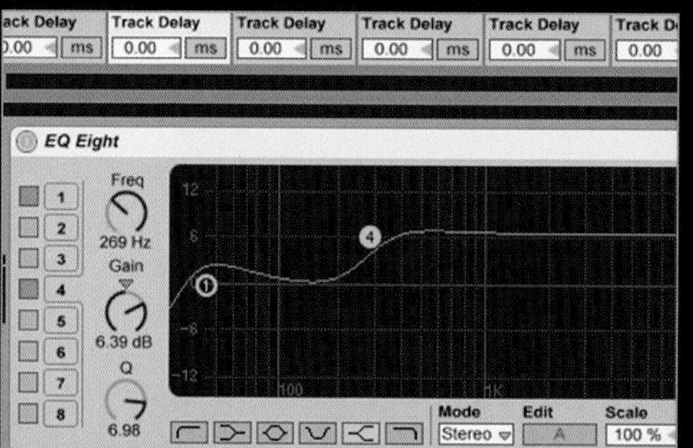

3 Use EQ to roll off the really low frequencies. Choose a 24dB high-pass filter, set it to 20Hz and work up from there until you feel like you are cutting into the audible range of the sub. Use a high-shelf EQ with a gentle Q to cut or boost the notes in the higher octave. Use a narrower Q to tame notes that stick out of the mix.

4 If the sub is carefully programmed and the synth supplies a complementary tone, the bassline shouldn't need much compression. Use a fast attack to reduce transients and a moderate release to keep the body consistent. Set ratio to 10:1 and lower the threshold so that it reduces peaks by 3–6dB. If the sub clashes with the kick, use sidechain compression

The ideal tech-house bass is warm and deep. It sits in the pocket of the groove, holding down the rhythm and pushing it forwards in an infectious way, like a hypnotic, dubbed-out bass guitar. Start by outlining the groove using the root key of the track and expand from there by adding extra notes, changing the pitches and playing with the accents.

Tech basslines can be short and stabbing or long and deep, the amp envelope release left wide open, the rhythm shaped by heavy sidechain compression.

The bassline pictured uses a two note riff in the key of E minor. It works nicely with a medium swing quantise, helping to give it some bounce. Keep the note lengths fixed to one beat except the final note, which should be shorter to maintain the funk. The riff has two notes emphasised with higher velocity values. In the synth, map velocity to open the filter cutoff and increase amplitude.

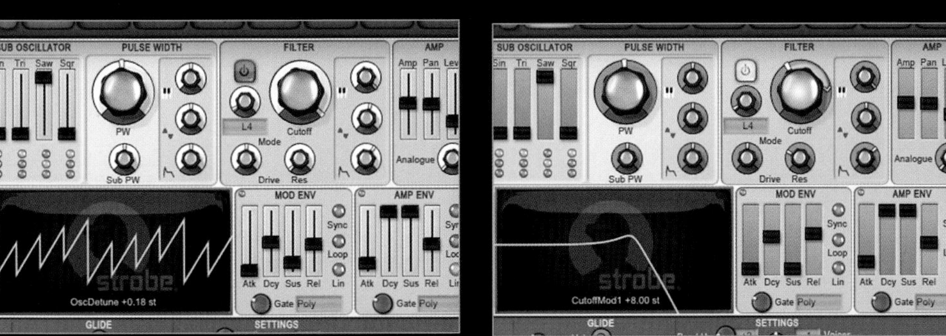

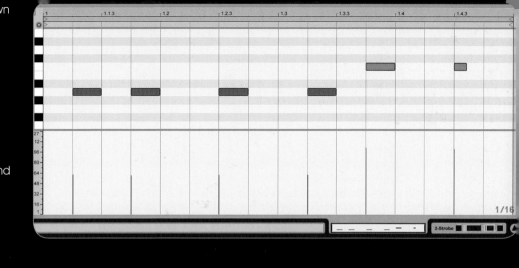

1 Create a synth patch with one saw wave at mid volume and another an octave below at maximum volume. Detune the upper saw a little for an analogue feel. Set the amp envelope to medium-fast attack, 100% decay and sustain, and 50% release.

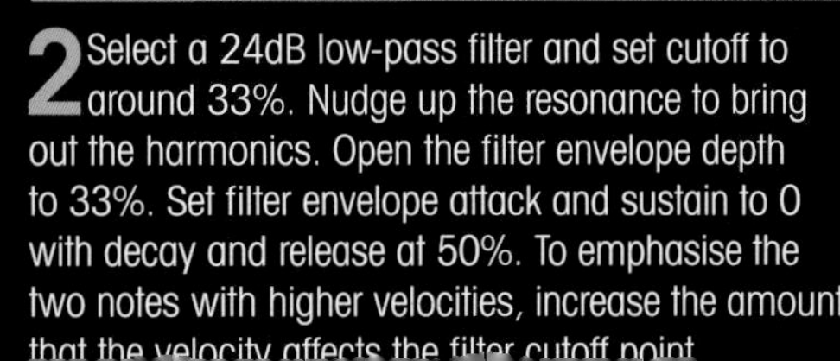

2 Select a 24dB low-pass filter and set cutoff to around 33%. Nudge up the resonance to bring out the harmonics. Open the filter envelope depth to 33%. Set filter envelope attack and sustain to 0 with decay and release at 50%. To emphasise the two notes with higher velocities, increase the amount that the velocity affects the filter cutoff point.

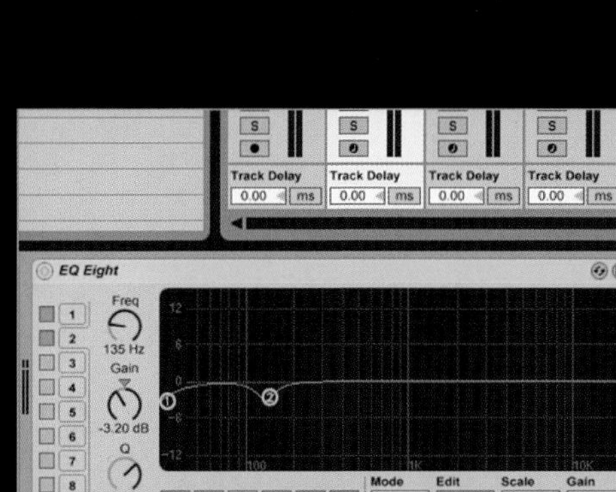

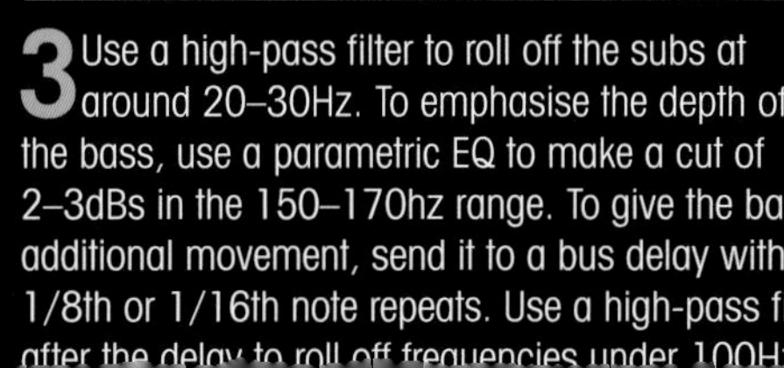

3 Use a high-pass filter to roll off the subs at around 20–30Hz. To emphasise the depth of the bass, use a parametric EQ to make a cut of 2–3dBs in the 150–170hz range. To give the bass additional movement, send it to a bus delay with 1/8th or 1/16th note repeats. Use a high-pass filter after the delay to roll off frequencies under 100Hz.

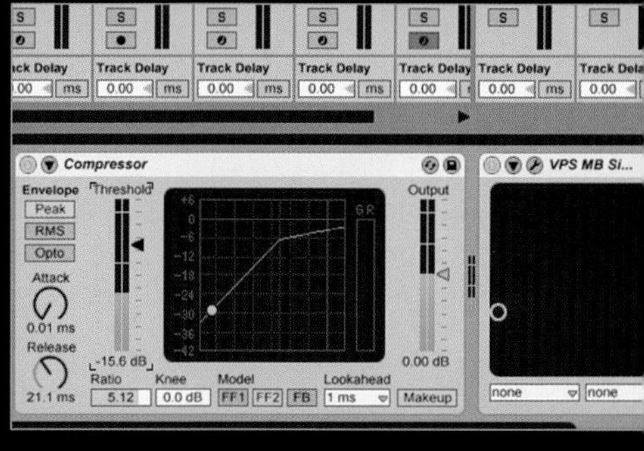

4 Make the bass growl with compression. Use a medium fast attack to let the initial transients through and turn up the release so that it adds a bit of grit to the signal. Use a 5:1 ratio and lower the threshold to reduce gain by 5–7dBs. For added character introduce an extra compressor on sidechain duties to reinforce the groove.

rog basses are a combination of form and function, working alongside the kick while following he chord progression of the lead line. For a simple, solid bass sound use a saw wave and louble it with a sub oscillator an octave below. For added harmonic quality, introduce a third oscillator and tune it to four, five or seven semitones above the initial saw. This produces chord harmonics at major third, fourth or fifth intervals.

asteful use of automation on the amp envelope and filter during the track shapes the bassline's journey from the first drop through to a twisted breakdown. (For advanced prog basslines try also automating the interval of the third oscillator so that it stays in tune with the ead line chords.)

his grid is 16 beats/four bars long, allowing for the longer duration of a four bar progression. Note how the note changes every bar but the rhythm stays the same. This musical progression starts on the route note (the first note of the scale and the key of the track) and shifts to the minor third, then down to the minor second, then resolves back to the route. The minor key gives the tune a dark, emotional feel. This can be changed to a happier, uplifiting vibe by moving the notes in bars two and three up by two semitones. This simple bassline works well with a straight groove or with a light amount of swing.

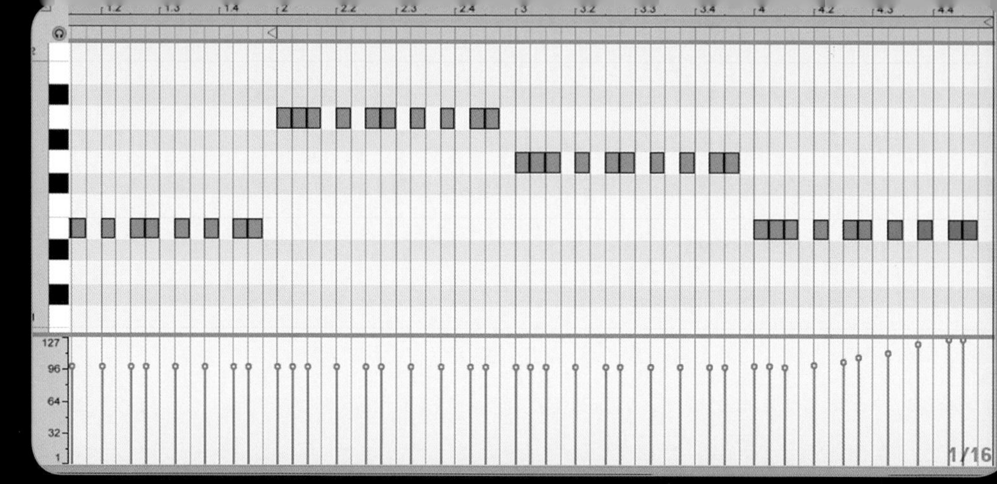

1 Create a simple synth patch with a saw wave on osc 1 and add a sine an octave below on the second oscillator. The saw wave provides the tone, while the sine acts as the sub, adding bottom-end girth. The amp envelope should be set with a fast attack, 30% decay, 70% sustain and fast release.

2 Use a 24dB low-pass filter set to 40% with resonance at a minimum to preserve thickness. Set the filter envelope depth to 65%. The velocity gets progressively louder on the last bar to help build intensity as the bassline comes round again. Velocity doesn't have to be mapped to volume. Try mapping it to filter cutoff and filter envelope depth.

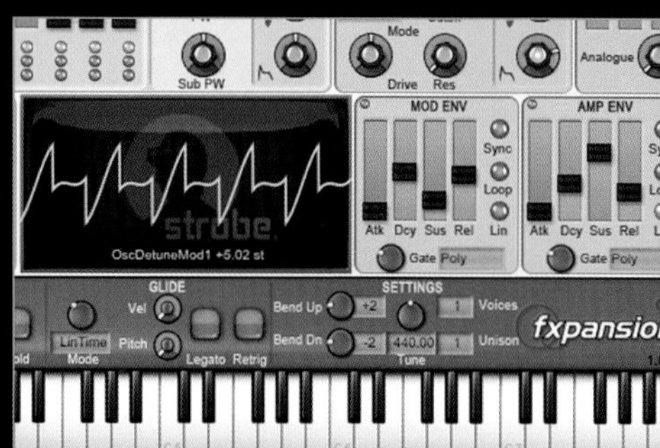

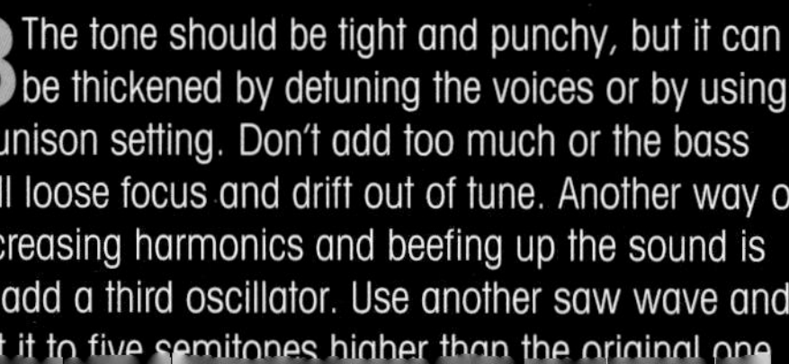

3 The tone should be tight and punchy, but it can be thickened by detuning the voices or by using a unison setting. Don't add too much or the bass will loose focus and drift out of tune. Another way of increasing harmonics and beefing up the sound is to add a third oscillator. Use another saw wave and set it to five semitones higher than the original one

4 The rhythm can be augmented by subtle use of sidechain compression. Use a small amount to reign in the attack, so that the bassline doesn't clash with the kick. Add a touch of room or plate reverb on an aux send to help place it in the mix and enrich the high-end harmonics. Place an EQ on the reverb return to cut the bass and mid-range

/walkthrough electro

Up-front electro-house bass sounds are loud and proud, taking equal inspiration from rhythmic and lead bass styles. Swing can be used to add more bounce and sidechain compression is used aggressively for added pump. A good synth is a prerequisite for authentic electro tones. Choose one with multiple oscillators and modulation sources. Try creating riffs with call and response lines, and juggle these between two or more synths to create variations of the hook.

Use an LFO to modulate the filter cutoff point and create tempo-driven wobbles that cut across the groove. To help keep things tight, ensure that the LFO is set to re-trigger with each new note and that it is bpm-synced.

It's also worth experimenting with the LFO phase and polarity/direction parameters as this can help tighten up or change the feel of the rhythm pattern – especially when using ramp and sine waves. In electro you will spend as much time fine-tuning the filter parameters as you will creating an original hook. And you won't stop when you've got the killer line: electro basslines rarely stay the same for long. Instead they keep changing, with ongoing automation of both the modulation depth and LFO rate throughout the track.

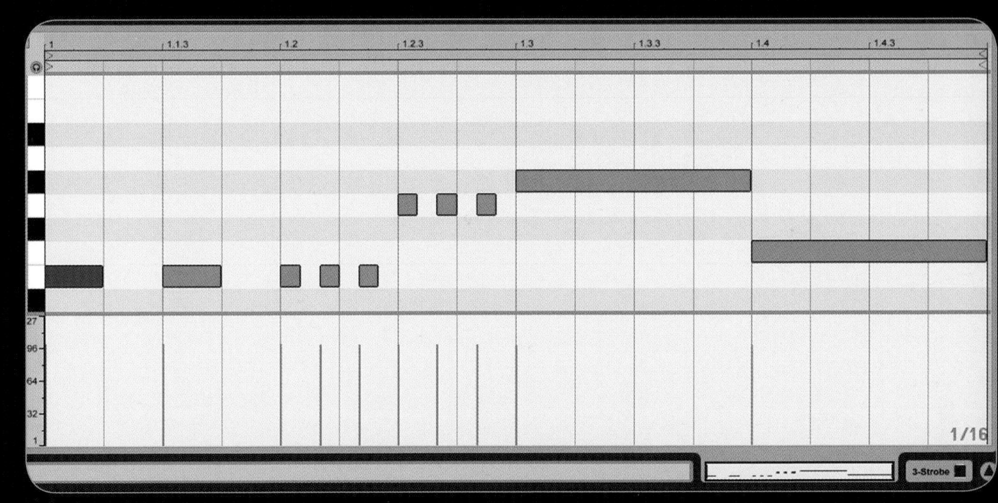

1 The key to a juicy electro-house bass starts with several stacked oscillators. Mix a saw wave with a sine wave an octave below and a square wave an octave higher. Then mix in some white noise to dirty it up and help it cut through the mix. Don't overdo it though as the bass will become too aggressive and trashy.

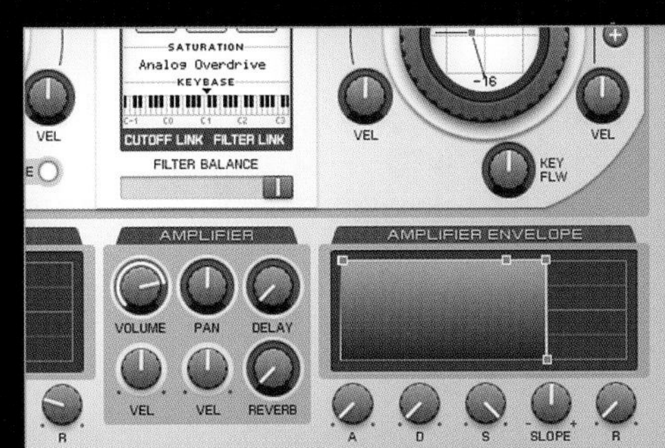

2 Set the amp envelope to minimum attack, decay and release, and maximum sustain. Select a low-pass filter and set the cutoff point to around 33%. Add some filter envelope modulation. Set the envelope to fast attack, medium decay, minimum sustain and fast release. This produces a nice chunky, throbbing bass sound.

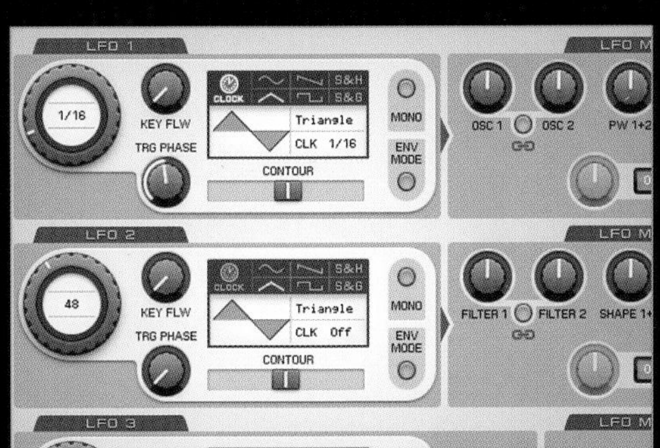

3 Add extra interest by modulating the filter with the LFO. Choose an upwards ramp with a rate of 1/16th. Set the LFO to re-trigger on key press and increase the modulation depth to get a bubbling rhythm. Sometimes the LFO shape doesn't fit with the groove: if it this happens try changing the LFO phase from 0 degrees to 90, 180 or 270.

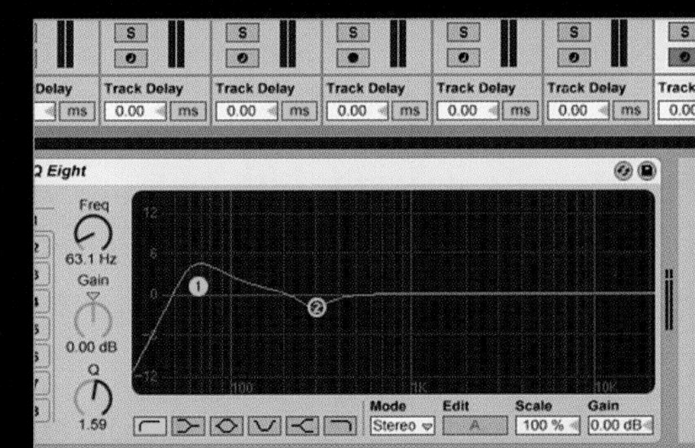

4 Remove the lowest frequencies with a low-cut filter, starting at 20–30Hz and working up until the sound gains clarity. Carve out a small notch around 200–500Hz. If the bass needs extra density boost around 60–70Hz. Squeeze it together with some compression, with fast attack, medium release and a 10:1 ratio.

/walkthrough fidget

Fidget is the punky brother of electro-house, which doesn't care about breaking a few of the engineering rules to create hooky bass noises. With its jackin' groove, big cone-bending pitch drops, wonky LFOs and rave references, it can be hypnotic and deranged in equal measures while providing a few snatches of melody too.

Copious use of distortion adds to the filthy hardcore feel and it's almost mandatory to use sidechain compression to bring out the rhythmic whomp of the beat.

One of the key features in fidget basslines is the use of melodic changes on every fourth or eighth bar. The variations can be made by changing some of the filter or modulation settings, swapping oscillators to create different tones and textures, or jumping up an octave to cause a shift in bass pressure.

The sliding, bendy character can be programmed in several different ways. One way is to use the synth's pitch bend to produce the dives manually. A second is to use automation (**pictured right**): increase the bend range on the synth to one octave either way to get a two-octave slide range. A third way is to use portamento, ensuring that the synth sound is monophonic. As new notes are triggered and held the sound will glide between them.

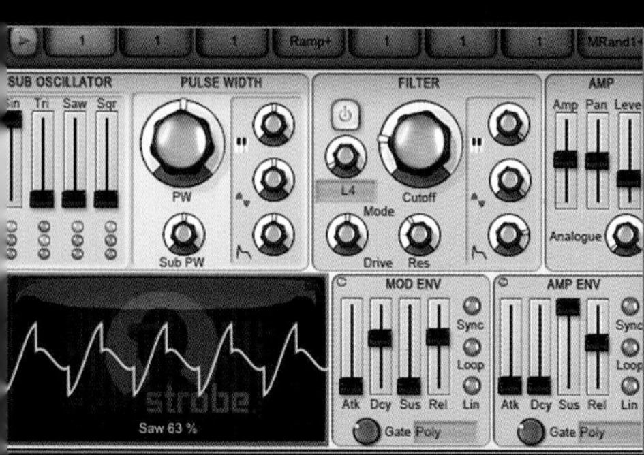

1 Start with two saw wave oscillators and detune them in opposite directions by a few fine-tones. This creates an analogue chorus effect. Add a sine wave oscillator and tune it down an octave. Turn the saw waves' volumes up to 60% and the sine sub to 100%. The relationship between the three influences how much low-end welly the bass has.

2 Select a 24dB low-pass filter and set cutoff to around 500Hz and resonance to around 50%. Set a sine wave LFO to modulate the filter cutoff. Ensure it is bpm-synced to 1/8th note and triggers at the start of each note. Increase the amount of resonance and modulation depth to bring out the flapping sound. Modulate the parameters to taste

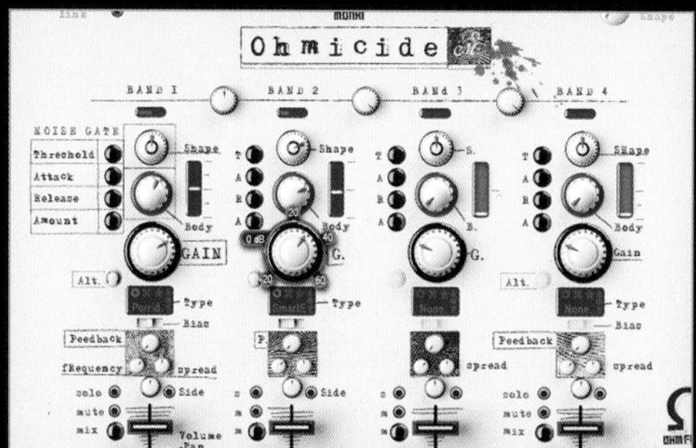

3 Get filthy with some overdrive, distortion or bit-crusher effects. These can be stuck on an insert for a fully coated sound or blended with the dry signal on an aux bus. With the bus method, use EQ after the effect to get a more polished sound. Listen for honky mid-range and muddy low-end frequencies and scoop them out using parametric EQ

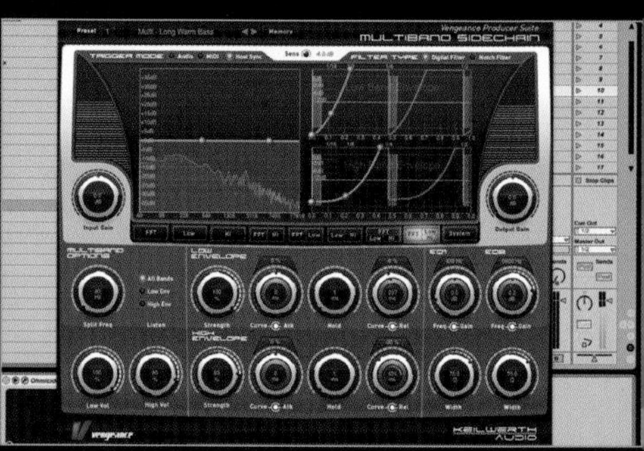

4 Set up a sidechain compressor driven by the kick and max out both the threshold and ratio. This will cut the volume to silence when the kick drops. Set attack to minimum and release to maximum. Lower the release until the bassline bounces. Experiment with different compressors. Finally, add some stereo width – see page 39

/walkthrough disco and funky house

Away from the more electronic-led basslines are the myriad that exist in the disco / latin / deep genres, which use a mix of sample-derived live lines alongside cleverely programmed synths.

Programming live bass can be daunting, but a little knowledge of how the instrument is played will get you a long way. Any synth capable of generating a nice warm monophonic signal is up to the job of producing the raw tone: in many ways the simpler the better. You're looking for a saw wave with a sine or square sub layered an octave below to thicken it up.

To recreate the sound of a real bassist, change the velocity of the hits and note lengths. Keep some notes short to recreate muted plucks. Use subtle amounts of portamento to mimic slides and don't be afraid to push notes 'off-grid' so that they weave into the groove, either before the beat, giving the rhythm a feel of urgency, or just behind, to give a lazier feel.

The example on the right uses classic stepped disco octaves with a few short 'plucked' notes to drive the groove.

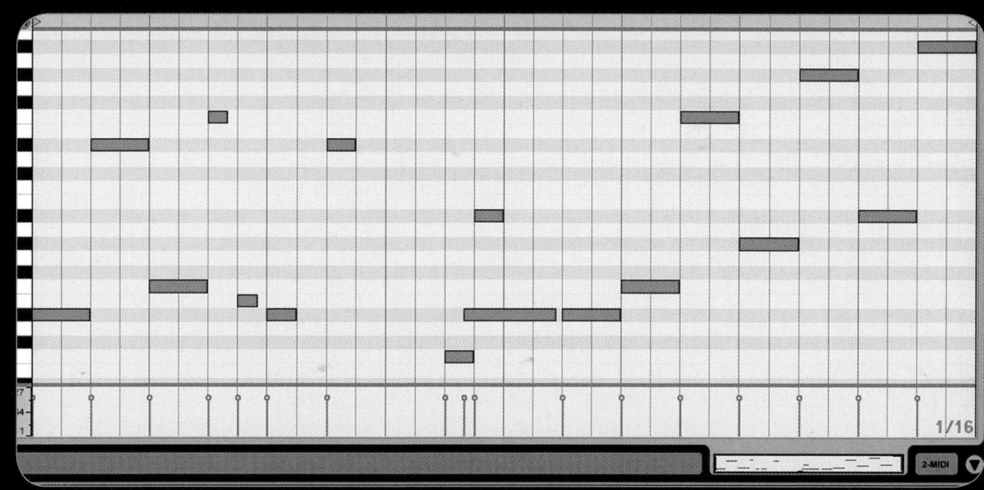

1 The Novation BassStation is loaded as the sound source. The patch is simple: here there's a saw wave on oscillator 1 and a square on the sub. Attack is at 0 with sustain at 100% and release at 0 too. This yields instant attack and decay, just like a tight disco bass. Resonance sits at around 20% to give the sound a warm edge.

2 The BassStation is run through Logic's native AutoFilter, a powerful filter that can boost the lower mids to create the classic funky house sound. Here resonance sits at 48% with cutoff at 38%, rolling off the higher frequencies but adding a rich resonant sweet spot. Fatness is at 99%.

3 The compressor supplies additional energy to the bassline, overdriving the signal by a few dB while adding some attack bite and a fast release to keep the it sitting tight in the groove. Note the threshold is set fairly low – only taking in the louder hits so as not to squash the life from them.

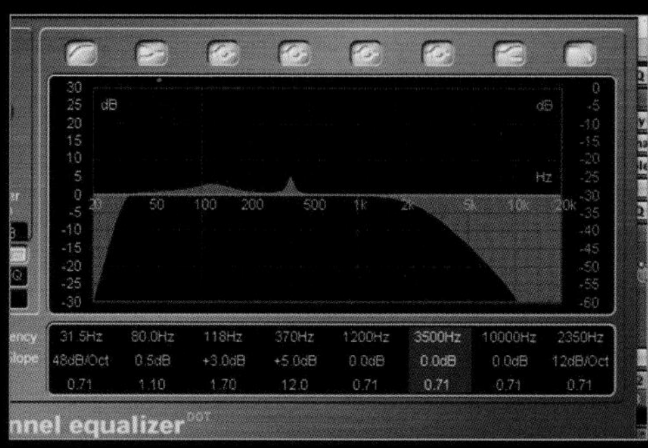

4 Last in the insert chain is the EQ. A steep low-cut removes the unnecessary bottom end. A gently-shelving high-cut filter rolls off the tops that would interfere with keys and guitars. A notch at 370Hz gives the bass some bite, while a gentle boost at 118Hz gives it some oomph.

/pro tips
the young punx

Hal Ritson from The Young Punx played on Eric Prydz' classic 'Call On Me', he's fighting for a fair deal for musicians in the digital age, and he REALLY HATES over-mastered mixes.

What is the key ingredient in a track? Breakdown? Style of production? Bassline?
MUSIC! TUNES! HOOKS! IDEAS! A trawl through Beatport uncovers a depressing vat of uninspired, idea-free dirges. They probably have something about them – a production style, a breakdown, a bassline – but they are all samey nonsense with no creativity. Who buys this stuff? Over the past decade the music industry has opened up immensely: in the past to get a record released you needed major money, usually from a record company, to pay for the costs of recording and manufacturing. These days you can make a quality record on a home computer and distribute it digitally to the whole world. This is all great, but the downside is there is no longer any meaningful filter forcing people to raise their game musically. In the old days if you submitted a derivative idea-free track to an A&R man it was their job to tell you to go away and make it better. Nowadays that filter isn't there, and it makes for a massive wash of B-league rubbish.

At the end of the day you have to try and make something that will stick in people's heads, and hopefully something that hasn't been heard before. This is just as relevant if you are making minimal, bassline-driven music as if you're writing a symphony. It can't just be 'a bassline' – it has to be 'THE bassline' and hopefully 'THE bassline the like of which people have never heard before'.

Do you mainly use analogue or digital soft synth sources? Do you think analogue really makes a difference?
I have been a fan of soft synths for a long time. They are so much more convenient: to bring up a track from two years back and find all the patches right straight away is great. They take up so much less space in a small studio, too. And they enable you to own £50,000 of vintage gear for £500. That said, I am slowly creeping back to analogue. I bought a Minimoog Voyager this year and it really is incredible. All the sounds are ultra simple, but so present, so 'right there', so mixable, so easy to play, so creative. It's a real instrument and it always sounds right first time. So there you have it: analogue is better. It really is. But it's only 10 per cent better, and it has a lot of downsides. It just depends how much you care about that 10 per cent.

How do you see the dance music industry developing over the next three years?
More power will move to the artist. The major labels will become a vehicle for a certain niche of commercial music. At the same time, more and more musicians with some business sense will start running their own labels and controlling their own destiny.

Any advice on monitoring? Quiet? Loud? Do you prefer flat and boring speakers, headphones or big, fat and chunky monitors?
When spending your budget never skimp on good monitoring. Always get the best monitors you can afford, rather than getting loads of synths and plugins. You can make a hit record on one instrument – even a toy instrument – as long as you can hear clearly what you are doing.

Volume is a quandary. If you're monitoring loud – i.e. loud enough that you have to shout a bit to talk to the person with you in the room – you can be sure your ears are modifying the sound, and you aren't REALLY hearing what is going on. You need to monitor at a moderate volume. That said, if you are working on a new track and you need to get a vibe going, that can require a bit of welly.

My own set-up features a pair of main monitors that never go too loud alongside a PA system that plays up to club volume. Typically we monitor at a moderate level, then every hour or so, smash it onto the super loud PA. This gives a second perspective on the sound – showing which parts get lost at higher volumes, and which can be muted. Finally, we have a really quiet listen on a pair of £5 walkman speakers. If you've mixed your record correctly you will be able to hear every element, both when the mix is really loud and really quiet.

How important do you think it is to have your music mastered commercially? Can you do it yourself as effectively and what tools would you recommend?
When I started out, the logic was that you could do everything on a track yourself apart from the mastering, where you needed to hire an expert. However, as styles have developed, the effects on the master mix (compression / limiting) have become such an integral part of the overall sound of the mix that it is now pretty much impossible to tell where mixing / producing ends and where mastering begins.

Avoid slamming the master mix hard against a limiter through some random plugin to make it 'loud'. You *will* make it loud and it will sound like shit. This 'race to be loud' has become a blight on the whole industry, and the commercial mastering houses are as guilty as bedroom DJs. Here's how you get round it: master your tracks more subtly and then turn tunes up louder when you play them out. Your records will sound so much better. Imagine you have a snare drum with a snappy bite at the beginning. Picture its waveform. Now imagine it after you limit the track heavily. All you've done is removed that nice snappy snare attack and replaced it with a flat line. Your track will kick less ass. Back off on the limiter by 2dB. Don't ask your mastering engineer to "just make it loud". Ask them to make it sound good and boost the PA to make it loud.

“These days you can make a quality record on a home computer and distribute it digitally worldwide. This is great, but the downside is there is no longer any meaningful filter forcing people to raise their game”

/part three

vocals

How many classic house tracks can you name that don't have a vocal in them?

They're not for everyone, but a vocal can take an underground smash and turn it into a crossover anthem, ensuring it a place in house history and significant royalties at the same time.

Whether they're vocoded, distorted, glitched, warped, Auto-Tuned or just left to shine alone, vocals provide instant hooks and toplines. What's more, a great vocalist can take a mediocre idea and work it into something sublime.

The process of writing lyrics, melodies and hooks requires creativity in its rawest form. There are no shortcuts to thinking up golden hooks, and the writing of great lyrics is an art in itself.

The recording, editing and production of vocals requires specific skills – not least in getting the very best performance from a vocalist.

So is the extra work worth it? That's one to answer after watching a floor full of clubbers all mouthing the same words...

/what kind of vocal?

they may not be the flavour of the moment but vocal lines in house have a long and proud tradition.

So you've got a backing track, maybe you've got a few melody ideas and a lyric or two bouncing around your head. Now all you need to do is bring them together to create a vocal house masterpiece. But where do you start?

In house music there are two main approaches to vocals: **riff vocals** and **song vocals**. With **riff vocals** the vocal part provides a lyrical, and potentially melodic, hook that repeats throughout the song, often getting warped along the way. Examples of this approach include Daft Punk's **Around the World**, Mylo's **Drop the Pressure** (**right**) and Eric Prydz's **Call on Me**. In each of these examples a strong lyrical line carries the main song hook, supplying a single memorable phrase and instant chart appeal. A second, more complex approach is taken with **song vocals**, where the track is structured around a more traditional 'verse, chorus, verse, chorus, chorus' form. Here the chorus usually supplies the track's main hook. The verses are used to pad out the song.

This form is less popular than in the heady days of the late 90s, where chart classics such as The Supermen Lovers' **Starlight**, ATFC's **Bad Habit** and Spiller's **Groovejet** (with lyrics!) combined instant-appeal choruses with well crafted verses. Brands such as Hed Kandi and later Ministry of Sound capitalised on the crossover appeal of house tunes that were also great songs, spawning a near never-ending product line in the process.

Each vocal method requires different approaches to sourcing and recording, although many of the production methods are shared by both.

Riff vocals

The riff vocal relies on just one thing: an awesome hook. The hook can be spoken or sung. But it has to be original, and it has to be memorable.

Sources

The cheapest, and most accessible, source of a riff vocal is your own voice. If you've got a hook idea then all you need to get it into your DAW is a mic. You don't even need a good mic: there are many high-profile artists recording vocal hooks using nothing more expensive than a £20 desktop microphone. Of course, if you have access to something better – a proper studio mic and a reasonable channel strip – then you'll get a better result. But the truth is that a lot of riff vocals are so mangled in the track, by vocoders, bit-crushers, harsh EQ and so on, that a less-than-perfect initial signal is often no bad thing. If you're going down the vocoder route then on-board mics offered with kit like the MicroKorg can be effective too.

A second source for riff vocals is sample libraries. Sample producers have never been that good at catering for the vocal market – partly because no-one wants to give away their best hooks. But there are some good products on the market, including the Vocal Forge / Foundry products from Zero-G and Sample Magic's Dance Vox. Another relatively unknown goldmine for messed-up vocals is Soundscan's excellent Funky Vox (available at www.soundstosample.com), which features talkboxes, vocoders, shouts and more. Some are cheesily unusable, but others might fill a vox-sized gap in your track. There is also a growing web-based market in dance vocals, with companies of varying sizes offering sample collections featuring different singers. It goes without saying that there's a lot of dross out there, with some dreadful lyrics and not much better vocal performances, but among the fluff you may find a gem.

A third source is the ubiquitous dance **a cappella**. An a cappella is a vocal mix with no musical or beat elements included. In the days of vinyl you would sometimes get the a cappella vocal for a track on the B-side, enabling producers to remix the track using the vocals supplied. Nowadays a cappellas are the meat of a million websites – all offering access to hundreds of raw vocals. Although it can be fun to play with a cappellas, if you create a killer track with another artist's vocals you'll be paying most, if not all, royalties back to the original artist or songwriter. This is all fine, of course, unless you want to earn some cash from your music.

Tip / The much maligned vocal sample CD has been the source of at least one top 40 chart hit. The lead line in MJ Cole's 1998 release **Sincere** is widely reported to have come from a sample CD.

Tip / Often sample packs contain hooks or melodic ideas that can become springboards on which to build songs. Auditioning individual lines in the context of a track may bring about new creative ideas that can then be expanded on by either yourself or a singer. As so often with samples, they can be used as much as inspirational means to an end as ends in themselves.

Ultimately a vocal riff stands or falls on the content of the lyric, and finding great lyrics is not easy. The truth is that a hook can be as senseless as 'Around the world, around the world', as effortlessly simple as 'Be sincere' or, in Moby's case, as odd as the word 'Go', repeated 30 times. The point is, there's no magic formula for finding a great hook. If you find something catchy just go with it.

Song vocals

Despite the recent move away from vocal content – and more specifically, the song form – in house music, there are still many records being produced that are built using great lyrics, beautiful vocals and hooky melodies. The West Coast sounds of artists like Miguel Migs and the Om and Naked Music labels make use of more traditional song vocals, mixing them with up-to-the-moment production techniques often taken from other house genres. At the same time, underground punk influences are bringing a resurgence of song formats among the new-wave Parisian house producers. It's true: the verse-chorus format is as old as pop music itself, but there's a reason it persists: it works, and clubbers as well as home listeners (and the big-buck radio stations) still respond to the chorus line.

Writing the song

If you choose to go down the 'song vocals' path then you're in territory that this book can cover only briefly. Here your lyrical choices are as wide as human experience and the only limitation is your imagination. Song-writers work in a million different ways, but a common approach among dance producers is to build a backing track until it starts to sound good, then to play it again and again, humming along, trying melodic ideas, maybe incorporating some vocal samples to fuel inspiration, until you have a few melody lines that you like. At this point you can start fleshing your ideas out with lyrics.

Other writers start with a hook: they find a line they think is strong, maybe also work it to a melody, and then build the song around that. There's no right approach: you can take a run and see what ideas come as you get sweaty or you can take the backing track to the pub on an ipod and sketch lyrical ideas over a pint. At the end of the day writing songs is a personal and creative activity and you'll find your own way of working.

It can be a daunting business, thinking up lyrics. What do you write about? How personal should you be? How do you avoid the clichés? Fortunately practise plays a major part in refining lyrical skills: keep writing lyrics and they'll get better. There's also a lot you can do to increase your understanding of song-writing. First of all, listen to the songs that you admire lyrically. They don't have to be house tracks: the lyrics of Bob Dylan or Joni Mitchell may seem a world away from pumping club classics, but the masters have lots to teach as songwriters. There are also a healthy number of books – some of them good – that discuss techniques for writing lyrics. If you like feedback about your writing, you might also find a local song-writer's group, where like-minded people meet to give positive feedback about each others' work. In the quest for the better lyric arm yourself as well as you can.

The key aim – some might say the sole aim – of the dance song-writer is to create a single devastating hook, with memorable lyrics and a hooky as hell melody. It can be as simple as the 'down, down, down, down' of Paul Johnson's **Get Get Down**, as witty as ATFC's 'I've got a bad, bad habit – baby it's you' from **Bad Habit** or as suggestive as Mousse T's **Horny**. Your hook will be the part people sing along to on the dancefloor, which raises hands in the air when it bangs back in after the verse. However you get there, what you're aiming for is a simple statement – probably no more than 10 words in length – that says something everyone can relate to in a way that's not been said before.

It's not an easy proposition of course, which explains why top song-writers earn very good money indeed. The most enduring topics among dance producers include music, sunshine, night time, sexual passion and the age-old favourite, love (or the loss of it). It's worth noting that if you're aiming for a hands-in-the-air-feel-good-classic some topics will be pretty much off-limits: the slow deterioration of a once-close relationship, for example, is not likely to bring a smile to anyone's face. For better or worse, it's often best to stick with sex, drugs and rock and roll.

six step song: one approach

1. Prepare. Create a reasonably full backing track with basic beats, bassline and musical elements. It doesn't need to be structured – an eight bar section is fine.

2. Brainstorm. Set your sequencer to loop the eight-bar section and immerse yourself in it. Allow lyrical and melodic ideas to form in your mind and when one sticks record it onto a dictaphone, your mobile, or into the computer.

3. Take a break. Go for a run. Walk the dog. Have a cup of tea. Come back after a break and do the same thing again. Put the backing track on your ipod and play it on your way to work or in the gym. Your goal is always the same: word and musical ideas that come from nowhere that may become the track's killer hook.

4. Decide. When you've got a few ideas make some decisions. Is there an obvious hook? Are some lines and melodies better suited to the chorus or the verse?

5. Consolidate. Get the verse and chorus lyrics down on paper. Write and re-write, edit and re-edit until the words work with the melody. Some settings are better than others for this process – often the studio isn't the best place. Take your backing track and notepad to a café and write. Always bear in mind that someone will have to sing your lyrics, so give the singer space for breaths (it can help to sing the lines yourself out loud to see how they flow).

6. Finalise. Make a rough early recording of your vocal line to see how it works in context. Refine and repeat until happy.

Structure

Once you've got a killer hook, the good news is you're governed by no structural rules. You can follow the classic verse–chorus–verse–chorus–chorus formula, you can throw in a bridge (to play between the two final choruses), you can use adlibs as a bridge; you can even open your song with a chorus and move on from there.

If you enjoy writing lyrics then two or three verses may appeal, but you don't need that many: you might opt to repeat the same verse a couple of times. Alternatively you could bin the rulebook altogether and jettison the chorus in favour of a single-line hook that repeats at the end of each verse.

Study the arrangements of vocal house records for long enough and you'll find a vast range of structures. Respond to the vibe of your track and shape the vocal accordingly. **For more see Structure, page 98.**

/the vocal session

lisa shaw, jocelyn brown, india – where would house music be without the divas? and where do you find them?

There are some music producers who would add singers to the popular entertainment adage 'never work with animals or children'. Studio folklore is awash with tales of demanding diva antics in the recording booth – including tales of singers who require certain lighting before performing, or who get into a J-Lo sized strop if the headphone mix isn't quite right.

Most of this is urban myth and the majority of singers are professional and easy to work with: if they aren't they don't get repeat bookings. That said, finding and working with a vocalist can be daunting if you've not done it before, requiring a set of skills not usually called upon by the dance producer. The following pages offer some advice on working with vocalists.

Finding a singer

Before you even think about recording, you need to find a vocalist. The search will be governed by both budget and your creative requirements. At this stage you should think carefully about the kind of sound you're after. Do you want a male or female? Are you looking for a smooth soulful sound or a big, belting performance? Do you want an off-beat, jazzy voice or a pure, ethereal trancey one? Now is the time to get this right: if you're making a funky house record then don't book a sultry jazz singer, however good they are, because although a high calibre session musician, like a top guitarist or keyboard player, should be expected to turn their hand to whatever style is asked of them, singers have specific sounds and strengths that they will find it difficult to stray far from.

When you've decided on the kind of voice you're after it's time to start researching. If you have a big budget your job will be easier: there are plenty of agencies with singers on their books and if you know a singer whose work you like then some targeted web-surfing will find the name of their agent. From there agree on the terms of the particular project and a fee for the session.

If you don't have a big budget then you will be looking at working with someone who either sings as a hobby, or who does it professionally part-time. There are a variety of ways of finding these kinds of singers:

Myspace. Few vocalists are not on Myspace. All you need to do is find their pages, which is usually a mix of persistence and luck.

Magazine 'wanted' lists. Most pro-audio magazines have free listings pages, which you can either use to find singers who are advertising themselves, or to post your own

'Wanted: Singer' ad. If you post an ad keep it brief but informative. Give a link to some of your songs and, if you have one, an indication of budget. Magazines also often have online versions of these directories, which are free to post on. Sound on Sound's website, www.soundonsound.com (**below**) has a busy 'Wanted' bulletin board. Try the Future Publishing forums too.

Music shop ads. Local independent record shops and instrument stores often have pinboards where musicians place ads. Check them out. One advantage of meeting someone advertising locally is that they will probably also live locally – meaning you can meet up and run through songs without incurring travel expenses.

Backing vocalist I am looking for a backing singers to work with me on forthcoming gigs. Please take a look at and if the music I perform is interesting to you, please get in touch. I am holding auditions in north west London within the next few weeks. Professionally trained, experienced people please :-).
Email (London) 04/10/09

(About the advertiser)

Singer/ Songwriters/ Musicians Music producer/ writer with a studio. US Top10. Specialising in most styles inc R+B/ Rock. Based in Chelsea.
Phone or Email (London) 01/10/09

(About the advertiser)

Keyboard Ipayer Keyboard player required for the prog-rock band Strang Quartet.
Phone Martin or Email (Meldreth, Cambridgeshire) 30/09/09

(About the advertiser)

FEMALE SESSION SINGER AVAILABLE for remote / in loco recordings
Email (London) 28/09/09

Studio demos. Recording studios often get sent demos from session musicians keen to get on their books. Next time you're in a studio and you have a spare ten minutes ask if they can recommend any singers or if you can listen to demos they've been sent. Even if you haven't booked a session a studio will often be happy to pass on recommendations.

Get online. There are several online directories of singers. A useful first stop in the UK is the Musicians' Union website, which has an online database of musicians.

Get out and about. Go to gigs, visit showcases; whenever you see a singer whose voice you like approach them and ask if they do session work. If they do, take a number or a business card. Sometimes you can find awesome voices in the most unlikely places – busking on the tube, or singing in a restaurant.

Word of mouth. Speak to fellow producers, labels you've worked for, mates in bands, theatrical friends, musicians, club night promoters – anyone who mixes with singers. Everyone knows someone who they think has a good voice. Personal recommendations go a long way and really do sort the musical wheat from the chaff.

Cash and legal stuff

Once you've found a vocalist with the kind of voice you're after for a fee you can afford it's time to negotiate terms. At this stage you should be looking at deciding two things; firstly, how much they will be paid for the session and secondly, whether they will take a share of any song-writing credits and royalties.

If you have no budget then cash will not enter the equation: you'll have to sell them the idea of working on your track for free as something they want to do because of your charm / awesome track / good looks.

If you want the vocalist to co-write any lyrics / top-lines then you will need to offer some form of song-share agreement entitling them to a share of royalties made from the song.

All writers on a song are entitled to a split of the publishing royalties. Traditionally words were worth 50 per cent of the publishing and music the other 50. But this was in the days when the melody top-line was already written.

Such arrangements are rare now. This is partly because some vocal lines consist of nothing more than a single lyric. And it's partly because some song-writers end up writing everything, from chord structure to the lyrics, leaving the producer to polish the production. Every situation is unique and the arrangement you come to with your singer should fairly reflect the efforts of all involved.

There are several ways to pay a singer:

Session fee. A one-off fee for the singer's time and work on the day of the session. This can take the form of a one-off payment (check Musician Union rates in the UK to see what the union recommends for singers) or a recoupable advance against future royalties made from the song.

Song-share agreement. If you are going to ask the singer to provide lyrics and/ or vocal melodies then sign a song-share agreement with them, identifying the fact that you are both co-writers, and specifying the percentage of the song you have written (a 50/50 agreement works well if you are providing the backing track and they the lyrics and top-lines). Ensure that you both sign and date this and specify the name/s of the song/s. You can find sample song-share agreements online.

Doing all this before the session is good practise and will help avoid disagreements afterwards – or worse, during it.

In reality, if the song you are recording is a mix of your work and the singer's you will probably want to offer both a one-off fee to reflect their work on the day plus a share of the song's future royalties. This is a fair way of operating and might also give the singer an added incentive to give their best performance during the session. Once you've agreed to this, and got it in writing, go ahead and arrange the session, taking a copy of the agreed documents for you to both sign.

The session

Where to record

If your home setup is suitable then you won't need a studio, but many producers with good home setups still end up booking a studio purely for the vocal recording – as much for the recording space as the high-end equipment.

Ensure any studio you pick has, at the very least, a good vocal booth and a range of high-end mics to capture the vocal performance. Set aside between three and four hours for each song; many vocalists will be able to turn around a recording sooner – especially if they have practiced beforehand – but if you're planning on recording harmonies, adlibs, potential double tracks and nail the lead lines you will need time to do it: the last thing you want is to rush the recording or, worse still, run out of time mid-way through. Also bear in mind that the singer's voice will need time to warm up, and that they will need regular breaks. Denying them these is neither conducive for top vocals, nor for a good working relationship.

Preparation

When you've booked the session and sent the backing tracks to the singer, it's time to make the final preparations for your visit to the studio. There are a few things to prepare.

The first thing is the backing tracks that your singer will record to. Bounce them down as 16-bit Wavs and mp3s. Copy the Wavs onto USB drive and load the mp3s onto an iPod. This means if either doesn't work you've got a backup. Email one to a hotmail or gmail account as an additional safeguard: there's nothing worse than not having a working backing track when you reach the studio.

The next thing you need are the lyric sheets, Print two or three copies of the lyrics, preferably in big 16 or 20 point Arial, so that your singer is able to read them when they're in the booth. Take a copy for yourself as well.

Stock up on water (studio air conditioning can dry you up fast) and / or caffeine drinks to keep your energy levels up – the amount of concentration required during a session is enough to knock out the most energetic of producers. Some food isn't a bad idea either, though most studios prefer you not to eat at the mixing desk.

Finally, take some blank DVDs for your recorded material (many studios charge extra for these), and don't forget some cash.

all about the the range

It may be obvious but it's worth re-stating: every singer has a range – a region of notes in which their voice sounds best. Deviate outside this range and they will struggle and their vocals will sound weak.

A euphoric trance singer, for example, will be able to soar to the highest notes, but will struggle with the lower, earthier tones that a gospel vocalist will excel at. Every producer's nightmare is discovering the song they've written is in the wrong range for their singer – especially if they discover this at the studio!

The risk of this is mitigated by sending the vocalist a backing track with guide vocals on it before booking the session, getting their feedback on how well it suits their range and then transposing the track either up or down a few tones accordingly. If this isn't possible then you may need to consider choosing a different singer for the particular song.

A nifty work-around, if there are just a few notes that the singer can't easily hit, is to transpose the backing track up or down into the singer's range for the phrases they are struggling with during the session itself. Record these line/s in a range more comfortable for the singer then when you get back to your studio transpose the lines back into their original key. This technique can be a life-saver but is not recommended for entire sessions.

Using high-end pitch editors like Melodyne is essential if you use this method, which – however well it's done – will always introduce unnatural and often undesirable artefacts to the recording.

The recording

Practice

Plan for your first hour in the studio to be fruitless as far as nailing vocals goes. It's the hour in which you'll get the tracks loaded into the studio's sequencer, the singer will warm up and the engineer will set up and test the mics.

While the engineer does the stuff they're good at go through each of the songs with the singer, identifying awkward lyrics, singing the track along together to check they're happy with the melody and answering any questions about the vocal lines as they arise.

When the engineer's happy with the setup get the singer into the vocal booth, fire up the first backing track and do an initial run-through. The singer will use this time to ask for changes to the 'can mix' that they are getting through their headphones. They may want reverb on the vocals (the verb tail can help them identify if they're drifting from a note), or they may want the relative volumes between the backing track and their fed-back vocals changed. This is not the time to comment on the quality of their singing. That comes later.

When the singer is as happy as the engineer with the recording levels then have a first full-song run-through. Don't worry if every word is wrong: the singer is warming up, probably flexing their vocal cords to a routine they've used many times before. Never record cold: the majority of voices require a good half-hour warm-up before recording.

Tip / Experiment with the signal path before recording. Some producers track through a hardware compressor, using the unit to calm volume spikes and to introduce subtle analogue flavours to the sound. Others prefer to record the sound in its raw form, recording straight to disc without any processing. The latter option is non-destructive, providing you with vanilla stems that you can process to your heart's desire later. Your decision may also be shaped by the studio experience of the singer: some singers are able to interact with the mic so that they pull back durng loud passages and move in during quieter ones, ensuring a similar dynamic range throughout. For singers who don't have this level of control, a certain amount of compression may be desirable or indeed necessary.

Recording

Overseeing a recording requires a strange mix of qualities that will see you become part engineer, part producer, part writer, part psychologist and part manager. You must balance perfectionism with an acceptance that the singer may never quite capture what you have in your head. You must be willing to offer endless positive feedback – even if you hate the first few takes. You will need to get the best from the singer when you're both knackered. And you will need to be a control freak – ensuring you get every word nailed – while also allowing new ideas to inform the recording, from both your singer and anyone else in the studio (engineers often come up with good feedback: they will have attended many hundreds of sessions and will always have an opinion on the recording, if asked).

Your job is, in theory at least, very simple. All you have to do is get every line recorded, and sounding as good as it possibly can. There are no set ways of structuring the recording. There are, however, a couple of favoured approaches, each with their merits.

Verse by verse: Work through the track one verse at a time, then record chorus, harmonies and adlibs in that order. This sequential approach leaves the chorus until relatively late in the process – when the singer is warmed up and has found their voice. This should ensure a confident sounding chorus.

Rough mix: This approach is similar to the above, except when you're happy with the chorus you go back and re-record the verses. The rationale is that when the chorus is nailed the singer will be in the right voice and mind for the song, and may be able to perfect verses that they struggled with earlier.

Whichever way you choose, it will take time – even after the warm-up – for your singer to 'find the voice' of the song. Although a fairly ambiguous concept, this 'voice' is usually found when the singer has warmed their vocal cords and are confident about the melody, lyrics and feel of the track.

When all of these things are in place you should get a feeling that what you're recording sounds 'right'. Like the moment you find the perfect snare to sit in the rhythm track, your ears and heart will both tell you you're getting what you're after.

If you're struggling to get to this stage, and your vocals just don't sound as you want them, then you'll need to work with the vocalist to alter anything from intonation to delivery. This can be tricky to get right – and is often something of a diplomatic mission, especially if the singer is not easy to work with. There are, however, some tried and tested methods of getting the sound closer to what you want.

it's all take, take, take

Unless you are recording an inhuman superstar, or you have mega bucks to blow on a two-week session, then you're not going to leave the studio with a single perfect vocal recording.

Instead, what you're after is a series of 'takes' of each vocal line (a single take might be as long as a whole verse, or as short as a phrase). When you return to your studio you will sort through these takes (there may be as few as three or four and as many as 20 or more for each line), select the strongest parts of each take and then compile (or 'comp') them together to create a single seamless vocal line – see **Comping walkthrough, page 57**. Knowing you'll be comping later rids you (and the singer) of the pressure of capturing the elusive 'single perfect take'.

This has certain implications while recording. First, however many takes you record, you must ensure the singer maintains the tone and character of their voice across takes. If they sing loud on one take then go much softer on another you'll have trouble comping them together.

The second, related requirement, is that the singer maintains the same proximity to the mic so that the raw timbre of sound that is recorded remains the same. (Although this can be varied for choruses, see **Tip, right**.)

It can be helpful to do a rough 'comp mix' as you go to ensure you're getting this continuity of tone across different sections of the song. It will also help identify any weak lines that may require re-recording.

Delivery suggestions: Do the vocals sound too harsh? Suggest that the singer calms the energy, maybe leaning closer to the mic for a slightly warmer sound. Use adjectives to explain what you're after, but avoid negative feedback. So do say: "Can it sound a bit calmer; a bit more chilled?" and don't SAY: "That line is so angry I'm afraid for my life."

Sing along: If the singer just can't nail a specific line or rhythm get them to leave the vocal booth and come and sit with you. Sing the line together until they are happy, then re-record it. If they still can't get it record the line yourself as a guide, feed it into their cans and let them sing along.

Vocal tone: A microphone accentuates lower frequencies the closer the singer gets to it (the so-called 'proximity effect'). This can, and should, be used to your advantage. For beautifully soft, quasi-whispered Lisa Shaw-style vocals get the singer as close to the mic as you can (but beyond the pop-shield!). For huge, diva-style voices, push them back – as far as 30cm to a metre. Experiment with different placings, and remember that the further a vocalist is from the mic, the more room sound will enter the signal. This can be a good thing in a nice sounding room and one of the qualities that makes a good pro studio a great one is the room sound they have.

Breaths: Good lyrics allow the singer to get the breaths they need while singing. If they can't – or you've rammed in lots of syllables for effect – then you may need to drop in to record on certain lines.

Be flexible: If a particular line just isn't working – for either melodic or rhythmic reasons (it may be too high, or the lyrics too dense) then don't be afraid to change it. It's never too late to amend a track, even in the studio.

Drop-ins: Sure, it's nice to capture a full verse or a line in a single take, but sometimes your singer will be unable to get a particular word. If so don't keep re-recording the line; you'll be wasting studio time. Instead set up a drop-in point so the vocalist can sing just the awkward word. It's worth getting them to sing the previous part of the line quietly too, so that their voice is already in the zone before dropping in for the required word.

Beware line ends: It's not unusual for a singer to run out of breath towards the end of a long line. Doing so will weaken the line end, affecting pitch and energy. In these cases try dropping in mid way through a line or verse to ensure you have at least one take with a strong line ending. You can comp it together with a strong line start later.

The X-Factor: Sometimes it's bizarre suggestions from the producer that make a vocal line come alive. If the vocals sound a bit dead try explaining the mood of the song you're trying to get across. Statements like: "The narrator of this song has just lost her lover! I want to feel more sadness in your voice!" might help the singer visualise the mood you're aiming for. Some singers respond well by picturing themselves singing the track live. Studios are, by any standard, fairly passion-free built environments. Get the singer to imagine they're in front of a crowd of thousands, about to deliver the best performance of their life. Sound a bit daft? Who cares – if it works.

Push, push: Even when you think you've got the perfect take, go for one more. To get an extra five per cent say to the singer: "Awesome, awesome, but I know you can do one better! Let's do one final take!" If it isn't as good as its predecessor you've lost nothing. If it is better, you've got a killer take.

/pro tips
the chorus block

For really big choruses get your singer to record the same line using different timbres of voice (some whispered, some shouted) and to move around the vocal booth so you get some close mic'd takes alongside ones where they are standing back from the mic. When mixed down this can give the illusion of many different voices singing, rather than just one, in a way reminiscent of tight gospel choirs. You can recreate this effect to some extent during the mixdown too by strapping different compressor and EQ settings across constituent chorus parts to give the illusion of different timbres of voice.

Tip / To ensure you record every word of every line to the quality you're after, manually score out lyrics on a lyric sheet when – and only when – you've got the take you're after. In a high-stress recording environment this technique allows you to keep track of what you've done and what still needs recording. It can also be useful to build a rough mix as you go, to help you hear how new lines work alongside the previously recorded vocals.

What to record

The material you take home from the recording will depend on the kind of track you've written. If you just need a few takes of a single line then your job's easy. If you've gone down the more traditional song route you will need to consider:

Verses: Record each verse. If you want to repeat a verse in the breakdown try recording a different version of it, with an amended melody and different intonation (a more whispered version maybe). To emphasise certain words or phrases, double-track them or build harmony blocks around them.

To give body to a verse add full-verse harmonies below the lead line. When recording harmonies and double-tracks remember to keep the rhythm tight.

Chorus: Ensure you have one near-as-damnit perfect take of the lead chorus line. Then use this as an 'anchor' on which to build others. Play the singer this anchor take in their cans and get them to double and triple-track it, adding as many harmonies as you need. Record octaves of the lead line (either above or below) to subtly bulk up the mix.

Double-tracks: A double-track is, as the name suggests, a form of overdub of the original line. Double-tracking verse and chorus vocals is an age-old trick to get them sounding stronger and fuller, introducing a pleasing pseudo-chorus feel. To record double-tracks simply nail the first take, then send the take to the singer's headphone mix so that they can sing along with it in sync. They may need a few takes to get it sitting tight. Triple tracks add a third replicar, and can also sound good, particularly on the lead chorus line.

Adlibs: The bits that aren't verses or choruses but which you can drop in – during the bridge or intro, or closing chorus – are best recorded last above a rough vocal mix. It's worth doing three adlib takes. The first should be to just the backing track. The second should be with the rough vocal mix in the cans so the singer can respond to that. The third should be over a few passes of the chorus to ensure you have enough material for the final choruses. Some forms of adlibs have a proud tradition in house music, including scats, breathy delays and the diva wail.

/editing the vocals

it can be a tiresome experience, but fine-tuning and comping the vocals is an important part of the mixing process.

Vocal editing takes place in the period between recording and mixing. It is the process of tranforming the numerous audio stems you've recorded into polished single 'comped' stems. The edit will see you push harmonies into time, re-tune duff notes, tidy up breaths and select the best adlibs. It is a hugely important part of vocal production and is best done when you're in the mood for a period of painstaking and quite dull work.

Vocal editing requires specific tools that do two things: push out-of-tune notes back into tune, and move notes in time to correct them rhythmically.

For the past few years the decision on which bit of kit to use was made for you: Celemony's Melodyne allows you to alter not just a vocal's pitch, but also nudge notes backwards and forwards in time.

Although Melodyne remains the application of choice for many vocal producers, the major DAWs have all taken lessons from Melodyne's flexibility and, to a greater or lesser extent, have integrated its key tools.

Logic 9's Flex Tool: Can change lengths of notes and move them back and forward in time, but must be used alongside a pitch corrector for re-pitching.

Cubase 5's VariAudio: Offers vocal editing and pitch alteration of individual notes in monophonic vocal recordings and can solve both intonation and timing problems.

There are other options for editing pitch too, including:

Antares' Auto-Tune: Graphical mode offers extremely powerful pitch processing options, but no ability to shift notes in time.

Native pitch correction plugins: Like Logic's Pitch Corrector or Cubase's PitchCorrect.

The words and walkthroughs over the following pages are relevant whichever tools you use.

Comping the vocal

Verses

Before you start re-pitching, you need to get the best comped take of each vocal line that you can. Do this in your DAW's arrange page.

This process sees you taking on the role of a TV talent show judge: you will audition hundreds of takes and pick the best. To start the process, set the sequencer to loop around a section (a verse, for example) and audition each take. Have a careful listen to every one. Some may be so bad you can delete them immediately. Run through them all a couple of times to remind yourself what material you have (see **Comping from multiple takes walkthrough, right**).

Now select the best parts of each take. Get busy with your DAW's scissors tool, deleting weak parts and keeping the best. It doesn't matter how short a section is: if it sounds great, keep it.

A good way of keeping track of the best takes, and grading them, is to colour each segment of a take according to its quality.

When you've finished going through all the takes in a section you will be left with a series of the best parts. Now you need to make the final master selection of the best of the best. Listen through them again, for character of vocals, delivery and the elusive 'soul' factor. Tuning is important, but it's not the most important factor – you can re-tune later.

When you're left with a single track worth of vocals that combine to make a great sounding verse, strap a compressor and reverb over the vocal track to get an idea of how they will sound in the mix. If they still sound good bounce them down without effects. That's your comped vocal line. Repeat this process for all verses.

Chorus

Comping for the chorus follows the same procedure as for verses. The main difference is that it is useful set up a rough mix as you go, building the chorus block up gradually on top of one near-perfect 'anchor' line.

This anchor should be the best comped take of the lead chorus line. When you have chosen this, play it with the backing track and use it as a guide while you comp the remaining supporting lines and harmonies. This will help ensure you get the tightest possible chorus block.

When comping for block harmonies pitch (and bum or weak notes) is far less important than rhythm. Pitch correctors work well on harmony lines – even on extreme settings – as they are usually mixed quite low, meaning any artificial characteristics introduced are buried in the mix. Concentrate on comping for rhythm instead, choosing sections of takes that are bang in time with the anchor.

(It's worth noting that relaxed chorus blocks without the precision of rhythmic uniformity can also sound great. This kind of lazy-sounding approach is used to popular effect by chillout producers and has found its way into occasional house choruses, like in the sublime **Good Enough** by Gaspard.)

Adlibs

The final cherry on the vocal cake is supplied by adlibs, which may be used at the start of a track, in the breakdown and during the final choruses. Select adlibs in the same way you did the verses, but set up a rough mix first so that you can get an idea of how they work in context. Keep more adlibs than you need: you will make most of the decisions about their placement later in the writing and production process.

/walkthrough
comping from multiple takes

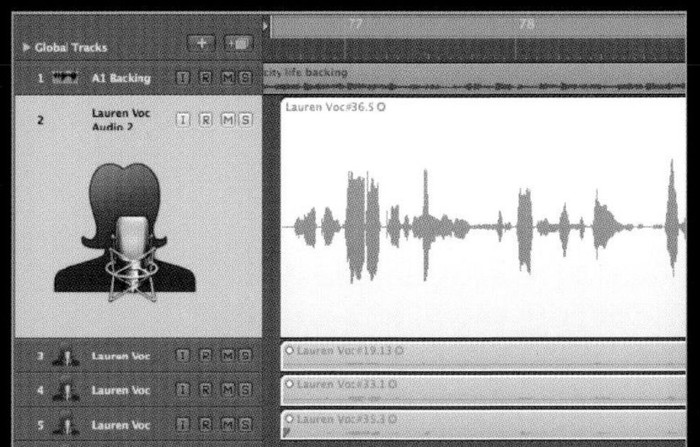

1 Loop the section of the track you want to work on. Arrange all vocal takes on different tracks outputting on the same channel. Mute all but one. In loop mode listen to each take several times before moving on to the next and muting the others. Get a good feel for the different takes, noting the strengths and weaknesses of each.

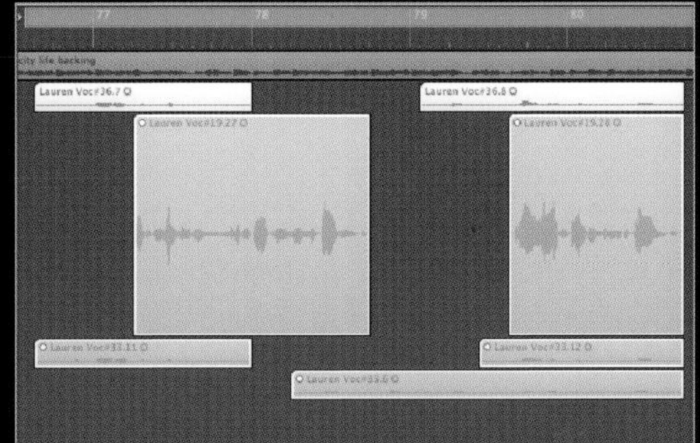

2 On first audition you will find some parts of each take that can be immediately discarded – maybe the rhythm is wrong or the melody's way out of tune. Using the scissors tool cut the offending sections, leaving the good parts in place. Don't delete them completely from your hard drive as you may need to reinstate them later if you've got nothing better.

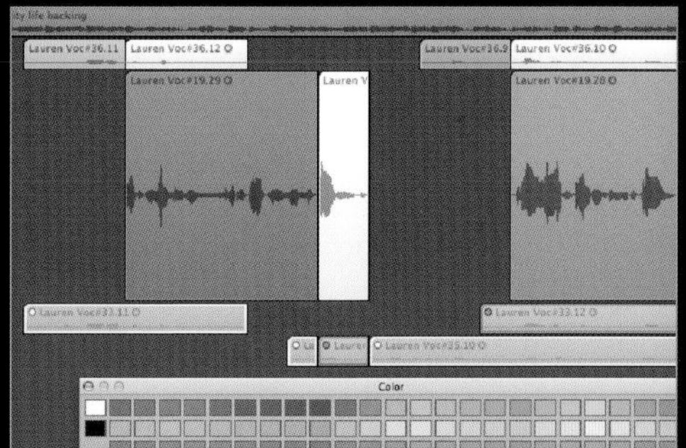

3 After losing the worst of each take, it's time to pick the best of the rest to make the comped line. Open the colour window (View > Colours) then loop through the takes again, making further edits to isolate particularly good words or lines. Colour the best segments in one colour, and less good but still usable ones with another.

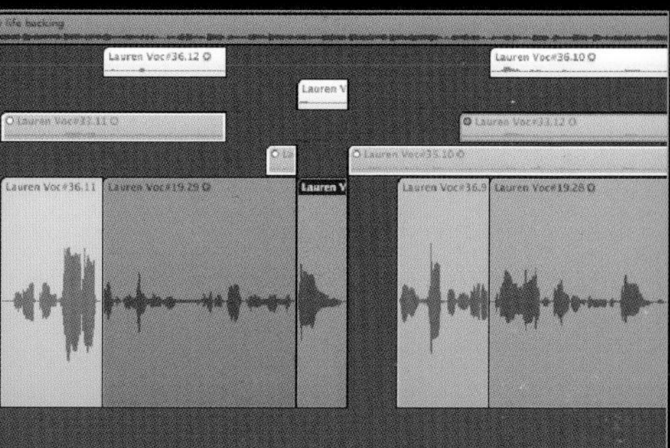

4 When you've finished selecting and colouring make an initial rough comp by dragging the good coloured sections onto a different audio track. Strap a compressor and vocal reverb on the track – don't worry too much about settings for now. Have a listen to this early comp alone and with the backing track.

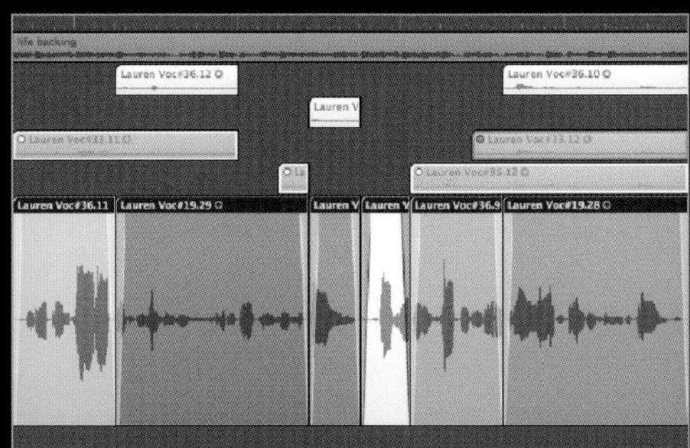

5 It's not unusual to have certain words or phrases that are weak, where you have to fall back on a mediocre uncoloured take. So be it. Pull it into the master comp track. Tidy things up by adding fades and crossfades to avoid pops and clicks. You may also need to adjust start, end and crossover points to make the phrase sound like a unified vocal take.

6 When you're happy with this final comped line bounce it down to a single audio file. Bounce the file down dry as a mono 24-bit Wav or AIFF. Mute your earlier workings (don't delete them! you may need them again later!) and create a new lead vocal audio track. Place the new master vocal on this track. Repeat steps 1–5 for the other verses.

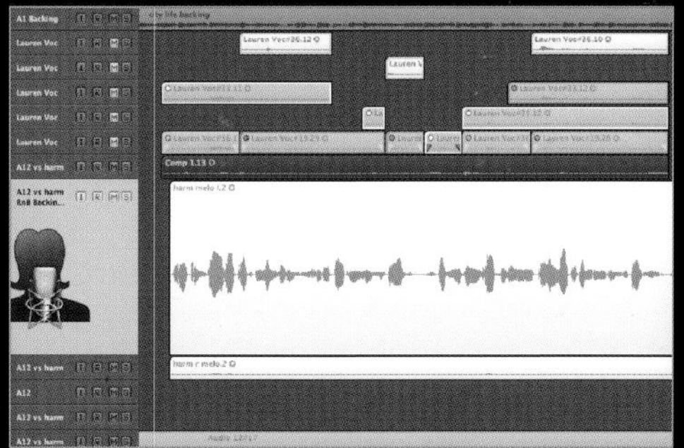

7 If you've recorded vocal harmonies then you should use a similar approach to comping as outlined in the previous steps. Keep playing the backing loop but this time include the comped lead vocal so that you can audition harmonies against it. Above you can see the bounced lead line coloured brown with the two potential harmony lines below.

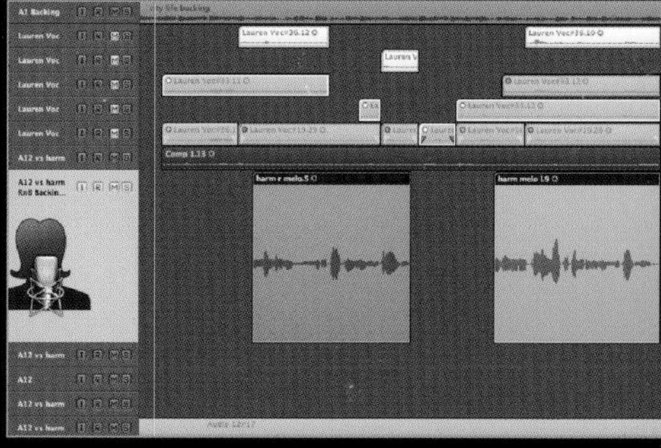

8 Sometimes you will want verse harmonies to play for a whole verse, but they can be more effective emphasising certain lines. Use the colouring technique to choose the best harmony lines and mute different sections until you're left with parts that complement and strengthen the verses.

Tweaking the vocal

When you've bounced down all of the best comped takes, it's time to do the fine-tuning and rhythmic tweaking. A good vocalist won't need much re-tuning, but the majority need a bit of artificial help, and – for better or worse – years of the (over) use of Auto-Tune and Melodyne have created an expectation among listeners for a sometimes artificially in-tune vocal sound. Of course you don't need to re-tune. A brave producer with a top singer and a desire to keep the vocal as natural as possible can use the vocal as is. But in today's dance music the vast majority of vocal lines are re-tuned to some extent, some very gently and some unnaturally for effect (as with the classic 100 per cent Auto-Tuned sound popularised in Cher's **Believe**).

For the re-tuning process you have two main tools at your disposal:

Auto-Tune

Antares' Auto-Tune was the first realtime tuning plugin to find a mass following. The principal was simple: insert it on the audio track of a vocal line, set the correct key and then let it do its magic as the song plays, automatically pulling notes closer to 100% pitch perfection according to the settings programmed.
It was – and is – simple and devastatingly effective, particularly for harmonies. It has two key drawbacks: it can sound unnatural, particularly at extreme settings, and it offers no control over the rhythm of a line.

Auto-Tune has a second, very powerful, 'Graphical' mode, that allows you to program in individual settings for each note. Although it requires some patience to get used to, this mode offers a high level of control and can mitigate many of the more artificial artefacts introduced in Automatic mode.

Melodyne

Celemony's Melodyne re-thought the tuning challenge and came up with a new ground-up approach offering complete control of tuning, timing and formant for monophonic (and polyphonic, as of Melodyne Editor) material. Used standalone or as a plugin via Bridge, Melodyne allows producers to retune individual notes, push and pull specific syllables into shape, change the amplitude of a signal – even alter the formant of a note. It can be used to make extreme changes to a part or subtle – and very natural – alterations that introduce few noticeable artefacts. It is this ability that found it a legion of fans among vocal producers.

Melodyne can deal with more than one part at a time, enabling producers to work with and stack up multiple harmonies and tweak them so that they all sit in time. (See **Chorus blocks walkthrough, page 60**.)

It also allows users to create new harmony parts from scratch. If you failed to record a harmony in the studio, or your singer made a dog's dinner of one of the lines, all you need to do is copy the lead line, paste it onto a new track and then transpose it lower (or higher) by a few semitones for a new harmony. Adjust the formant and push it back in the mix for a harmony that can sound as near-natural as any recorded during the session. (See **New harmony lines walkthrough, page 61**.)

Tip / Melodyne – like Logic's Flex and Cubase's VariAudio – makes life easier. But you don't need it. You can achieve good results the 'old-school' way by cutting and time-stretching notes so that they are in time and then feeding them through Auto-Tune or similar to pull them into tune.

/walkthrough auto-tune basics

1 The much abused autotune vocal sound originates from the Antares Auto-Tune plugin. It's designed to correct the pitch of vocals automatically by re-tuning them to a pre-programmed set of notes. The first thing to do is to set the key and scale of the track. In this case we are using Dm.

2 Jump to the 'Pitch Correction' controls and set retune speed to maximum. This forces the pitch to jump to the correct note almost instantly to give it the characteristic robotic effect. If you're after something more natural back off on the retune speed.

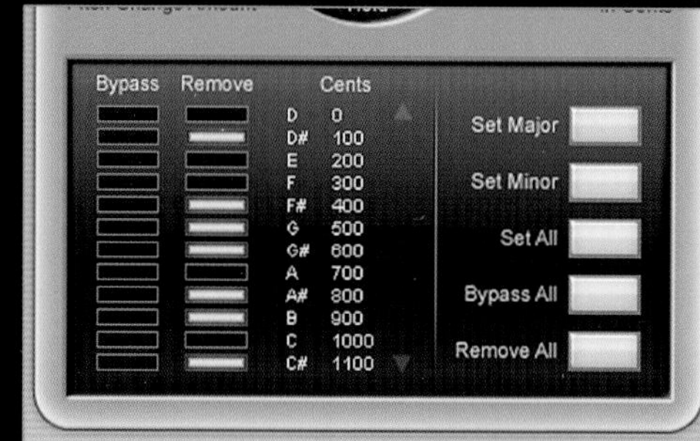

3 You can edit the scale manually so that Auto-Tune only uses notes from the melody. This keeps it from correcting pitches wrongly, but it can also be used as a creative effect. Switch the scale type to 'chromatic' and highlight the relevant 'remove' buttons to remove notes from the scale. In the above example we are left with just D, E, F, A and C.

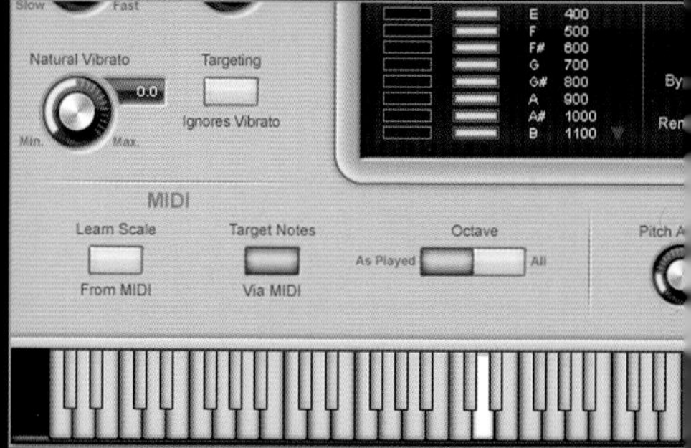

4 AutoTune can also be played like a synthesiser. It responds to Midi data, allowing you to programme a precise melody line. To switch this function on press the 'Target Notes Via Midi' button at the bottom left. Now route a Midi pattern and the audio to the plugin inputs for some French-influenced robotic workouts.

/walkthrough
melodyne basics

1 Bounce down the backing track (without vocals) and any vocal lines you want to re-tune. Bounce the vocals dry, without any effects or processing, as 24-bit mono Wavs or AIFFs. Remember to set fades on comped vocal lines to avoid clicks or pops. Be sensitive to breaths in the vocal – don't cut them off half way. Keep them for now. They can be cut later.

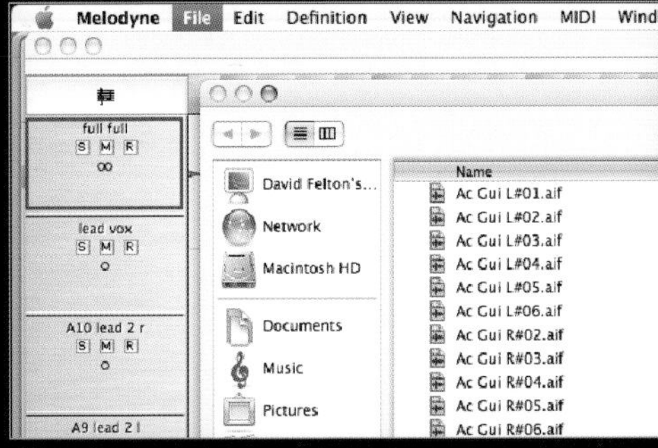

2 Open Melodyne (not in Bridge mode). Select File > Import Audio File. Choose the file (or multiple files) that you want to edit. The Melody Manager (File > Melody Manager) allows you to browse audio files and audition them – useful if you're working on a big project with multiple files. When you're done click Open.

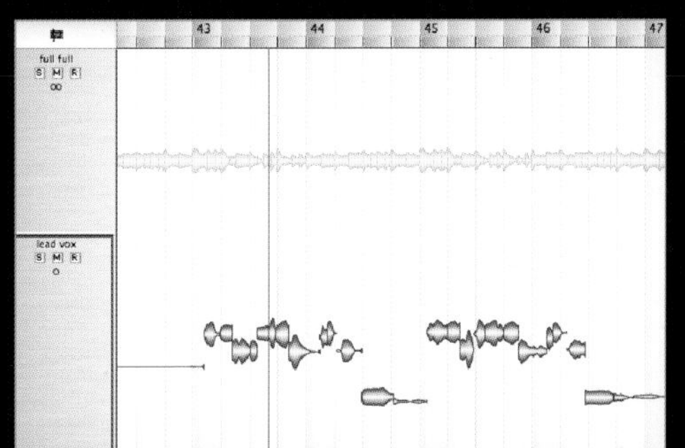

3 Melodyne spends a few moments processing the audio files and assigns them to tracks in the arrangement window. Above, the backing track (in yellow) hasn't been assigned pitches. That's because it's too complex. The lead vocal line in red, however, has been processed, giving a visual representation of the line's notes and velocities.

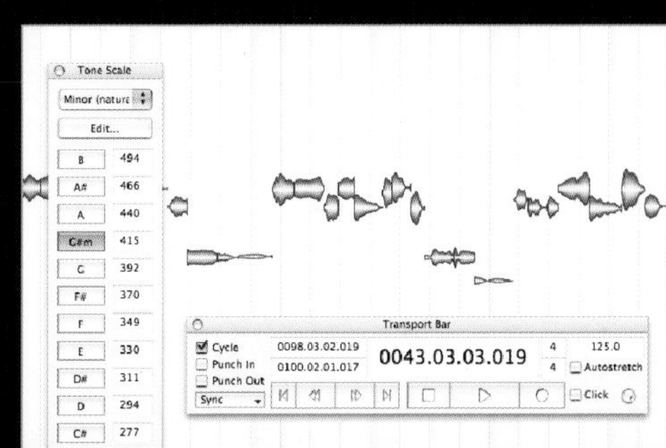

4 Before you begin editing change a few global settings to make life easier. Open the Transport window (Window > Mixer) and change the tempo (top right) to reflect the tempo of the track. This changes the alignment of the bar guidelines. Tick the Autostretch box and the Cycle box. If you know the track key select Window > Key Scale.

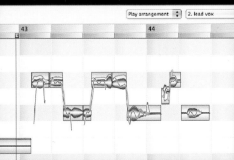

5 Double-click a note in the lead vocal line. This opens the edit window. At the top right of the window click on the Play Visible pull-down menu

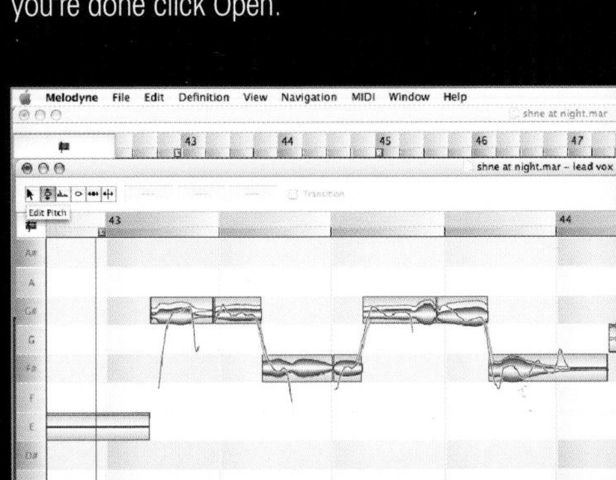

6 At the top left of the window select Edit Pitch. This reveals additional detail in the window, with the thin wavy orange line giving a visual

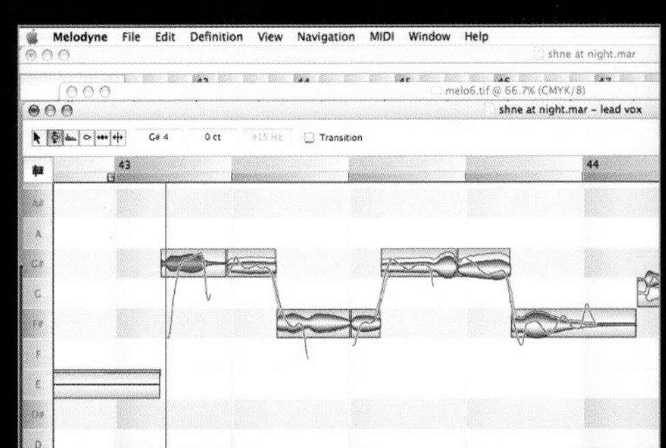

7 To 'correct' a note, move the mouse over it, click and hold, then shift it up or down. For semitone changes click and drag. For more subtle

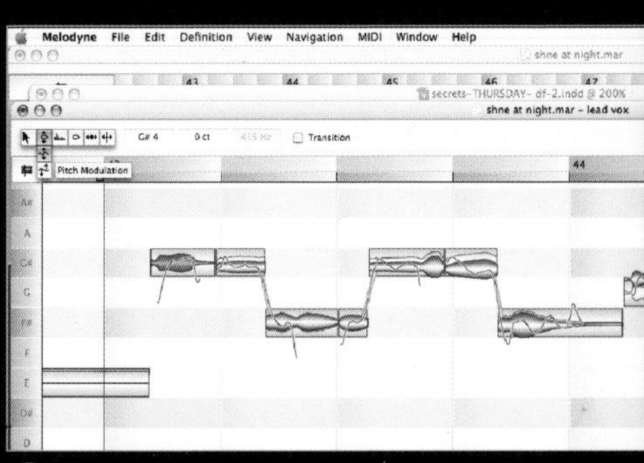

8 Most of the time you'll be making much subtler changes than full-note shifts. In the toolbar, select the Pitch Modulation tool. Select an individual

/walkthrough next steps in melodyne

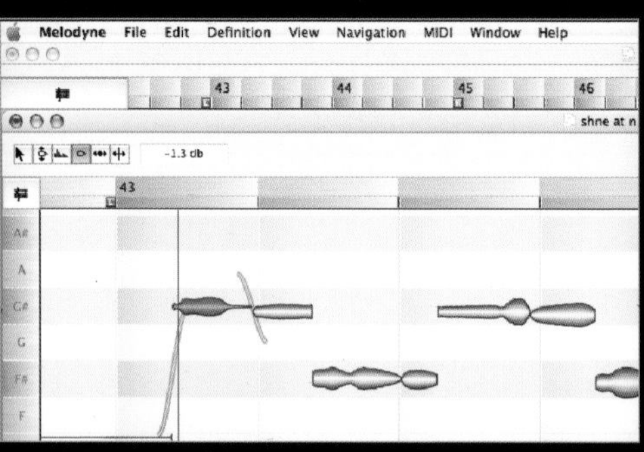

1 Melodyne isn't just useful for tuning a line; it can also be used to alter the amplitude of different notes, allowing you to pull back on overloud parts, or it can be used to shift notes in time. Here we've selected the Edit Amplitude tool from the toolbox. Click the offending note and drag up or down to alter its volume.

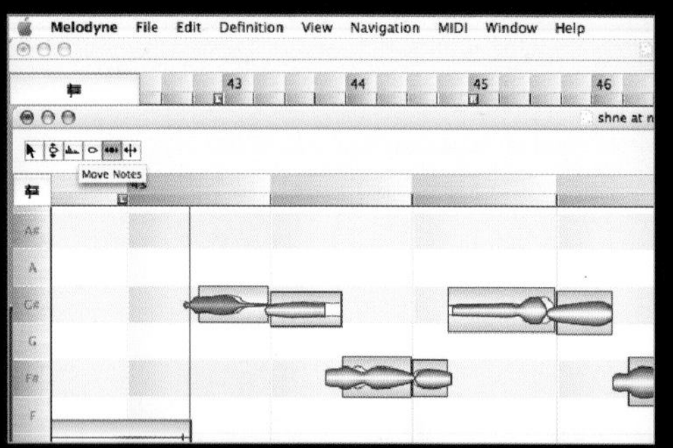

2 Moving notes is just as easy but it requires more care than the other operations as it can introduce unwanted artefacts. To shift a lazy note back in time select the Move Notes tool, then highlight the offending note.

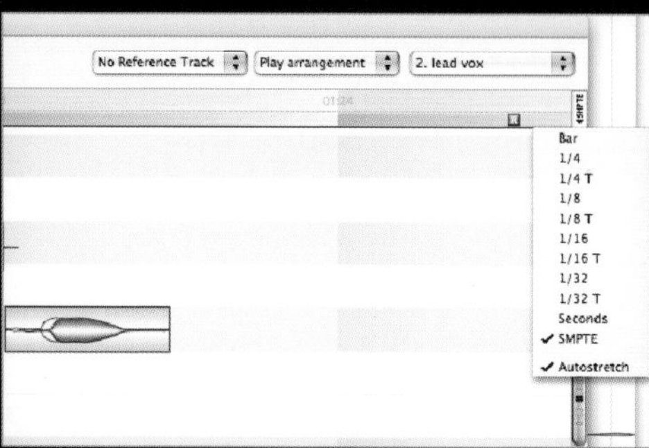

3 In the top right corner of the window is a drop-down box entitled SMPTE. Click on it. It shows you the bar divisions – including triplets – that time shifts will automatically snap to. For fine tweaks it is unlikely you will want it on, so change the settings to SMPTE and Autostretch. This gives you the freedom to move the notes as much as you like.

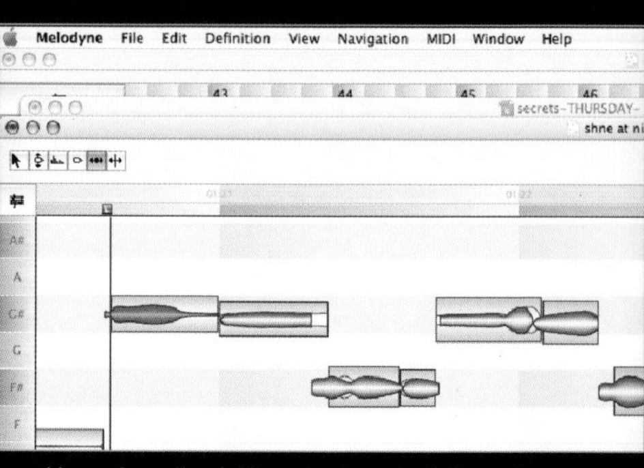

4 Now drag the left or right end of the note you want to shift into the location you want it. If whole phrases are late you can lassoo multiple notes and shift them as one. Be wary of introducing unpleasant digital artefacts. If you do, you may need to resort to the next tool along – Note Separation – and split an individual note before shifting part of it.

/walkthrough chorus blocks

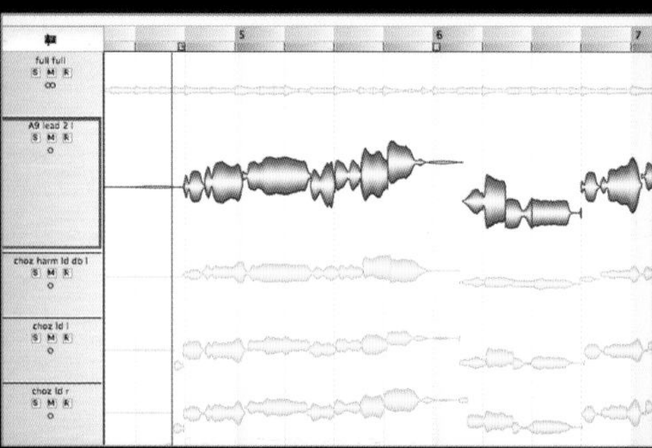

1 Melodyne comes into its own when creating multi-part chorus blocks. First, pick the strongest lead chorus line and edit it using the steps in the previous pages until it is as you want it, in terms of both rhythm and tuning. Import the other chorus lines using File > Import Audio File.

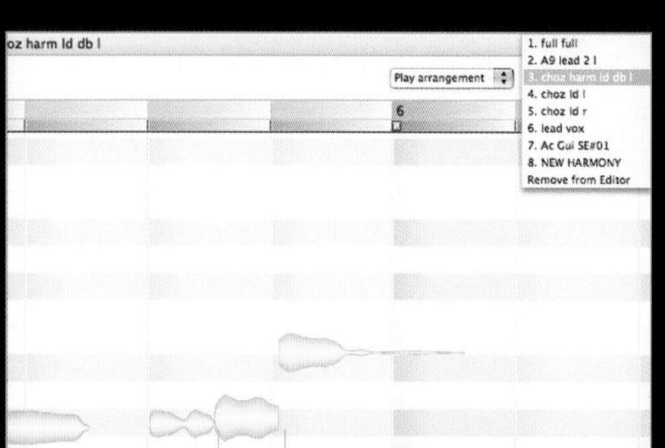

2 Double-click the next line you want to edit. In the top right of the Editor window select 'Play arrangement' and in the selection drop-down menu alongside choose the name of your original anchor chorus part. This introduces the chorus anchor into the Editor grid in yellow so that you can use it as a graphical guide when editing new lines.

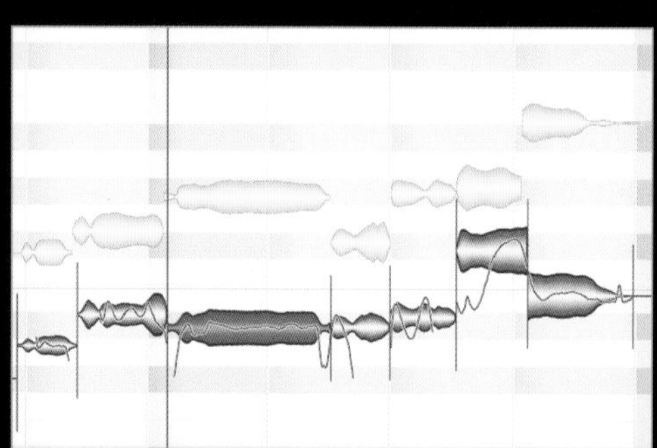

3 Using all of the tools at your disposal nudge the notes in the new chorus line so that they are in time and in tune with (or harmony with) the original anchor. Use the graphics to help you. Note that if you become too perfectionist while editing you may lose some of the soul and humanity that give the vocal its character and power.

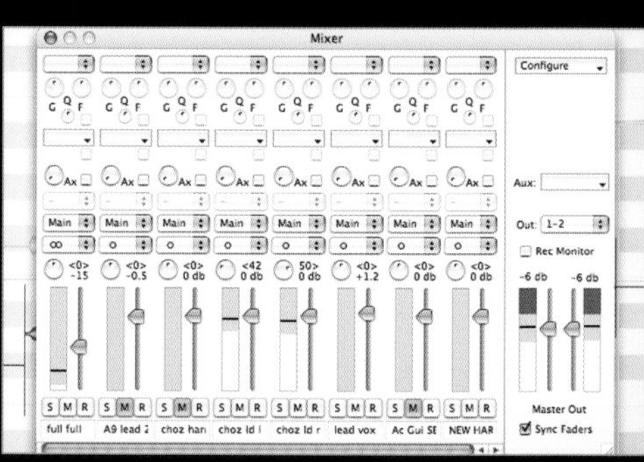

4 While editing multiple chorus parts into time with a chorus anchor what you listen to is important. As a general rule keep the backing track low and separate the two vocal lines you are working with (anchor plus new line) by panning them apart. Working with headphones can also be beneficial: this is precision work.

/walkthrough
new harmony lines

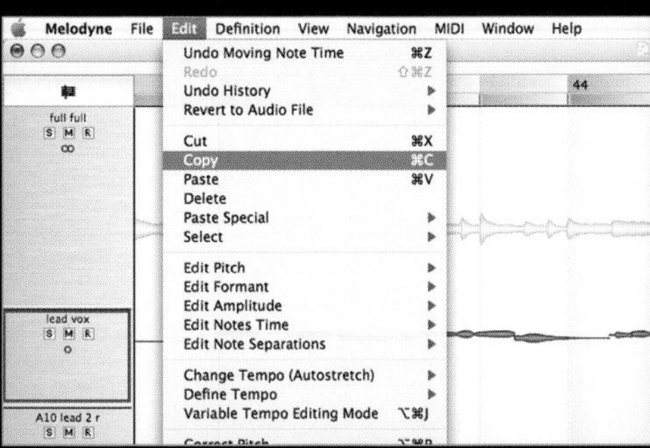

1 If you didn't find time to record a harmony during the vocal session, or you missed a great one you've thought of since, or you just need to fill out a chorus, Melodyne makes it easy to create harmonies artificially. First, in the arrangement window select the line you want to make a harmony from. Then go to Edit > Copy.

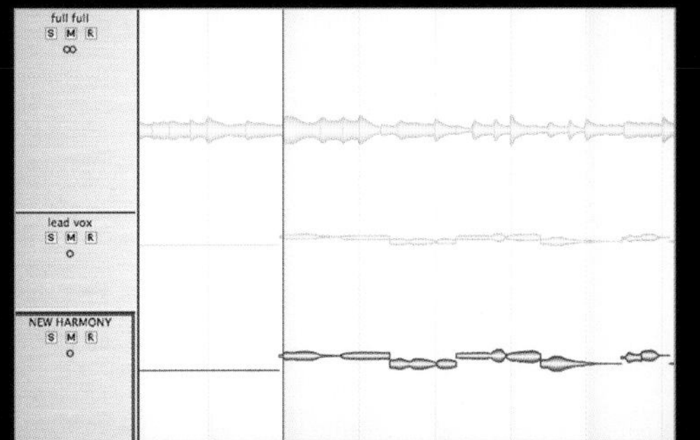

2 Paste the selection into the next available track. Melodyne can be awkward when positioning. If it's in the wrong place, drag the copied melody so that it plays in unison with the original. In the mixer (Window > Mixer) pan the original lead and the new harmony a little apart to separate them and make your editing job easier.

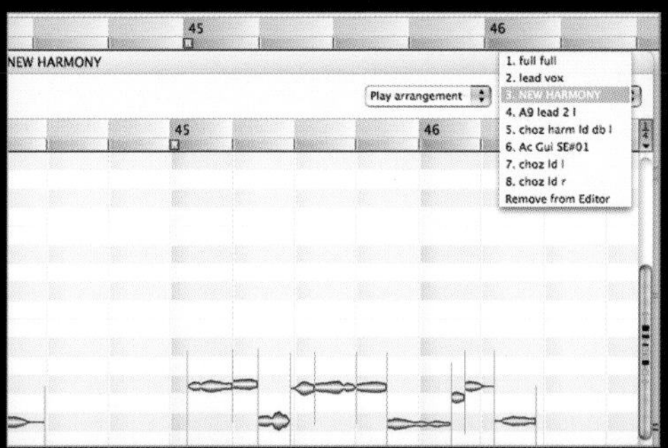

3 Double-click the new harmony to open the Editor. In the top right change the Play Visible drop-down to Play Arrangement and change the display track pull-down on the left so it shows the original lead line too. This is a nifty option, allowing you to display any lines you wish. Select 'Remove from Editor' to remove a part at any time.

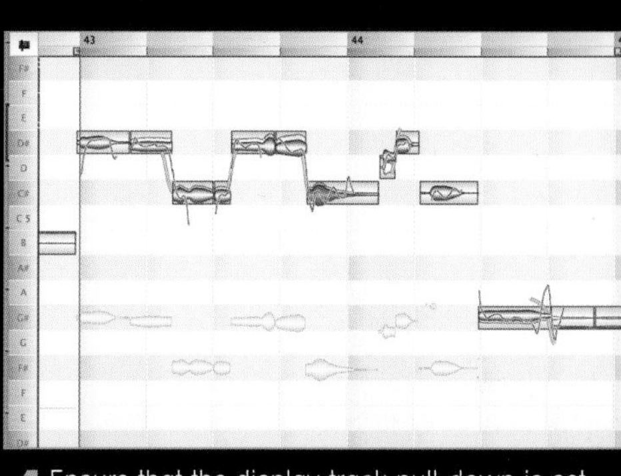

4 Ensure that the display track pull-down is set to the new harmony line. Move all the notes by going to Edit > Select > All, then with the Edit Pitch tool, move the notes up or down until you start getting nice sounding harmonies (thirds or fifths are good starting points). In the above example, the harmony is moved up by a third.

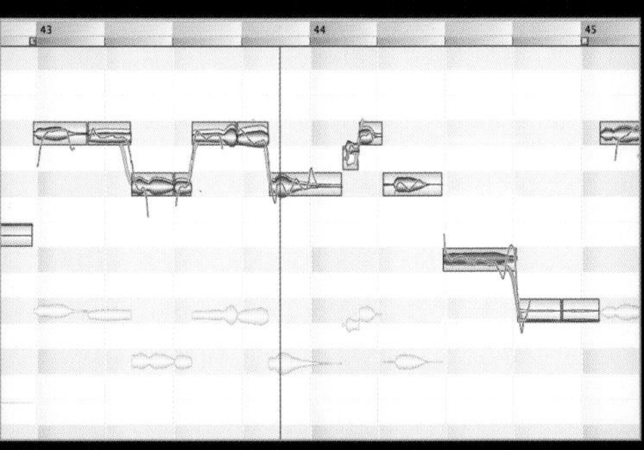

5 If you've moved an entire block of notes then it's unlikely every one will work with the lead line. You will need to alter any rogue notes manually.

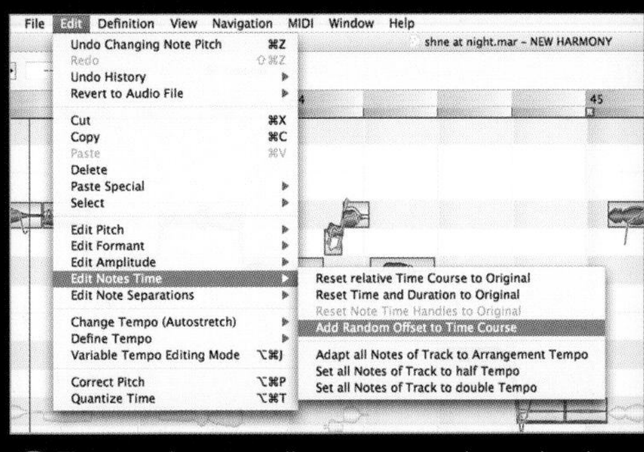

6 The new harmony line may sound unnatural. There are a few tools for making it sound more human. First, introduce some timing imperfections

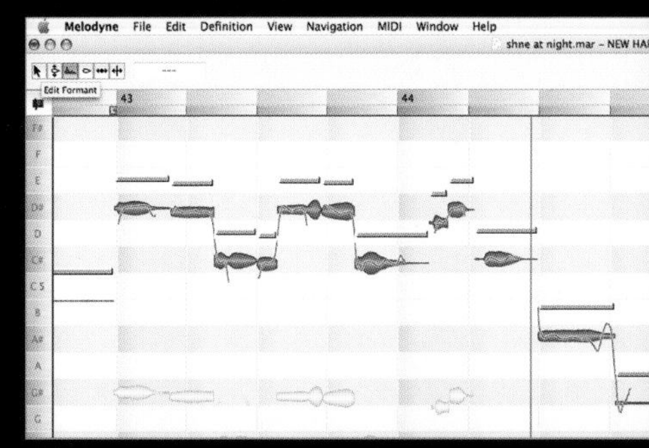

7 Next choose Edit Formant in the toolbox. This alters the tonal characteristics of a line, helping mitigate some of the more unnatural by-products

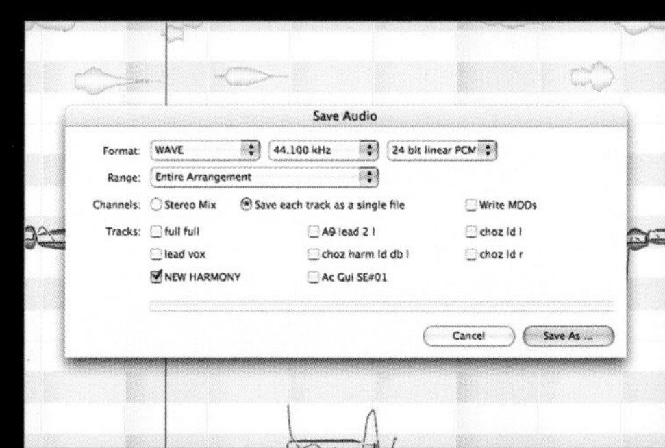

8 When you're happy with the new harmony bounce it down (File > Save Audio). Bounce it as a 24-bit Wav (or whatever format you're working

/vocal production

compression, eq and reverb are the main tools in the vocal producer's toolbox.

Whichever vocal approach you decide on – riff vocals or song vocals – there will come a time when you've recorded, edited, fine-tuned and bounced down, and you're ready to introduce the vocals into the mix. If you are using riff vocals then you are more likely to use production techniques involving the creative and outlandish effects outlined from **page 67**. Otherwise you'll be using the more traditional production techniques outlined over the following pages.

In both cases decide on the number of audio tracks you need for the vocals. If you have song vocals allow one for the lead (and a second if you've double-tracked), one for each chorus line, one or more for adlibs, one for each harmony, one for spins and so on. If you have riff vocals create one main track, and then additional ones for FX variants. If you have a complex vocal arrangement it can be helpful to set up a new project in which to pre-mix the vocals, before bouncing down blocks and harmonies to be used in the main project later.

Vocal processing

Compression

The most important tool at your disposal for processing vocals is the compressor. Singers have a wide dynamic range. The compressor tames the peaks to give a usable signal. Pick the best compressor you have at your disposal. Vocals carry both melody and meaning: don't scrimp on the quality of plugins you use on them.

The compressor settings you use will depend on the nature of the recording and the kind of sound you're after. If you're aiming for a **relaxed, natural sound** the compressor shouldn't shave off any more than 3–6dB from peaks. Start with a fast attack of 5–20ms, a release of 50–200ms and a ratio of between 1.5:1 and 4:1. For a more **artificial, heavily compressed sound**, similar to that used in X-Press 2's **Lazy** – where the compressor acts as an effect, squeezing the sound so tight that everything, including breaths, are the same volume – you can reduce as much as 15–18dB worth of gain. Start with a fast attack, release of around 0.5s and ratio of between 5:1 and 10:1. Use a hard knee setting.

Tip / The compressor isn't the only tool for controlling dynamics. Limiters can be used too – often as the last plugin in an insert chain. Automation plays a key role, allowing you to manually dip the volume during particularly loud sections (see Free riders, page 64). In practise the combined use of compressor and/or limiter alongside automation will usually yield the best results.

Tip / Although single-band compression is effective in most instances, **multi-band compression** (**see page 111**) can be used to shape the tone of a vocal if it isn't quite sitting in the mix. Bring out some warmth and body by increasing the ratio of the lower-mids, or add presence by bringing up the gain in the 5–8kHz region. Multi-band compression is particularly useful for processing bussed chorus blocks.

NOTE: Unless you're after extreme compression, be very careful when processing the lead vocal. It is easy to squeeze the life from it and render it soulless. Keep comparing the processed version with the original to see that any changes are improving the raw material, rather than stifling it.

EQ

EQing a vocal line so that it sits comfortably in the mix is probably the hardest part of mixing. Use EQ to cut problem frequencies, to shape the sound into its surroundings and to boost certain qualities, like 'air' and 'body'.

Remove rogue frequencies: One of the hazards of recording is introducing rogue frequencies caused by standing waves shaped by the dimensions of the recording environment. To remove them use a parametric EQ, dial in the lowest Q you can, whack up the gain to plus 20dB, then slowly dial through the frequencies until you find ones that ring out in an obvious and unpleasant way (you'll know when you find them!). Tame them by widening the Q a little then cutting by anything between 2–8dB.

Low-cut: Even the deepest singers don't produce sound below 60–80Hz: the average voice's fundamental frequency is above 120Hz. Remove rumble using a low-cut filter.

Air and warmth: Depending on the vocalist, 'presence' sits at around 4–6kHz. A gentle boost there will help lift the vocals, particularly if they are fighting with hi-hats or shakers. For more bass 'body' apply boost in the 200–700Hz range. For breathy air increase around 11–12kHz+.

Problem solvers: If the vocal is grating, try cutting using a medium Q somewhere in the 2.8–4kHz area. Nasal frequencies sit around the 1kHz mark. If it sounds muddy cut around 250Hz. Remember that boosting between 5kHz–10kHz will increase sibilant frequencies, so boost gently and keep a de-esser to hand.

Tip / Often EQing vocals is less important than EQing other mix elements to make space for the vocals (it's invariably better to cut using EQ, rather than boost). Because vocals span a large range of the frequency spectrum, they jostle for attention with guitars, keys, pads, synths and sometimes fx, as well as rhythmic percussive elements. Re-consider the choice of sounds playing alongside the vocal. Do you need them all? Can any be changed? If you need them, set up a 'music bus' for musical elements that inhabit the same space as the lead vocal. Identify the key frequencies you need in the vocal and then carve an EQ notch in the music bus at the same frequency.

/walkthrough
the lead vocal

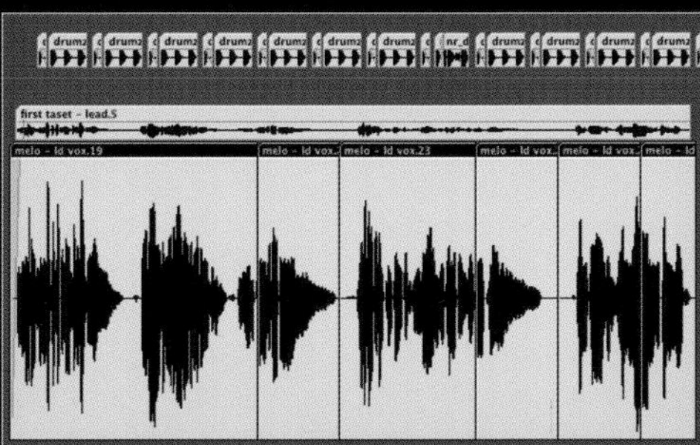

1 Loop up a vocal section that has been pre-edited. The above line has already been comped and edited until the tuning and timing is as required. If the vocal line is made up of different audio files then remember to introduce fades – in, out or across – between different sections to remove clicks and pops.

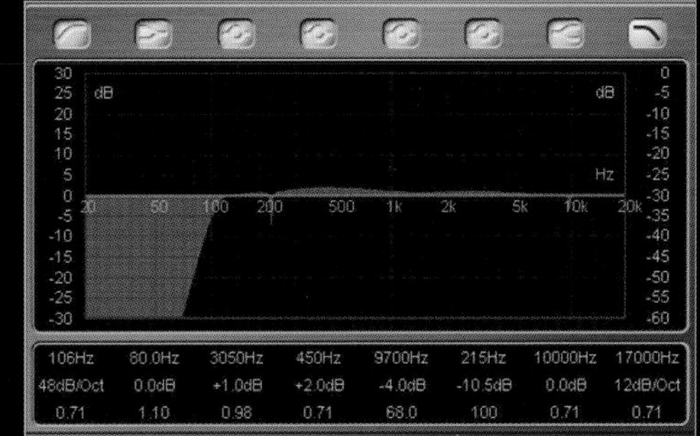

2 First in line is the EQ. Roll off below around 100Hz to reduce microphone rumble and unnecessary muddiness. The narrow cut at 215Hz removes a boomy room sound. The cut at 9.7kHz removes spiky sibilance. A subtle 2dB boost at 450Hz adds warmth.

3 Next is a compressor with a relatively subtle setting, trimming off only 3–6dB at peaks, with an attack of 19ms and release of 310ms. The settings are enough to pull back peaks and raise the overall volume without impacting on the natural sound of the lines. Peaks that still stick out of the mix can be calmed with automation later.

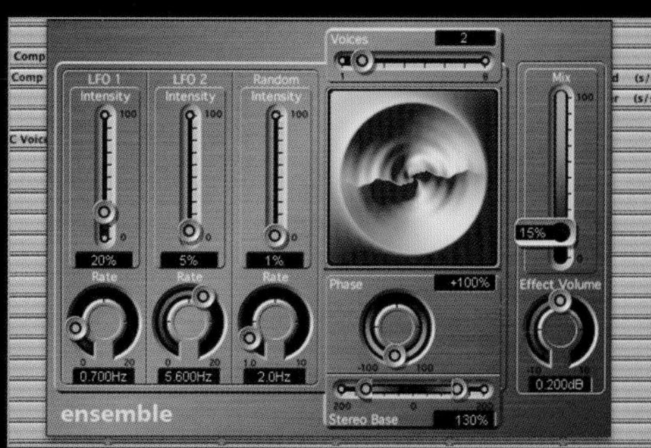

4 Logic's Ensemble is a chorus effect that also allows for stereo widening. In this example, the stereo base has been widened to 130% to give the vocal more spread. It is mixed into the main signal at a subtle 15%. The effect is barely audible, but it supplies a character that is missed when the effect is bypassed.

5 TC Electronic's VoiceStrip offers voice-specific processing tools. In this example the de-esser is switched on to remove offending sibilant syllables. The voice-optimised EQ re-introduces a little high-end sparkle and some mid bite lost in the previous processing. Last in line is a limiter with a subtle 3dB worth of gain applied.

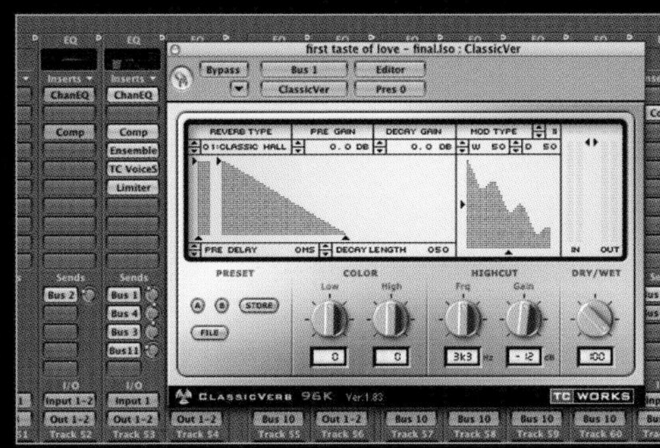

6 All reverb and delay effects on this track are applied using sends. In all, four are used: a hall reverb on bus 1, a mono delay on bus 3, an ambient stereo delay on bus 4 and a warm room reverb on Bus 11. The reverb pictured – TC's ClassicVerb – is the bus 1 verb, a medium length hall setting that helps the vocal sit in the mix.

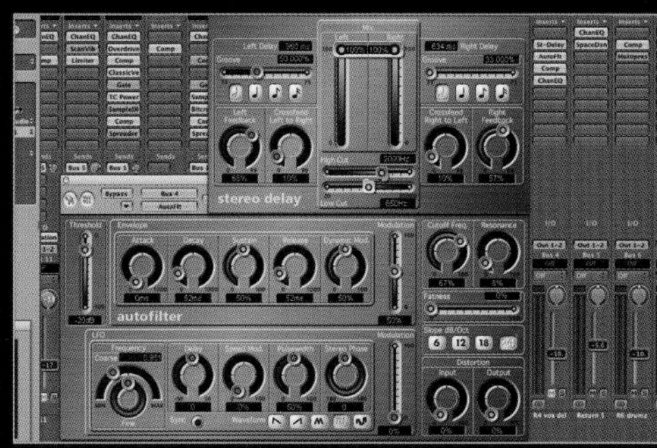

7 The ambient stereo delay on bus 4 gives the vocal stereo support and some additional low-end body to help it gel with some of the lower parts in the mix. Note the different delay lengths on right and left channels and the use of the autofilter to cut the high frequencies and introduce a little resonance. An EQ rolls off the return's bottom end.

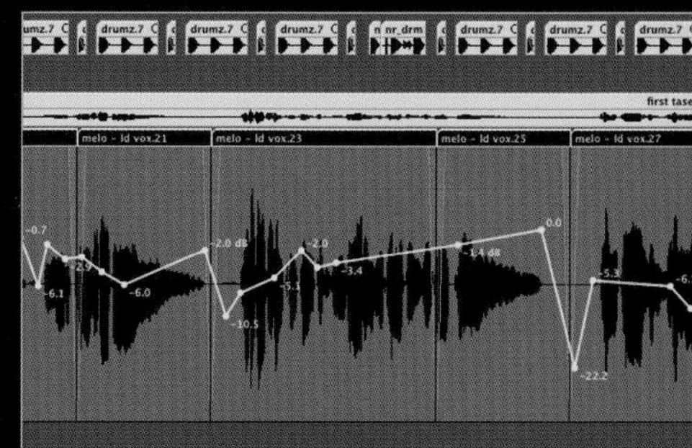

8 When the vocals are sounding good, get automating. The combined use of compression, limiting and automation allow you to preserve the innate character of the line, while also making it work in the mix. Note the sudden dips that reduce the level of breaths in the mix, whose volumes have been raised by the compressor and limiter.

Reverb and delay

Vocals have a nasty habit of sticking out of a mix. Helping them fit into their sonic surroundings is helped greatly by reverb and delay, which give dry recordings life and sparkle, and a sense of space. The kind of reverb you use will depend on both the recording you start with and the kind of sound you're after. Big, diva-style leads demand longer hall settings, while intimate, whispered vocals are best served by tight, in-your-ear room algorithms and early reflections.

The settings you'll be changing for vocals include **reverb time** (the longer the reverb tail, the bigger the sound and the further away the vocalist will sound), **type**, **pre-delay** (this should work with the tempo of the track: longer pre-delay values allow more vocal to sound dry before the verb tail kicks in – great for intimate sounding vocals), and **density**.

Tip / Many lead vocal lines are sent to two reverbs, one supplying the dry-sounding roomy 'body' of the sound (ambience), the second supplying a longer hall-type tail. By placing each on a different bus you can change the character of the vocal by altering the amount of send that goes to each.

Tip / Reverbs can be used as insert or bus effects. Using a reverb on the bus allows you to route all vocal parts – including harmonies and adlibs – to it, which will help them sound like a consistent and uniform section when playing together.

Delays play a similar role to reverbs, giving the vocal a place in the mix. Indeed clever use of delays can mitigate the need for any reverb. Play with return **timings** (usually the standard 1/8 or 1/4 note delay will be best; triplet values may throw the groove), and the number of **delays** (the more, the bigger the vocal sound). **EQ** the delay return to remove low and high frequencies that might interfere with the main vocal line.

For big vocals: Use a hall / chamber reverb with a long tail. Add between 50–80ms of pre-delay to seperate the raw voice from the effected signal. Change density to taste.

For soft, sultry vocals: Try plate or room settings. Balance a short tail with high levels of early reflections for a more intimate sound. Plate tails add sparkle and air to make breathy female vocals in particular shine.

Up-front vocals: Use a mix of early reflections and stereo-widened dry signal. See **page 115** for more on this popular technique.

Chorus

Fortunately the use of chorus as an audible vocal effect in house music (Enya style) never really caught on, but a subtle use of chorus, ensemble or other stereo widening effect can give the vocal additional character in the mix. Either use it as an insert or a bussed effect and keep it unobtrusive (if you can actually hear it then it is probably too loud).

Overdrive and bit-crushers

Use overdrive to introduce new harmonics to a vocal and give a lead line more balls and body. As with chorus, you're not looking to make the effect noticeable – just to introduce a character that wasn't there before. Subtle overdrive will not make your sultry vocal into a mighty diva, but it will make the signal warmer and will help your mighty diva sound slightly mightier. An overdrive value of anything between 0.5dB and 2dB should yield useable results. Bit-crushers yield similar results.

automation: free riders

Automation is a must in most vocal productions. Where producers-of-old rode the mixing desk faders to level out spiky vocal lines, we have the luxury of automation, allowing us to drop the level at over-loud peaks and nudge it up during quieter sections.

Programming automation is all about patience and should only be done when a mix is in its closing stages (if you do it earlier you risk rendering your work pointless as wider mix changes inevitably impact on the relative volume of the vocal).

To program automation simply loop one section at a time (verse, chorus ec), listen to which notes are quieter and which are louder, then program in compensatory volume changes (higher in quiet lines, lower in loud lines). You will end up returning to your edits time and again, fine-tuning the automation to get it completely right.

Automation is particularly useful for non-destructively editing out (or lowering the volume of) breaths between lines, which inevitably get raised in volume when compressed.

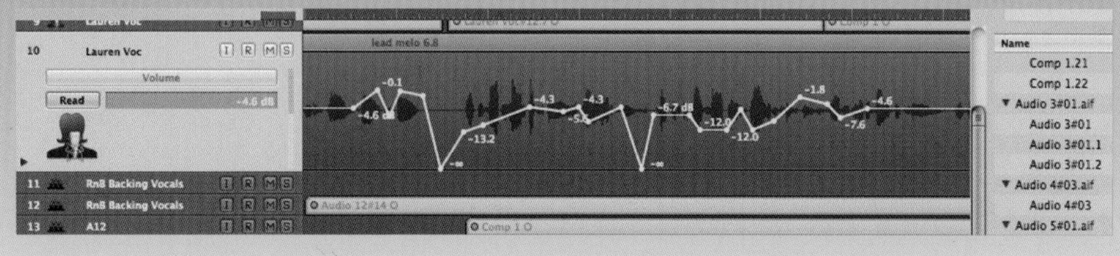

De-essers

Sibilant syllables are the scourge of the vocal producer. You can reduce them on a practical level by avoiding including too many S's in lyrics (particularly during the chorus). But you'll never avoid them completely. A **de-esser** is a specialised compressor with a sidechain that is driven by sibilant frequencies so that it reduces the sibilant range of a signal when Ssss's hit the chain. Experiment with the de-esser's settings to avoid it impacting on the rest of the signal, and use the monitor facility to hear exactly what it's reacting to (**see page 112**). Often a better (or at least complementary) result can be achieved by ducking the volume of sibilant syllables with automation.

Warmers and beyond

There are a range of other plugins, including specific vocal channel strips, that will up the game of your vocal production. Experiment with analogue saturation plugins to warm up a lifeless digital signal.

A postscript on plugin order

The order you place insert effects on the vocal channel has an impact on the final sound. Try the following as a start:

1) Initial EQ – to remove rogue frequencies and bottom end
2) Overdrive (very subtle, if relevant)
3) Compressor
4) Chorus or stereo enhancer / widener (subtle)
5) Body reverb (assuming not on bus)
6) Final EQ (adding shine or body and refining processed sound)
7) Final limiter (entirely optional)

NB: Assumes delays and main verb are located on the busses.

/walkthrough
the chorus block

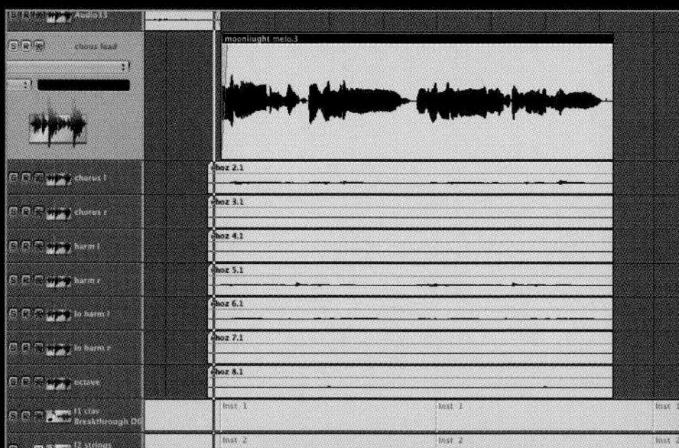

1 Load the audio tracks that make up the chorus block into your DAW. Some or all of the lines may have been treated to correct pitch and rhythm. Here the top three lines carry the lead. There are also two double-tracked harmony parts and a single line an octave below the lead, making 8 chorus lines in all.

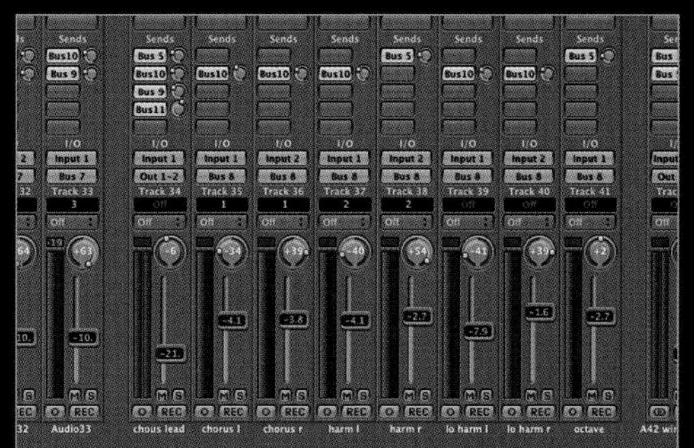

2 The lead chorus line is triple-tracked, with the main line taking centre stage. This is processed in the same way as the verse vocal, with the same bussed effects. Supporting this are the triple-tracks that are mixed low and panned left and right.

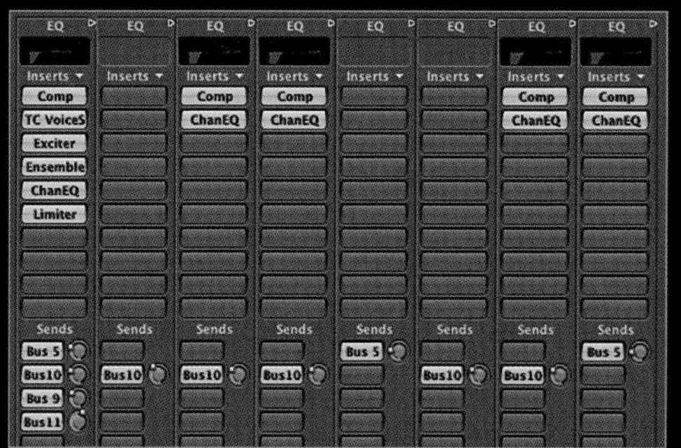

3 Every chorus part except the lead line is sent to a bus for block processing. Some are also processed before the bus, with gentle compression and EQ. It can be useful to use different EQ and compression settings to create a range of different vocal timbres and make the chorus sound bigger.

4 Each harmony line is sent to one of the two reverbs used by the chorus lead. The amount sent is more than for the lead, to sit the harmonies behind it. The main verb bus has a vocal ambience setting followed by a limiter to bulk up the sound. An EQ rolls off the low and high ends.

5 First in line on the chorus bus is a stereo widener that introduces some spread and helps settle the chorus in the mix. Next is a compressor that reduces 8–10dB worth of gain, with a fast 8ms attack and 190ms release for a tight feel, punching with energy. You can be fairly tough with settings here to ensure the chorus parts all gel together.

6 Next in line is a tape delay. This supplies delay across the entire chorus block, placing it in the mix behind the lead chorus line. The mix level is set to 25% with feedback at 30% for a fairly subtle effect. Note that a reverb could have done a similar job. For in-your-face chorus vocals keep the settings low and roomy.

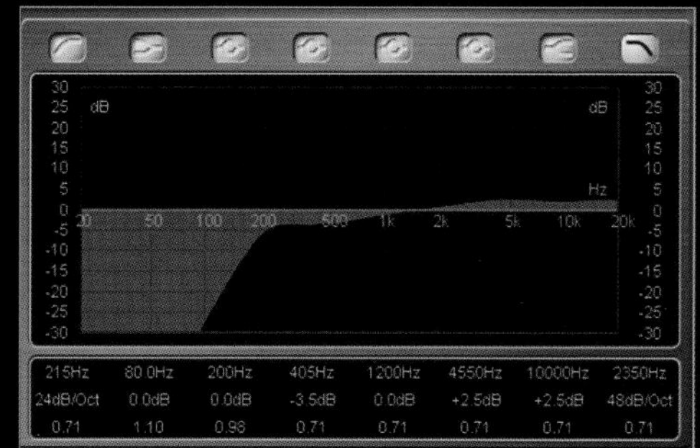

7 A parametric EQ is last in line. A shelving low-cut filter removes the muddy bottom. It can roll away signal as far up as 250Hz. A gentle scoop at 405Hz takes out some body, while a wide boost at 4.5kHz adds definition and clarity to the block, helping it cut through the mix. A further gentle boost at 10kHz gives it some air.

8 Every chorus treatment is different. This second example shows a different sequence of effects, including EQ, a multi-band compressor, stereo widener, de-esser, limiter, a second EQ and then a bit-crusher to bulk up the sound and give the chorus more bite. This kind of treatment served a big gospel-style block well.

The chorus

The chorus may contain just one vocal line or have as many as 100 (sometimes even more!). Usually in house productions it will be made up of between 4 and 10. Often it will include harmonies that work with the lead chorus line (the line that carries the main chorus melody). There may also be versions of the lead line sung an octave below and above to thicken it and reinforce it, in the way an additional oscillator thickens a synth sound. Harmonies are often double-tracked.

How you mix the various parts in the chorus vocal block will depend on the song and material available. Options include:

Simple chorus. The lead line is supported by a single or double-tracked harmony. Can be very effective with a strong vocal, but not recommended for big gospel-style choruses.

Lead
Harmony

The double-track. The lead line is double-tracked with the parts panned a little apart. Supporting harmonies and octaves are sent to a bus for processing.

Lead Lead
Harm block

The triple-track. The chorus lead line is processed using the same channel strip as the verse vocal. It is supported by double-tracks singing the same lead chorus line mixed lower and panned left and right, as well as harmonies and octaves sent to a bus for processing.

Lead
Lead Lead
Harm block

Note that although all vocal parts can be sent to the same bus for processing, it is often more useful to treat the lead vocal line separately, without sending it to the bus.

Even before hitting the bus, a rough mix can be set up using volume and panning to get the chorus block sounding good. The lead line should usually sit centrally, with potential double or triple tracks either panned a little to the left and right, or further out, with harmonies panned to different areas to create a stereo chorus mix that sounds full and works as a whole, with no single line sticking. Deciding on the stereo positions of double tracks is a matter of trial and error: they should be far enough apart to get the classic chorus effect, but they shouldn't lose contact with each other.

Chorus processing and effects

Start by treating the lead chorus line in the same way as the lead verse vocal, with the same compression, EQ and reverbs. This helps maintain a seamless tonal continuity between verse and chorus.

The double tracks and harmonies can be treated alone or together on the chorus bus. It is good practise to do some basic processing on each track before it is sent to the bus – removing low-end EQ, using gentle compression – but the main processing should happen on the bus, where all parts can be treated together to blend them into a tight, unified whole.

Compression on the chorus block can be fairly brutal, with gain reduction as high as 8–12dB. Experiment with the attack and release settings and aim for a mix between a full, round sound and one that still punches with energy. Note that higher compression settings will raise the volume of breaths – a particular worry if there are lots of vocals singing the same line. Either edit them out of the audio files or automate the chorus bus volume to dip down at breath points (see **Holding breath, opposite**).

You can be ruthless with EQ too. Roll away low-end energy (sweep up from 100Hz to as high as 250Hz). It's often worth trimming some high-end too so that the chorus block doesn't fight with the lead line in the upper-mids and highs: remember that they are there to support the lead, not overshadow it.

Other tools that may be useful include a last-in-chain limiter (be careful of squashing the life out of the block), a subtle overdrive or bit-crusher to add additional harmonics and stereo wideners to give the chorus block additional width in the mix.

As far as reverbs and/or delays go, the rule is generally to use the same reverbs on chorus lines that are used on the lead vocal line, but to send more signal their way so that the chorus block as a whole appears to sit further back in the mix.

Tip / Chorus blocks feature many lines singing the same lyrics at the same time. This can cause sibilance problems as all the S's hit at once. Power up a de-esser to tame them or, for more drastic measures, edit out the S's on the actual audio file in all but a couple of the harmony tracks. (Some producers even ask their vocalist not to sing sibilant and plosive syllables on chorus harmonies during the tracking stage.)

Tip / Multi-band compression can be useful on chorus blocks, as it enables you to process different frequency areas differently. You could, for example, push up a weak lower-end and pull back on the highs that threaten to overwhelm the lead vocal line.

Tip / If the chorus block sounds weak, route it through a reverb with either a short plate or room reverb. Mix the signal 20% wet and 80% dry to introduce body to the sound.

/walkthrough adlibs

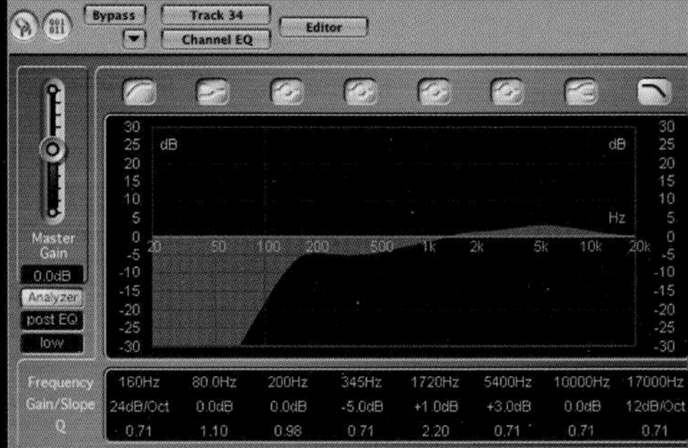

1 Adlibs can be a nightmare to fit into the mix. The secret is treating them slightly differently to the lead vocal. Here the adlibs are panned a little to the left of the lead line, with an EQ scoop of lower-end energy and added high-mids. At the same time, automation on the lead vocal cuts the same upper-mids to open space for the adlib line.

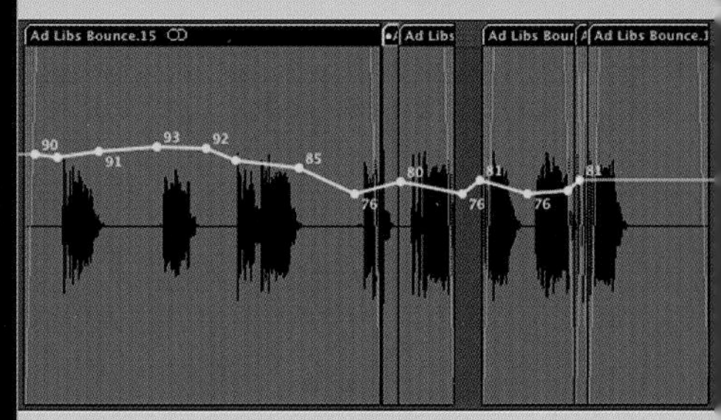

2 Automation also plays an important role. The compression settings are relatively light (only removing 3-4dB worth of gain) so that the raw power of the adlibs is preserved. Automation tames the peaks and raises the troughs. The adlibs are mixed up-front, with little reverb but some obvious delays to create a bigger sound.

/vocal fx

turn a tired one-phrase loop into a classic hook by abusing a whole handful of tried-and-tested effects.

Where would vocals be without extreme effects processing? The number of classic house tracks with screwed-up vocals is almost endless, from the auto-tuned melodies of Daft Punk's **One More Time**, through the vocoded mayhem of Mylo's **Drop the Pressure** to the sleaze-fests of a dozen Justice offerings.

All effects are fair game when it comes to extreme vocal processing, but some have found their way into the house hall of fame.

Vocoder

The godfather of house vocal effects creates singing robotic lines from raw vocals. It does this by mixing the characteristics of a human voice with the body of a synth tone. (See **Vocoder vox walkthough, page 69**). Keep the input notes and rhythms changing for ever evolving sounds. Add bit-crushers and EQ to help the signal cut through the mix.

Talk box

Often confused with the vocoder, talk boxes produce the classic 'talking guitar' sound. The sound of an instrument (usually a guitar) is modified by the shape of the performer's lips and vocal cavities, resulting in vowel-like musical phrases. Using spoken phrases to modulate the instrument can yield great results. If you don't own a talk box, try using the 'Talk-wah' setting in NI's Guitar Rig 3.

Overdrive

Use overdrive or bit-crushing to introduce warmth to a signal or to break it down into digital splinters. Somewhere between the two you'll get ballsy 4 and 8-bit sounds. Automate bit-crushing parameters for extra dirt.

Auto-Tune abuse

It's clichéd as hell now, but time was when every other record featured overly auto-tuned vocals, á la Cher. It's the easiest effect in the book to get: strap Antares Auto-Tune across the lead vocal as an insert effect, turn the 'Retuning' threshold to as fast as possible – start at zero – and program the scale to taste. For more control enter Graphical mode. You can similar sounds using Logic and Cubase's native pitch correctors on extreme settings. Take the effect to the next level and create artificial – but perfectly tuned – harmonies by copying a single vocal line onto different tracks and then automating the scales being played, or manually programming the notes played using Auto-Tune's Graphical mode for instant digital choirs.

Glitched vocals

Vocal processing isn't just about abuse. You can program interesting vocal lines from single spoken or sung phrases by using nothing more than a step sequencer and a sample's start and end points. See **Minimal vocals in Ultrabeat walkthrough, page 68**.

Ring modulation

The supplier of vocals to the Daleks and Clangers allows for serious creative exploration. Specialising in metallic sounds, the ring modulator produces a range of tones, from subtle wobbling to discordant clangs. Although not massively useful across an entire vocal line, it can be used as a spot effect to pick out particular words and phrases to give them an other-worldly twist.

P-P-P-Programming

However many tools you have at your fingertips, it's often imaginative programming that makes for a memorable effected vocal line. Cutting up and re-arranging the vocal loop and experimenting with fade times, loop times and so on, either on the arrange page or using a sampler, can generate a wealth of memorable riffs. Try reversing select sections into others for wonky ins and outs.

Old-school timestretching

Get all Fatboy Slim and timestretch the vocal way beyond acceptable parameters. This will degrade the signal and introduce grainy effects. Re-sample the resulting audio file and introduce cut up sections of that into the main mix. Note you can do something similar with Apple Loops by turning a vocal loop into an Apple Loop, reducing Logic's tempo to, say, 12bpm, and then bouncing down the loop. It will disintegrate, making it ripe for use in a lo-fi electro or nu-rave mix.

Automation

Whatever you do, keep it changing. Automate everything from tuning through bit-crush parameters to EQ and beyond. Intricate programming across time can keep a single vocal phrase interesting for an entire song.

/pro tips

holding breath

It's a perennial question for the vocal producer: to keep or ditch the breaths? On the one hand breaths can sound messy in the mix – particularly when you have multiple vocal lines playing (and breathing) at the same time – but removing them can make the vocal sound unnatural.

Most producers find a happy medium, preserving them in the lead line, using automation to dip their volume when necessary, and editing out breaths in harmonies and often chorus backing lines too.

Breaths can sound great as effects, giving an in-yer-face whisper-in-the-ear quality when heavily compressed. Run a breath through a big reverb plate and ping-pong delays for the occasional sensual spot spin.

/walkthrough
minimal vocals in ultrabeat

1 Set a simple beat loop running against which you'll create the minimal vocal line. Create a new instrument track and open an instance of Logic's Ultrabeat drum machine. Open the Drag & Drop Samples preset.

2 On the bottom panel of Ultrabeat change length to 16 clicks, introduce a little swing using the swing dial and then either drag and drop or load a sample into the sample player. The sound is introduced by default onto the highlighted C1 pad. The kind of sample you're after is a tight spoken word or sung clip with plenty of rhythmic content.

3 Turn on the sequencer using the power button and press play. Now click on each of the 16 numbered pads in the sequencer so that they light up. This triggers the vocal sample on each 16th note.

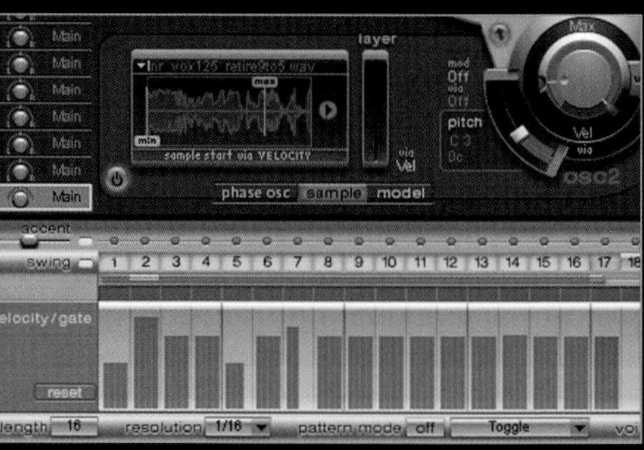

4 In the sample preview pane, click and drag the blue 'max' slider to the right – try a point a third of the way through the sample. This changes the sample start point depending on the velocity of the hit. To see how it works in practise, program in a few velocity changes in the sequence by clicking on the blue bars and dragging them up or down.

5 With the beat playing, refine the sequence by changing note lengths, muting some and changing velocities. A single note can play across beats by dragging the right edge of the blue block across divisions. Experiment with the position of the 'max' and 'min' sliders in the sample preview pane.

6 When you've got a good groove going, it's time to fire up Ultrabeat's more advanced settings. Click on the step edit button (bottom left). This allows you to set values for everything from cutoff frequency to distortion amount for each step. Alter the pitch on a couple of notes by clicking on a step and changing its pitch value.

7 Everything is fair game for tweaking. Change any of the gold highlighted values for each individual step. In this example the cutoff frequency has been pushed up and some drive introduced on a single step. Tweak until you're happy, although for minimal vocals you'll probably want to keep tweaks relatively subtle.

8 Finally, export the data from Ultrabeat by clicking the 'Drag to arrange window' button at the bottom left of the Ultrabeat window and dragging it onto your Ultrabeat instrument track. This will give you the note information, which you can edit further in the Matrix Editor. You could use the same Midi loop to power a different instrument altogether.

/walkthrough
vocoder vox

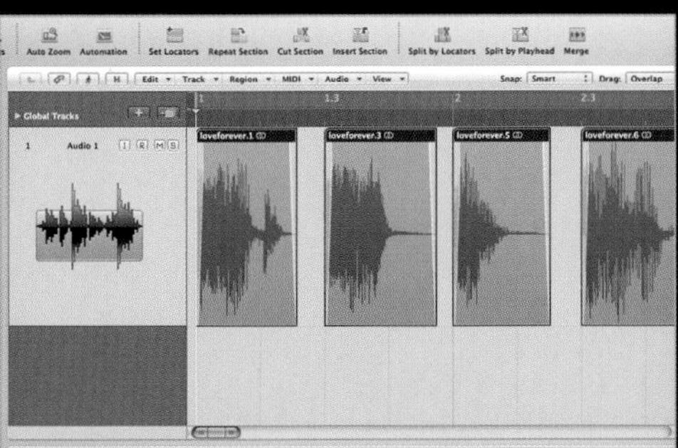

1 Record or load an audio file with vocal content. Ideally it will be a spoken word line without a melody. The cleaner the sound the better at this stage. Place the audio file on a dedicated audio track. Perform any micro-edits to pull the vocal into time and add fades to remove clicks and pops.

2 Create a new instrument track. Load the EVOC 20 Vocoder (or equivalent). Vocoders work by imprinting the frequency spectrum of one signal onto the sound energy of another. Hence it has two inputs, speech (the voc in vocoder) and carrier. Set up the EVOC so that the sidechain (top right) is fed by the audio track. Load one of the 'Vintage' presets.

3 Mute the original vocal part and, on the EVOC track, create a Midi loop and draw in the notes you want the vocoder to play. The original vocal line will now play through the vocoder at the pitches you've drawn in. To start with program a simple monophonic line.

4 It can be hard to get the vocoder to 'read' the vocal material. If so try inserting an EQ on the vocal track to emphasise the higher frequencies where the consonants sit. Roll off the lows. Use firm compression to get the line sitting even. Try high ratios, fast attacks and decays, and remove as much as 15dB gain. An exciter can help too.

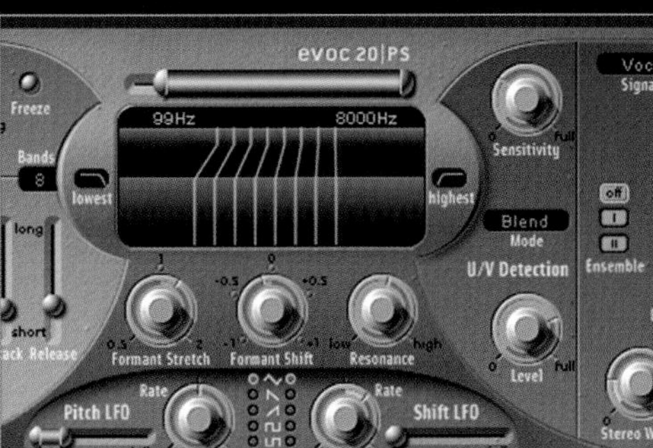

5 The main vocoder controls allow you to change the number of filter bands and the amount of formant shift. The more bands you have, the more the voice will sound like the synth input. Choose low numbers for the classic vocoder sound. Shift the formant for higher and lower toned variations.

6 You can program the vocoder to respond in a range of different ways to the source material. The attack and release settings in the 'Sidechain Analysis In' section allow you to alter the envelopes. In the Mode section select Dual and then play with the value next to Wave 1 for a range of different timbres. Try also detuning Wave 2 by +5 or +7.

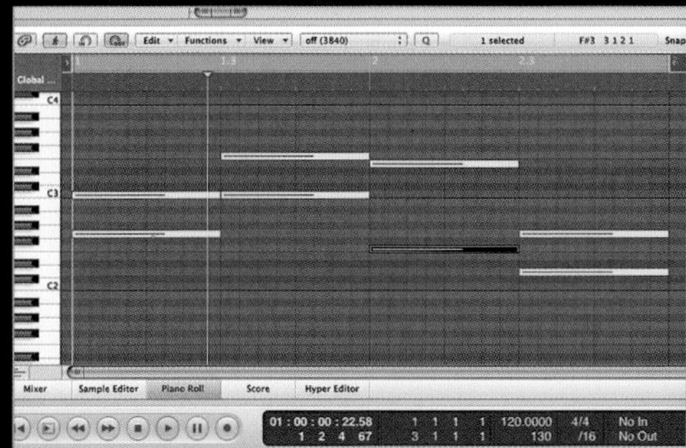

7 Now return to the looped sequence and alter the notes. Big chords (including 5ths and 7ths) work as well as monophonic lines (note the poly, mono and legato settings on the top left of the EVOC, which you should amend depending on what a sequence is doing).

8 Vocoders are ripe for abuse and automation. Here you can see the source vocal material has been cut up for a glitchy nu-rave style sound with automation on the vocoder controlling the octave tuning of oscillator 1. This sweeps the tuning up towards the end of the two-bar section, where the amount of glide is also increased for a funky end.

/walkthrough
sleazy tuned electro vox in logic

1 Either record or import a short audio file with strong lyrical content. You want a line that makes people take note and listen. Roll off some low-end at around 125Hz and power up an initial compressor to tame the peaks. Keep the release value low to maintain dynamics.

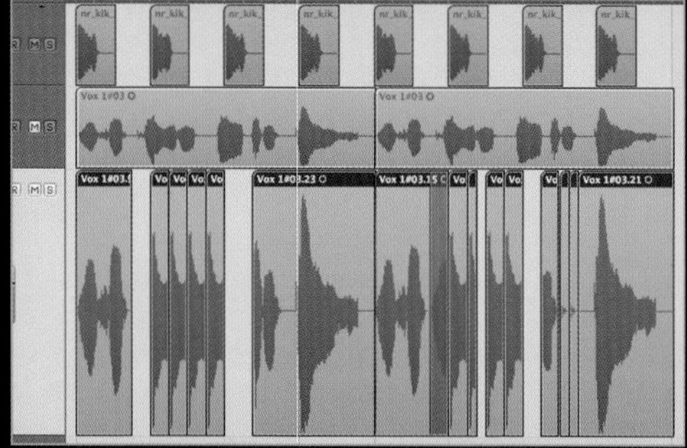

2 Working against a simple kick drum loop, start cutting up and re-arranging the vocal line. Your aim is to maintain lyrical meaning (unless you're deliberately seeking nonsense), while also messing up the loop. This may mean keeping specific words while triggering short sections of others. Experiment and bin substandard attempts.

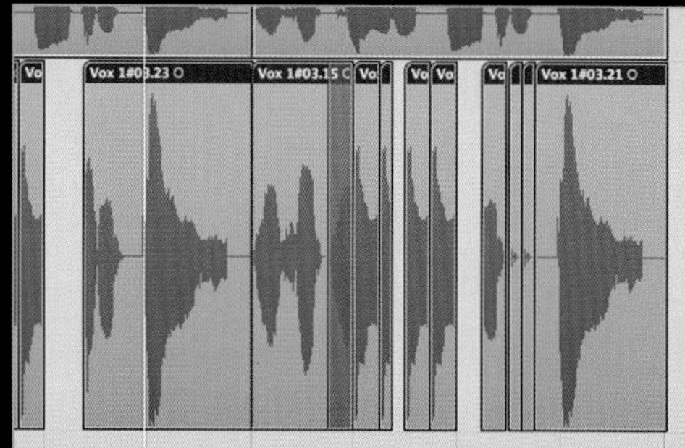

3 Some techniques have a tried-and-tested track record. Re-triggering hard edged 'plosive' consonants (Ps, Bs, Ts) in quick succession can work well. Try reversing small sections of audio for freaky fade-in and out effects. Note that silence also plays an important role, cutting the rhythm and leaving space for other mix elements – like drums.

4 When you're happy with the line it's time to dirty the signal. A bit-crusher is a good place to start. Here drive is set to 4dB, resolution has been pulled back to crunchy 8-bit, with downsampling at 3x. After this comes the kooky Logic Speech Enhancer, set to a mic model of the iSight to introduce further signal deterioration.

5 Now the fun part. Insert a vocal transformer (it's under the pitch plugin menu). Set mix to 100%, turn the Robotize function on. This discards existing melodic values and forces the pitch to the value indicated on the left hand pitch dial. Play with the formant on the right. Small changes can sound good – artificial but still identifiable.

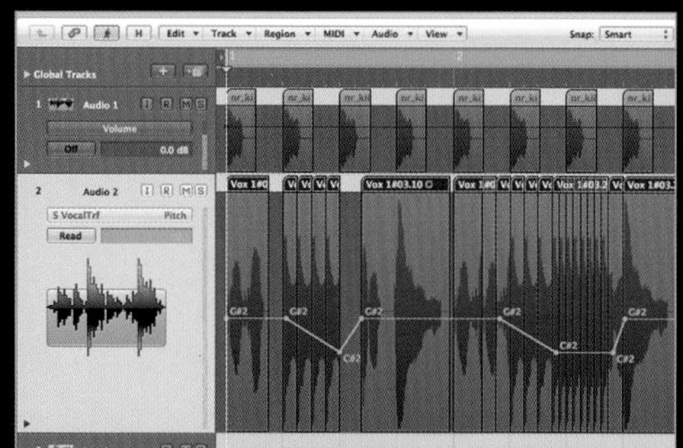

6 Return to the arrange window and start programming automation. You want to automate the Vocal Transformer pitch value over time to introduce a melody into the glitched vox line. In this example the pitch slips down to C# on the re-triggered sections, returning to the root of G#. It gives a funky nu-disco sound.

7 Try introducing other automation throughout the sequence. Real-time formant changes work well, as do changes to the grain size. Try automating the bit-crusher values too – downsampling sweeps can give you a ripping vocal sound. Finally, add reverb and / or delays for the final polish.

8 Create a digital harmony by copying the glitch sequence to a new audio track with the same plugins on. Now program a different set of Vocal Transformer pitch values. In this example the original pitch drop is mirrored by a rise resolving to the same note an octave above on the second line. Add more lines for bigger vox blocks.

/walkthrough reverse reverb

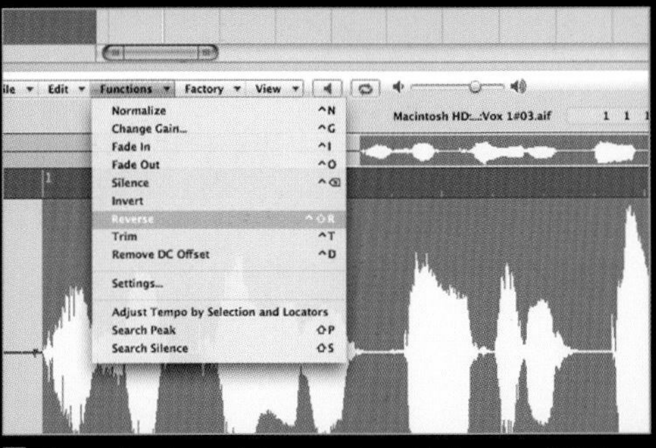

1 Record or import the vocal part into your DAW and place it on an audio track. Reverse it using the in-built audio editor (Functions > Reverse).

2 Run the vocal line through a hall or plate reverb with a long tail and 70-80% of reflectivity. In this instance we've ignored the high-end Space Designer for the more lo-fi SilverVerb. The mix should be set to 100% wet. Bounce down the effected vocal (remember to catch the full tail!).

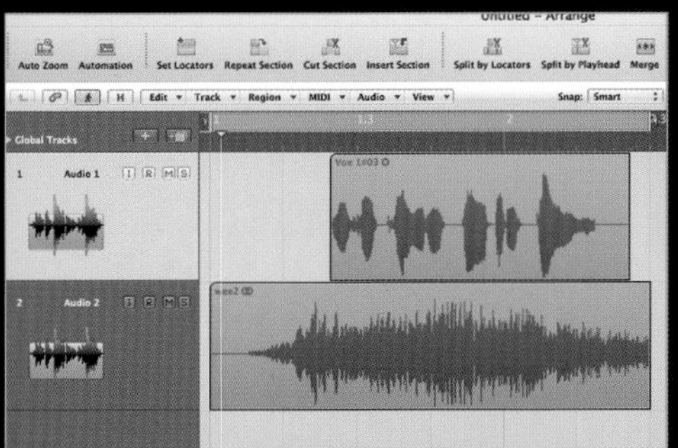

3 Add a new audio track and import the bounced effected vocal onto it. Reverse it. At the same time remove the reverb plugin from the original vocal line and reverse that too so it plays forward again as it did when you first imported or recorded it.

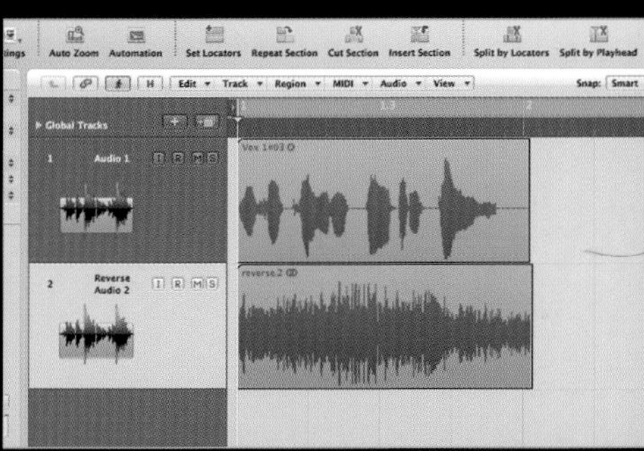

4 Now you need to align the two parts so that they work together. It's a matter of trial and error, although listening out for common consonants can help. When the two are working, lower the volume of the effected version. Add modulation effects to introduce additional movement.

/walkthrough phone filter and riser

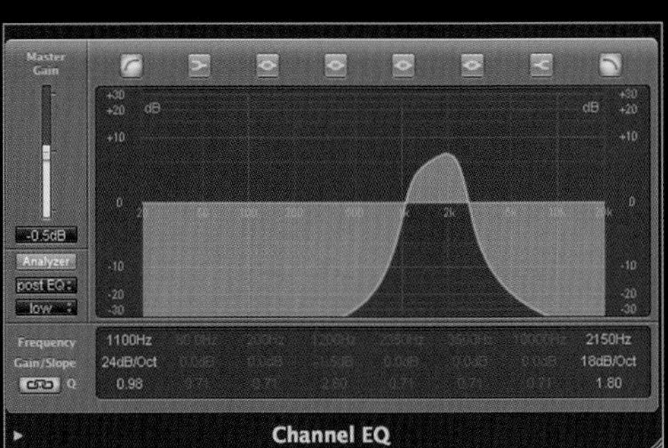

1 Useful for vocal spins, spoken word passages and during breakdowns, the classic phone filter effect is made using an EQ that only allows a narrow range of frequencies through. Specifically, set up a low-cut filter at around 1.1kHz with a Q value of 0.98 and slope of 24dB. Add a high-cut filter at 2.1kHz with a Q of 1.8 and a filter slope of 18dB.

2 It can be effective to follow a phone EQ with a brick-wall style compressor, making an artificially flat vocal sound. Here the threshold is set to -40dB, with a short attack and release and ratio of 5.6:1. Note the VCA circuit. If the consonants are too harsh try raising the threshold or extending the release a little.

3 Add some lo-fi grit by powering up an overdrive unit or bit-crusher. Here the crusher is set to reduce the signal to 10-bit, with a downsampling value of x2. A 16th note slapback delay is added last in the chain, mixed at a relatively low 10%, to add some ambience. Longer delay values – including dubby triplets – can also work nicely.

4 The 'rising EQ' trick has been used on many classic records. Just set up the automation so the low-cut frequency steadily rises through a given phrase. It will remove low-frequency content until you're left with just the light, brittle top-end. Add additional automation to increase the delay send value towards the end for an additional twist.

/pro tips

way out west

Way Out West's Jody Wisternoff has done remixes and production duties for James Holden, Echo & The Bunnymen, The Orb and Roni Size. He spills all on monitoring and mastering, soft synths and hard work.

Do you mainly use analogue or digital soft synth sources? Do you think analogue really makes a difference?
I'm really into analogue synths and I've become more so over the last few years. I seem to get more usable and inspiring results from old synths, as opposed to vst plugins. I think a major reason is that I like to alter my sounds as I play riffs and to do this with a VST requires a lot of mouse movement and automation, which can kill inspiration. There's something special about genuine synths – they seem to have individual characters and personalities of their own. It's not just vintage analogue stuff I love but also digital classics like the DX7. However, everything has its place, and I'm a huge fan of programs like Reaktor and Massive when it comes to complex rhythmic stuff, soundscapes and effects. It's also true that sometimes VSTs are just easier: they never give you tuning issues, you can write on the road, total recall is standard, and – above all – for better or worse most listeners can't hear the difference between the two anyway.

Any arrangement secrets you want to share?
It pays to start arranging a track sooner rather than later. If you start building a rough structure fairly early on then you can work out how many different ideas you need in a track, as opposed to working over an eight bar loop and just adding and adding. Simplicity is often the key, and even though it's hard to keep a track interesting over seven minutes with only a few essential elements, when you achieve it it can be a beautiful thing. Complexity is often a substitute for a lack of really good ideas. I also think that you either need to be a DJ, or spend a lot of time clubbing, to really understand how dance tracks should be structured.

What's your opinion on processing the mix bus? Leave it clean or drive it to the extreme?
If you have a lot of plugins strapped across the mix bus you are giving the mastering engineer less room to manoeuvre. That said, some compression can definitely help glue the mix together, and a bit of EQ is sometimes needed. When I mix, I tend to set up three main busses for drums, bass and music. It's on these busses – rather than the main outputs – that I apply compression and sidechaining. Usually if I find myself wanting to EQ the master it's a sign that I need to work on the mix a bit more. At the end of the day though, just trust your ears. Dance music has always been about breaking the rules, and some of the most exciting sounds have been made by accident. If it sounds good but is technically wrong, fuck it and run with it!

When building a track how do you normally work? Do you start with the beat and build your way up from that?
I normally start with a riff or bassline. When I used to make breakbeat music I would start with a selection of beats and loops, but these days I find it more inspiring to begin with a musical element: either a sample, a vocal or a really catchy riff. I start adding the drums in afterwards and build the groove from there. If you've got a great hook the track usually flows a lot better. Another thing I do from the start is loop up a kick drum to be used as the sidechain trigger. I can then build the track against this sidechained backbone.

How important do you think it is to have your music mastered commercially? Can you do it yourself as effectively and what tools would you recommend?
Commercial mastering is an extremely important process and is not something I would ever attempt using plugins. You need a proper mastering rig consisting of a selection of dedicated compressors and EQs, all of which shape the sound in their own specific ways. You also need years of experience to call yourself a mastering engineer. It's a specialist job and is often underestimated. On demos it's fine to throw a limiter plugin over the master bus, but for a commercial release mastering is a job best left to the pros.

Loops or programming your own beats from single hits, and why?
A bit of both really. It depends on the vibe of the track, but I usually run a few loops behind programmed beats. They help fill out the groove and magical things can happen when you start layering.

You do have to be careful that things don't clash though, and I do a lot of subtractive EQing to help different elements sit in the mix. For example, you don't usually want more than one kick drum in loops or things start to get messy. It's a lot harder getting a groove going when programming from single hits, but if you can do it it's great because you have control over all the individual elements.

Which sounds do you find the hardest to create from scratch?
Really interesting electronic sounds that have never been heard before are the hardest to create; sounds that are unusual but also harmonically pleasing and give a good feeling. It's one thing using presets, but when you come up with amazing noises from the ground-up it's really satisfying.

What is the secret to being a successful producer?
I think the most important thing is remaining consistent and also keeping your profile strong with a continuous flow of output. The industry is more competitive than ever right now and you really cannot rest on your laurels: you have to be driven to create music as if your life depends on it. Making music is not a shortcut to an easy life, but more like an addiction that needs to be fed. In order to be successful you need to give 110 per cent, have a bit of talent, and a whole lot of luck.

"The main thing is remaining consistent and keeping your profile strong with a continuous flow of output."

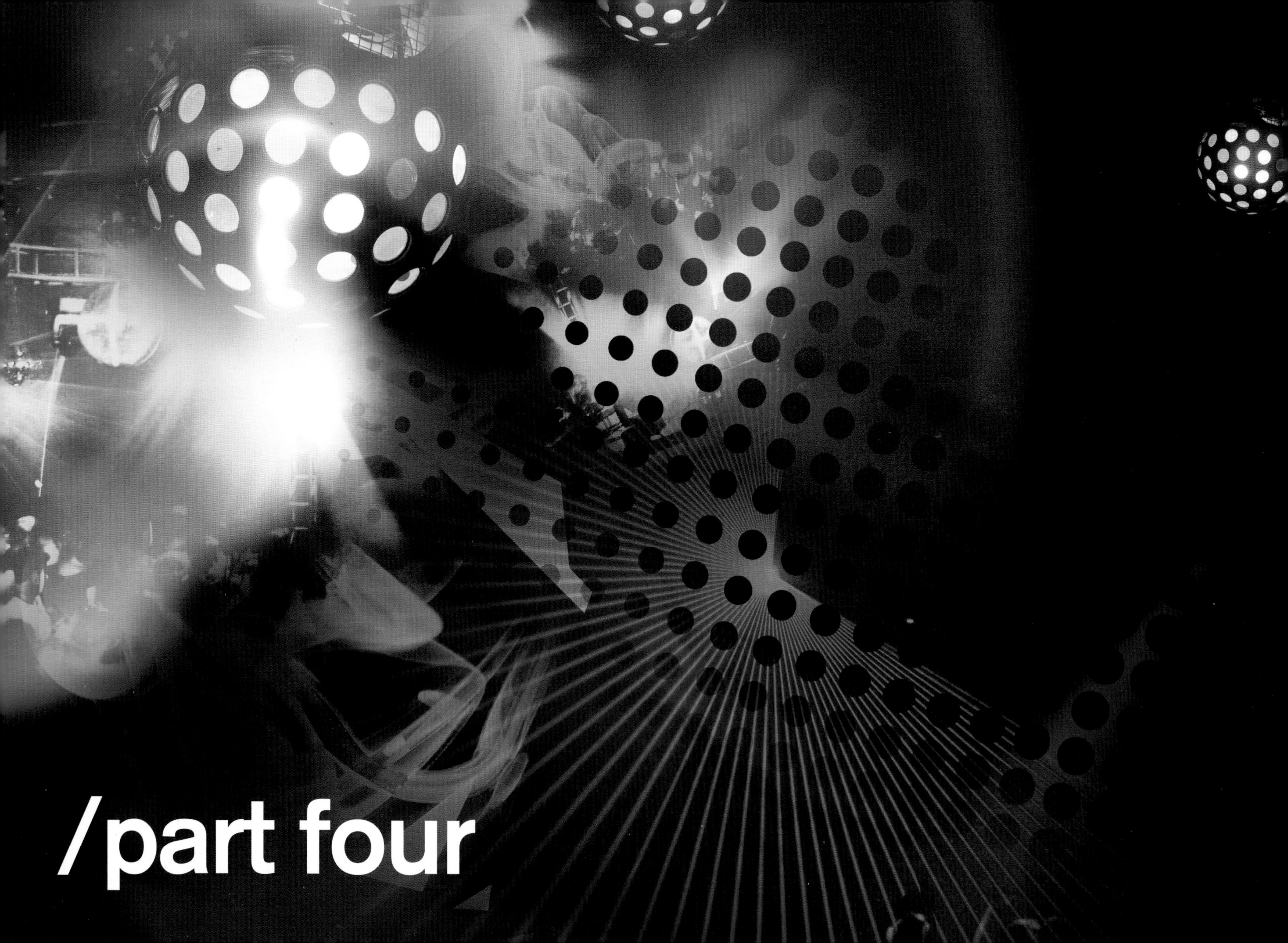

/part four

the music

Whether it's a full-on stacked saw lead, a pounding filtered progressive line, a slinky minimal arp or a sublime Rhodes backing, the musical elements of a track supply not just soul and sonic candy to the mix, but also the all-important hook.

Although organic instruments like keys and guitar play important roles in some productions, it's the synth that takes centre stage in most: an all-in-one sound generation powerhouse that delivers basslines, leads, pads, drum sounds and mighty wobbling FX.

Creating music parts is not just about technical wizardry though: it's about understanding a little theory too, knowing when to use major and minor scales, sevenths and ninths, roots and inversions. Time spent learning the basics can pay significant dividends in the long-run.

When great sounds combine with solid musical understanding the magic starts to happen.

/synth anatomy

the synth supplies bass, leads, fx and more to the mix. spend some time getting to know how it makes and shapes sounds.

The synthesiser is the most essential and versatile instrument in the dance music studio. It can be used to create every element in a track, from bass and drums to leads, pads and effects. It can even be used to process vocals and other instruments to open up a whole new world of timbres.

It is worth investing in at least one great sounding, versatile synth. Look for one with plenty of oscillators, filter types and modulation options to give you as much power and programming flexibility as possible. There are many fine sounding synths on the market that will do the job well, but it's better to find one or two that provide the features you need and learn to use them well, rather than owning a dozen synths that only get used for preset surfing.

There are many breeds of synthesiser offering different flavours of synthesis, including **analogue**, **digital**, **additive**, **FM**, **wavetable**, **PCM** and **granular**. But the most commonly used is the good old analogue or virtual-analogue **subtractive** synth. As its name suggests, this takes a raw waveform and runs it through a filter, which 'subtracts' frequency content, before it is further shaped by a series of modules – like envelopes and LFOs – to give the final waveform that reaches the ears.

Oscillators

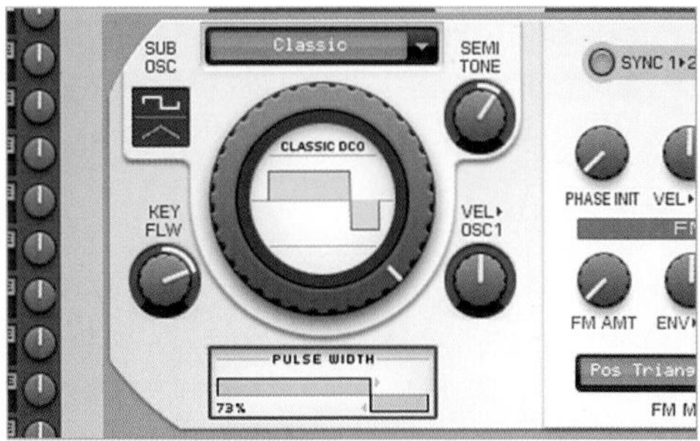

It all starts with the oscillators. These supply the basic waveforms that make the synth sing. The waveforms can be combined to produce complex tones. The classic analogue waveforms are sine, triangle, sawtooth, square (or pulse) and noise. Each one has a distinctive sound based on its harmonic content.

Sine waves are the simplest and purest waveforms, producing just the fundamental frequency and no harmonics. **Triangle** waves have some harmonic overtones.

Saw waves have both odd and even harmonics, giving them a rich, full sound much like brass instruments. They are the raw waveform used for many basses and a generation of raw electro lead lines. **Square** waves have only odd harmonics and sound hollow, like woodwind and reed instruments.

Noise comes in white and pink shades and is used for making edgier sounds, percussive noises and special effects.

Sub oscillator: A slave to the main oscillator, the sub sits one or two octaves below the master and is used to add thickness and character, especially to bass sounds.

Fine tuning: Use this to detune the oscillators slightly for a wider, richer tone. Detuning by a few cents causes the oscillators to breathe or 'beat' against each other like in an old analogue synth. Detune by semitone intervals like fifths for the classic D.Ramirez sound.

PWM (Pulse width modulation): The symmetry of a square wave can be adjusted to produce changes in timbre. Pulse width may be modulated using an LFO or envelope. As the pulse width is increased a sound starts to loose bass frequencies. Use PWM for shimmering pads and leads.

Unison: Thickens the sound by adding extra slave oscillators which are detuned slightly, producing a wider, richer tone from a single oscillator. Unison is used a lot for pads and big, fat leads.

Envelope

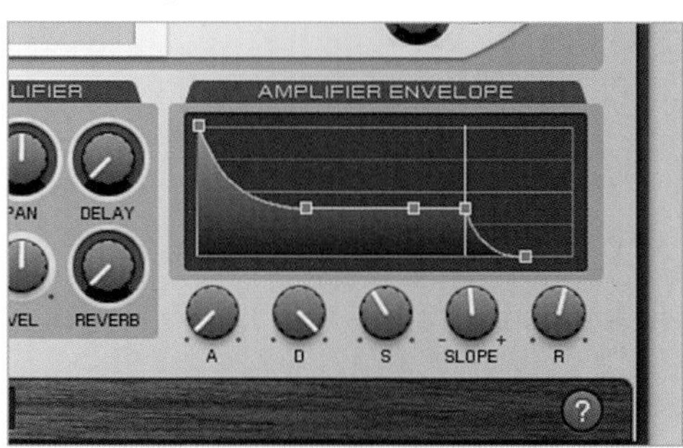

When a note is pressed the synth generates not just a waveform, but also an envelope. The envelope generator (EG) is a modulation source used to control a parameter so that it changes over time. It is most commonly used to control a sound's volume. The envelope consists of several 'stages' or points, which can be programmed to specific values.

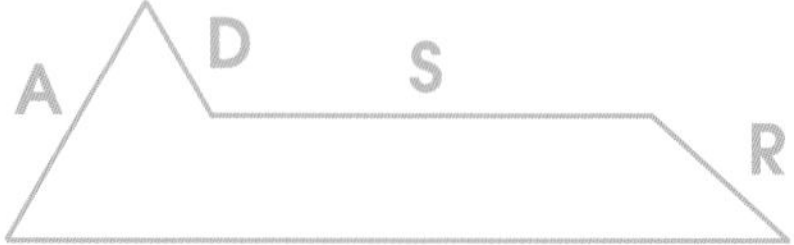

The most common envelope is the ADSR envelope, which has four stages; Attack, Decay, Sustain and Release.

The **Attack** stage starts when the key is pressed and dictates how quickly the sound goes from silent to loud. Low values are used for percussive instruments.

Decay determines how quickly the amplitude decreases after the peak of the attack.

Sustain is the level the sound holds at until the key is released, at which point it passes onto the release stage.

Release indicates how quickly the sound fades away. Use long values for pads.

Filters

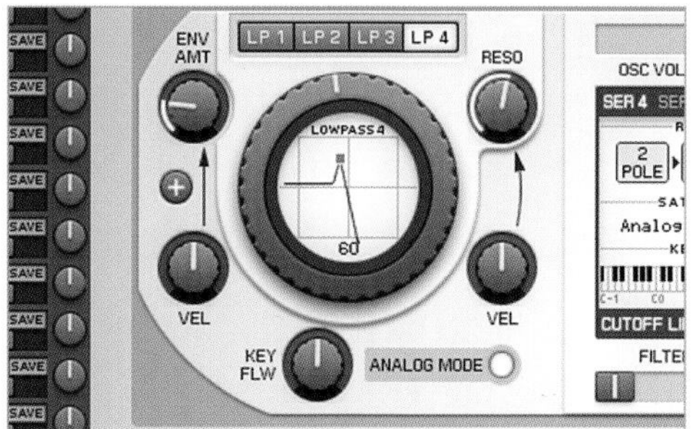

The filter is a type of EQ (**see page 110**) used to shape the harmonic content of a tone. It does this by removing some frequencies while letting the rest pass through untouched.

The three most common types are **low-pass** (cuts high frequencies – ideal for bass sounds), **high-pass** (cuts low frequencies – good for pads) and **band-pass**. More exotic synths may offer band-reject and comb filters.

Cutoff (Hz): Controls the frequency at which the filter cuts off the signal. It is probably the most widely used feature of the synth in electronic music.

Resonance (dB): Boosts the volume of the frequencies around the cutoff point. At higher levels resonance introduces pleasing harmonic overtones. When pushed to the max it becomes louder than the original signal, generating a raw 'screaming' sound. This is referred to as **self-oscillation**. Probably the most recognisable example of this is the tearing sound of the Roland TB-303 when resonance is set to more than 90 per cent.

Many synths offer dual filters and different ways of routing the sounds between them, either in series or parallel. Experiment with these routings for radically different sounds.

LFOs

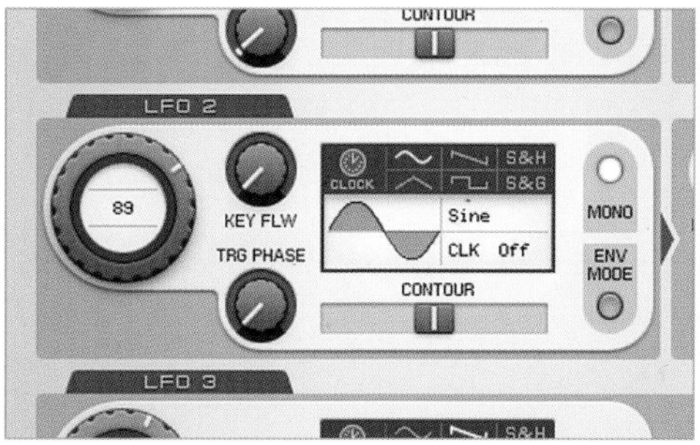

Low frequency oscillators (LFOs) are like regular oscillators, but are set to cycle below the 20Hz limit of human hearing and are used as **modulation** sources instead of sound sources. They can modulate anything from the filter cutoff level to an oscillator's pitch.

Shape: Selects the shape of the LFO waveform. This can range from the basic analogue shapes to reversed and inverted types and random generators such as S+H (sample and hold).

Speed: Can be set in Hz (cycles per second) or as a relative value of the bpm such as 1/8th bar or 4 beats.

'Note-on' triggering: The LFO is re-triggered each time a note is pressed. This is essential for programming predictable rhythm patterns and phrases that lock with the groove.

Phase: When the LFO is triggered, it can be set to start cycling from a specific point in the waveform cycle. Use this in conjunction with note-on triggering to fine tune how the LFO works rhythmically.

Fade in: Increases the amount of LFO to the specified depth over time, much like the attack stage of a modulation envelope. Can be useful on sustained sounds.

Modulation matrix

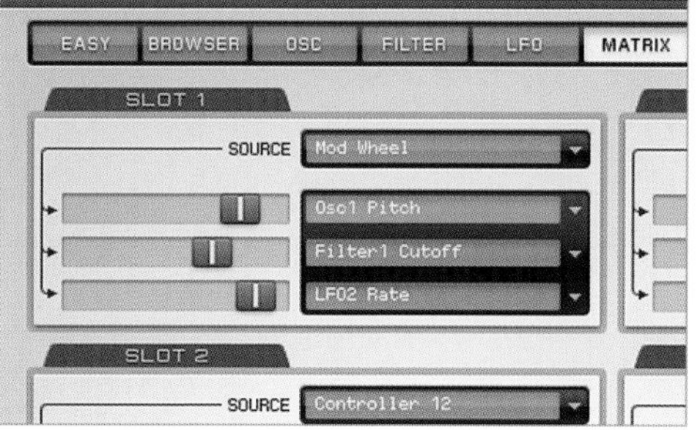

The modulation matrix is like a central telephone exchange that links modulation sources such as LFOs and envelopes to destinations such as oscillator pitch or filter cutoff frequency.

Once the source is routed to a destination, the amount of modulation is set using the **depth** parameter. This can be a positive or negative value depending on the synth and parameters involved. The flexibility of a mod matrix makes it possible to assign several sources to a single destination or vice versa. It's also possible to create complex morphing sounds by programming one modulation source (such as a Midi CC) to control the depth of several modulation routings at once.

Amplifier

The amplifier or 'amp' shapes the volume of the signal and has a dedicated envelope for the job. Many synths allow the volume level to be modulated by Midi note velocity for added dynamics.

Pitch bend

Hardware synths have pitch bend wheels for live performance. These can be programmed to bend the pitch up or down smoothly by a number of semitones. Vintage synths were restricted to two or three semitones, but virtual analogue and digital synths can have ranges spanning several octaves. When programming pitch bend values using Midi CCs the middle point is 0, with full bend up at +64 and full down at -64.

Mod wheel

The mod wheel is an assignable performance controller usually found next to the pitch bend on a synth. It is traditionally used for vibrato effects using Midi CC#1. Use the mod matrix to map the mod wheel to several parameters for complex morphing sounds.

Portamento/glide

This feature forces the pitch to slide smoothly between notes like a trombone. Depending on the synth, it can be programmed for all note events or overlapping notes (legato) only. The speed or rate parameter setS the speed of transition. Portamento can sound awesome used sparingly: use automation to switch it on for select notes only.

Key tracking

Key tracking follows the incoming Midi note and maps it to a parameter such as filter cutoff. Use this when a sound needs to be brighter when it is played higher up the keyboard and duller when it is played lower.

Polyphony

Refers to the amount of notes a synth can play simultaneously. Polyphonic synths play many notes and are useful for playing chords while classic machines such as the MiniMoog and TB-303 are monophonic, only playing one note at a time. To emulate this on a VST reduce a sound's polyphony to one.

/classic pianos and stabs
the rave sound

In 90s house, piano riffs were the indisputable stars of the show, used everywhere from euphoric breakdowns to melody lines that swooped above anthemic pads.

Many old-school piano/chord tracks were made 'ghetto style', with just one sample of a piano chord used to make the whole riff. These were sampled from a record so the chord was fixed at a particular interval. Moving the whole chord up a third or fifth created the familiar sequences.

The latest progressive and tech productions are embracing synth style piano chords and stabs. Although the sounds are different, their role and function in the track is the same.

One trick for capturing the classic sound is to program riffs and chord progressions with left and right hand syncopations. The left hand plays a single-note bass part that sits on the root of the chord (see **In theory, right**), while the right hand plays the chords.

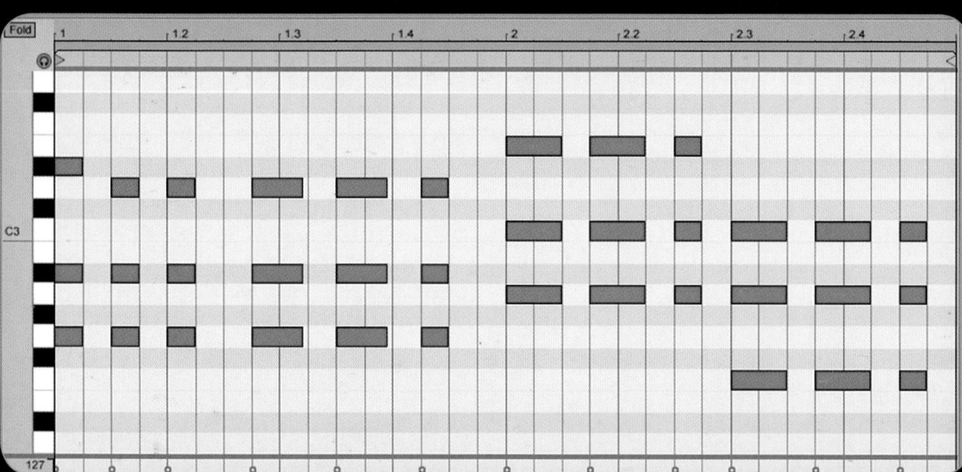

This euphoric rave-style pattern starts with an Eb major (Eb) chord but quickly flips to G minor (Gm) for the rest of the bar. The two chords are closely related and both use the G and Bb notes. The second bar is more dramatic and jumps from Am to F. This clever switch swaps the high E note for a low F note, helping to shape the melody line more dramatically than if it had moved to the high F instead. The other two notes A and C stay the same.

in theory... **roots and the minor scale**

Classic piano riffs and prog stabs work well using a standard minor scale, like C minor (or Cm), illustrated above. The Cm (natural minor) scale is made up of C D Eb F G Ab Bb. Pianists use both hands to construct melodies, with the left hand typically playing supporting bass notes. This is also the case in old-school rave, where the left hand plays the 'root note' while the right plays the associated chord an octave or two above. This 'root note' is the note on which the rest of the chord is built, so for a Cm chord, the root is C. For a Gm chord, the root is G. Before moving on any further it's also worth saying a few words about notation. When reading music or chord progressions major chords, like C major, are usually shortened simply to 'C', while minor chords have a small 'm' after them, like Cm. A 'b' symbol indicates a 'flattened' note (Eb means E flat) and # means 'sharp'. So C#m means C sharp minor.

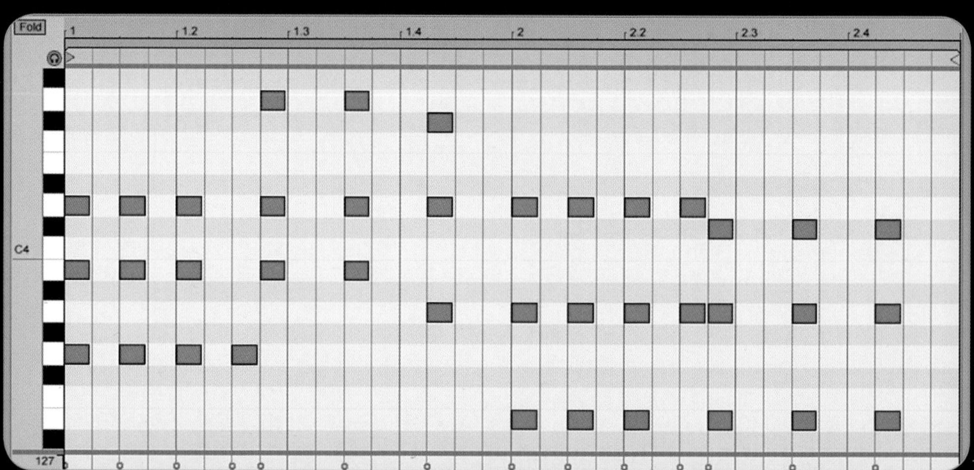

This pattern starts in G, using the first, third and fifth notes of the chord. The low G note jumps up an octave for the second bar, to make an inverted chord, before dropping one note down to the F# and harmonising to Bm. The third and fourth bars are both in A. It starts with an Asus4 chord which uses the fourth note of the scale, D, instead of the third, to make the distinctive sweet harmony with slight tension. The D drops down to the C# note as the chord resolves to A.

/walkthrough early 90s house

1 The only way to get the authentic rave tone is to use a real piano sample set, 90s keyboard or software sampler. The classic machine for early 90s house piano is the Korg M1. There is a virtual M1 supplied as part of the Korg Legacy Digital Edition. Look no further than preset 01, 'Piano 16', for the sound heard on all those old tunes.

2 To brighten the piano and help it cut through the mix use a parametric EQ and boost up to 4dB between 3–6kHz. If the piano is playing at the same time as a bass synth, use a high-pass or shelving EQ to roll away bass frequencies below 100Hz.

3 Add a limiter to the chain. Push the gain up a little so the piano hits the brick wall. This toughens the sound considerably, but be careful not to overdo it unless you are aiming for a deliberately roughed-up warehouse/hardcore sound.

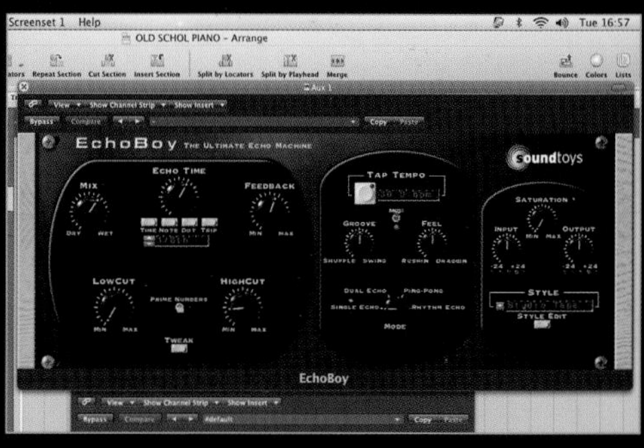

4 Part of the bounce comes from a ping-pong or stereo delay. Load a deay on an effects bus and send some signal its way with an echo time of 1/8th note and a medium number of repeats. EQ out a little top-end and add a touch of hall reverb for added sparkle.

/walkthrough synth chord stab - tech and prog style

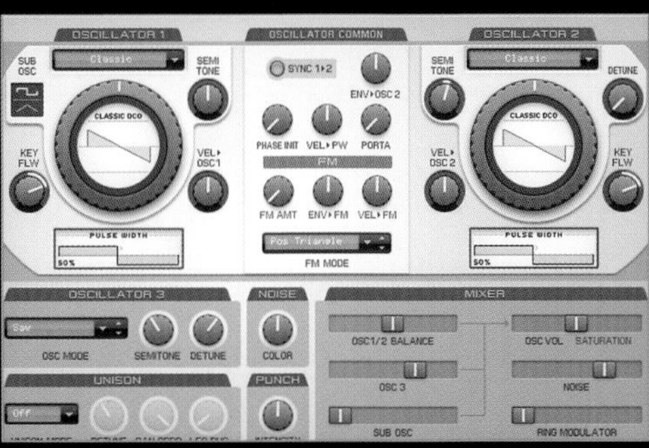

1 Synth-style piano chords are also a favourite with tech-house and prog producers. Use a two or preferably three-oscillator synth. Tune the second oscillator to a different note, creating a one-finger chord. For progressive styles tune up or down by 5 or 7 semitones. For darker, moody tech sounds,

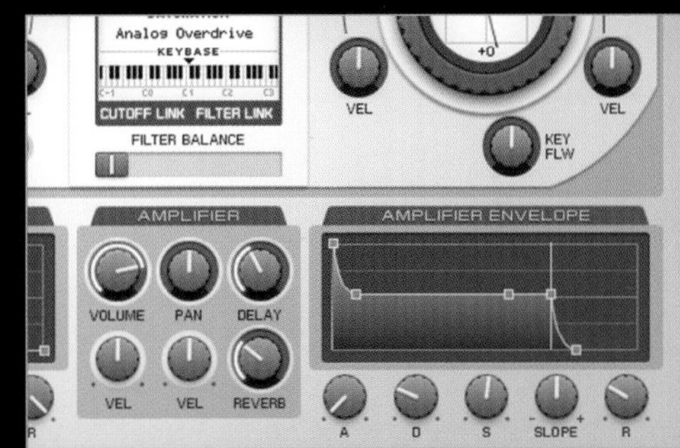

2 Use saw waves for all oscillators, and tune the third down an octave. Add some white noise for extra percussive texture. Set the amp envelope to mimic a real piano's volume curve, with a short attack, a slightly longer decay and release, and sustain at 50%.

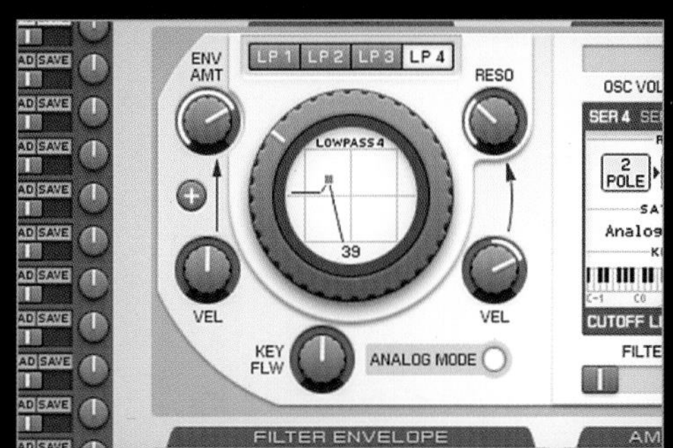

3 Choose a 24dB low-pass filter and add a touch of resonance. Set cutoff to 25% and filter envelope depth to 66%. The envelope shape should be tight like the amp's. To get the classic stab sound play with the filter decay and automate it to catch nice harmonics. This can be done by using the

4 Run the stab through a bit-crusher to roughen it up and introduce some lo-fi grit. Tweak the down-sampling value to introduce harmonic variations. Accentuate these harmonics by adding a ping-pong delay and a hall reverb to the effects chain.

/fat leads and arps
the electro sound

=at lead sounds and killer hooks go hand in hand. Sitting loud and proud at the front of the nix, the lead line is the defining element in electro, jackin' and nu-rave productions, blasting out the signature melody and getting lodged firmly in peoples' heads.

t's important to find a good match between bass and lead sounds. If the bass sits deep, with a low-pass filtering its upper harmonics, there will be plenty of space to position the lead line. If he bass is busy, or has a bright searing tone, use a simple percussive lead to support it.

he retro revival means a three-oscillator synth and a handful of basic effects is all that's needed to create fat leads. Stack saw and square waves at octave intervals to increase harmonic richness and use detuning and unison voices to expand the width.

Once you have a basic lead pattern, start shaping the synth sound using envelopes, LFOs and modulation to make it more unique. Use automation to shape the lead through the track.

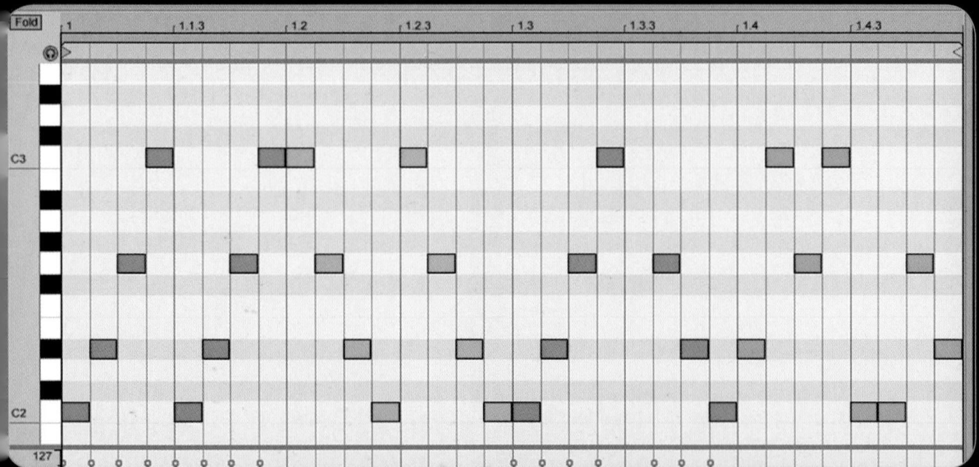

f you are struggling with a killer melody but have some good chords, copy the chords to another track and arpeggiate them. Arpeggiators take the notes in a chord and re-trigger them in sequence with various parameters to edit. One of the most important decisions to make is over the direction the notes play. Basic arpeggiators offer up, down, up and down, and random. Above is an illustration of how the four patterns ook when using a Cm chord, with a different pattern in each beat of the bar (up, down, up-down, random).

in theory... major vs minor

Lead lines usually play single note patterns using a monophonic synth sound. The melody line will be related to the track's chord progression, which is in turn related to the key of the track. The two main types of keys are 'major' – which gives music a happy, uplifting feel – and 'minor' – a key that evokes melancholy emotions but can also have a darker, bluesy vibe to it. The first, and most important, note in the scale is known as the root/tonic. The minor third is three semitones up from the root (see the orange symbol above) while the major third is four semitones above the root (the pink symbol). A standard chord is finished with the 'fifth', five notes above the root, meaning the chord of C major consists of C, E and G. C minor, on the other hand, consists of C, Eb and G.

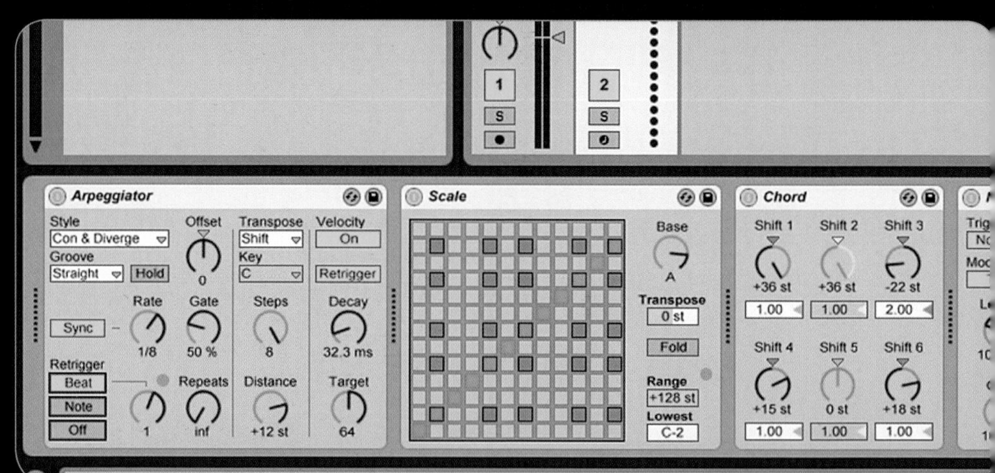

Another important parameter is speed. This is usually clocked to a track's bpm, with values on offer between 1/4 of a bar to 1/64 note. Use a fast speed of around 1/32 note and a 3 octave span with up and down direction to simulate the sounds of 80s video games. Experiment by changing the order the notes are triggered in the chord, as well as length, volume and octave span parameters. It doesn't matter i your synth doesn't have an arp function as most sequencers have Midi data generators to do the job.

/walkthrough mighty lead

1 Take two saw wave oscillators and detune them to create a wide, chorused sound. For a sharper version, keep detuning to a minimum. For a big wobbly electro blast max out on the detuning, adding additional oscillators to taste. Add a saw or square wave oscillator and tune it an octave down to fill out the bottom end.

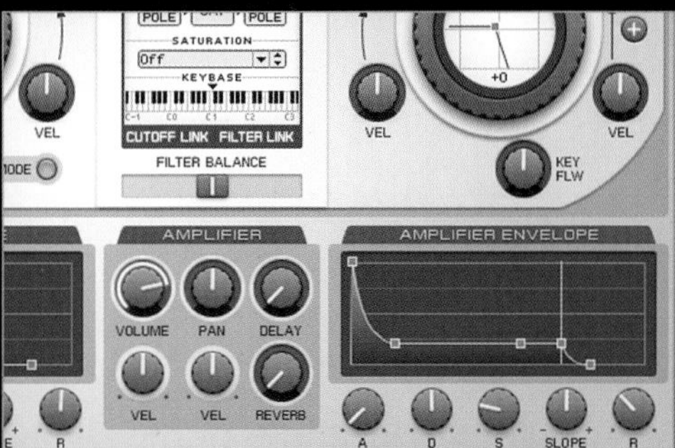

2 Use a 24dB low-pass filter with cutoff point and resonance at around 30%. Increase the filter envelope depth to 70% and set the ADSR so that attack and sustain are 0 with decay and release at 50%. Set the amp ADSR so that attack is instant, decay is 100%, sustain 50% and release 33%.

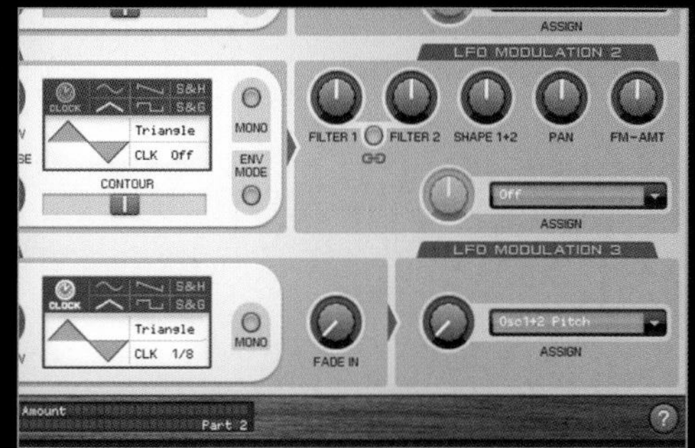

3 To introduce a wild guitar flavour use LFO 3 to modulate the pitch to accentuate certain parts of the riff for a vibrato feel. This is done in two parts. First set the LFO speed to between 4–8Hz. This translates to around one cycle per 1/8th note at 125bpm. Assign the LFO to modulate the pitch of all oscillators but leave the depth at 0.

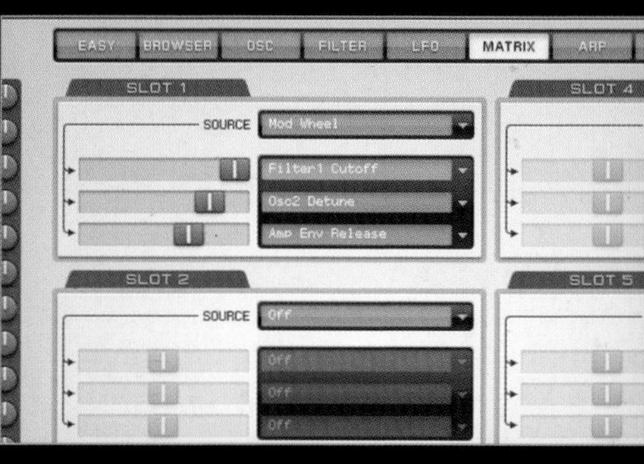

4 The next step is to control how much the LFO affects the pitch. Use the modulation matrix to assign the mod wheel as the source and LFO depth as the target. Set the depth to around 30%. For nu-rave and fidget leads add extra distortion and bit-crusher to the chain. Increase the resonance to make it scream.

/walkthrough d.ramirez portamento slides and tuning

1 This lead is a variation of the one-finger chord trick, which uses a major third chord to give the melody an uplifting feel. Power up a three oscillator analogue-style synth with saw waves for all three oscillators. Tune the second four semitones up and the third one octave down. Set the volumes of oscillators one and two to 50% and three to 100%.

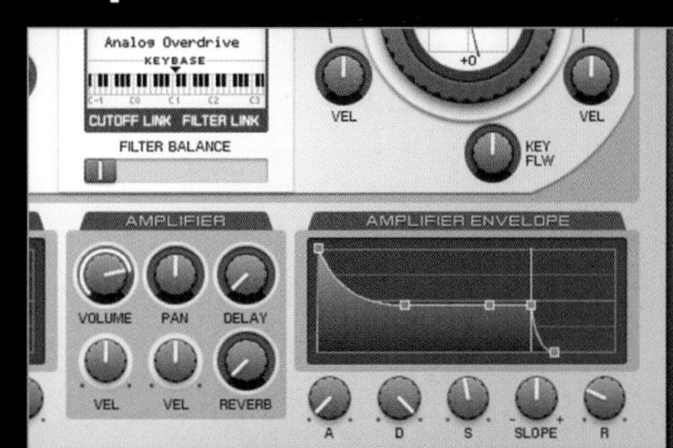

2 Detune one of the oscillators very slowly. It will start to sweep like a phaser, picking out harmonics. Set the amp envelope with attack at 0, decay 50% and sustain 33%. The tail should linger a little after the note has been released, so set release to around 33%.

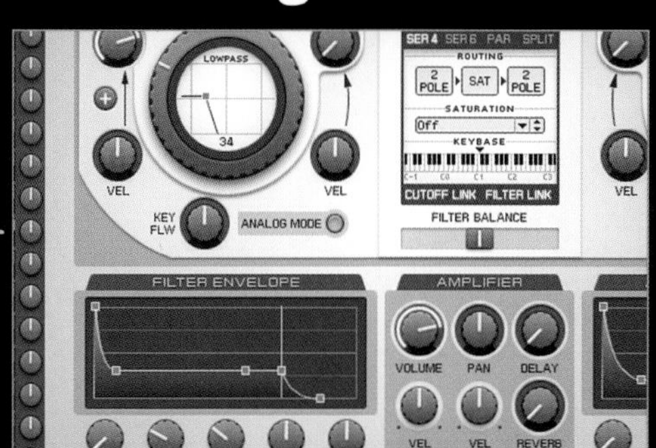

3 Use a 24dB low-pass filter to mellow out the brightness. Set the cutoff point to 33% and leave resonance at 0. The cutoff needs to be modulated by an envelope to get the cutting edge while filtering the body of the sound down to the warmer mid-range frequencies. Set attack to 0, decay to 33%, sustain and release to 50%.

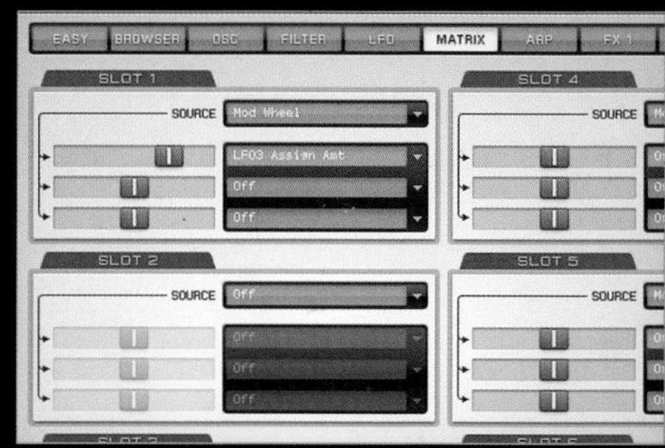

4 Increase the portamento amount until it swoops quickly. To get an ever-changing sound that opens up during breakdowns and snaps back for drops, assign multiple parameters – such as filter cutoff, detune amount and amp release – to one source like the modulation wheel. Now program automation of the mod wheel throughout the track.

/pads
the backing sound

Pads are to the synth world what the string section is to the orchestra. They primarily occupy a space in the mid-range, adding a rich tonal bed that 'pads' out the mix. Sounds can range from smooth and warm to shimmering, ghostly textures. Thanks to their strong, but often subtle, mid-range presence, they are ideal for mapping out a track's chord progression and reinforcing the lead.

The simplest pad sounds come from old analogue polysynths like the Roland Jupiter 8. Newer digital synths have a far wider palette for creating exotic textures than the classic analogues, especially wavetable synths, which are ideal for creating interesting moving textures. To make a big pad stack several oscillators in ascending octaves and use subtle amounts of detuning and chorus/ensemble effects on them to create extra width. Saw waves and square waves are both ideal oscillator candidates. Pads tend to fade in (and often out) softly so set the volume attack and release envelopes accordingly.

in theory... inversions

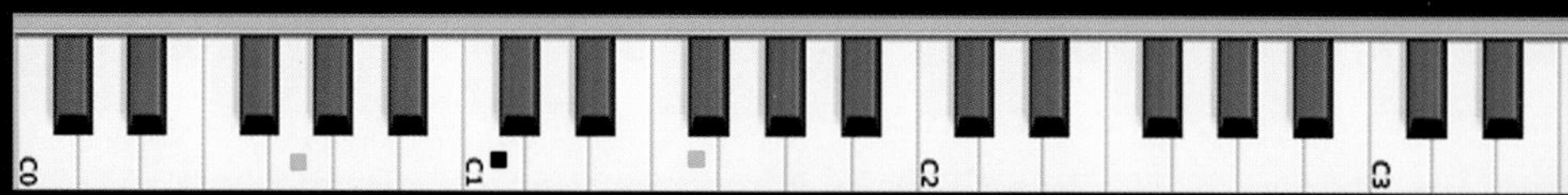

When building a chord it's normal to start with the root note and then place the fifth above. Adding the third in-between – either major or minor – supplies the emotional content. The next step is to experiment with the order of the notes in the chord. Instead of having the lowest note as the root try a different one in the chord, like a G or E in the case of C major. Doing so gives 'inversions' of the standard C chord, all of which sound different. Try placing the lead melody note at the top of a chord and then getting creative with the positions of the notes below. Using inversions allows you to maintain common notes when the chord changes, keeping some held down while others shift. Using inversions opens a whole new range of programming options and allow you to escape from the limitations of standard chords into writing territory in which new possibilities abound.

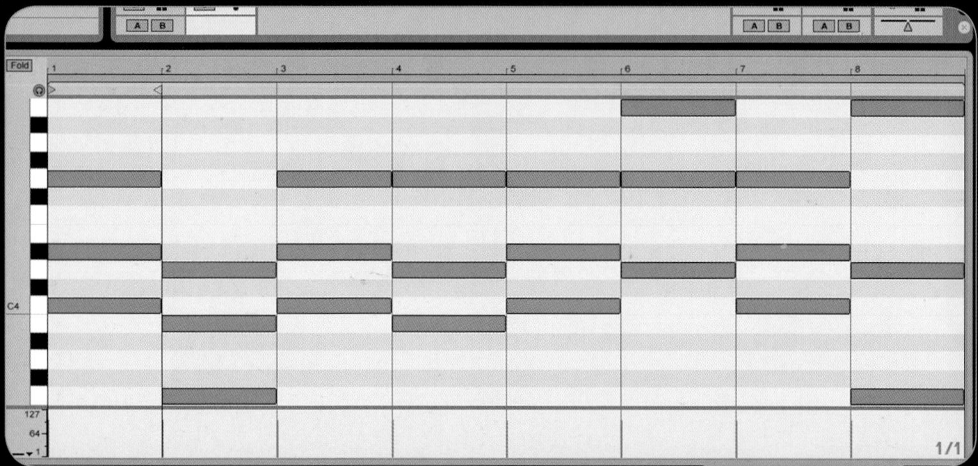

In this pattern the chord shifts from Cm to G in four different ways, using inversions of the original chord. In bar one, it moves down, keeping the harmony notes in the same order. In bar two the top and bottom notes shift but the central note stays the same. In bar three it moves upwards slightly, keeping the G common. In bar four, the whole chord moves up at the same interval, with the melody note at the top of the chord. If the tone of the pad is thick or buzzy, try spreading out the notes so that the harmony is more clearly defined.

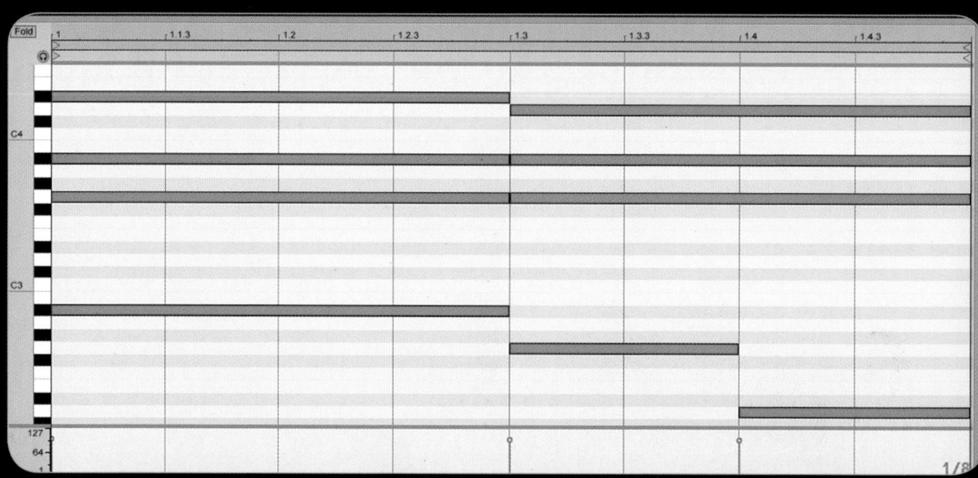

This deep, moody Moby-style pattern is built around a chord progression in the key of Gm. A lower bass part plays the root note of each chord while the upper notes contribute harmonies. It starts with a Bsus4 chord in the first bar, which gives a feeling of slight tension. Then as the Eb slides down to D, and the bass moves to G, it creates a feeling of resolution. When the bass shifts to D at the end, it forms a Gm inversion with the 5th at the bottom. The new feeling of tension sets it up for the next cycle.

/walkthrough analogue anthem pads

1 To make full-frequency anthem pads take two identical sawtooth oscillators and detune them slightly so that they subtly 'breathe'. Add a square wave on the third oscillator an octave above. Set its volume to 50% and the other two to full. Set the amp envelope attack to 0, decay and sustain to 100% and release to 50%.

2 Modulate the pulse width of the square wave on osc 3 with a sine-shaped LFO. Set the speed to around 1/4 note and increase the depth until it begins to shimmer. Increase the brightness by adding a little resonance and position the cutoff point somewhere near maximum.

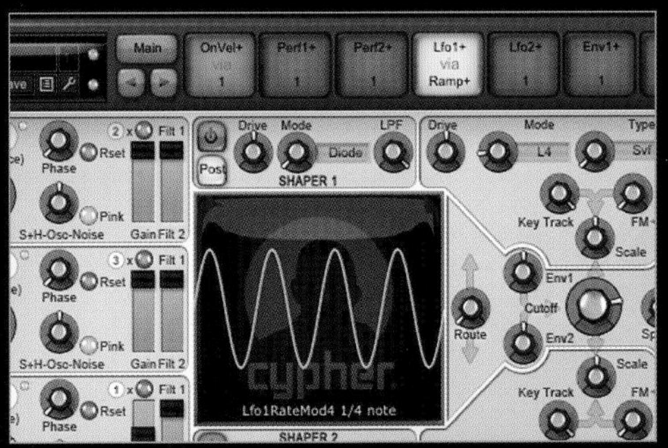

3 Old analogue synths have various unison, chorus and ensemble functions on them which can be activated to get an even wider, more detuned synth sound. Switch on your equivalent and then increase the depth of the pulse width modulation and LFO speed for additional width.

4 Lay down a simple chord sequence which triggers on every beat and follows a C to Gm progression. Stack the root note of the chord at the bottom, followed by the fifth and the octave on top. Add a simple melody line above for additional character. Make the whole pad throb by adding heavy kick-linked sidechain compression.

/walkthrough gated pads

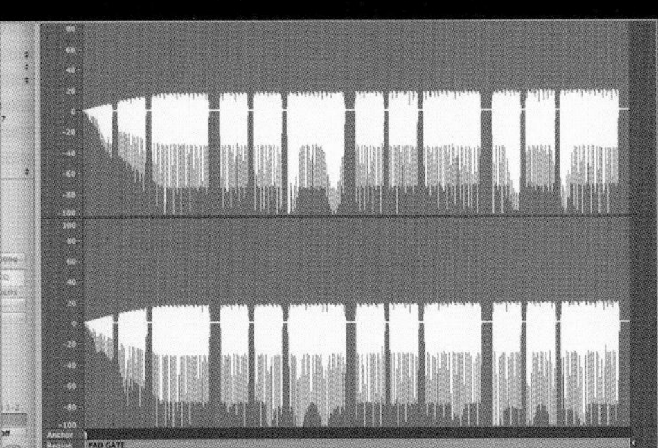

1 Pad sounds are associated with washy textures, but by adding a noise gate to the signal path, they can become part of the rhythm section. Triggering the noise gate allows you to shape the volume of the pad in tight formation, without re-triggering its own envelopes or interfering with evolving textures essential to the pad's character.

2 With the pad line playing, set up a separate trigger track with a basic synth. Load a preset sound that's short and snappy, with instant attack and decay. Now strap a noise gate across the pad track. Open the noise gate's sidechain function and route the trigger track to the input. Turn the output of the trigger track off so it isn't heard in the mix.

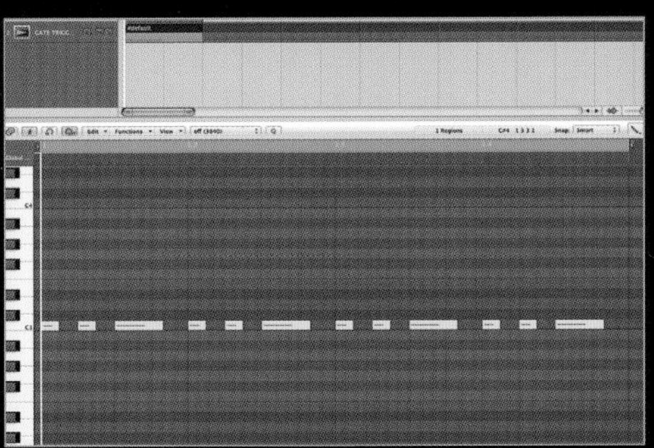

3 Program a note sequence on the trigger track: it doesn't matter what note as it's just a trigger. Treat the length just like a regular Midi note. This will affect the length of time the noise gate stays open for. Start with short 16th notes so that the gate triggers for 32nd note durations. This gives a regular pattern throughout the bar.

4 By default the gate will have a simple on-off shape, so open the attack and/or release to soften the edges and lengthen the decay. The last control worth investigating is the reduction level. It works like a wet/dry mix control. Increasing it will let a little of the original dry signal through. This can be used to soften the gating effect.

/soulful rhodes
the deep sound

It's the sound that spawned a genre, fuelled by the West Coast labels of Naked and Om: the classic deep house sound, featuring lush Rhodes and sparse instrumentation with silky smooth vocals on top. Although there's no such thing as 'the soulful Rhodes chord' there are some tried and tested chords that are good starting points.

Of these, the best to kick off with is the minor 9 chord (written as m9). To get this chord in the key of C, play the root C with the left hand and with the right play a chord made up of Bb, D, Eb and G in ascending order (note that this is an inversion of a minor 9th chord). This gives you the classic soulful sound. Move the same chord down four semitones to Abm7add9, then down a further semitone to Gm7 for a nice progression.

For a more chilled sound introduce an Fm9 (F, Bb, G, Ab, C) and try the progression Cm9 to Fm9. Add and remove notes as you see fit, altering the order for variations.

in theory... sevenths, ninths and beyond

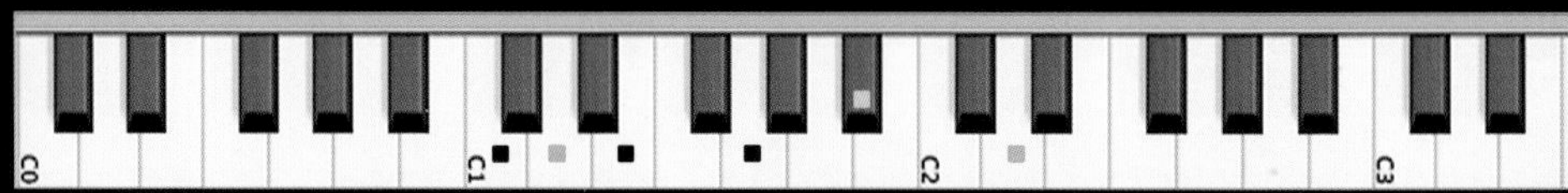

Even using inversions, standard chords – featuring the root, third and fifth – only take you so far. You can breathe new life into your programming by introducing new intervals, like sevenths and ninths. Although daunting at first, these chords simply add new notes to the standard chord in the same way as the third and fifth, only using the seventh and ninth notes instead. In the case of a C7, you add the seventh note in the scale of C, which is Bb (see pink symbol). In the case of a 9th, because the ninth note of a chord overlaps into a new octave, you are essentially adding the second note of the scale, the note D in the key of C. You can either add this between the C and E or you can play it in the octave above (see the orange symbols above), which sounds nicer. Experiment with inversions for many, many new chords.

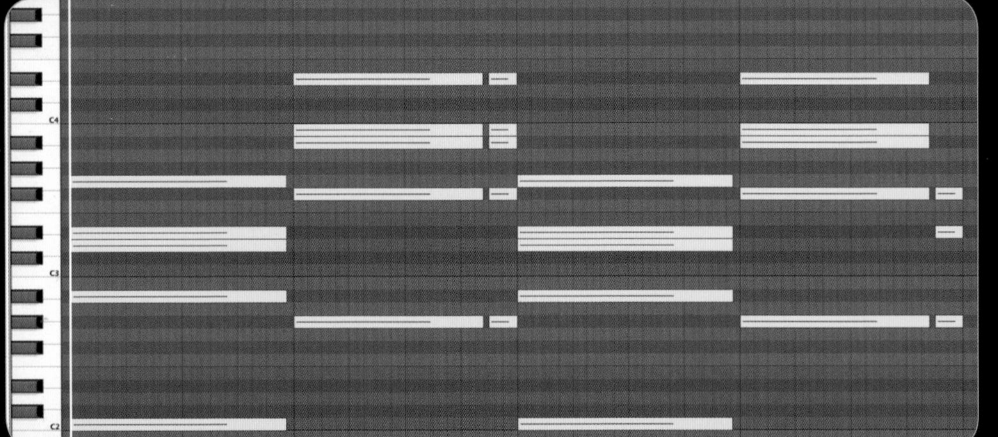

Start with a laid back four-bar progression that moves between Cm9 and Abm9 before introducing a final short Abm7 stab (omitting the C) that moves into the next bar. Note how the second chord comes in a 16th before the beat, giving a nice pre-emptive push to the groove. The short chord before the third beat pushes the rhythm forward.

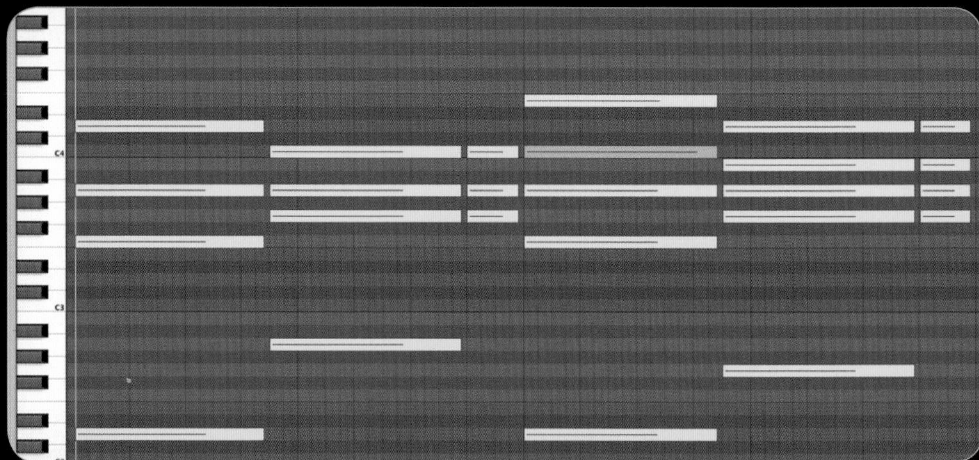

This progression moves from Dm to Am7, then back to Dm9 to resolve at Gadd9. It follows a I-V-I-IV sequence with the bass playing the root of each chord (D, A, D, G). The Gadd9 chord differs in two ways from Dm9. Firstly, it's a major chord, employing the major third (B). Secondly, it doesn't use the seventh note to form its harmony. The result is uplifting, but less complex than the sound of a full ninth chord. The orange note indicates a higher velocity which adds a different flavour to the Cm9 chord on beat 3.

/walkthrough soulful house chords

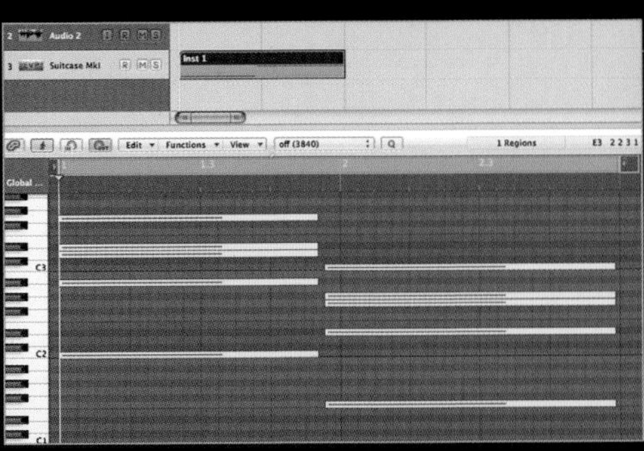

1 With a beat rolling, open the EVP88 electric piano, or similar Rhodes virtual instrument – don't worry about the setting for now – and program some simple chords. This four bar sequence rolls through a Cm9 and an Fm9. Quantise is set to 16C to help the chords sit with the groove.

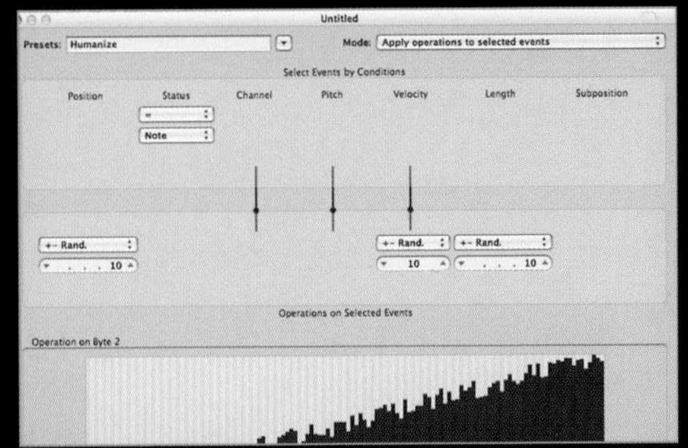

2 Programming using a matrix or piano-roll editor leaves a part sounding mechanical, however lovely the chords. Either mess with the volumes of individual notes or power up a humanising editor. Here we use the Tranform editor's humanise algorithm in Logic. It pushes all notes off grid and changes velocities subtly for a more human sound.

3 Open your electric piano plugin and select a Rhodes Mk I or Mk II setting. These model the classic Fender Rhodes Electric Piano Mk I (1970) and Rhodes Electric Piano Mk II (1979) and are staples of the soulful house sound. Applied Acoustics Systems' Lounge Lizard VST is also a favourite among house producers.

4 Soulful Rhodes parts sit beautifully wide in the mix, almost like pads. To get this sound power up a chorus or, better, an ensemble. Here Logic's native Ensemble has 5 voices, two different LFO rates, phase at +100% and a stereo spread of 200%. The result is a lush and wide sound that gently moves in the stereo spectrum.

5 Use compression on the Rhodes to do two things. Firstly tame peaks with a medium high ratio (here 2.1:1) and long release, cutting around 5-8dB of gain. Secondly, if appropriate in the context of the song, set the compressor to respond to a kick drum powering its sidechain for a gentle breathing feel.

6 Give the Rhodes chords space in the mix by sending part of the signal to a reverb or delay bus. Here it is sent to a bus with a stereo delay. The stereo delay has a 1/2 note (L) and 1/2 note triplet (R) setting, with a small amount of feedback. Note the EQ low-cut value sitting at 1700Hz, cutting low-end material that would muddy the mix.

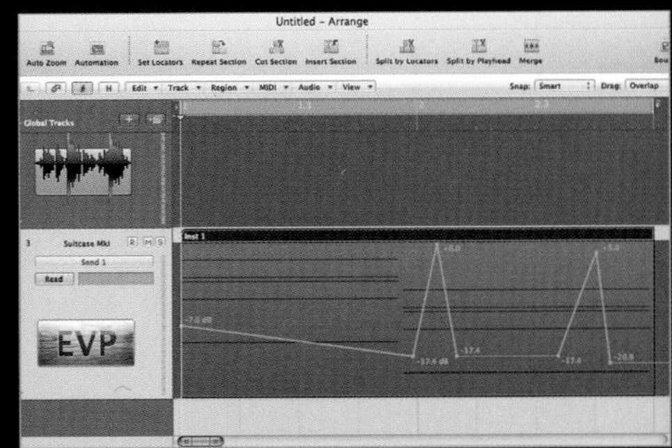

7 For sublime moments automate the delay send to trigger occasional delay swells. An increase will send more signal to the stereo delay, bringing momentary splashes of sound that echo into the mix – ideal at the end of phrases or to pick out particular chords. For even greater control automate the delay bus itself.

8 For added movement, depth and interest try a tremolo or filter plugin. Logic's Autofilter sounds great on Rhodes. Here a band-pass filter is selected with fatness at 90%, resonance at 46% and cutoff at 33%. A long attack envelope gives a nice resonant fade in. The cutoff point is automated during each chord for pure soulful bliss. Yum.

/working with loops

loops provide both creative building blocks and inspiration. personalise them for endless options.

Love them or loathe them, loops are all-pervasive in house music. Not only do they offer a quick way to get an idea up and running with minimum programming time, they also offer inspiration when creative juices run dry and supply sounds that are simply too difficult to program yourself – either because you don't have the kit, or the session musicians, or the programming know-how. Loops can come from old records or the very latest sample collection. If it's the former be aware of legal issues surrounding copyright. That's why sample CDs are so popular: most are sold to you 100% copyright free, meaning you don't need to pay additional royalties if you use them to create a chart-topper.

Pitch and stretch

Loops are a great way to build up drum and percussive tracks in layers, but if the loops are at a different bpm to the track then they will need to be sped up or slowed down to fit. In the early days of dance music there was no such thing as time-stretching – you had to pitch a loop up or down vinyl-style – but nowadays all the major DAWs have extensive native stretching features.

Not all time and pitch manipulation tools sound the same, and at high settings the process introduces audible artefacts that change the quality of a sound. These include weird tonalities and sharp metallic overtones caused by granular stretching algorithms.

Most DAWs offer several different time-stretching settings, each of which is optimised to work with different types of audio material. Categories include 'percussive', 'pads', 'monophonic' and so on. Although these different presets are useful as starting points, it's best to use your ears to see which does the best job on a specific sound source.

It's also worth noting that you can get some interesting effects by abusing time-stretch functions, sending beats, for example, through pad algorithms for twisted effects. A case in point is the Akai S950 time-stretch function, whose characteristic lo-fi processing has been abused on vocal samples by the likes of Fatboy Slim and Armand Van Helden.

Rex files

Until the mid 1990s if you were using loops, you were using Wavs. Propellerheads opened up a powerful alternative with the introduction of the Rex (and later Rex2) formats. This format was devised to enable the tempo of a loop to be changed with minimal audible artefacts. Producers use ReCycle to slice a loop into separate sections or 'hits', embedding the hit points into the Rex file along with a Midi pattern that preserves the rhythmical position of each hit. This allows a loop to be played back at different speeds.

This slicing process unlocks the creative potential of a loop and allows the producer to access each individual hit for re-tuning, length adustments and additional FX processing. As it also analyses the loop and creates a Midi file of the groove, it makes it possible to easily change the order of playback or even re-program the loop entirely. Finally, if the groove is hot, but the samples are not, you can extract the Midi pattern from a Rex loop and update it by replacing the original hits with new samples.

Rex files are geared towards percussive sounds and get excellent results, but they are not so good for long, sustained sounds with few transients. This comes down to the way ReCycle spaces the slices, not filling the gaps when the tempo is slowed down.

You don't need ReCycle to use Rex files, as many sample collections come pre-Rexed, but you will need it if you want to create your own Rex loops. There are three things you should do when making Rex loops. Firstly, start with an accurately trimmed loop. Next, make sure you set the correct guide tempo. Finally, add the right amount of hit-points before exporting. (See **Creating a Rex file, page 88**).

Using Rex loops

Most of the major DAWs and soft samples can make use of Rex files in one way or another. Some allow you to drop entire Rex loops into their arrangement windows, mapping the loop's tempo to that of the track.

For more advanced manipulation use a soft sampler that can read Rex files, like Guru, Logic's EXS24 or Battery. These automatically map the different slices to different notes / pads, where each slice can be treated separately with different amp and filter envelopes and start / end times to either help you fit the Rex to the groove, or to create whole new rhythmic timbres.

Tip / If you like the rhythm of a Rex loop, import it into your DAW and use it as a groove template to quantise drum or rhythm sounds.

> /overview
>
> **what is...?**
>
> **Wav loops:** The most pervasive loop file format. Wavs can be given additional meta properties to make them into 'Acidized' Wavs – optimised for Sony's Acid software.
>
> **Apple Loops:** The propriety loop format for Logic and GarageBand. Apple Loops can be transposed. They lock to bpm.
>
> **Rex loops:** Format devised by Propellerheads to allow loops to be used at different tempos, and to allow easy rearrangement of loop 'slices'.

/walkthrough logic flex

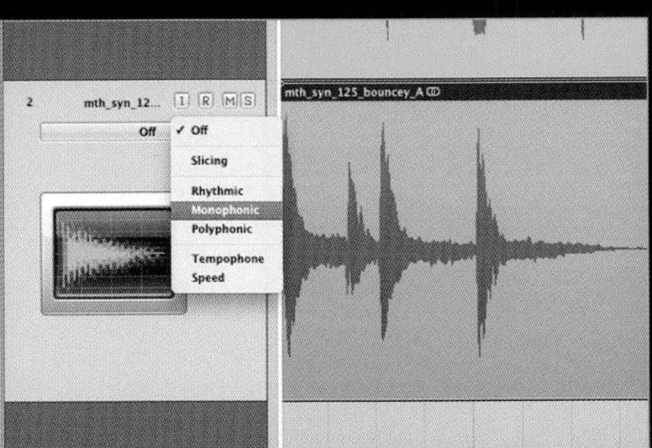

1 To activate Flex Time click on View > Flex View. The track header will show a new selection box. Click on it and select from one of the three slicing modes. Monophonic mode is best suited to simple, monophonic sound sources. Polyphonic is designed for complex processed material. For drum and percussion loops use Rhythmic mode.

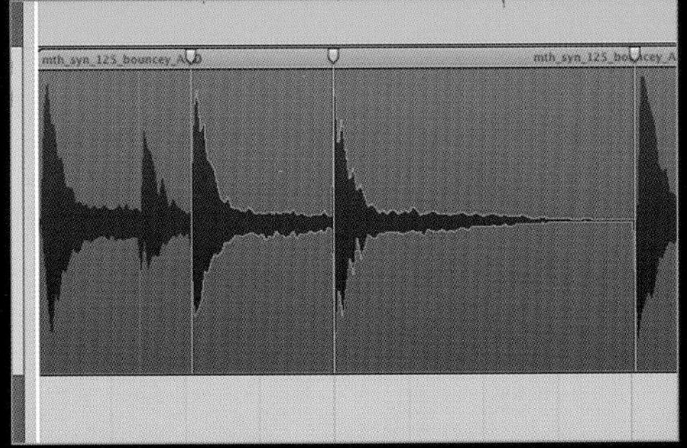

2 Once it is analysed, the audio file will change colour and the anchor points will become visible and ready to edit. There may also be faint white lines in the background. These are transient markers that haven't been assigned a flex anchor yet.

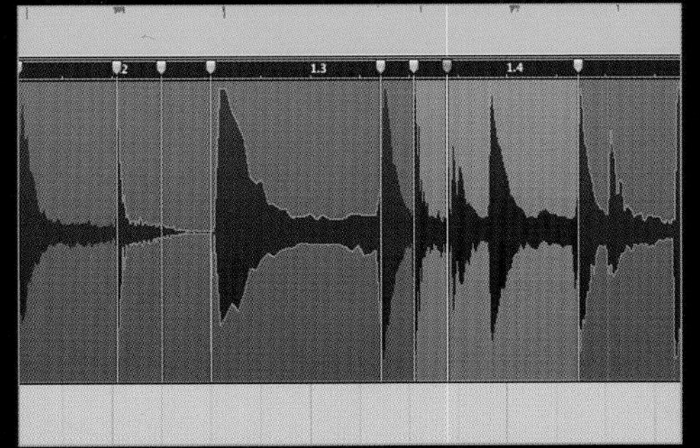

3 To move an anchor point, hover the mouse over the line. The cursor will change shape. Click and hold as you drag the anchor to its new position: the affected regions will be highlighted. In addition, quantise markers will be momentarily displayed to help you line up the new position of the anchor. Use Snap Mode to set the resolution to speed things up.

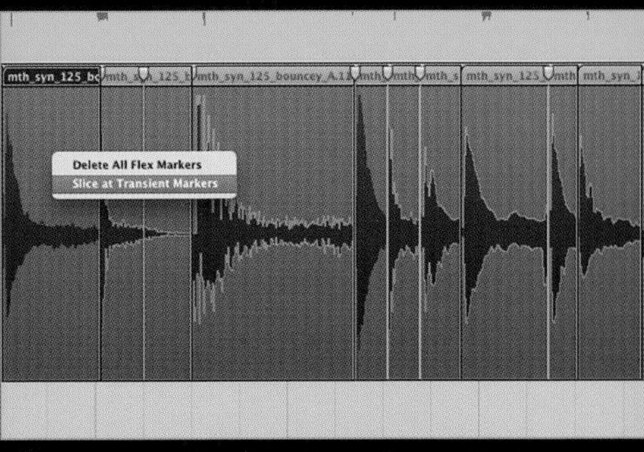

4 To add additional anchors, line up the cursor and click once on the waveform. To delete an anchor or restore it to its original position, right click on a point and select one of the options. To re-arrange the order of events, chop the audio file into regions. Right click anywhere on the file other than an anchor point and select 'Slice at transient markers'.

/walkthrough slice to exs

1 Logic can quickly convert an audio file into an EXS sampler instrument by chopping it into regions and mapping the regions across the keyboard. The process is useful, but not entirely fool-proof, so follow these steps for the best results. First open the file in the sample editor and click the button (highlighted) to launch 'Transient Editing Mode'.

2 The waveform display will show a number of white lines dividing the file at the transient peaks. To move a marker, hover around it until the cursor changes, then click, hold and drag the line to a new position. To audition a specific region, click between the white lines and press the space bar to play.

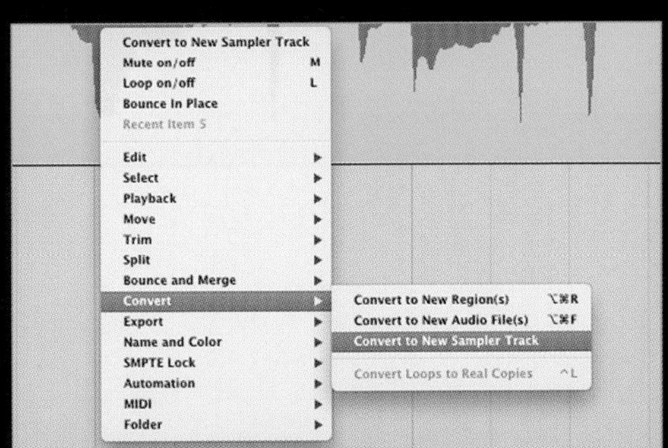

3 Use the plus and minus buttons to the right of the transient button to increase or decrease the number of markers. To delete a marker double-click on it. Close the sample editor and return to the arrange page. Right-click on the audio file and choose 'Convert to New Sampler Track' from the menu.

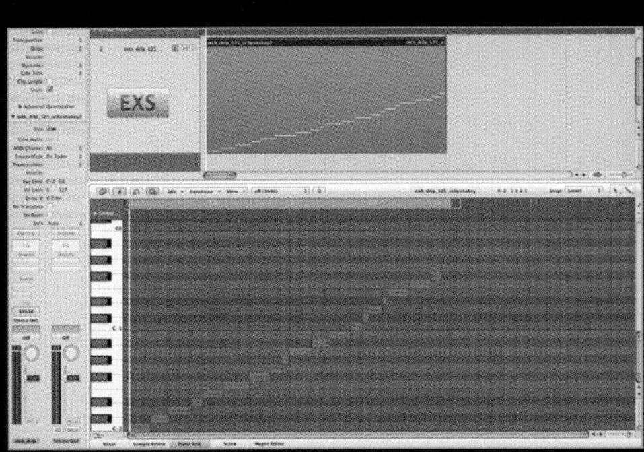

4 A pop-up box asks you to choose how the sample zones will be created. Select the 'Transient Markers' option, and the file will be split at the points specified in the sample editor and make an EXS instrument complete with a Midi pattern to play it back. Re-arrange the Midi notes to make a thousand new grooves.

/walkthrough
creating a rex file

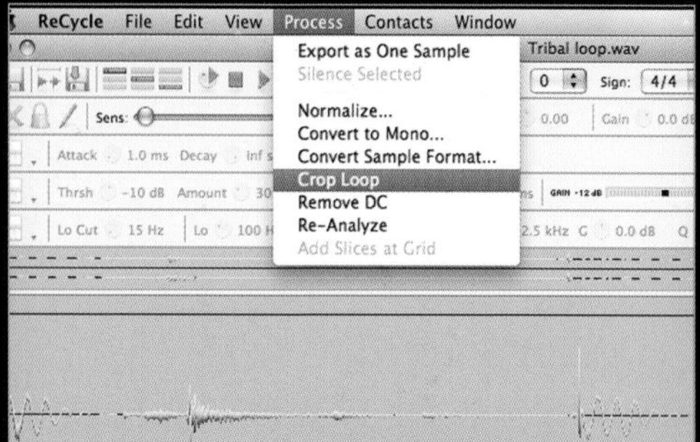

1 Open the file and set the left and right markers around the area of the loop you want to convert. To crop the loop to the new length choose 'crop loop' from the Process menu.

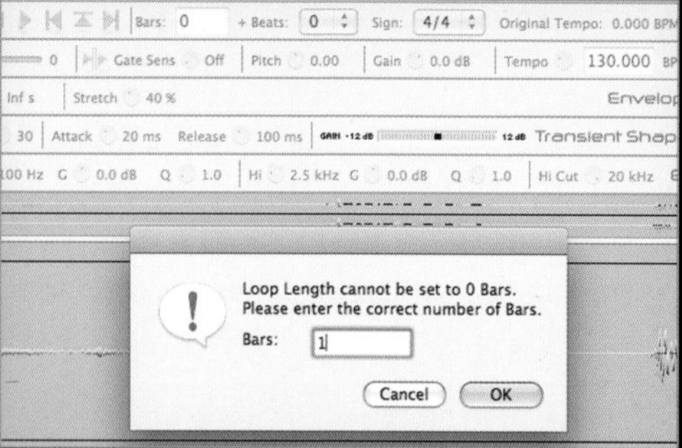

2 Enter the number of bars and beats and original time signature in the empty boxes. This helps ReCycle create a Midi pattern that will play back properly and enables the preview effects.

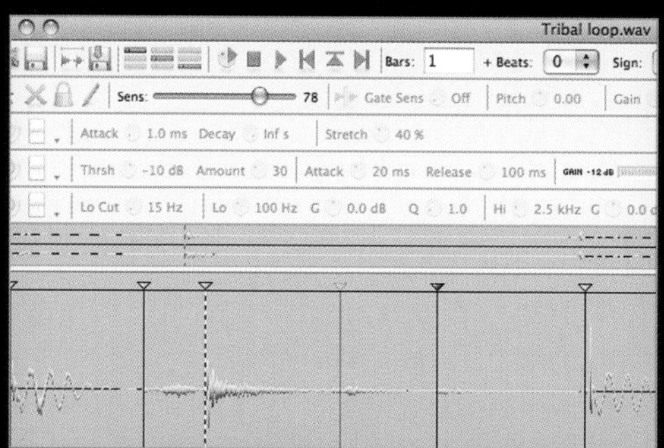

3 To add slice points move the sensitivity slider from left to right. To move them, click, hold and drag the arrow-heads. If a particular marker isn't required, delete it.

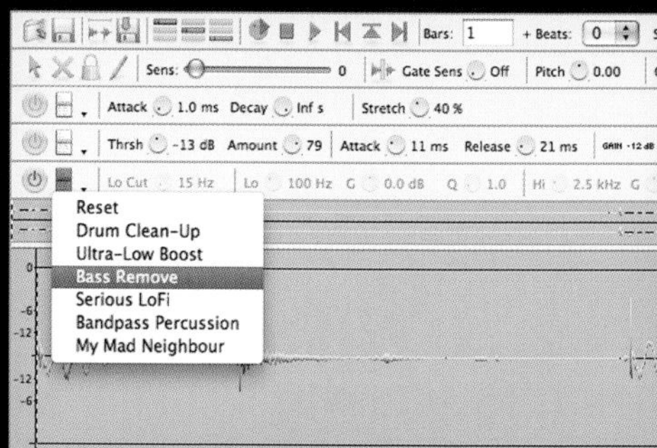

4 There are three FX blocks to process the loop: a volume enveloper, a transient shaper and an EQ. These can be used to modify the overall sound of the loop and affect each slice evenly.

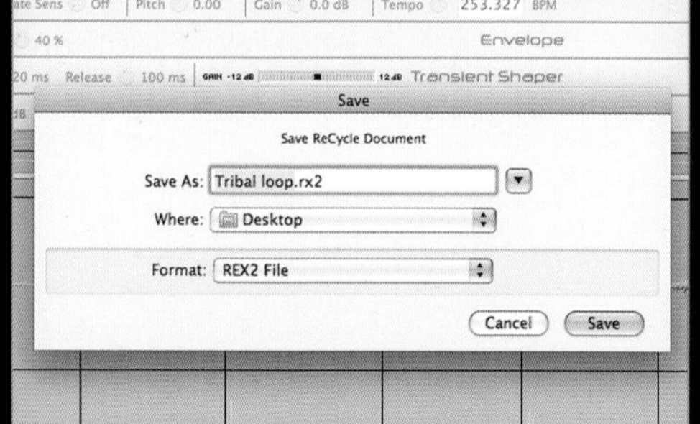

/walkthrough percussion loop edits in ableton live

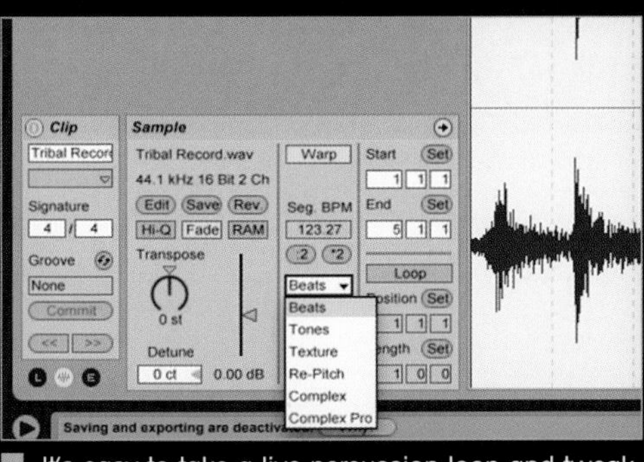

1 It's easy to take a live percussion loop and tweak it into something new in Live using a few editing functions. Record or load the clip and click on the Warp button in the sample box. The wave form display will change to show the loop points in beats and bars with a number of anchor points at the top. Select the 'Beats' time-stretch algorithm.

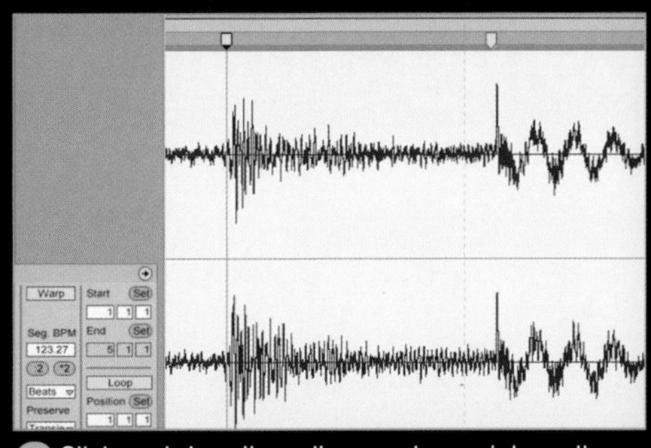

2 Click and drag the yellow anchor points so they float over each percussive hit. Selecting the appropriate quantise resolution, like 8th or 16th notes, can help speed up the process. In some cases though it's better to turn quantise off and use the zoom tool to get right in close and fine-tune the anchor positions manually.

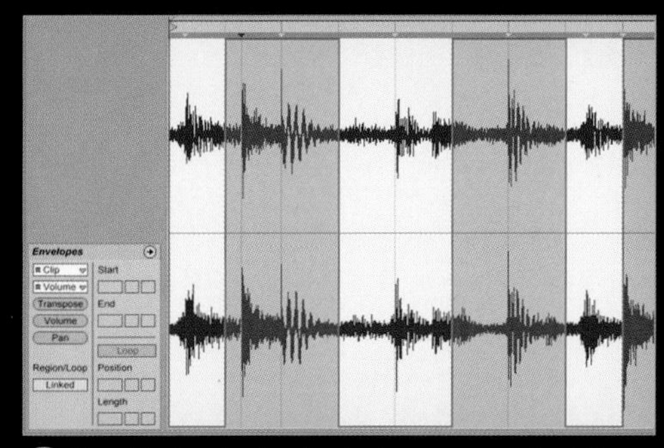

3 Simplify the rhythm by losing some of the hits. Click the 'E' button in the bottom left corner. The display will turn pink to indicate Envelope Edit Mode. Select 'clip' from the top box, and 'volume' from the one underneath it. Switch to draw mode and choose the 16th note grid to get started. Use the pencil to edit the volume so that some hits are softer, and parts of the groove that you don't need are silent.

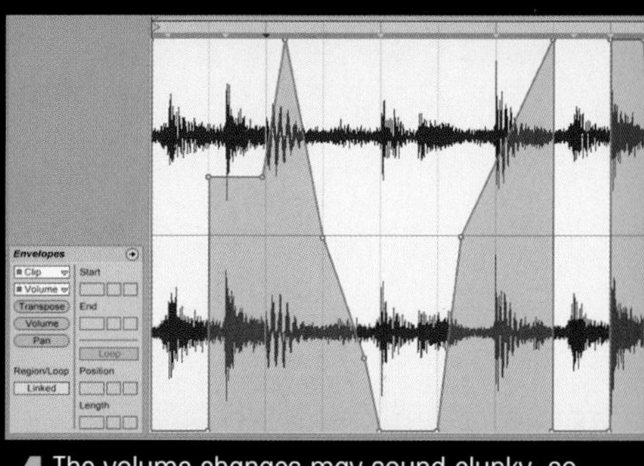

4 The volume changes may sound clunky, so switch out of draw mode and manually edit the points to fade the volume up and down. This will help smooth things out and remove clicks and pops. Drag the volume lines up and down to change the relative volume between hits, making a quiet one loud and a loud one softer. To make the changes permanent use the Export Clip function.

/walkthrough re-grooving drum and percussion loops in ableton

1 Sometimes a percussion loop has the right sound but the groove doesn't fit with the track. The easiest way to re-groove it is to slice it up and re-program it using Midi. Drop the loop into a new clip slot. Make sure it is trimmed to an even number of beats.

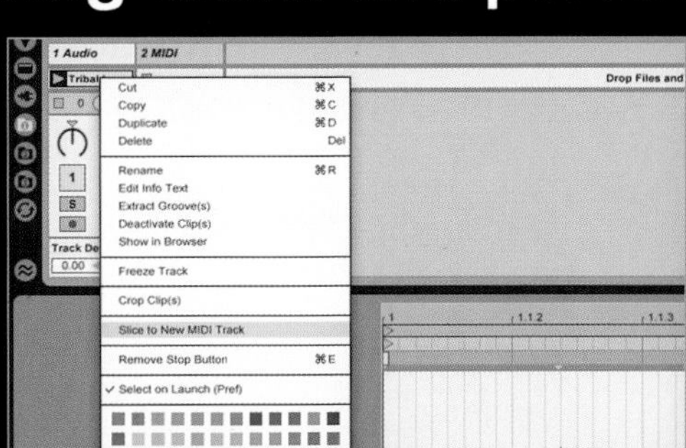

2 Ableton automatically slices loops with the 'Slice to new Midi track' command. Right-click (option click on Mac) and select the command from the drop-down. A new window opens asking you to select the slicing method. If the riff is syncopated choose 'Transient'. If there are an even number of hits use the beat slice preset with 8/16/32 hits.

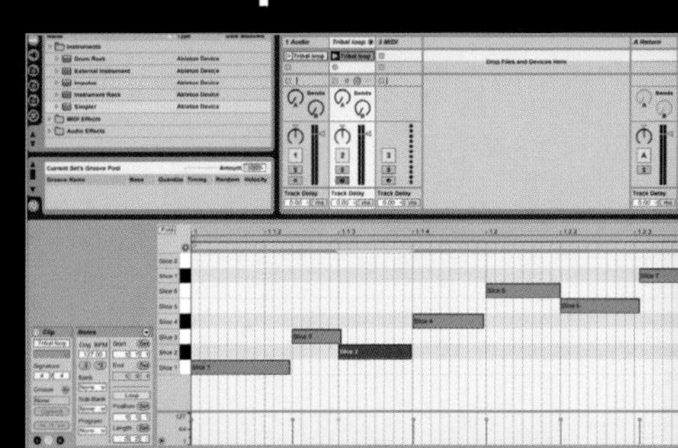

3 Ableton creates a new Midi track and part for the sliced riff, as well as a sampler instrument with all the slices pre-mapped to individual key zones. Press play on the Midi part and the new sliced riff should sound identical to the original loop. Now it is just a matter of rearranging the Midi notes to make a new groove that fits the track perfectly.

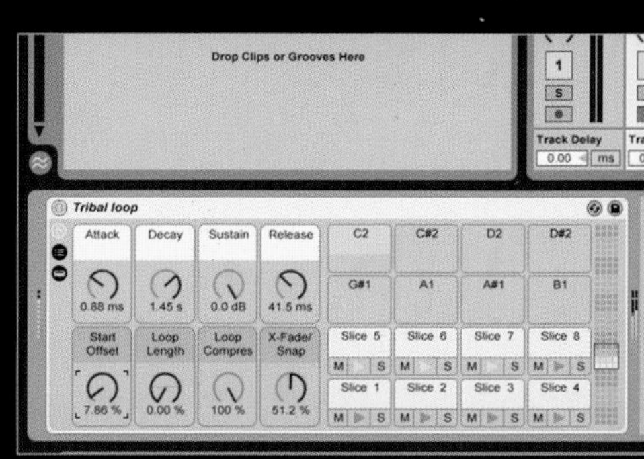

4 But that's only the start. The slice function offers many more creative options. Each slice has several editing options, including tuning and an amp envelope to individually shape volume and dynamics. If Ableton hasn't chopped a hit to the right transient marker you can use the start offset parameter to move it to the right point.

/apple loops

like wavs, but more versatile for the mac owner.

Apple's propriety loop format is available to users of Logic and GarageBand. Apple Loops (or AIFFs) can be both time-stretched and pitch-shifted within the arrange window, allowing a huge amount of freedom. They can also be tagged with various meta 'Tags' to indicate the type of sound it is (guitar, bass, keyboard etc), its author, its key and its characteristics (cheerful/dark, relaxed/intense). This tagging comes into its own when you have a large sound library, allowing you to quickly find the sound you're after without spending hours scrolling through gigabytes worth of samples.

Apple Loops Utility

Apple Loops are created using the Apple Loops Utility that comes bundled with Logic. Open it from within Logic by selecting a loop in the arrange window and selecting 'Open in Apple Loops Utility' from the pull-down audio menu. It can read both Wavs and AIFF files.

Like ReCycle, the Apple Loops Utility allows you to add, delete and move transients so that they sit at the right places within a loop. A second tab is where you program the loop's Tags (see **walkthrough, right**). Multiple files can be tagged at the same time by importing a selection of loops into the Utility, a process known as batch tagging.

Advanced Apple Loops

Quick additions to the library: You can add a loop, or a region, to the Apple Loops library from within the arrange window. Just select the region, then click on Region > Add to Apple Loops Library. This opens a window with a slimmed-down version of the Tag choices available in the Apple Loops Utility,

Lose the Apple: Sometimes you need to turn an Apple Loop into a Wav for precise editing. The easiest way to do this is to open the Apple Loop in the audio editor, then select Audio File > Save Selection As. Save it as a Wav and re-import.

Two colours of Apple: Not all Apple Loops are the same. Specifically, there are blue loops (regular audio files) and there are green ones. The green ones are Software Instrument Apple Loops (SIALs), loops with embedded Midi information and channel instrument settings. Drag one into the arrange window and it will create not just a Midi loop, but also a full channel strip.

Abuse 'em: Apple Loops adapt to the tempo of the track. At extreme settings they break down. Exploit this by running loops at very slow tempos and then bouncing the distorted signal down for lo-fi textures.

/walkthrough
using apple loops

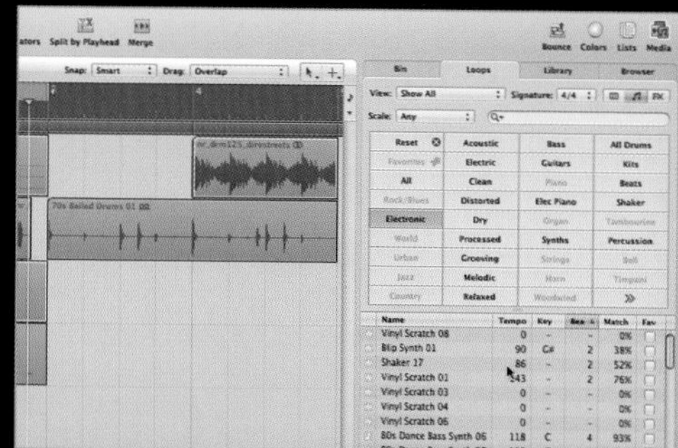

1 Open the Apple Loops library by clicking on the Media button and then the Loops tab. This opens the library selection window. Here you can narrow down your sample search by clicking on the relevant properties you want in your loop. Apple Loops are shown below: normal audio loops in blue, Midi loops in green.

2 Drag the chosen Apple Loop into the arrange window. In the top left loop properties box you can now transpose it so that it fits with the key of your track. You can nudge it forwards or backwards in time by changing the delay value or – if you wan to preserve its original tempo – you can uncheck the Follow Tempo checkbox.

3 For all their strengths, Apple Loops have a number of weaknesses. The main one is that it's impossible to quantise them or change their groove settings. You can work around this to some extent by adding the Grooveshifter plugin to the track in question. For a percussive loop, the Source Material has been changed to Beat, the Grid to 1/16th and the Swing setting pushed to a high 73%.

4 Importing a green Apple Loop into the arrange window introduces a Midi loop with an associated channel strip. The instrument can then be opened, and the sound edited. The Midi loop itself can be altered to create whole new loops. You can save a Midi loop you've programmed, and its associated instrument, by selecting it and then choosing Region > Add to Apple Loops Library.

/walkthrough
turn a wav into an apple loop

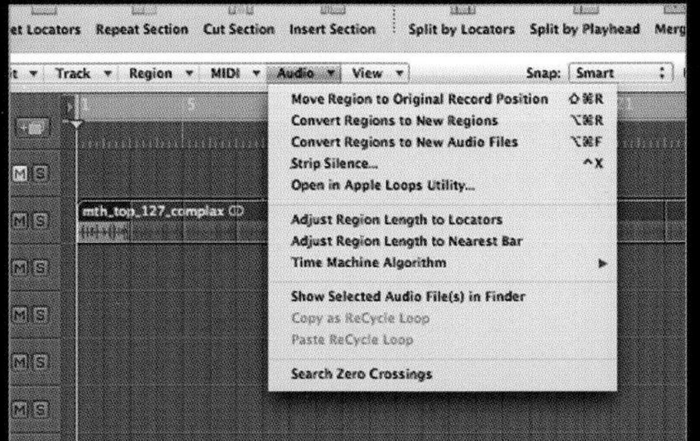

1 Select the Wav loop you want to make into an Apple Loop in the arrange Window. In the audio pull-down menu click on 'Open in Apple Loops Utility'.

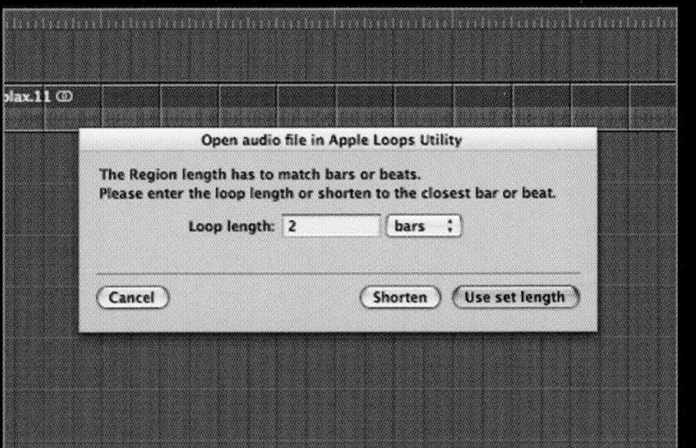

2 A dialogue box opens asking you to confirm the number of bars in the selected loop. If you prefer to think in terms of beats then click on 'bars' in the pull-down menu and change it to beats. When the number of beats or bars is correct click 'Use set length'. Note: Unless you're trying to edit an unusual loop, Logic usually defaults to the correct value.

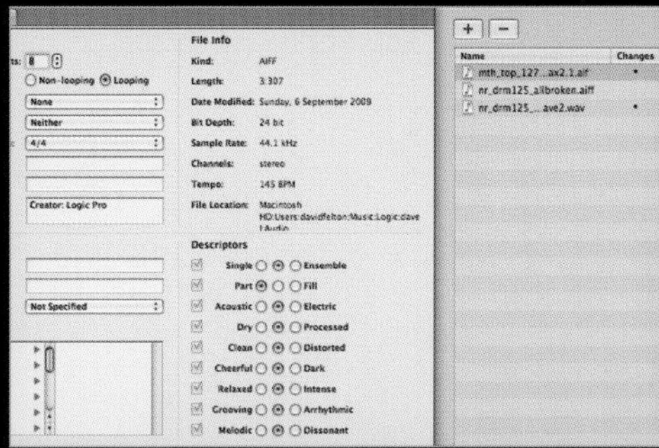

3 The Apple Loops Utility opens, with your loop in the right hand pane. If the loop was a Wav it is automatically saved as an .aiff file – the Apple standard for pro audio files. The left panel shows the various property tags, all of which can be changed to categorise a loop. You can change as many or few of these as you wish.

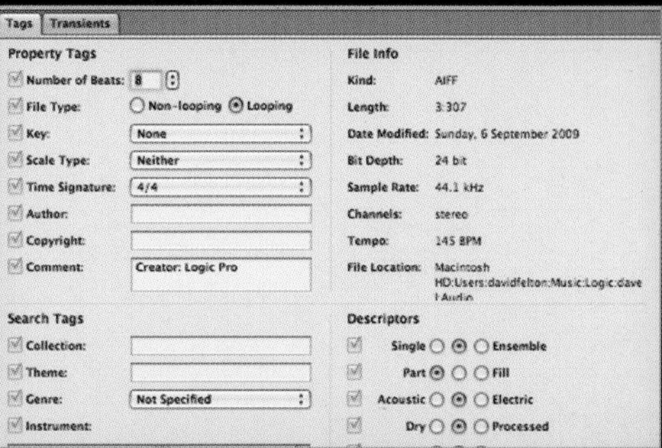

4 In this example – of a minimal house drum loop – we keep the time signature at 4/4, change the Genre to 'Electronic' and the Instrument to 'Electric Beat'. On the right side we change some of the descriptors to reflect the beat as 'Grooving', 'Processed' and 'Electric'. Ensure that the Looping check box in the top left is checked.

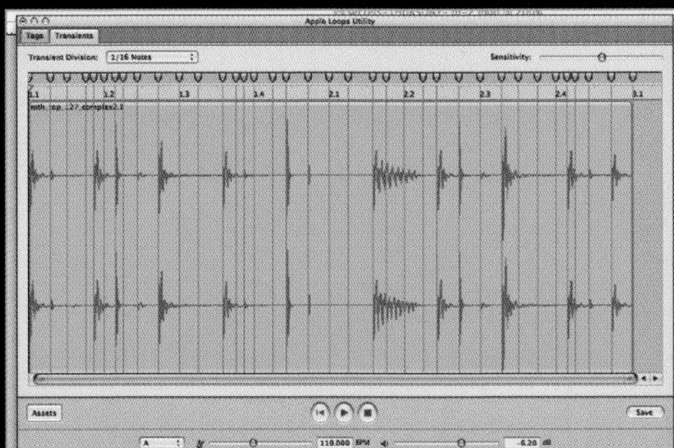

5 Click the transients tab on the top left of the window to see a waveform of your loop with overlaid transients. Press play. Alter the playback speed using the bpm slider and the key using the key drop-down menu. Changing these values lets you hear how the loop will react at different speeds and keys when imported into Logic.

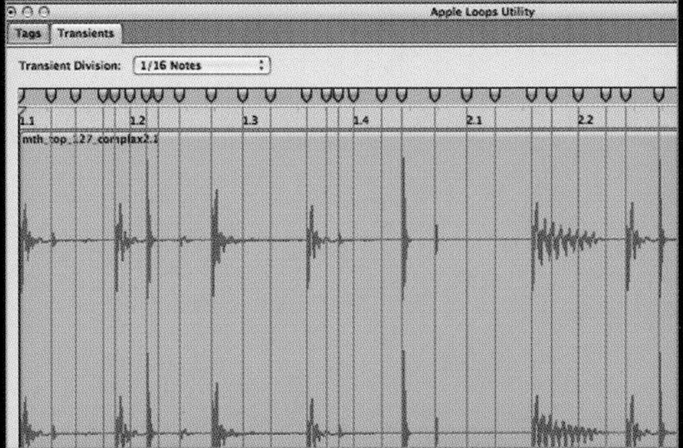

6 The transients are anchor points that tell Logic and Garageband how to process the sound when sped up or slowed down. Ensure there are transient points at the start of each event in a loop – in a drum loop this will be at each hit: kick, snare, hat and so on. For drum and percussion loops, transient divisions of 1/16 notes are usually fine.

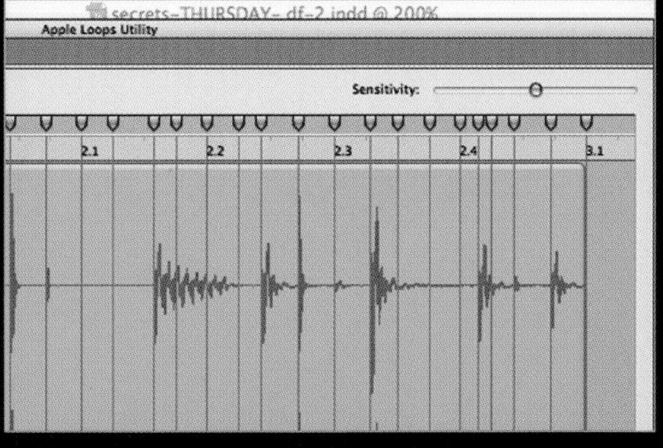

7 Use the sensitivity slider to add or reduce the number of transients. Keep auditioning to hear how this affects your loop. For loops that have heavy swing settings, you may need to move individual anchor points manually using the blue sliders. Add new transients by clicking in the grey bar. Delete points by selecting them and pressing delete.

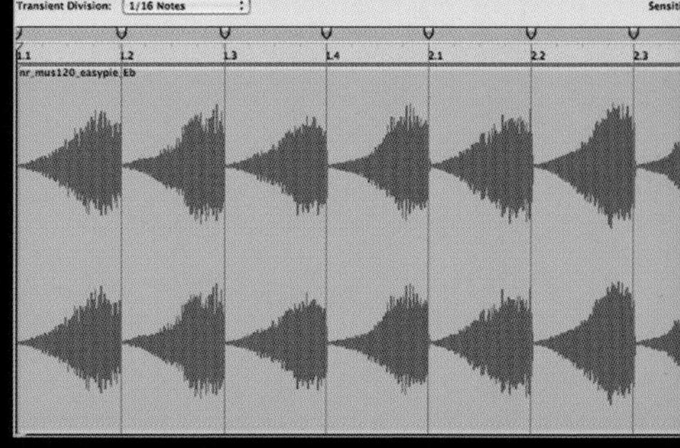

8 The hardest kinds of loops to work with are ones that feature extended chords – like pads or Rhodes lines. In this example all transients have been removed except the first in each bar. This gives the most natural sound when looped. In general, beats and loops defined by strong percussive elements make the best Apple Loops.

/fx

effects are the sonic icing on the production cake.

Sound effects (or 'fx') play a variety of important roles in a house track. They help ease transitions between different sections of a song, taking the traditional part of the drum fill. They supply background interest in the latter sections of a track – particularly during recapitulations and tweaked versions of the lead riff. They are also used to fill up a target set of frequencies that need additional excitement.

But it's during the breakdown that effects come into their own. Over the past decade the fairly simple sweeps and dives of old have become ever bigger and more complex so that they now take centre stage in many breakdowns. Whether it's the side-chained white noise rise, or crazy modulated lazer-fall, effects have an importance today they never did before.

They are also some of the most fun sounds to experiment with in the studio.

All in the synth

A great sounding and versatile synth is a must for making effects. Look for one with plenty of oscillators, filter types and modulation options to give yourself the widest possible palette. Get stuck in with automation and fine tuning to make the effect fit the track perfectly. Use envelopes to shape a sound's direction upwards or downwards and beat-synced LFOs to make time-based effects fit the groove.

Get into the habit of bouncing down any effects you make to build a personal fx library, which you can draw on in the future to add your signature sound to other tracks.

Five of the best

1. The white-noise riser: Frequently used to ratchet up the pressure approaching the drop. Pile on the reverb and delays for an even bigger sound. Pump it up with heavy sidechain compression.

2. The bomb: Ideal for entering the breakdown: a mighty verb-laden explosion to wind down the pressure.

3. The reverse crash: A deep and funky house favourite, this is simply a reverse crash followed by a normal crash.

4. Downshifter drop: Another classic for entering the breakdown, featuring a long, gradually descending synth tone.

5. Full-mix FX: Made much easier with the new generation of glitch plugins, this technique involves building crazy fills using bounced material from the track.

/walkthrough
alarm wind-up

1 The sound of an alarm speeding up is a tried-and-tested tension supplier for breakdowns and builds. Any analogue waveform can be used. Start with a saw. Saw waves have enough harmonics to really tear through the mix. Draw in a Midi note covering the length you want the sound to trigger for. Set sustain to 100% and release to 0.

2 To make the saw wave pulse like an alarm assign an LFO to modulate the pitch of the oscillator. The ramp wave LFO is a classic choice for this effect. Start with a slow speed – around 1Hz – or synchronise speed to the tempo of the track so that the pulses are in time.

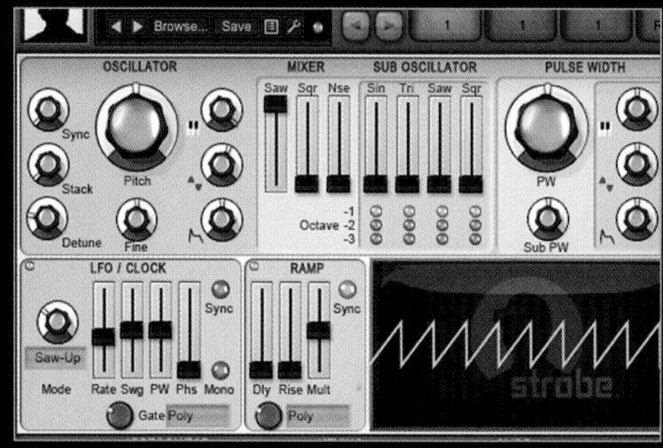

3 Increase the depth to hear the pitch modulation start working. Alarms sound convincing when the pitch spans around two octaves. However don't limit yourself to this: any depth setting can be used creatively.

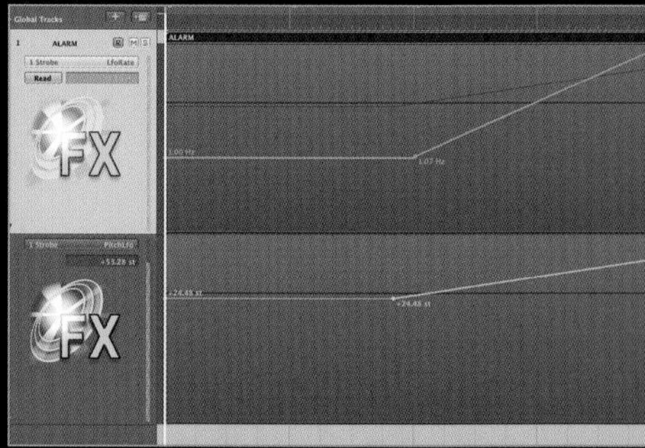

4 Now it's time to tweak. You can automate a range of parameters to increase tension throughout the build. Try changing the LFO rate, modulation depth and even the oscillator pitch. Add reverb and delay for depth and space.

/walkthrough the bomb

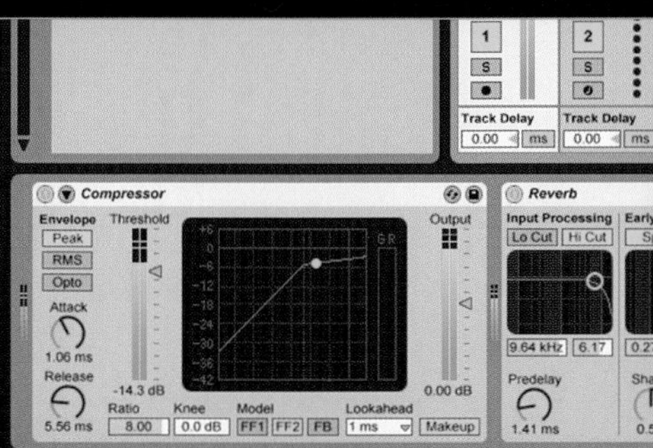

1 Cinematic-style impact effects are created by feeding a kick drum through a reverb unit. It's important to choose a kick with lots of mid and high frequencies to ensure it comes alive when it hits the reverb. Add a compressor if it needs beefing up. Start with an attack time of 1ms, release 5ms and a ratio of 8:1. Lower the threshold until it thickens up.

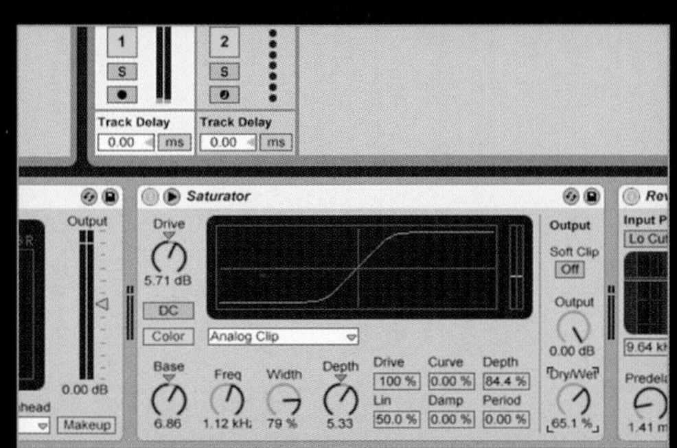

2 Make the kick edgier by feeding it through a clipper, overdrive or distortion effect. You are looking to boost the mid and high frequencies so use the filter or tone control to hone in on the right area. Boosting between 800Hz–2Khz will make it bang louder. Boosts above that will make the bomb cut through the mix more clearly.

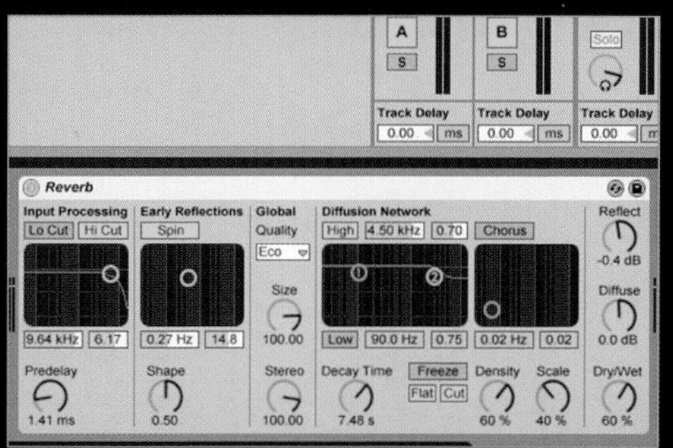

3 The reverb supplies the explosion so choose the right type. Halls work best with long decay times of around 5–10 seconds. If the reverb has a high-cut control open it so the high frequencies sparkle. Set wet/dry mix to 50%. The optimum balance will depend on whether the impact is used on top of the track's regular kick drum or on its own.

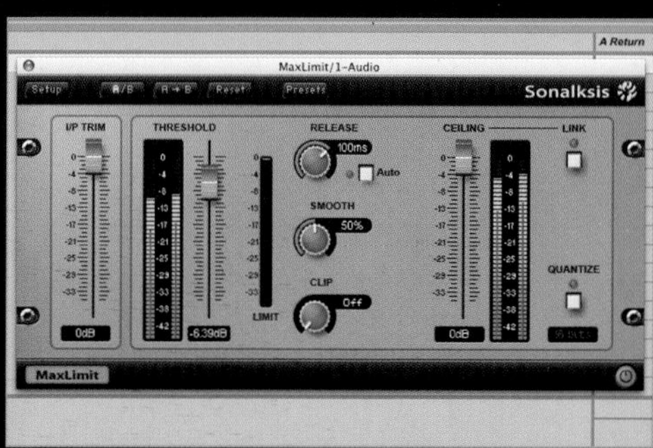

4 Make the explosion even louder and thicker by using a limiter plugin after the reverb. Aim for 2–3dBs of reduction to beef it up and make it cut through a busy mix. For added fun, sidechain the reverb tail to a kick drum to give it the full pump-factor.

/walkthrough fizzy sweeps

1 The fizzy synth sweep is a classic effect that dates back to the early days of analogue synths. It can be used alongside or in place of a regular crash or sweep effect at the start of a bar or to pre-empt a drop. Start with a single sine or triangle wave

2 We are going to use a second sine or triangle oscillator to modulate the pitch of the first one. This is called frequency modulation – also known as analogue FM. Some synths have mod routing pre-wired, but if not route the second oscillator (osc 3 in

3 The tone should sound fizzy and full of high frequencies. To make the sound sweep down automatically assign a modulation envelope to the pitch of oscillator one and set the depth to maximum. Set the mod envelope attack to

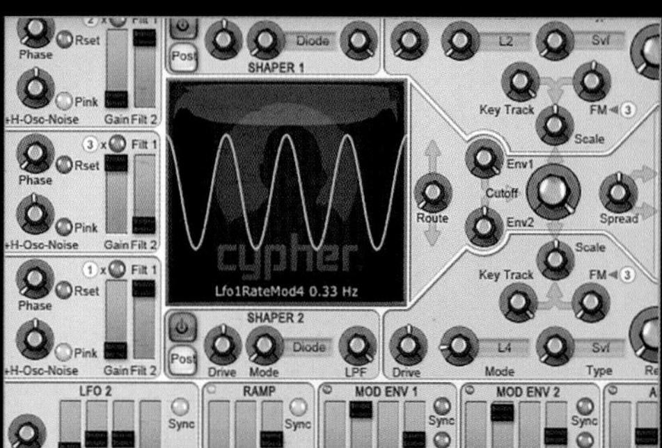

4 The effect can be further twisted to get an effect like tuning into a radio station. To do this modulate the pitch of the FM oscillator (osc 3) with a sine or triangle shaped LFO. Set the rate to .03Hz and depth to maximum. It should now sound like

/walkthrough
downshifter pitch drop

1 Sparkling downward synth sweeps are ideal for entering breakdowns. There are countless variations but the common element is the pitch drop that goes from high to low. Start by drawing in a Midi note to cover the desired length of the sweep. In this example it is two bars, or eight beats, long.

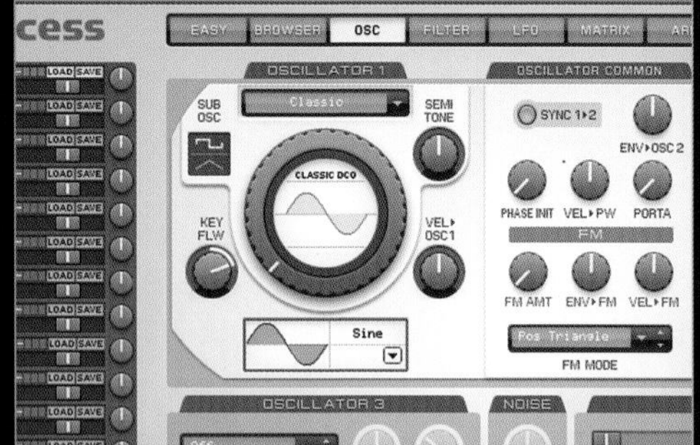

2 Only one oscillator is needed, so select a basic sine wave and turn the others off. To make the sound fade in and out, set the amp envelope attack to 66%, decay and sustain to 100%, and release to 66%.

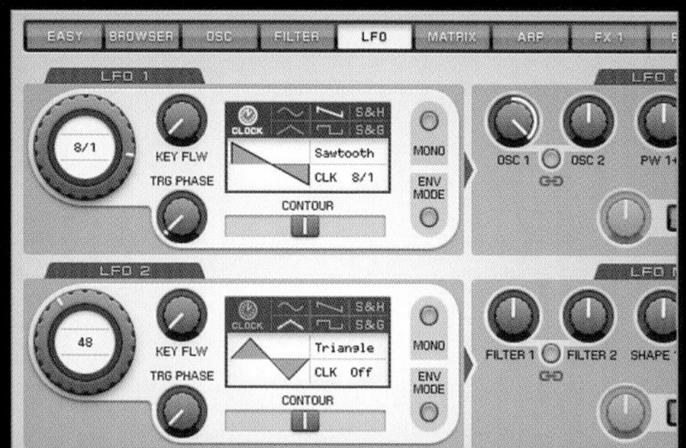

3 Make the pitch drop by modulating it with an LFO. Select a saw waveform and make sure the phase of the waveform starts at the highest point and ramps in a downwards direction. Set note re-trigger to 'on' to trigger the LFO when the note starts. To make it last the whole eight beats select bpm sync and set it to eight beats.

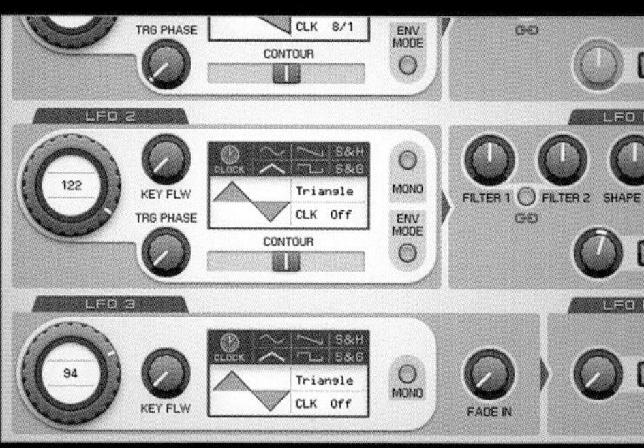

4 For added excitement use a second LFO to modulate the pitch of the oscillator. Use a sine or triangle LFO with a medium to fast rate. Set the depth to around 10%. It will make the sound warble or bubble depending on its speed.

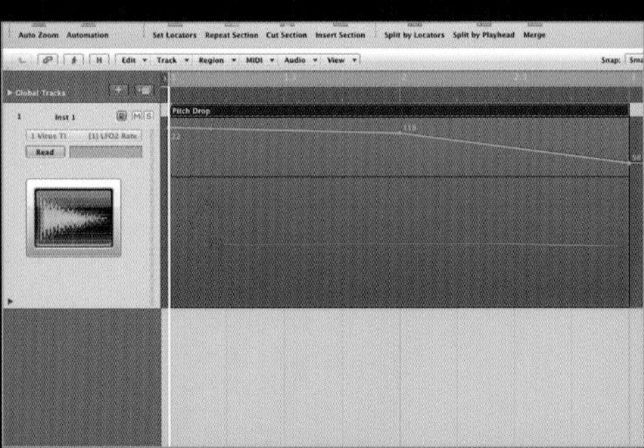

5 If you want to emphasise the sensation of winding down, automate the speed of LFO 2 so that it slows down a little over the course of the 8 beat period. Experiment with automating the modulation depth as well for added sonic candy.

6 Adding a chorus or flanger to the effects chain will expand the stereo width and make the wind-down smoother. You can set the intensity and mix levels fairly high without detracting from the tone of the effect. Try adding more than one modulation effect to increase harmonic richness and add additional colour to the sound.

7 Increase the size of the effect by adding a stereo or ping-pong delay. There is no exact delay time to use, but longer times will make the effect last longer, so start with 1/4 or 1/2 notes with a medium amount of feedback and work from there. Set the dry/wet ratio to 33%. Shave off the low end at around 250Hz to avoid muddying the bass.

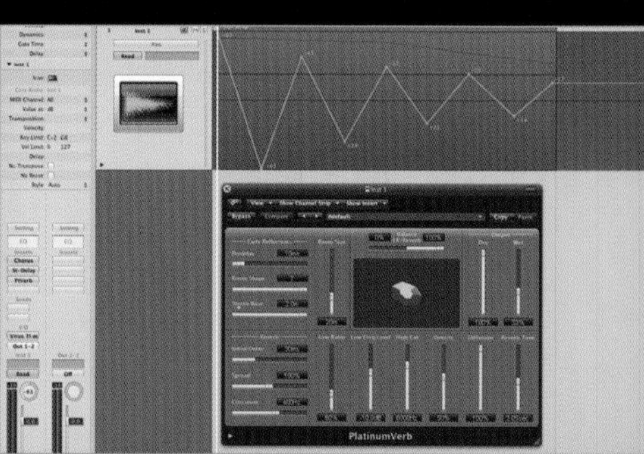

8 For extra space add a medium to large hall reverb. Use a decay time of between 2 and 5 seconds and set the dry/wet mix to between 33% and 50%. Wind-down effects are also ideally suited to panning and other stereo spreading effects. Experiment with a bpm-synced auto-panner or draw in the panning using automation.

/walkthrough white noise crash

1 Crash-style noise or 'gas' hits can be created using any synth with a white noise generator. Draw in a Midi note with a 1/2 beat length and set the amp envelope to minimum attack, 50% decay, minimum sustain and 25% release. This gives a hard impact transient that gradually fades out.

2 Select a 24dB low-pass filter and turn resonance to 33%. This brightens the sound. Now gradually lower the cutoff point until the sound cuts through the mix. Roll off any very high end (8–12kHz). This stops the crash from sounding too sharp and painful on a big system.

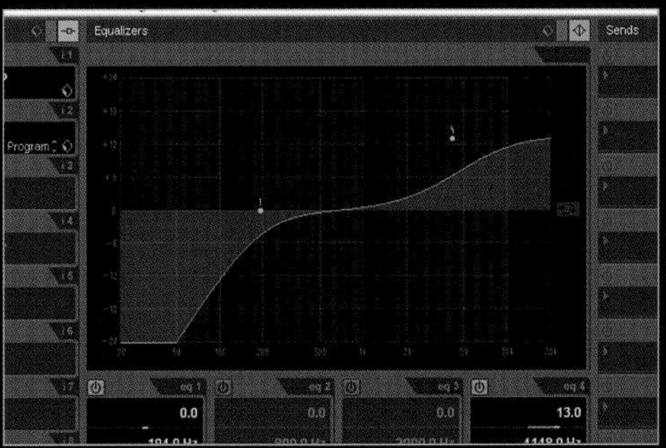

3 Use a high-pass filter and scoop it up to around 200Hz to cut mud from the low end. Add air by boosting up to 15dB from around 4KHz. This won't affect the high end which has already been removed. Give the noise stereo impact using a stereo widener.

4 For more of a warehouse vibe add a big reverb using a hall or plate algorithm. Get a lush sound by dialling up to 7 seconds of decay with 35ms pre-delay. Set size between medium and large and push all modulation and diffusion settings to maximum. Use a compressor sidechained to the kick drum to make it pump like a smoke machine.

/walkthrough crash swell

1 To make a long reverse crash that comes out of nowhere and swells in volume, load up a regular drum machine crash such as one from a 909. Experiment with the tuning: crashes at higher pitches are naturally brighter than those that have been tuned down. Note that crashes are pitched instruments so retune it until it works in the track.

2 To make it longer, add a tape echo or stereo/ping pong delay. Use the bpm sync and set delay time somewhere between 1/8 and 1/4 bar. Experiment with dotted and triplet values to see what blends best with the groove. Set the feedback around 50–75% and mix to 50%. Remove some of the high end using high-cut EQ.

3 A slow sweeping flanger adds an extra layer of sparkle to the effect. Use a slow rate that takes longer than 8 beats to sweep up. Set feedback to 50% and mix to 30%. Increase if for a sharper, more prominent sound. For a 'jet stream' sound use a very short delay time of between 0.1–2ms.

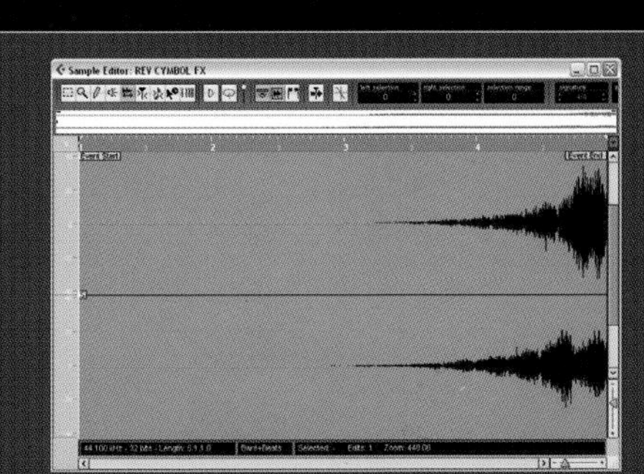

4 Set loop length to 8 beats and export the crash as an audio file that lasts the full 8 beats. Import it back into your DAW and place it on a new audio track. Open it in an audio editor and reverse the crash. Place it back in the mix. It can now be further effected. Try adding a compressor fed by a kick on the side-chain for added pump.

/walkthrough elevator / white noise woosh

1 Draw in a Midi note that lasts the desired length of the rise. The pitch doesn't matter as you'll be using the white noise generator on a simple analogue-style synth. Set the amp envelope to minimum for attack, decay and release, with 100% sustain.

2 To make the synth sweep up use a low-pass filter and tweak the cutoff point. For a thinner sound, use a band-bass filter instead. Adding resonance will introduce a whistling pitch, which can help the sound cut through a busy mix.

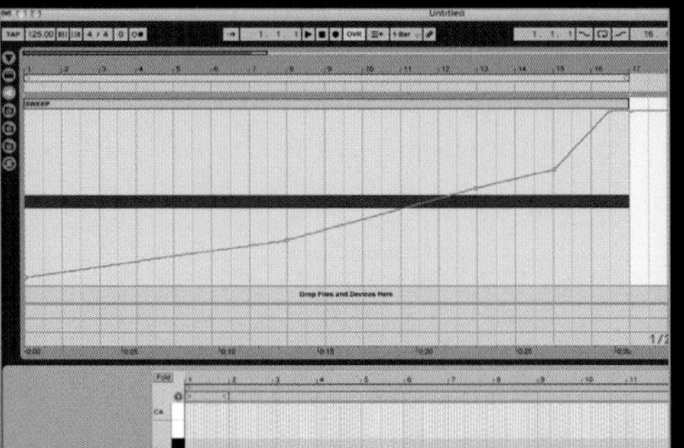

3 The easiest way to make the filter sweep up is by using automation to draw in the filter cutoff sweep over its length. This allows a huge amount of control over how the cutoff filter opens. One trick is to ramp it up to make the sweep accelerate near the end.

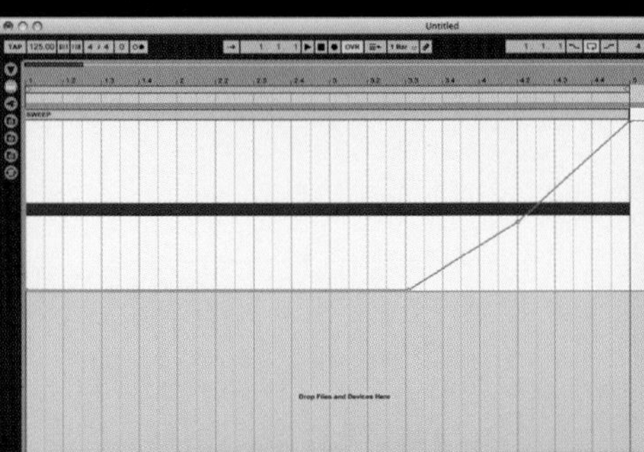

4 Reverb will smooth out the sound and help it blend into the mix, giving it additional atmosphere and depth. Use a reverb decay time of several seconds for a glossy, spatial whoosh effect. Add a high-pass filter after the reverb and automate it to rise towards the end. This filters up the reverb tail, adding to the lifting sensation.

/walkthrough minimal verb build

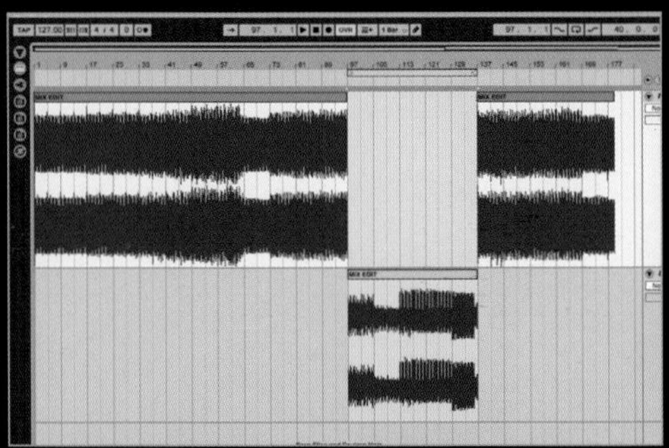

1 The classic 'building reverb' technique involves effecting a bounced version of the full mix. After you've mixed the track down, cut out the break you want to effect and place it on a new track.

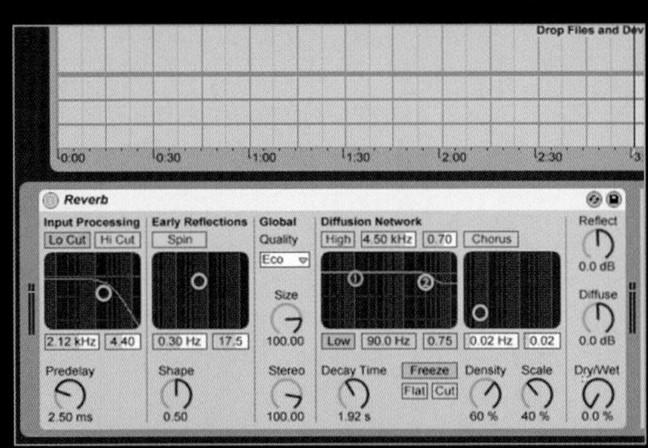

2 Insert a reverb plugin onto the track with the break in it. Choose a big hall preset and set the decay to around 2 seconds and mix to 100% dry.

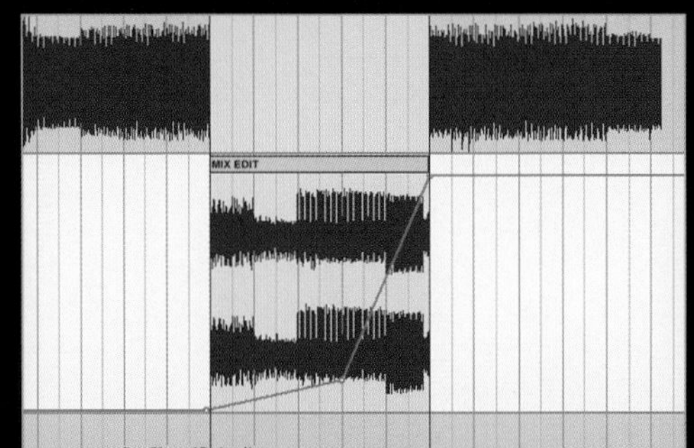

3 Next automate the reverb's wet/dry mix so that it goes from 100% dry at the start to 100% wet at the end. If there are parameters on the reverb that increase the stereo spread it's worth experimenting with these too for an even more intense build.

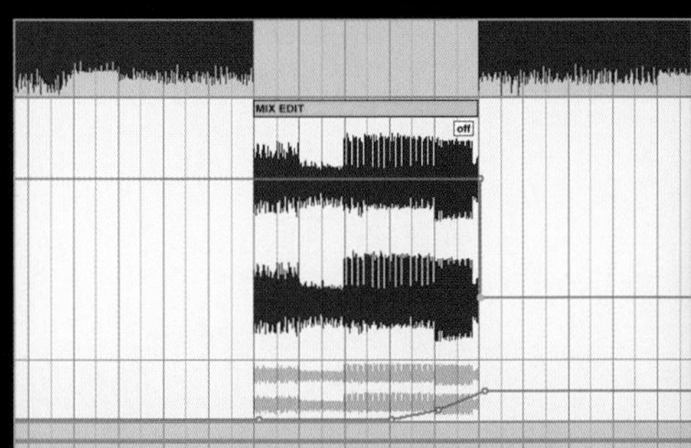

4 Add a high-pass filter after the reverb and automate the cutoff towards the end to take out the bass. It's not necessary to sweep all the way up – just enough to make a contrast between the breakdown and the kick back in. If you don't want the reverb tail hanging over when the track kicks back in, mute the verb track at the end of the break.

/walkthrough full mix fx

1 Some special effects tricks, like running the mix in reverse for one bar, are easiest to do post-mixdown. Open a new project and import a copy of the final stereo mix so that you can edit it without affecting the original. Set the tempo to match the track. This makes it easier to chop in and out of bars.

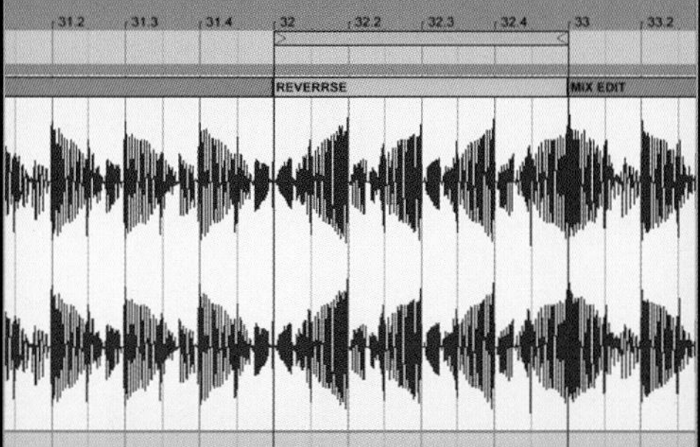

2 Using the scissors or selection tool, line up the cursor and chop the last four beats of the bar before the drop. Locate the reverse function from the edit menu and hit 'process'. The chosen section should now play backwards.

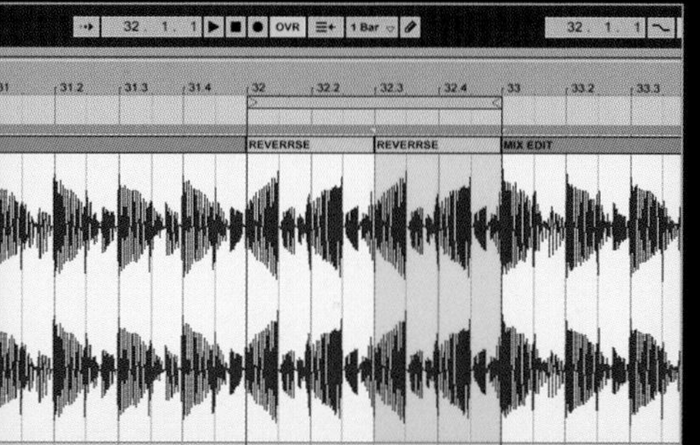

3 Sometimes the timing between the normal and reverse sections doesn't quite flow with the groove. To solve this problem and make the transition fit the groove better experiment by nudging the audio file forwards and backwards in time by very small amounts.

4 Take the edit to the next level by adding a filter effect over the reversing sound. Insert a low pass filter and automate the cutoff so that it sweeps down from high to low. This will add to the sensation of the track being sucked down into the bass bins before kicking back in.

/walkthrough dub siren

1 The dub siren is an instant hit of rebel vibes. Use a single square wave oscillator as the source. The other half of the magic comes from the smoky echo repeats. Set the amp envelope with attack and decay to minimum, sustain to max and release

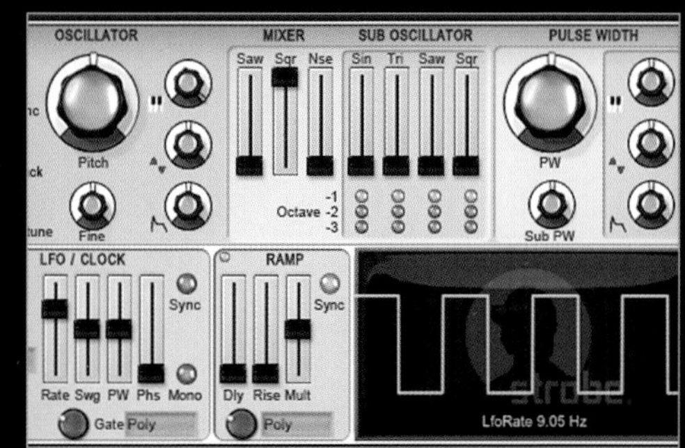

2 To get the warbling quality use an LFO to modulate the pitch of the oscillator. Use a square wave LFO. Start with a speed of around 9Hz or 1/16th note when using bpm sync.

3 Play C3 and increase the LFO modulation depth to change the pitch of the two notes. Experiment with odd tunings such as 15, 19 or 21 semitones by changing the LFO depth. This can add a musical edge to the effect by matching or clashing with the

4 To get dubby delays the Roland Space Echo is the authentic choice, but any tape delay emulator will work fine. Set feedback to a notch below the point of infinite repeats and use the high and low-pass filters to shave a bit off each end to

/part five

structure

The difference between a set of killer ideas and a killer track lies in the arrangement. Making the transition from one to the other requires a combination of know-how, experimentation and hard-draft decision-making.

Poetry has been described as 'all the right words, in the right order'.

The house producer's job is the same as the poet's: weaving ideas together into a single unified whole that is more than the sum of its parts.

This unified whole should toy with the dancefloor, teasing the tension with builds, drops and breakdowns.

In shaping a track's structure the producer is making decisions over how a crowd will react in the clubs.

Ask a DJ what drives clubbers most crazy: the answer will invariably be the breakdown and the drop.

No pressure...

/structure

perfect an eight bar loop, build a few fills, create a classic breakdown and above all, keep the dj happy. easy.

Loop first, song second

The tried and tested way of building an arrangement is by perfecting a killer four or eight bar loop consisting of all your track's major beat and signature musical elements – including drums, bass, synths, music parts and maybe even some fx sounds – and then building from there.

It's while programming this early looped section that the initial creative work happens, with decisions being made on everything from the track's tempo and key through chords to groove settings and instrumentation (as well as vocal lines if applicable). Only when a creative seed has flourished here will the producer consider developing it into a full track. Of course not all ideas get beyond this initial stage: if you can't get the seed of an idea to flourish at this stage, it almost certainly isn't worth taking it to the arrangement stage.

Use as many layers as you like when building this loop section. Although you don't need everything in yet – beds and textures are often best left until later in the mixing process when they can be used to 'pad' the sound – anything that shapes the personality of the track should be in. If a layer isn't adding to the soundscape, lose it and keep the mix free of clutter. It's never too early to cut flab.

Eight is the magic number

When you're happy with your four or eight bar loop, it's time to start the arrangement process. This is the often time-consuming business of deciding where different parts come in and out, and shaping the sounds at your disposal into a complete song.

If you spend a little time deconstructing arrangements of house tracks that work on the dancefloor, it becomes clear that there are a few structural techniques in common use. The three deconstructions over the coming pages take house tracks with dancefloor pedigree to highlight these.

It is important to note that structure in dance music is governed by two things: what the DJ needs and what the dancefloor wants.

As far as the former goes, the requirements are relatively simple: 16 or more usually 32 bars' worth of stripped beats at the start and end of the track (see **Intros and outros, right**). As for the latter, as a general rule, you will want to be introducing changes – new elements, fills and so on – in intervals of no less than eight bars, but more often 16 and in some cases, typically in prog-house arrangements, as many as 32. Deviating too far from this will throw your listeners. For better or worse there are some things dancefloors expect, and solid arrangements that don't deviate far from the norm is one. So don't do anything significant after six-and-a-half or two bars: it will sound odd, confuse people and interrupt the track's flow. Chances are the DJ will only play such a track once.

Plan and pace your arrangement for the energy of the dancefloor, and not the studio. Sections that sound over-long in the studio will often work much better on the dancefloor. If in doubt analyse tracks that you know drive dancefloors wild and replicate their structures.

A second element to consider is how the energy builds and drops around changes during the arrangement. This is often genre-dependent. Minimal, tech and progressive tracks build and drop subtly and smoothly, with new parts easing into the mix rather than blasting in. Even within eight or 16 bar blocks, elements can be introduced gradually by riding volume faders and automating effects so that sounds twist and morph as they come in and out. By contrast, electro and fidget bangers need to grab the attention immediately, with arrangements having a more direct 'cut and paste' structure with blatant verse / chorus sections and new elements banging in with all the subtlety of a brick wall.

Some tracks are consciously made as 'transitional' records, used by DJs to move from one mood to another, or to stitch together two tracks that can't easily be mixed. These club-minded arrangements are built around two or three sections, each of which has a slightly different energy level. The sections are intersected by stripped-back breakdowns that give the DJ the chance to easily mix in the next record.

/overview
what is...?

Breakdown: Section where kick drops out and track breaks down into its simplest elements. In some genres, specifically progressive house, this is where the main melodic hook is introduced. Sometimes the breakdown is the most memorable part of a track. Rarely lasts longer than two minutes.

Drop: When the track 'drops back in' – either after the breakdown or an extended fill – and the track reaches full energy. Occasionally used to describe the 'dropping out of a sound', like the kick for a bar.

Build: A build in energy, typically at the end of the breakdown, where risers, building crashes, opening filters and new elements fill the mix, building tension to a climax before the drop.

Playout: Outro. Elements stripped back to beats and atmospheric effects. Allows the DJ to mix in the next track.

Fill: Anything from traditional drum break to crazy noise sequence to round off a bar before a new section begins.

Fills

Fills are used to add interest and sonic lifts at the end of each eight or 16-bar cycle or to lead into transitions, like the chorus or a new riff. In the past, fills were made using drum breaks or old-school 909 snare rolls. Nowadays the raw material used to build them is sourced from synths, percussive sounds or heavily effected versions of the backing. Common tricks include reverse sections and filter swells (see **fx, page 92–97**).

A common way of producing interesting fills is to run the drums or even the whole track through a glitch / stutter effect such as MDSP's Livecut or Ableton's Beat Repeater. By making use of the randomisation parameters it's easy to generate an array of crazy, often impossible to program fills and edits that you can sort through to pick the best.

Smooth transitions

Placing big reverberated effects hits, long dubby delays and white noise (or traditional) crashes at the start of bars and sections plays two important roles. Firstly, it announces the beginning of a new cycle, and secondly it helps smooth out changes in tone and rhythm between sections, blurring the boundaries and helping to mould the song into a unified whole. Without these smoothing elements, transitions tend to sound abrupt and uncomfortable.

Tip / Just when you think you've reached the drop and you cant possibly tease a breakdown out any longer, strip to silence and insert an extra one bar fill before dropping back into the groove. Some producers don't like using these 'illegal' fills as they mess up the neatness of the arrangement page, but used sparingly they can take a build to the next level and provide a rare exception to the 'don't do anything structurally odd' mantra,

Mix as you go

Although the mixdown proper often happens after the major structural decisions have been made, a certain amount of mixing as you go is both inevitable and desirable. Usually this involves adjusting volume levels, basic EQ cuts and panning, as well as introducing key creative effects (See **The mix, page 121**).

For certain genres – particularly ones where ultra-clinical production is paramount, like minimal and IDM-influenced tech house – mixing as you go, often to exacting standards, is vital. This is because it's next to impossible to work out if you need more parts in a mix if the existing ones have not been fully treated.

Working with a mix that's 95 per cent there allows you to hear which frequencies are being tickled and which are missing. This will inform decisions on what to introduce next into the mix. When mixing in this way, perfect an 8 or 16 bar section and go as far as testing your mix on different systems to see how it stacks up.

Automation

Slick use of automation can add a whole new dimension to an arrangement. Whether it's used to change the intensity of effects, open a synth's filter, mute channels or smooth out volumes, each change will impact on the way a track progresses and will in turn affect arrangement decisions.

DAW tracks have the ability to record automation in a variety of ways. The most direct is by using a mouse and the pencil tool to draw it in. Alternatively, switch on live recording mode and wiggle the parameter button on your interface to capture changes. Return to the edit page to fine-tune it.

Breakdown

The breakdown has taken an ever more important place in house tracks over the past decade, to the point where two minute breakdowns are not unusual (a la Daft Punk **One More Time**), whipping the crowd into a frenzy before kicking back into the groove. There are countless approaches to the breakdown, but the common feature of all is that the kick drum drops away.

Breakdowns tend to have a feeling of movement and direction, with it beginning quietly – often in silence – and then building up, with ever more layers introduced until it swells to epic proportions. Not only does the breakdown grow, it also expands outwards in sonic space, so make use of opening filters, EQ, building reverbs and echoes, and plenty of automation. The breakdown should be a little quieter than the main section of the track or it will lose impact when it kicks back in.

Scatter writing: a second approach

Of course there's no single way to approach arrangement. Some producers prefer to write as they go. Instead of refining an eight bar section, they treat the page as a blank canvas and experiment with different sections of the song, jumping between them and creating pieces of a jigsaw puzzle that they work out how to fit together later. This less structured approach can open interesting creative avenues, not channeling you down a specific direction too early in the writing process.

Tip / If you have a track with a structure you want to replicate, import it into your DAW's arrange page and then build the track up alongside, constantly A/Bing between it and your arrangement to see if you're on the right track.

/how to intros and outros

In house music it's rare to hear a DJ play a track from the start. In most cases the intro and outro are used purely for mixing purposes.

It can be both annoying and potentially off-putting for the DJ to get a track without at least eight bars worth of stripped lead-in. In practise most lead-ins (and outs) occupy 16 or 32 bars.

To make the DJ's mixing job as easy as possible, the lead-in needs a strong rhythmic element to help them catch the pulse. This can be as simple as a kick and hi-hat. The uncluttered nature of a stripped rhythm part makes it easy to hear in a banging club through headphones.

Introducing elements slowly and leaving lots of mix space will get DJs on your side and make the track a breeze to play. Ideally there will be some kind of identifiable sound or fill that announces that the drop or break is coming. This will signal to the DJ that it's time to mix out the previous tune. Rising sounds, reverse swell and uplifiters all do the job nicely.

/anatomy of a track
electro-house

Introduction

Fat pumping basslines, searing synth leads and chunky beats are the key ingredients of an electro-house bomb. Putting them together into a workable arrangement requires a knack for creating memorable riffs, chopping up hooks and considering the effect of an arrangement on the dancefloor.

In contrast to the more linear arrangements typical of tech/minimal, electro-house and fidget tracks are made up of clear 'sections', usually based on a synth line or chord progression, that turn around every four, eight or, very occasionally, 16 bars. As the song progresses, these sections are repeated and modified by using different combinations of synth and drum elements.

A good technique is to perfect an eight or 16 bar segment of the hook first, with all drums and edits locked down, before laying out the rest of the track.

There's no need for massively long intros or outros for DJs: the days of the three minute build are long gone:16 or 32 bars is usually enough.

This arrangement is based on the track Pole Position by ***Stripper****, copyright control 2010. You can find it on the CD-Rom.*

In detail

1 The track starts with a solid four-on-the-floor groove with a rocking snare pattern driving through it. The funk is supplied by the swing; the energy by the relentless shaker line.

2 A reverse sucking effect introduces a dirty, bit-crushed atmospheric drone that rasps its way through to bar 17, with automation changing its texture as the bars fall.

3 A crash and downshifter signify the entry of a new rising electronic bubble sound, which lasts a full 16-bar measure and leads the track into the first breakdown. Note the spot delay effects that add washes of ear candy to the mix.

4 The first melodic breakdown starts with a deceptively simple four-chord turnaround that repeats every four bars. The filter opens slowly (both upwards and down) throughout the break to build the tension.

5 The hi-hat stops and the low end is cut from the pared-down beat to ease back the energy and focus all of the listener's attention on the melody.

6 A new synth topline, playing a slinky, syncopated pattern, enters here. It follows the same four-bar chord progression as the synth part in 5.

7 The drums drop out altogether now to allow the building melodic elements to take centre stage. At bar 57 an as-yet-unheard raucous cross-kick pattern enters the mix. The groove complements the funky snare part and serves to build anticipation towards the drop, along with a wild rising sound.

8 The pressure spirals as the cycle of synth parts changes. Instead of the four bar / four chord pattern continuing, both the backing and lead melodic synths resolve to the first chord and stick with it for the remainder of the build, easing an extra 10 per cent worth of tension from the crowd.

9 Apart from a single kick drum hit, the whole track is stripped to the squeaky lead riff for one bar.

10 The track drops back in with the main drum groove and bassline rocking. Careful production means the kick doesn't interfere with the stacked bass synth. Note how the bassline is tweaked throughout the track, with various filter rises and effects edits ensuring an ongoing sense of movement.

11 The squeaky riff returns to complement the rolling bassline. It is supported by an occasional tom pattern that fills in the synth gap in the latter part of the turnaround. At bar 89 an additional supporting synth line enters. It doubles part of the bassline to form a call and response phrase.

12 This cheeky little section features a Midi edit to the bassline that extends the notes longer than those on the dancefloor expect. It brings variance and ups the all-important pressure.

13 The track kicks in fully now, with all parts rocking as it builds towards the main breakdown.

14 The breakdown hits. The drums are stripped back to kick and hat only with the lows cut on the kick. The synth chords and melody from the first break return for a quicker build than the first one.

15 The cross-kick pattern re-enters, supported by a big, live-sounding clap and a series of layered rising sounds to start the build.

16 A specially tweaked version of the bassline is introduced. A low-pass filter begins its ascent. To reinforce the increase in energy, at bar 151 the bassline pitch begins to rise too, mirroring the pitch of the building riser effect. Note the dubbed out rave-style sirens and rhythmic panning filth crashes that get triggered in wonky triplets to start with, and then ever faster to become yet another element in the building FX wall. Note also the gradual increase in the amount of reverb and delay that is being sent to the effects busses, making an ever-wetter mix just waiting to be dried out...

17 ... Now! All parts are suddenly cut except for the signature lead line – served 100% dry for maximum dramatic effect before the track kicks back in. The top synth layer now initiates the call and response routine with the bassline. The squeaky lead re-enters at bar 169, layered this time with a white-noise snare to give it added definition. The rattly tom pattern continues its call/response noodling. To add variance the synth line is occasionally automated to send more signal to the reverb for messy verb spins.

18 All parts are dropped for a second one-bar edit – except for a tweaked version of the bassline (note the suck effect made by reversing the riff). The drum section kicks back in with a noise riser to lead us out of the final bass section.

19 As the track proceeds towards its mix-out phase the bassline drops and an atmospheric drone and siren effect inject some ear candy.

20 The track winds down with 16 bars of full drums, and then 16 bars without the hi-hat, during which EQ is automated to gradually filter out the lowest bass frequencies. A short reverse noise signals the end of the tune.

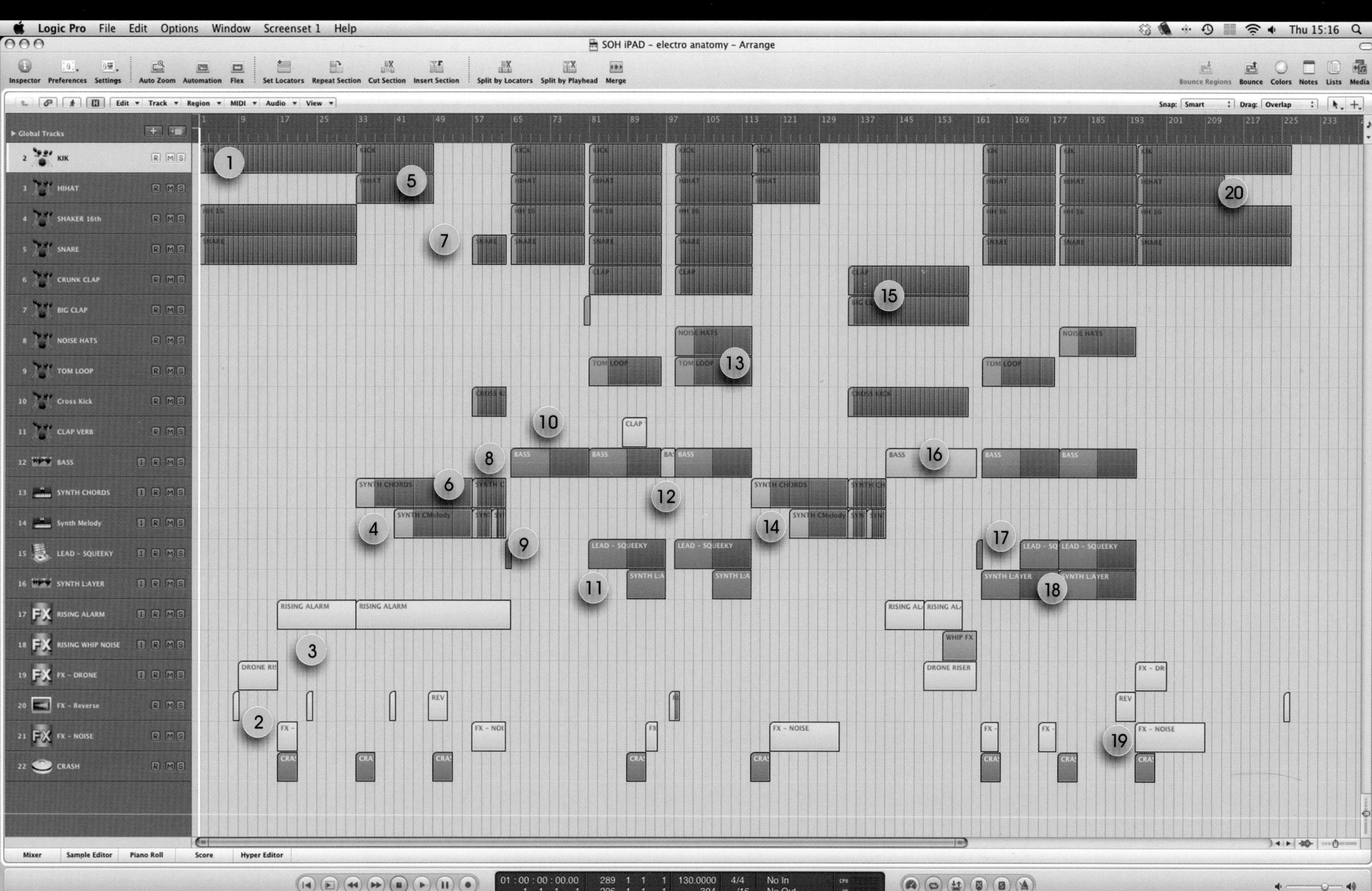
Logic Pro File Edit Options Window Screenset 1 Help
Thu 15:16
SOH iPAD - electro anatomy - Arrange
Global Tracks
KIK
HIHAT
SHAKER 16th
SNARE
CRUNK CLAP
BIG CLAP
NOISE HATS
TOM LOOP
Cross Kick
CLAP VERB
BASS
SYNTH CHORDS
Synth Melody
LEAD - SQUEEKY
SYNTH LAYER
RISING ALARM
RISING WHIP NOISE
FX - DRONE
FX - Reverse
FX - NOISE
CRASH
1
2
3
4
5
6
7
8
9
10
11
12
13
14
15
16
17
18
19
20

/anatomy of a track

minimal & tech-house

Introduction

Minimal and tech-house tracks share a common ethos when it comes to arrangements. They both have steadily-building – and fading – grooves, which allow plenty of opportunity and space for the DJ to mix in and out at various points.

Tracks are usually divided into three or four distinct sections, with one or two breakdowns interrupting the main groove.

It's important to keep the energy moving during the whole track. This can be achieved by adding and removing layers of drums and synths and tweaking automation.

Every tiny nuance will contribute to the vibe of a minimal or tech track and the very subtlest amounts of automation over a 16 or 32 bar section can turn a repetitive groove into a sublime masterpiece.

Where electro-house stands or falls on the strength of a riff, and where vocal house relies on a key lyrical hook, minimal is all about subtlety and cleverly-worked change over time.

This arrangement is based on the track Putting in the Work by ***Marc Adamo****, copyright control 2010. You can find it on the CD-Rom.*

In detail

1 The track opens with a solid groove made up of kick, open off-beat hi-hat and hypnotic 8th beat clave line. An additional soft 8th-note closed hat loop gels the kick and snare, maintaining a consistent energy throughout the track. An atmosphere loop – some sampled street noise or room ambience – sits far back in the mix, adding a unique vibe to the groove. It is sidechained with the kick to make it pump and give the beat a rhythmic pull.

2 A high pass version of the sub bass riff is introduced at bar 17. Rhythmically it pre-empts the full bassline that enters at 33. To counter this lower energy an additional lo-fi hi-hat supplies some high-end roughage.

3 A noise loop eases into the mix. Automation is used to increase its volume and raise the frequency of the low-pass filter.

4 A subtle crash signals the entry of the sub bass, which sits in the depths of the mix – some way below the kick, driving the rhythm forward. Additional energy comes with the introduction of a 16th note percussive topline, which is dominated by a synthesised shaker pattern.

5 A long reverse build increases the drama before the signature bassline enters. The beat drops out at bar 48 where a funky percussion fill introduces this main bassline – a raw, triangle wave-sourced affair that sits tight above the sub. Note the subtle variation that comes at the end of every 8th measure – a nice touch that nudges the energy onwards and tickles listener engagement. Note also the rhythmic interaction between the sub and main basslines, with both playing their own unique roles.

6 A big white noise hit drenched in reverb signals the arrival of the first breakdown. The main drums and shaker drop out and are replaced by a filtered percussion loop generated using white noise. A low-pass filter on the loop rises slowly throughout the breakdown to increase tension. At the same time the first musical element – a rhythmic synth riff – is introduced to the mix.

7 As the track nears the drop a dub echo effect notches up the pressure. The echo feedback is increased and the filter opened using automation on an FX bus. A pitch riser joins the mix for a final injection of sonic pressure to get clubbers' hands in the air.

8 In the bar before the track kicks back in, the shuffly fill from bar 33 – made using a combination of drum and percussion hits – returns. This fill becomes a motif of the track which gets used, occasionally in a varied form, in forthcoming drops to herald the return of the kick. In a genre that is not generally reliant on riffs these signature motifs act as rhythmic hooks.

9 A thin crash signals the end of the break and the return of the beat and sub bassline. The synth riff is stripped of dub effects to leave it sitting dry, brash and up-front, locked into the groove.

10 The mix will shortly be at its busiest – with the main bassline back in. But before it gets there, the groove is interrupted with a one-of-a-kind fill. It's made using a glitched variation of the main synth line combined with a reverse noise effect. It serves two purposes: it's a nice fill, and it's also a freaky variant of the main lead line, breaking the expected melodic flow in the run up to a new section. Using a separate audio channel for this fill can be quicker than using effects automation on the main synth chord track.

11 Automation on the synth riff raises the filter cutoff point while echo and reverb effects are intensified to build excitement through this section.

12 The one-bar fill at bar 112, preceded by a short build, signals the end of the synth riff – for now – as the bass groove returns to centre-stage.

13 A reverse build leads into the second breakdown, which opens with a blast of white noise. All beat elements are cut for maximum impact leaving the mix bare but for the overlapping white noise delays. The atmosphere loop is cut too, for the only time in the song. As the white noise fades out, the lead synth riff is filtered back in, creeping into the mix as a low-pass filter is slowly opened. Note the additional mounting verb on the (very) high passed sub bass line.

14 The build begins, with a big white noise crash reinforced with a rising effect and the filtered percussion loop from the first breakdown re-introduced. Automation is used to both raise the pitch of the synth tone loop and to increase the amount of echo on it to build the tension further. Several additional rising effects finish the picture.

15 The track drops back in with the trademark rhythm fill. It's time to give the dancefloor what it wants: a final full hit of the original synth and bass lines.

16 A big smash noise with a long reverb tail sounds and the bass and synth lines drop out leaving nothing but the drums and atmosphere loop playing. This lowers the pace and gives the DJ room to mix in the next track.

17 The track winds down with only the backbone of the rhythm left. A reverse build takes it to the finish line.

Logic Pro File Edit Options Window Screenset 2 Help
Fri 12:19
SOH – MINIMAL & TECH HOUSE – Arrange
Inspector
Preferences
Settings
Auto Zoom
Automation
Flex
Set Locators
Repeat Section
Cut Section
Insert Section
Split by Locators
Split by Playhead
Merge
Bounce Regions
Bounce
Colors
Notes
Lists
Media
Edit
Track
Region
MIDI
Audio
View
Snap: Smart
Drag: Overlap
Global Tracks
KICK
HAT GROOVE
HAT OFF
CALP
HAT 8TH
CLAVE
SHAKER 16TH
DRUM FILL
SUBBASS
BASS
HIGH SUB
SYNTH
Synth Fill
SYNTH HOISE ...
SYNTH TONE
SYNTH FX RET...
8 note Throug...
FX – DRUM RE...
DRUM BUSS
ATMOS
NOISE CRASH
CRASH
REV BUILD
DDFX_Tran...
UPLIFTER
OKO FX
DDFX_Blee...
FX HIT
RISE
1
2
3
4
5
6
7
8
9
10
11
12
13
14
15
16
17
Mixer
Sample Editor
Piano Roll
Score
Hyper Editor
01 : 00 : 00 : 00.00
128.0000
4/4
No In
No Out

/anatomy of a track
vocal-led house

Introduction

This kind of structure can cover a range of song-based styles, from deep and organic through US beach to classic disco and Latin house. It uses a fairly standard verse/chorus approach with a bridge formed by using an edited version of the first verse.

Although the beats and instrumentation are important here – the song will fail if they aren't rock solid – it's the vocals, and particularly the chorus hook, that need to shine. Other instrumental parts serve as backing – like the chorus strings, Rhodes and pervasive synth lead, which plays throughout almost all of the track. Additional instrumental parts – like the clav – throw in some variation and maintain the listener's interest, but again, they are supportive: it's the vocals that should be the focus.

It's worth noting that a large amount of work has happened before getting to the layout opposite. Specifically the chorus vocals have all been fine-tuned and edited, then mixed in a separate project to get the single bounced stereo file shown. A chorus can be made up of more than 30–40 audio tracks, which are worth bouncing down before building the final arrangement to free up tracks and CPU.

*This arrangement is based on First Taste of Love by **Jake Island**, copyright Toolroom Records 2010. You can find it on the CD-Rom.*

In detail

1 The track opens with a stripped version of the main beat, featuring a layered kick with a snare/clap combo. The snare is mixed dry and up-front, with a heavily reverbed clap lower in the mix giving a sense of space. This basic beat is accompanied by the main synth hook – a simple eight-bar loop that plays throughout the song and is sidechained to the kick to give an audible pump. A low-cut filter ensures it doesn't interfere with the kick or bassline.

2 A sweet bell-tree glissando (taking the place of a crash) brings in the Rhodes chords, which support the lead synth line, occupying a different place in the frequency spectrum. A simple 8th note hi-hat picks up the pace of the track.

3 The beat drops away in the intro break leaving the kick to support the bassline: a busy, jazz-tinged workout that contrasts with the fairly straight drum part. A filtered echo line supplies a dubby background sound bed, with automated filter cutoff tweaks and triplet delays that cut across the beat.

4 A short FX rise drives the track into the first verse. A shaker line and subtle percussive loop fill out the top end, while a pad sits back in the mix, pulling together the many melodic elements. The lead and chorus synths are sent to a bus along with this pad and the Rhodes so that they can all be EQd and compressed together.

5 A vocal spin takes a select word or phrase and delays it to add interest to a line. The effect can be achieved in a number of ways. In this instance the words to be spun are copied from the lead line, inserted onto a second track, pushed back by a 1/4 note and then sent to a heavily reverbed delay. The sparse spread of the lyrics means there is plenty of space for the spins in the mix.

6 A key motif in this track is the lazy Latin trumpet hook that plays between verses. A velocity-controlled filter on it gives the sound a nice analogue squelch when louder notes are played.

7 Verse 2 comes in, accompanied this time by a noodly clavinet part. This new element keeps the listener interested while subtly pushing the rhythm forward. A guitar could have done the same job in a similar part of the frequency spectrum.

8 The build to the first chorus occurs in the verse line, where the melody climbs and the singer increases the energy in her voice. An FX climb rises and in the bar before the chorus hits a sampled live drum fill interrupts the rhythm and prepares the listener for their first taste of the chorus hook.

9 The noodly clav drops out and is replaced by a chorus synth line that plays a counterpoint melody to support the chorus hook and a high string part that supplies big washes of sonic colour to fill the the mix. The chorus vocal track features a 14-part pre-mixed set of harmonies and leads, all with their own place in the stereo spectrum. A stereo widener gives the backing even more width, while the lead chorus line sits in the centre.

10 In a vocal-led track, where the majority of interest is generated by the voice and its hooks, drops and breakdowns are given slightly less prominence than in other house styles. In this track, the main breakdown comes after a double chorus, when the bassline leaves the arrangement along with the top percussive elements to slow the pace of the track. The filter echo from earlier is re-introduced, filling the stripped mix with dubby delays.

11 The breakdown begins, with all beat elements silenced bar the percussion, which plays a shuffly backing against which a softer, more soulful version of the verse 1 vocal plays. With just Rhodes and the pad for backing, the vocal can shine, with spins and automated verb swells adding interest.

12 Next up is a variant of the chorus – featuring a single female voice in the first pass, and then additional harmonies in the second. It's a nice way to introduce variety into the song and build anticipation before the drop. The return of the shaker pins down the rhythm.

13 With the mix still sparse a filtered line is introduced. This is a bounced version of the full chorus instrumental backing, including bass and drums, fed through a resonant low-pass filter, its cutoff point rising towards the drop. It's the classic disco-house filter trick used sparingly: a classic that can still make a dancefloor go wild.

14 The trumpet hook returns to move the track towards the drop. A reverse crash and a long FX rise further add to the tension...

15 ...then, just as the listener expects the track to bang back in, a two-bar rest is inserted, in which the last note of the chorus vocal block is dub-delayed, and the one-bar fill plays.

16 The full track kicks back, with all elements in now, including the trumpet part. Vocal adlibs weave in and out of the last two choruses, supplying additional interest and energy in the last sections of the song. These are fed through varying strengths of delay to merge them into the mix.

17 The bass is cut, along with the percussion and chorus instrumentals, leaving just the trumpet and clav above the chords. These soon drop out too to leave the kick and shaker for the DJ to mix into the next track. Subtle use of automation makes the stripping of elements more natural.

SOH – Song house arrangement – Arrange
Inspector
Preferences
Settings
Auto Zoom
Automation
Set Locators
Repeat Section
Cut Section
Insert Section
Split by Locators
Split by Playhead
Merge
Bounce
Colors
Lists
Media
Edit
Track
Region
MIDI
Audio
View
Snap:
Smart
Drag:
Overlap
Global Tracks
Marker 1
Marker 2
1 KICK
2 SNARE
3 CLAP
4 HH
5 SHAKER 8th
6 PERCUSSION
7 DRUM FILL
8 BASSLINE
9 SYNTH LEAD
10 CHORUS SYNTH
11 RHODES
12 PAD
13 STRINGS
14 FILTERED MUSIC
15 CLAVINET
16 TRUMPET SOLO
17 LEAD VOCAL
18 VOCAL SPINS
19 VOCAL CHORUS
20 VOCAL ADLIBS
21 FILTER ECHO
22 REV CRASH
23 BELL TREE
24 FX RISER
HH - OFF
CH SYNTH
FILTER
TRUMPET
VERSE 1
VERSE 2
VERSE 3
CHORUS
ADLIBS
REV
RISER
1
2
3
4
5
6
7
8
9
10
11
12
13
14
15
16
17
Mixer
Sample Editor
Piano Roll
Score
Hyper Editor
01 : 00 : 00 : 00.00
127.0000
4/4
/16
No In
No Out

/part six

effects

A good mix can be transformed into a great one with a handful of quality effects.

Effects play two key roles. On the one hand they are used to enhance sounds – refining and shaping them until they sit perfectly in the mix.

Their second role is more creative: warping sounds to make new and original textures; to bring a pump to the track; to make lead lines wider-than-wide; and to conjure singing robots from bog-standard voices.

Using effects sees the producer dabble in the world of physics, getting their hands dirty with phase inversions, wave cycles and all kinds of filters.

But it's important to know what each effect is capable of, and to familiarise yourself with them so you get a feel for the best times to use them.

Effects bring colour to a mix. Use them liberally.

/effects in detail

getting to grips with effects will give you a greater insight into their abilities and make your mixes stronger.

EQ (equalisation)

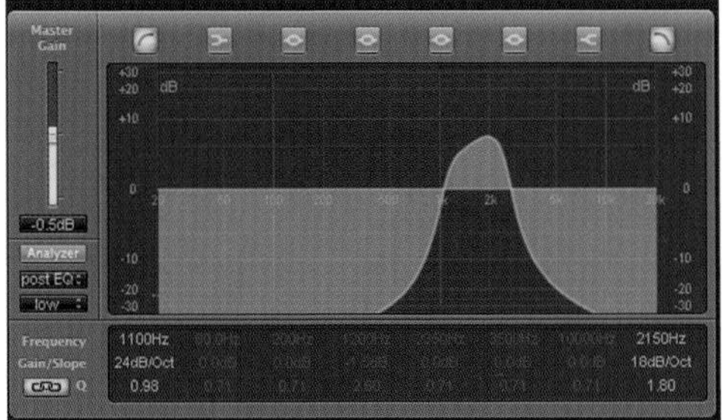

Equalisation, shortened to EQ, is used to cut and boost the volume of specific frequencies in a sound. This is usually to correct the tonal balance so that a certain range of the sound is emphasised or reduced.

A traditional analogue mixing desk typically had a simple three-band EQ on each channel, allowing producers to shape the bass, mid-range and treble independently. We have much more freedom these days, but an EQ's purpose remains the same: to make sounds brighter, duller, thinner, sharper, softer, warmer and so on. Note that EQs can only manipulate frequencies if they already exist in a sound: they can't add new ones or additional overtones.

There are several types of EQ, including **parametric**, **shelving**, **graphic**, **linear phase** and simple **filters**, like low-cut, high-cut, band-cut and band-pass. These all do slightly different jobs.

Filters and shelving EQs are ideal for topping and tailing a sound, rolling off unwanted highs and lows. It's good practice to use these on most channels to preserve headroom and reduce clutter, particularly in the bass area.

Parametric and graphic EQs cut and boost select areas of the frequency spectrum, either in a general way or with pinpoint precision. It can be handy to use a spectrum meter before this kind of EQ to help locate problem frequencies and spot rogue tones that your speakers might not expose.

Most EQ plugins address several bands independently and offer a combination of different EQ shapes.

It is useful to understand the relationship between the key of the track and the frequencies that are being tweaked. Each note occupies a specific frequency (C3 sits at 130.81Hz, for example). You can find a note-to-frequency chart on **page 127**. Knowing these values allows you to boost frequencies that match the key of a track. This can greatly improve the clarity of a mix, and is particularly useful for tuned drums, like kicks and snares.

Controls

Frequency (Hz): Sets the point in the frequency range to cut or boost. One trick to help locate the spot for cutting is to make a significant boost first to help emphasise any problems. Then slowly sweep up and down listening for obvious trouble spots. When you find them reduce the gain to make the cut.

Gain / Cut / Boost: Increases or decreases the volume of the selected frequency range. The overall volume of the signal might need to be adjusted afterwards to compensate.

Width or Q: On a parametric EQ this changes the width of the frequency range being treated. Higher Q values treat wider areas of the sound. This is usually indicated graphically with a bell shape. As a rule of thumb it is better not to make sharp boosts with a narrow Q, but it is fine to make surgical cuts to reduce sibilant and resonant frequencies.

Slope: On filters and shelving EQs this value dictates how steeply the shelf drops away (and hence how abruptly frequencies above or below the selected value drop or rise in the mix). A 24/dB slope means that 24dB worth of cut (or gain) takes place over a single octave. A gentle slope, of 6dB say, sounds more natural, with frequencies falling away – or rising – much more gently.

Compression

Compressors control the dynamic range of a signal, changing the relationship between its loudest and quietest parts and shaping the transients of a sound. It is an essential tool for creating clear and punchy mixes and can be used on many parts, including drums, synths, basslines, vocals and aux busses, as well as full mixes.

A compressor's main function is to reduce the dynamic range of a signal by reducing the volume of its loudest peaks.

Compressors can make a sound seem louder, clearer, punchier, firmer and thicker without increasing its overall volume. There is a common misconception that compressors not only tame peaks, but also boost troughs. This is not so: they only deal with peaks. Any subsequent rise in signal volume is powered by make-up gain after the compressor has done its work.

Compressors are effective when used on groups of sounds, including on bussed groups, to help glue parts together into a cohesive block, as on the drum bus or chorus vocal bus. They are used during recording too, to prevent clipping by keeping peak levels below the point of distortion.

Not all compressors are made equal and some engineers use two or more different compressors in series to achieve a unique blend of compression flavours. A trained ear can tune into different aspects of a sound, such as transients or bass harmonics, in order to bring out the specific qualities of each.

Classic units include the 1176 and LA-2A from Universal Audio, the SSL Bus and the Fairchild 670 tube compressor, all of which are available in original hardware form and software emulations. The Alesis 3060 has been a favourite budget-priced unit, springing to fame when it was used on Stardust's **Music Sound Better With You**.

Controls

Threshold: The level (measured in dB) at which the compressor kicks in. Only sounds that go above the threshold are affected. When dealing with a quiet signal, the threshold will need to be lowered significantly before the compressor starts to have an effect.

Ratio: The difference between input and output levels. With a 4:1 ratio, four is the input level and one the output. This means that for every 4dB of signal above the threshold, only 1dB will be output. As the ratio gets higher, a compressor starts to work as a **limiter**.

Attack: How quickly the compressor responds when the signal breaches the threshold, usually measured in ms (milliseconds). High values will preserve, and accentuate, peaks. Software compressors use a 'look ahead' function to scan for when peaks are coming and can therefore offer 0ms attack time. This kills transients that would spike the mix.

Release: Length of time the compressor takes to return to 0dB worth of reduction after the signal has dropped back below the threshold. A fast release setting can introduce a pumping or breathing sound. A slow setting may leave the volume too low, as the compressor never lets the signal return to 0dB worth of reduction.

Make-up gain: The compression stage lowers the volume of the signal. Consequently the level needs to be boosted again to fit the sound back into the mix. Some compressors offer an 'auto make-up gain' function as default. All offer it manually. Try to ensure that the volume of uncompressed (bypassed) signal is the same as the volume of the compressed signal. This will help you make better decisions when comparing the dry with the effected signal.

Knee: Not essential, so not found on every compressor. The choice is usually between soft and hard knee, with the soft option providing a more gentle, natural quality. If you like your sounds banging stick with hard.

Sidechain input: Can be used to route a control signal into the compressor for pumping and ducking effects. The most common use of the sidechain input is to drive it using a kick drum for the classic pumping house sound. By using an EQ in the signal chain, the compressor can be used for select frequency ducking – as with de-essers.

Some suggested settings

Kick drum smash: 0.1ms attack, 0.6ms release, 4:1 ratio, 2–8dB gain reduction.
Synth lead: 0.3ms attack, auto release, 8:1 ratio, 2–4dB gain reduction.
Vocal: Fast attack, 0.5s release, 2:1–8:1 ratio, 3–9dB gain reduction.
Bassline: 0–15ms attack, 0.5–2s release, 3–12:1 ratio, 3–6dB gain reduction.
Mix bus pump: 0.1–0.3ms attack, 0.2–0.5ms release, 10:1 ratio, 4–8dB gain reduction.
Mix bus glue: 0.1ms attack, auto release, 2:1 ratio, 2–4dB gain reduction.

/pro-tips

parallel and multi-band compression

The technique of mixing a heavily compressed version of a sound in with a more dynamic, less compressed signal, is known as **parallel** or **'New York'-style** compression.

Parallel compression maintains the subtleties of a performance while also stabilising the dynamics, allowing you to produce very solid mixed signals.

Additionally, the attack and release settings of the parallel compressor can be set in a manner that causes the signal to pump in sync with the song's tempo, adding an identifiable character to the sound.

Setting up parallel compression is easy. Simply strap a compressor across the part in question with relatively subtle settings. Then send some of the same signal to a bus and on the bus place a second compressor with more extreme, pumping settings. Blend the two signals together and hey presto, you are able to control the dynamics with the first compressor and add bulk, body and slam with the second.

This technique works on a variety of different sound sources but is most commonly used to add body to a weak vocal line, for effects where the two compressors work against each other – with one attacking as the other is releasing – and on drum groups, where the mix between the two compressors can be anything from 70/30 to 50/50 in more extreme cases.

When processing complex mixes using a standard single-band compressor gain pumping can become a problem. This happens when a kick drum or bassline dominates the mix and the compressor reacts by pulling back the volume of the whole mix. In these cases it is possible to achieve higher compression levels with less audible pumping by splitting the mix into separate zones and processing each one independently using a multi-band compressor.

A **multi-band compressor** splits the mix into two or three bands so that bass, mid and high frequencies get treated with separate compressors, the three signals mixed back together at the output stage. This makes it possible to apply heavier compression to the bass end while leaving the mids and highs sounding more natural. By playing with the crossover points and volume levels of each zone it is possible to completely alter the tonal and transient balance of a mix.

Limiter

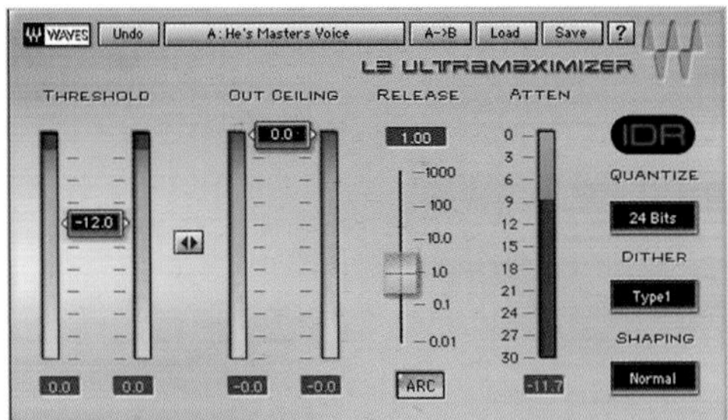

A limiter is a type of compressor that stops the volume of a signal from going above a set level. It has a super-fast attack time that stops transients dead in their tracks, without there being any signal overshoots. The limiter allows the overall volume of a signal to be raised without risk of clipping or distortion. It can be used to make sounds louder in the mix.

A limiter is often used last in the signal chain when mastering a final mix and some producers like to mix with a limiter on the master output to avoid clipping. It is also often used to cut a few dBs on a group bus to help gel the grouped elements together. Slam it hard for a crunchy, pumping Paris-style mix.

Because a limiter is essentially a compressor with a fixed attack time of zero and a fixed ratio of infinite:1, the only controls it offers are threshold and release.

Controls

Threshold: Level in dB at which limiter kicks in. Anything above is flattened to the same level.

Release: How quickly the limiter reacts to incoming changes in volume. As with the release setting on a compressor, there will be a midway point between too fast (the sound will become thick and claustrophobic) and too slow (short transients will disappear).

Noise gate

The noise gate was originally designed to stop the build-up of noise while recording using analogue equipment. It still serves an important role today, keeping unwanted noise in a signal to a minimum.

A gate works by monitoring the volume level of the signal passing through it. When the signal reaches a certain volume the gate opens, allowing sound to flow through. When it drops below the threshold again, the gate closes and the signal is silenced.

The gate has obvious benefits for recorded material – particularly vocals – where low-level studio ambience can easily be blocked from the mix, the gate only opening to allow the vocals through. If a compressor is used on the same channel as the noise gate, the gate always comes before the compressor. This allows the gate to remove any noise before the compressor has a chance to make it louder.

Tip / Gates can be triggered using an external signal through the sidechain input. This has been artfully used to chop up vocals and pads into rhythmic phrases by feeding percussive parts into the sidechain.

Controls

Threshold: The minimum level in dB that the signal must reach before the gate opens.

Reduction: Sets the volume level when the gate is closed. The default position is silent (0dB), but it can be raised to let some of the sound bleed through. This can be useful for creative gating sounds, allowing some of the dry signal to blend with the gated signal for more subtle effects.

AHR envelopes: Attack, hold and release values can be altered in the same way as on a synth, allowing you to shape the volume response each time the gate is triggered.

De-esser

Designed primarily for use on vocals, de-essers help reduce the volume of sibilant frequencies, especially harsh Ss and Ts.

The de-esser works just like a compressor, only instead of altering the volume of the whole signal, it hones in on a very select range of frequencies. When they exceed a given threshold the de-esser dips them.

With vocals, the problem area is usually between 4–10kHz, although this depends on the individual vocalist. You may find sibilant frequencies as low down as 2kHz.

Hi-hats can be fed through a de-esser to help them sit in the mix or even as a creative effect, giving them a lispy feel.

The de-esser also has mastering uses, helping the engineer counterbalance and control any unwanted high frequencies introduced during the high frequency boosting needed prior to cutting vinyl (**see page 133**).

An alternative to de-essing is programming in short volume dips or EQ cuts using automation on the vocal line to dip problem syllables. For greater control still, automate the de-esser to come on only when needed.

Controls

Detection frequency: Central frequency that triggers the ducking process.

Target frequency: Central frequency to be ducked.

Sensitivity: Determines how quickly the de-esser reacts. This control is a kind of equivalent to the release setting on a compressor. You can program it to allow very short syllables through but to catch longer, nasty sibilant frequencies.

Strength: Controls how much ducking will occur, measured in dB. Be careful not to overdo this, as it will leave the vocalist sounding like they are lisping.

Monitor: Switch on to hear only the signal being affected by the de-esser. Can be useful when solo'd for honing in on the correct sibilant frequencies.

Overdrive, distortion and clipping

These are three variations of the same effect, which can be used to rough up a drum sound, inject filth into a bassline or simply put a little warmth into a sterile-sounding digital signal. In the analogue world, these effects boost the volume of the signal so that it clips and folds, producing all kinds of additional harmonics and overtones, and creating a richer tone.

Overdrive processors can be used as insert effects or on a bus. The latter option lets you apply heavier distortion and then mix this distorted signal back into the dry signal at a low volume to beef it up subtly.

Controls

Drive: Increases the intensity of the effect, boosting the volume of the signal before clipping it, introducing distortion and additional harmonic overtones. Use a small amount to warm the signal and add pleasing new harmonics. It can also add natural compression, firming up a flabby signal.

Tone: The classic tone control uses a low-pass filter to back off some of the high frequencies. This helps keep the signal sounding warm, rather than overly bright or tinny. It can be useful to roll off some of the lows to prevent the lower mids from getting too muddy.

Mix / Level: Simple stomp-box style units are either on or off, but some plugins have a mix control to blend the effect. Usually the overall volume gets boosted, so some also have an output level control to help equalise input and output gain.

Amp and speaker simulators

Mainly designed for guitarists, simulators model the sound of re-amping through all kinds of instrument pre-amps and speaker cabinets. Use it to add grit, heaviness or distortion to a sound – particularly on lead lines and subtly on the bass. Guitar Rig and Line 6's Amp Farm both model classic guitar and bass gear, but Speakerphone from Audio-ease goes one better and models everything from broken mobile phones to old gramophone speakers: great for lo-fi effects.

Controls

Amp: Typically has controls for drive, volume and a three-band EQ. Use the drive to increase distortion and compensate for the difference between pre and post-processed signal levels.

Cabinet: A cabinet needs to be mic'd up in order to be recorded, so there are usually a choice of microphone types and placement positions. There is a difference in tone between the front and back of the cabinet, with more mid-range content derived from a mic positioned close to the cab's front.

Bit-crusher

A type of distortion unit that produces its distinctive sound by reducing the sample-rate resolution and bit-rate of a signal in the digital realm. It is often associated with the sound of old-school drum machines, including the LinnDrum and Akai MPC60. Both of these units were digital but used lower sample rates to give them a tough, grainy quality.

At low settings a bit-crusher can make a sound chunkier and thicker, while also warming up the mid range and gradually cutting out the highest frequencies. At more extreme settings, it can massively transform a simple sine wave bass. Drive it hard and reduce the sample rate for all kinds of robotic vowel shapes and talking overtones.

Controls

Bit-rate: Reduces the digital bit-rate of the signal, from 24-bit down to 1-bit. Settings below 8-bit will add background noise. As you hit 2-bit, the sound will begin to break up and splinter – ideal for processing tight, glitchy percussion.

Downsampling / frequency: Reduces the sample frequency below the normal 44.1Khz. As this drops, new overtones begin to creep in and interfere with the original signal before it breaks down completely.

Waveform shape: The shape in which the bits get decimated. Square folding is the most common and results in warmer overtones.

Tape saturation

The sound you get from overloading analogue gear such as valve pre-amps and half-inch multitrack tape machines is known as saturation or soft-clipping.

It is a gentle kind of overdrive that adds warmth and richness to a signal by boosting harmonic overtones. It can re-introduce a little analogue mojo to soft-synths and drums that have been created and treated entirely in the cold digital domain.

insert or aux bus?

There are two ways that effects can be added to an audio channel using a hardware or virtual mixer.

The Logic channel on the right features EQ and compression as insert effects, with some signal also sent to bus 1 (reverb) and bus 2 (delay)

The simplest way is to **insert** the effect onto the audio channel itself. The insert points on a hardware mixer were designed to add effect in-line, so that the whole signal was processed. EQs, compressors, panners and pitch correctors are the most regular insert effects as they are used to process 100% of the signal, rather than a part of it. (In practise most plugins have a mix control so they can still be blended with the original signal, even when used as an insert.)

The second way to add effects is to use an **aux** (auxiliary) **bus** (or buss). The send takes a feed from the audio channel and directs part of the signal to a separate aux channel, or 'bus'. This allows you to send as much of the signal as you wish to be effected and to balance the amount of effected signal – known as the 'return' level.

Some software sequencers – notably Logic – use the terms aux and bus interchangeably. Don't let this confuse you: at the end of the day the aux, bus or aux bus is just another channel in the mixer with a volume fader, insert points and so on that you can send other sounds to.

One advantage of aux sends is that all the channels on the desk can be fed to the same bus, making it possible for many channels to share the same effect. This is ideal for reverbs and ambiences where several sounds need to be positioned in the same acoustic space. It can also help save CPU resources.

It's worth noting that a signal can be sent to the aux bus 'pre or post-fade' (i.e. before or after the channel's volume fader). In pre-fade mode the signal is sent at a set level, regardless of the position of the volume fader. This is ideal when all you want to hear is the effected sound.

Busses can be used in a second powerful way. A number of tracks can be sent to the same bus for treatment. You might, for example, set up a 'drum bus' to which you send kick, snare, hats and so on, across which is strapped a single compressor and EQ, gelling the different elements into a single block. Busses allow you to quickly change the volume of entire sections of a mix, like the vocal chorus block or all musical elements.

Finally, busses can simplify the process of making remix stems, allowing you to bounce down entire sections of a mix.

Reverb

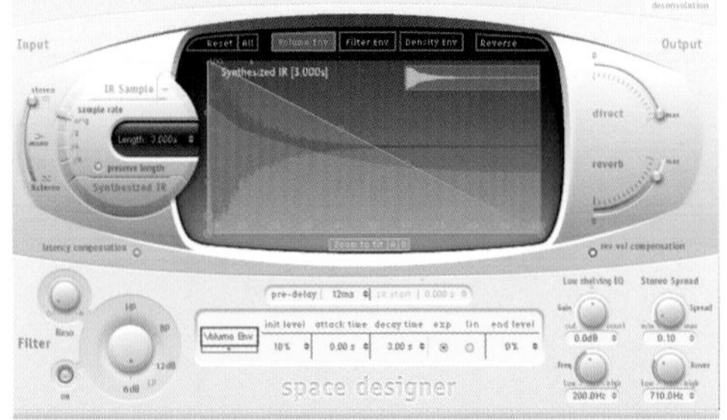

Reverb is used to simulate spaces such as rooms, halls and chambers, adding space and depth to a mix.

Sounds become richer and harmonically brighter when fed through short reverbs. With big, long ones the sound becomes smudged, its contours blurred so that it seems further away in the distance. Reverb can be used to push a sound back in the mix or separate it from others that are left dry.

Many units let you shape early and late reflections separately. EQ, decay and dampening parameters give you additional control.

Traditionally one or two reverbs were placed on different busses, with tracks feeding one or both of them to create mixes that sounded as if they were recorded in the same acoustic space.

The earliest reverbs were designed around springs or metal plates, while in the 80s digital reverbs came of age.

In many genres of house music it's not as important for the reverb to sound realistic as it is to sound interesting. With modern studio computers boasting tonnes of DSP power it is common to use different reverbs on different parts, albeit with one or two common reverbs on the busses.

Most plugin reverbs are designed around the same kind of digital algorithms to generate reflections, but there are also **Impulse Response** or **Convolution** reverbs. These use a snapshot sample of another reverb, such as a hardware unit, as the basis instead. Because they just use a single sample, these units don't offer true emulations of the real thing. That said, they do have a range of controls to maximise their creative uses.

Controls

Time / Length / Decay: How long it takes the sound to fade away after its initial impulse. The general rule is the bigger the space, the longer the tail. Use a long tail on a clap or kick to create a dramatic hit that pushes back into the mix.

Pre-delay: The gap between the dry sound and start of the reverb. A little pre-delay helps separation, suggesting a longer distance from the listening point. It can also be used to set the reverb in time with the track's tempo.

Density: Controls the quantity and thickness of the reflections. High values sound smoother because they are composed of more reflections.

Diffusion: Sets the complexity and distribution of the reflections across the stereo spread and over time.

Early reflections: Some reverbs have a separate control for early reflections. These are the reflections that bounce off the surfaces closest to our ears, so there is almost no delay time, and virtually no tail.

Some suggested settings

Snare: A short room or cabinet setting will bring a live feel to a snare. Longer hall settings are ideal for snares that sit back in the mix: program a reverb tail that leads into the next kick. For the classic gated verb sound use a noise gate after the reverb. See **The gated snare walkthough, page 16**.

Kick: Reverb is best avoided on kicks – it wil muffle the low frequencies, cloud your mix and the kick will lose impact.

Vocals: Anything goes here. Traditionally plates have been used to give lush, often bright, reflections to lead vocals. Hall settings work well too. Tastes have changed though, and a more modern sound – borrowed from hip-hop producers – sees reverb used sparingly, with vocals sitting whisperingly up-front in the mix. This sound is made using early reflections or very short room settings to give the vocal more body but no audible reverb tail. A different effect – useful for more soulful house vocals – is made by setting up a long and short verb on two different busses, with some of the signal sent to each. This gives a mix of body and space. For twisted vocals try any number of crazy effected convolution settings, although if there is any rhythmic content in the tail match the verb to the track bpm. Send backing vocals to the same reverb/s as the lead so that they sit in the same acoustic space, but treat more of their signal so they sit further back in the mix.

Tip / Create strange textures by using your own stereo audio files as convolution impulse responses. Do this by loading a file into the convolution unit. Files work best when they are more than a second long in order to create some kind of trailing texture.

Tip / To stop reverb from interfering with the sound it's effecting, sidechain it to the original signal so that it only increases in volume when the original decays. Sidechaining the reverb channel to the kick can contribute to the classic deep tech-house breathing sound.

Echo and delay

Echo and delay are variations of the same naturally occurring audio effect. With **echo**, the sound is repeated after a given time and continues to repeat over and over until it fades away.

Echo and **delay** effects are used in the mix for many different reasons. Subtle echoes are used to smooth out vocals and lead lines, make a percussion line pick up the pace or add some depth and space to a part alongside or instead of reverb. Very short delay times are used in chorus, flanger and resonator effects and variations of all of these can be produced using delay plugins.

Ping-pong or **stereo** delays pan repeats across the stereo spectrum automatically or have separate delay times on each side for true stereo operation.

Sophisticated echo patterns can be created using **multi-tap delays**. Each of the taps can be set to a different delay time, with echoes cascading into the next until they reach the feedback point and the sequence repeats. Of particular use to house producers is the ability to program taps to a bpm grid, allowing the sound to bounce around the stereo field in a tight, rhythmic sequence. Good multi-tap delays offer independent filtering, pan and volume controls for each tap.

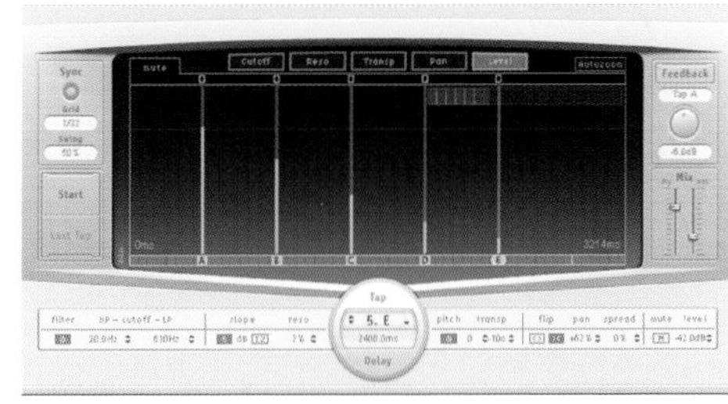

Note that when mixing for club systems the use of stereo or ping-pong delays can be rendered redundant: many systems work in mono and those that operate in stereo are unlikely to give listeners the full effect unless they happen to be standing drinking a gin and tonic directly between the two speakers.

Tape echo plugins give a nod to the tape echo units of the past. These had a distinctive flavour, with repeats getting progressively more distorted and lo-fi as they faded out, while high amounts of feedback result in overload and distortion.

Tape echo plays a significant part in dub music, with machines like the Roland Space Echo synonymous with the vibe. The next best thing is one of the many tape echo plugins, which do a similar job without fear of the tape jamming. The best even replicate the way the pitch wavers up and down.

Grain delay is the newest delay type to hit the market. As its name suggests, it is geared towards experimental textures and glitch effects.

Controls

Time / Groove: Either measured in ms or expressed as a factor of the groove such as 1/8th or 16th notes. Some units offer triplets, dotted notes and swing amounts.

Feedback / Regeneration: The amount of repeats, from one to infinite. Digital delays remain crystal clear, but tape echoes start to distort on higher settings.

EQ / Filter: Most units have built-in EQ or high and low-pass filters to shape the echo. It is good practise to thin out the echoes by rolling off the high and low end of the return. This helps the delays fit comfortably into the wider mix and stops them clashing with the original signal. Automate delay time, EQ and feedback for spectacular dub-outs.

Tip / To get the 'crash-fading-to-infinity' sound popular in funky house circles, insert a compressor after an 1/8th note delay with medium feedback to ensure the delayed signal doesn't fade too soon. For greater control, automate the volume of the delays so that they fade out over a specific period.

Chorus and ensemble

Chorus

When a choir sings, the multiple singers all vary slightly in their timing and pitch, creating a bigger 'chorus' sound. As a plugin effect, chorus does the same thing, making a signal richer and thicker by mixing the original with a version of itself that is very slightly delayed. The delay time – usually somewhere in the region of 20–30ms – is modulated over time by an LFO that causes the effected signal to fluctuate in pitch. The original and effected signals are then mixed together to produce a wider, wobbly sound.

Many analogue synths, including the classic Roland Junos, have built-in chorus effects. Roland was also responsible for the legendary Dimension D Chorus, widely regarded as the most sublime stereo chorus unit ever made. UAD offer a very good plugin version.

Ensemble

Ensemble effects combine several chorus units together. Extra voices can be added, and different LFOs can be used to modulate the pitch or pitches. The overall effect is richer than a single chorus, but less focused. it suits wide pad sounds, big detuned synths and occasionally backing vocals. Some ensembles offer stereo spread by inverting the phase between left and right channels.

Controls

Depth / Intensity: Controls the amount of pitch detuning, but can also affect the stereo spread. If the unit allows you to set the delay time and depth is set to zero, increasing the feedback of the delay will start to produce a resonant frequency. The frequency is linked to the delay time, so use that to tune the resonating frequency to the key of the track.

Rate: The speed of the LFO that controls the pitch. There is a golden ratio based on the law of opposites. A fast rate at low intensity produces a nice shimmering chorus, while a slow rate at high intensity results in thick detuning – ideal for lead synths.

Delay: Sets the amount of time delay between the original and effected signals. Short times are more focused, while longer times make the sound blurry. This control can also be used to offset the left and right sides to increase stereo width.

Mix: Used to blend the dry and chorused versions. Use small values for subtle effects.

Voices: Only applies to ensemble effects, and adds extra voices. Add more for ever thicker sounds.

Flanger

The crazier cousin of chorus, flange was originally produced by running two identical tape recordings of the same sound together, slowing one down fractionally by leaning on the tape. The very short delay between the two produces a harmonic overtone that can sound like a plane taking off as it sweeps up and down the frequency spectrum.

The difference between chorus and flange is twofold: firstly the delay time between the original and effected signal in flange is shorter – somewhere around 1–10ms rather than 20–30 – and flange units also have a feedback control.

In house production, flange works well on crashes, white-noise, reverse builds and other high-frequency audio to create a rush or suction quality without affecting the original pitch. It is widely used, often very subtly, on hi-hat lines to introduce some movement into them.

Controls

Depth / Intensity: Sets the range of the sweep. Try reducing the depth to zero for metallic resonances.

Speed / Rate: How quickly the LFO sweeps through the spectrum. Slow settings create subtle results while fast settings yield a sound more reminiscent of chorus.

Delay: The minimum delay time used on the copy of the input signal. This is usually between 1–10ms.

Feedback / Regeneration: Increases the intensity of the effect by emphasising the resonant frequency. At high settings it produces a comb filtering effect.

Shape / Direction: Advanced digital and plug-in flangers offer all kinds of LFO shapes aside from the archetypal sine wave.

Phase invert: Some flangers enhance the stereo image by inverting the phase of the dry and effected signals. This produces a noticeable change in the quality of the harmonics.

Phaser

Often mistaken for the flanger because of its similar sweeping quality, phasers work by taking part of the original signal, shifting its phase with an all-pass filter and then mixing it back in with the original signal. When these signals are mixed, the frequencies that are out of phase cancel each other out, creating the phaser's unique sound. The LFO controls the way this frequency sweeps up and down.

A phaser's character is shaped by the number of all-pass filter stages. The more stages you have, the more pronounced the effect will be. A two or four stage phaser gives a soft, whooshing effect ideal for pads. By contrast, a 12 stage phaser brings results that are much sharper and more clearly defined, with the resonant frequency far more obvious. This can be useful on hi-hats and fast percussion lines or when you want to introduce harmonic content to a dead sound.

Aside from the number of filter stages, the phaser shares most of the same controls as a flanger.

Pitch shifter

Doing exactly what its name suggests, a pitch shifter moves the pitch of a signal. It can be used to thicken a sound or to completely re-pitch it, transposing a vocal line so that it matches the key of a track.

Very small amounts of pitch shifting can be used instead of chorus effects. Such an approach is often used in conjunction with a few ms of delay.

Controls

Shift: The amount of transposition, usually measured in semitones for large steps, or in cents (100 cents = 1 semitone) for micro-shifting. It is possible to write whole new melody lines by automating this parameter.

Scale: Intelligent pitch shifters can be programmed to harmonise to a set scale. To do so you will need to manually set the harmony note to follow, e.g. minor 3rd or 5th. These kinds of advanced pitch shifters are used to produce instant backing vocals, although better results are often achieved by using specially designed plugins or applications like Celemony's Melodyne.

Type / Algorithm: Some plugins offer different shift types, designed to produce the most realistic results with different types of audio material. Categories can include drum, vocal, monophonic and complex polyphonic. It's always worth experimenting with the wrong type of algorithm to produce unusual new effects.

Formant: Affects the tone of the shift and can alter the perceived gender of a vocal to sound more male or female. Helps make the resulting sound more realistic, especially in the case of voices and acoustic instruments.

A variant of the pitch shifter is the **pitch corrector**, which corrects the tuning of a signal without affecting other aspects of it. Antares' Auto-Tune was the first to offer real-time processing and continues to play a key part in studios today, although both Logic and Cubase offer something similar as standard.

Pitch correctors offer a response time (the faster the value, the quicker out-of-tune passages are pulled into line) and the ability to set a song's key

tonal enhancers

Sometimes you need to generate additional frequencies to make a sound fuller in the mix. You may have a hi-hat that doesn't cut through the top end or a kick that lacks definition in the sub-bass zone. Gentle use of overdrive generates additional harmonics and EQ can help enliven dull frequencies, but there is also a family of plugins that are specifically designed to enhance and generate tones.

Sub bass enhancers

Much like the Octaver guitar pedals of the 60s, sub bass enhancers reinforce the low end of a sound by generating new frequencies. They analyse the pitch of the source material and then add a synthesised sine wave either one or two octaves below. This can be amazingly effective on weedy kick drums, toms or basslines that need extra body. Sub bass enhancers work best on material with a clearly defined pitch to track. They also work on complex tones, but can require a little extra fine-tuning.

Controls

Octave / Ratio: Set how many octaves below the original signal the new signal will be generated.

Centre: On complex material this can help steer the tracking frequency to the optimum range for clearer results.

Bandwidth: Allows fine-tuning of the width of the generated waveform. A narrow band will generate a distinguishable pitch.

Exciter

There are a range of enhancer or exciter plugins designed to sweeten a sound or mix. Their methods are closely guarded secrets, but most are built using the same principle as overdrive units, generating additional frequencies in a signal.

More specifically, exciters create 'even order' harmonics above a user-selectable frequency. They are particularly good at getting sweet breathy sounds from airy vocals and to bring additional bite or gloss to dull sounding guitars (both acoustic and electric) and synth sounds.

Exciters and enhancers are best used sparingly. Overuse can cause ear fatigue.

Ring modulation and frequency shifters

These two effects are related in that they both modulate the pitch of the audio to produce a range of tones from subtle wobbling to discordant clangs. They have been used extensively by sound effects designers to create unusual tones and textures, especially in sci-fi movies for robot voices like those of the Daleks and the Clangers.

The classic Bode frequency shifter takes the incoming signal and shifts it up or down by a fixed number of Hz. Use a very small amount to add a spacey, phaser-like shimmer to a pad or synth line.

A ring modulator works slightly differently by multiplying two signals, one the input signal, the second typically a sine-wave or other simple waveform. The output signal is the sum and difference of the frequencies present in each waveform.

Both effects have a huge amount of creative potential. Try using a ring modulator on a send before it hits the reverb to create weird atonal reflections or on a vocal to create odd backing harmonies.

Controls

Speed / Frequency: Tune the LFO to the key of the track or a harmony note to produce nice melodic overtones. Higher frequencies produce more metallic timbres, while slower speeds introduce a bell-like quality.

Mix: Although traditionally used as an insert effect, it can be useful to have a mix control to adjust the wet/dry balance, especially with a frequency shifter. If none is available use it on a bus instead.

Vocoders

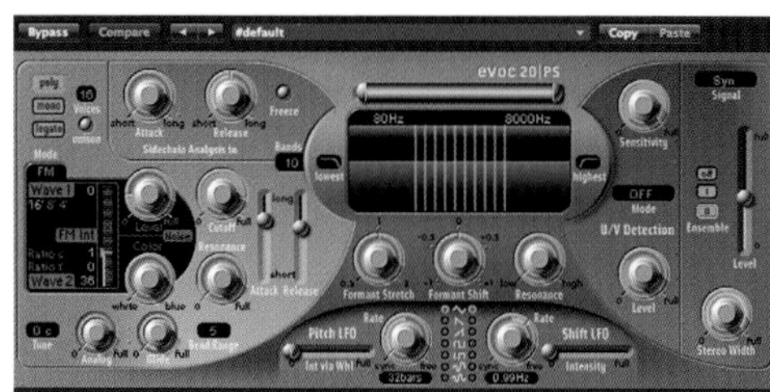

Vocoders were originally invented as a mechanism for encoding speech, but since then have become synonymous with synthetic robot voices and post-Daft Punk style French electronica.

Vocoders use two separate signals to work their magic. The 'modulator' signal is usually a vocal while the 'carrier' signal is typically a rich pad or synth sound. The modulator signal is filtered through a number of band-bass filters so that only the transients are left. These formant bands are modulated onto the carrier bands with the resulting bands mixed together to form the output signal. The result is a combined signal that speaks or sings.

Some vocoders – including Logic's EVOC20 – feature a built in carrier oscillator or even a whole synth unit for the job. The carrier signal provides the tone and texture. It's here you can alter how the vocoder sounds and it's worth experimenting with all kinds of synth sounds. Depending on what you feed in, you can make voices that are silky smooth, melodic and soulful or downright nasty. In order to get the speech sounding good, it's necessary to have a rich sound with clean harmonics. Keep any vocal recordings dry, well articulated and high quality if you want to send them to a vocoder.

Controls

Filter bank: Use the individual bands to cut and boost frequencies to alter the spectral balance. Playing with these can help make the speech clearer and more defined.

Bands: Number of bands in use, usually between one and 32. Lower values will give a tight and robotic sound, while higher values will sound more synthy and sophisticated.

Carrier envelope: Attack and decay parameters can be used to make the speech transients tighter or more relaxed.

Input mode: Determines which signals are used as carrier and modulator. Most vocoders require the modulator to be fed via the sidechain input. If there is no on-board oscillator, you must in a carrier too.

Tip / It's not just vocals that work well with vocoders: rhythmic sounds are ideal too, especially percussion and drum parts. It's also worth experimenting with melodic loops from instruments like guitars, using the vocoder to force them into a new key.

Tip / Although it's tempting to program just one sequence to control the vocoder's pitch, you can get awesome effects by creating stuttering or busy monophonic lines.

Tremolo

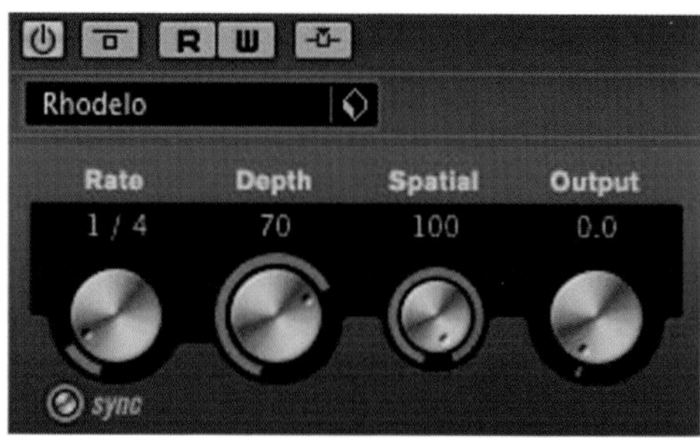

This effect is used a lot by guitarists and keyboard players to lend a vibrating tone to a sound. It does this by using an LFO to modulate the volume of the audio signal. Adjust the LFO shape and depth for different sonic possibilities.

Controls

Speed / Rate: Some tremolos can be locked to the track's bpm. This is ideal for creating choppy rhythmic patterns when depth is set to 100%. Set it to 16ths to create a hi-hat pattern from white noise.

Depth: Sets how much the volume drops. At full strength it should chop to silence.

Phase: Lets you alter the phase between left and right channels. This can boost the stereo impression and help widen a mono signal. At 180 degrees phase you can get the tremolo to behave like an auto-panner.

Auto-panner

Moves the sound between the speakers automatically, creating a sense of movement. Can be used on mono and stereo signals to add extra excitement and space to the mix. As with stereo delays, avoid if your tracks are going to be played in mono.

Controls

Speed: How fast the sound travels between speakers. As the speed gets faster, it becomes more difficult for the ear to keep up with the movement.

Depth: How wide the panning effect is. At 100% the sound should pan hard left and right.

Shape: Auto-panning usually uses an LFO as the modulator so chances are there will be a variety of wave shapes to choose from. A sine wave produces the smoothest results. Ramp waves direct the sound in one direction while a square shape offers hard panning only.

Stereo enhancers

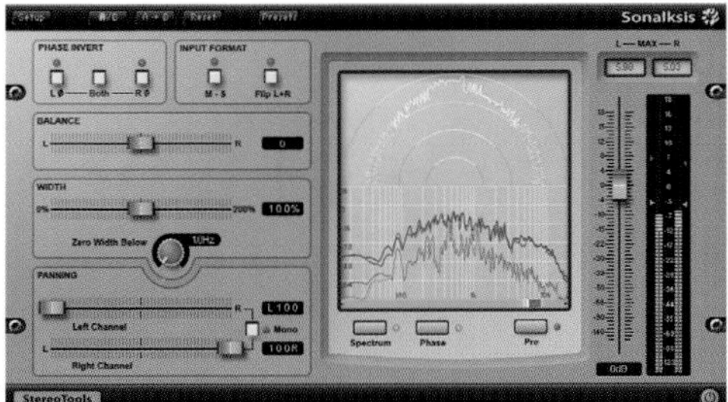

Stereo enhancers come in all shapes and sizes, but the most common is the width enhancer. This uses phase inversion on the audio waveform to reduce the volume of the mono part of the sound in the centre of the mix. As this is lowered the signal in the extreme left and right sides of the stereo spectrum becomes more prominent, creating the impression of a wider sound.

Enhancers work best on pads and other sounds with a decent amount of stereo information, such as reverbs. Since it reduces the volume at the centre of the stereo field, stereo enhancers are not commonly used on the whole mix or any sound that has a strong mono element, such as drums or bass.

Controls

Stereo width: Makes the image wider by reducing the volume in the centre of the mix.

Bass: Helps preserve the bass component by leaving lower frequencies untouched.

Stereo spread

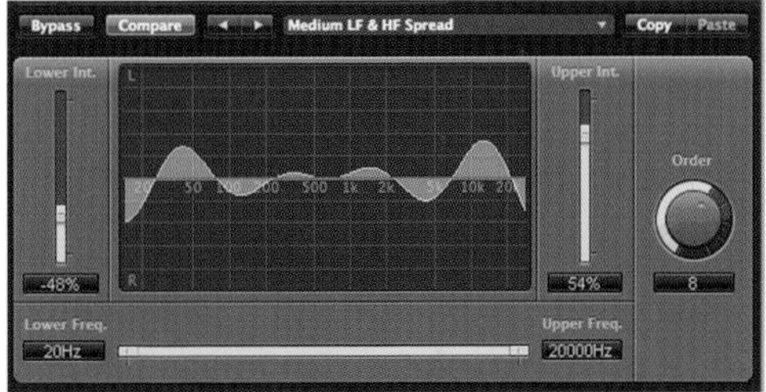

A stereo spreader divides the frequency range into a number of even bands and then pans each band in an opposite direction. This creates a vastly different stereo image to the basic width enhancer and because it doesn't use phase inversion tricks it doesn't collapse and cancel itself out when summed to mono.

Controls

Order / Bands: Number of divisions to be panned. Lower values make the effect sound obvious while higher ones give a more blended and natural result.

Range: Sets the high and low limits in the frequency range of the stereo spread.

Intensity: Width of pan effect. Increase this to make it more noticeable. Some units let you control the bass and treble separately, making them potential candidates for subtle use over a full mix.

effects of the new-school

DSP

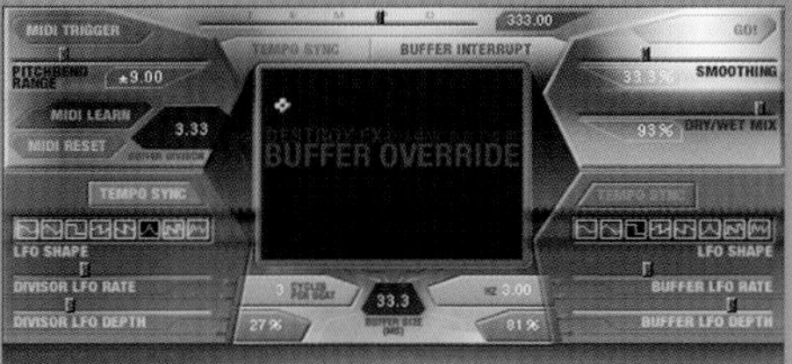

DSP-style effects are lo-fi plugins that recreate the sounds of computers gone wrong. They exploit things such as loop buffers to create a stuttering, glitch-laden frenzy from material they are fed. There are many variations on the theme that expand the scope by adding pitch shifters, echoes and so on into the mix. The must-have in this category is Buffer Override, a classic in donation-ware from DestroyFX.

Repeaters

These new-school effects create instant stuttering, glitchy, chopped up loops from raw audio signals. They use sequence patterns and random chaos generators to trigger various repeating and looping parameters. Use them on drum loops and hi-hat patterns for instant variations that would be hard to program manually. They can be relied upon to generate mad stuttering edits from vocal hooks and are also great for producing fill ideas.

Controls

Repeat time / Length: How long the repeated loop will be, usually set in fractions of a beat e.g. 1/4 note.

Repeat amount: Sets the number of repeats. There may also be a decay parameter to make the repeats fade out in a style similar to an echo effect.

Randomness: Higher amounts increase the chance of the repeater getting triggered and vary the quantity of repeats or change the length. A good tip is to bounce down a bunch of random versions and edit the best bits into final takes.

Multi-effects

These combine several processors together, sometimes in a semi-modular environment, with step sequencers to modulate the parameters. Simple variations, like re-arranging the order of effects, or assigning random modulators, can lead to all kinds of audio trickery that would be all-but impossible to program.

Plugins such as Sugar Bytes' Effectrix and BigSeq2 from Audio Damage are both great for experimental, groove-based processing. As with repeaters, they are ideal for generating original fills.

/part seven

the mix

Whether you mix as you go, or you do it the 'old-school' way, pulling tracks together at the end, it's the mixdown that brings the different elements of a record together and moulds them into a single unified whole.

In many ways it's the toughest job of all – that's why we've left it until last – and you'll be drawing on all that's gone before in this book to help you get it right.

Your aim is a mix in which every element has its own space and where the lead parts are supported by, and can shine against, a solid backing.

The mixing process is as much about listening as it is tweaking: switching between monitors and changing volumes until you know every sound, and what is happening in each part of the frequency spectrum, intimately.

We've included a mammoth 32-part walkthrough to guide you through a typical mix.

Start from there then go your own way...

/mixing

before you start the mixdown, there are a few fundamental concepts to bear in mind.

There are two broad approaches to mixing: **mixing as you go** and **mixing when you've done everything else**. The latter is the traditional way. When the producer had recorded the various instrumental and vocal tracks they would perform the 'mixdown', powering up the effects units and riding the faders to make a final **master mix**.

Nowadays mixing as you go is the norm in dance circles, with producers loading effects and making processing decisions as they arrange the track so that by the time they reach the final mixdown there's often little left do to but make a few last-minute tweaks. Whichever way you do it – and the truth is most producers end up doing a bit of both – the goal is the same.

There are no rules when it comes to mixing. A mix made a year ago will sound different to the same one made today. Effects and processing approaches go in and out of fashion and the best way to keep abreast of the latest techniques is to keep an ear on what's rocking the clubs and the charts.

Mixing is at the same time an art and an exacting science. It is about fitting the different sounds that inhabit a track together into a single unified whole. It is the process where creative ideas meet the tools that let them shine. The golden rule when mixing is: 'if it sounds good, it is good'.

You can make the mixing process easier by choosing sounds that work together from the off. A kick and snare that fit like hand and glove will need little additional work during the mixing stage, while a keyboard and guitar playing in the same frequency zone will require mix fixes to help both find their unique sonic identities. Selecting complementary sounds makes mixing more about creative decisions and less about problem solving – and therefore a more enjoyable process.

(It is worth noting that in 'old-school' mixing, involving multiple recordings of real instruments, producers went to some lengths during tracking (recording) to ensure that sounds would fit together later by using mic techniques and insightful arrangements. Their goal was an end mix in which the parts were already balanced and needed little corrective surgery. Dance producers are in a different boat. For a start it's rare for them to record many real instruments themselves – often their raw building blocks are sourced from records, sample collections or virtual recreations. Secondly, the majority of sounds in a house track are synthetically generated, making EQ tweaks essential. And thirdly, the overuse and abuse of effects and processors is a key part of the dance sound. That all acknowledged, it remains true that picking sounds which work well together not only saves time during mixdown, it generally yields stronger tracks too.)

/pro tips
which tools?

The best tools to use for...

Punch: Compressor, Limiter, Transient designer, Clipper

Depth: Reverb, Delay

Width: Auto-panner, Stereo enhancer, Chorus, Reverb, Delay

Clarity: EQ, High-pass filter, Exciter

Harmonics: Clipper, Overdrive / Distortion, Phaser, Flanger, Reverb, Exciter, Filter

All sounds in their own space

The job of the mix engineer is to balance the relationship between sounds so that all have their own defined space in the track. This is achieved by changing a sound's volume, **frequency content** and **spatial location**. It can be helpful to visualise a mix in 3D, with volume the first dimension, pan position the second, and depth the third. The **volume** of a sound is dictated by the position of the volume fader, EQ and compression; **stereo position** is altered by using the pan control; and **depth** is affected by EQ, volume, reverb and delay. A strong mix is one that works in all three dimensions.

Volume

Big dance records demand big, loud sounds. But not all sounds in a mix can be loud. Good food recipes often have one key ingredient with the 'wow factor'. The others ingredients support it, contributing to the overall taste and texture of the dish. The same is true in dance music: not every part can and should shine. Select the ones you want to stand loud and proud and let the others take their equally important supporting roles. There's a reason we speak about 'lead vocals' and 'lead synths': they lead, their supporters follow.

There's a second reason why not every part in a mix can be loud: an overloud mix will **clip** when **headroom** is depleted. Here's how to visualise headroom. Stand in a room. The space between your head and the ceiling is the headroom. It is wasted space. Until, that is, you want to jump in the air at a moment of excitement. Then you need that headroom. If it wasn't there you could never jump up. Now think about mixing. A signal can sit with an average volume of -6dB (that's with 6dB worth of headroom). If during a particularly loud part the signal hits 0dB then it has run out of headroom and will clip. When using analogue equipment clipping can sound OK – even good – but digital clipping is nasty and should be avoided at all costs.

Fortunately it's easy to avoid. When tracking and mixing in the digital domain aim for several dBs worth of headroom on each channel. This keeps the mix clean, punchy and open, and reduces the chance of overloading the master bus. As a rule it's better to keep track levels down than to slam the channels and then lower the master to keep it out of the red.

Dynamics

In music production the term **dynamics** refers to the difference in volume between the quietest and loudest parts of a signal. Dance music needs to be loud, but still have dynamics, otherwise it loses punch.

Let's think back to headroom briefly. The momentary peaks of volume in a signal are transients. These bring life and energy to a signal, but they also max out headroom and mean you can't turn up a channel without introducing clipping. You can avoid this by running the signal through a compressor or limiter. These catch and calm signal peaks, allowing you to increase the track's volume fader while reducing (or removing) the chance of clipping.

Compression, limiting and distortion/clipping all reduce the dynamic range of a signal. They can be used to add weight and fatness to sounds in a mix. But overuse them and you end up with new problems. Firstly, you can get sounds that just don't punch any more – like that snare with the previously fast attack transient. Secondly, when everything is turned to 11 it's easy to end up with a flat mix that is tiring on the ears and in which everything fights for space. (When you hear producers complain that a mix has had 'the life squeezed out of it' they're talking about overly compressed, undynamic mixes.)

An example of using EQ to help two similar signals sit together. The guitar (left) and synth (right) occupy similar frequency ranges and are fighting for space and identity in the mix. To avoid this a notch is taken out of the guitar at 630Hz, while the same frequency is gently boosted in the synth part. The opposite treatment happens at 1200Hz.

This means there is a happy halfway point between a **dynamic mix**, which punches through the speakers at given points and a **loud mix**, which is loud for its duration.

How do you get the best of both worlds? One way to keep things loud while maintaining dynamics is to use sidechain compression to duck the volume of a channel momentarily. This is used most commonly with the kick and bass to prevent overloading and mud in the low end (see **Sidechaining the bass walkthrough, page 37**). Sidechain compression can also be used on effects channels and vocals.

Bus compression is used to bring elements together as part of a single unit. This is done by routing individual tracks to a bus track and inserting a compressor or limiter across the group, gluing them together. This technique is most commonly used with drums and backing vocals. Busses can also be EQd, allowing you to carve space in backing sounds for lead lines to sit in, for example.

EQ

During the mix EQ is used for three main purposes: to **remove harsh frequencies** in specific sounds; to **change the tone of sounds** that inhabit the same frequency space so that they don't clash (by either boosting or cutting specific frequency regions), and to **place mix elements spatially**.

In the first instance, EQ is a corrective tool that allows you to pinpoint specific problem frequencies in a signal and dial in precise cuts. Like a laser-surgeon, you can get in close and cut or boost frequencies. Note that any changes you make to a part's EQ will

before you start...

Take some time out to think about the intention of the track. Is there a particular vibe or feeling that you want to bring out? Are you after a mix that is clean, dirty, smooth or aggressive? What key things should be happening at different points in the track? Which sounds are the focus and which are the supporting elements?

Next up, do some mix housekeeping. Arrange the order of tracks so you know where everything is. You might arrange them in order of when elements enter the mix, or by grouping drums, bass, leads, FX and so on. Using different colours also helps. This work will reduce the amount of time you spend jumping between channels searching for specific tracks when you're in the heat of the mix.

While you're doing this spend some time labelling tracks. It's a bore but it's another time saver. Delete or move any unused parts out of the way and switch off or remove plugins that are no longer in use.

Listen through the mix for clicks and pops, and for any parts that aren't properly in sync. Check the start points of sloppy audio files to ensure they line up with the beat. Midi parts might also need to be quantised to swing better, or nudged in time to compensate for latency. If any parts are running live from hardware record them into the DAW so that they are permanently part of the project and can be easily re-called for remixing.

have an effect on its volume too, so use the volume fader and EQ in tandem. Also note that changing a part's EQ content will affect its relation to other parts, and so will have a wider impact on the whole mix.

Use EQ to remove frequencies from a signal that aren't needed. Every sound has a fundamental frequency and most have harmonics above. Some parts of a sound may be unnecessary in the context of the mix. Use EQ to roll these away, cutting the low frequencies of a guitar or synth, for example, to open space for the bass. In fact it's good practise to roll off the lows on all tracks other than the kick and bass to open up the bottom end. The same process can be used at the high-end too to maintain airy space for hats, vocals and lead synths.

The second use of EQ comes into its own during the mixing process. Some sounds occupy a narrow band of frequencies, while others – the majority – are much fuller, taking up a large part of the spectrum. The result of this is that sounds often 'overlap' in the mix. A piano, for example, shares frequencies with the guitar, while the human voice shares frequencies with synths, guitar, keys and more (see **What goes where?, right**).

Sounds that overlap fight for space and if too many rub against each other you end up with a mix that is boomy, muddy or phasey, depending on the frequency range that is overloaded (see **Diagram 1, right**). This kind of mix is tiring and confusing to listen to, with no elements given the space to shine. Imagine you are painting a picture. If you use all the colours available across the whole canvas the picture will end up a muddy brown. Better to use yellows in one area, greens in another, reds elsewhere. So is the same when balancing frequencies.

/pro tips
what goes where?

Kick: Lows at 20–120Hz. Weight and warmth at 60–80Hz. Knock/thump at 120–800Hz. Edge and bite at 2–4kHz. High-end crack at 3–8kHz. 808 peaks at 60Hz, 909 at 90–100Hz.

Snare: Balls at 120–250Hz. Body at 200–400Hz. Crack at 1kHz upwards. Snap at 8–10kHz. If kick is a high, snappy kind, roll off snare lows. Can grate at 1kHz.

Hats: Body at 1–3kHz. Sparkle at 8–11kHz. Sibilance at 5–6kHz. EQ hats to fit wider rhythm. With synthetic hats, roll off lows from 400Hz.

Percussion: Can sit anywhere, depending on sound and purpose. Congas have body at 150–200Hz and slap at 5kHz. Tambourines have sparkle above 5kHz,

Bass: Critical power at 50–120Hz. Small changes here will have big impacts and can make the bass sound fat or thin. Additional harmonics up to 8kHz. Refer to Note to frequency chart, page 127, for specific frequencies.

Sub bass: 16–60Hz. Bear in mind club speakers rarely duplicate below 30Hz. Too much sub bass will eat headroom.

Bass guitar: Bottom at 50–80Hz. Fat and chunky at 260Hz. Growl at 600–700Hz. Finger noise 700–800Hz. Snap at 2.5kHz.

Lead synth: Can be hot anywhere from 60Hz–8kHz. Must work alongside bass. If dominant bass, cut lows. If lead synth is also bassline, add sub.

Pads: Body and warmth at 200–400Hz. Presence from 1.2kHz. Roll off lows / highs.

Electric guitar: Body at 250–450Hz. Presence at 1.3–2.8kHz. Clarity at 3kHz. Muddy below 80Hz. Roll off lows.

Keys: Fullness as far down as 80Hz. Presence at 2.5–4kHz. Roll off lows.

Vocal: Body at 200–700Hz. Nasal at 1kHz. Presence at 4–6kHz. Male vocal range from 100Hz–8kHz. Female from 250Hz–9kHz. Air at 11–12kHz+. Roll off below 80Hz. Boosting at 5–10kHz risks increasing sibilance.

When you get sounds that overlap EQ can be used to shape both so that they don't interfere, and so that their dominant frequencies don't clash. Mixing in this way is known as spectral mixing. The dual EQ image on **page 123** shows a situation where two parts that share similar frequencies are treated to give both their own space. The technique involves cutting a notch in one part and then gently boosting the second in the same area (when deciding the frequency to boost it will generally be where the sound in question has its core energy).

Finally, EQ can be used to position sounds spatially too. Sound sources that are further away have fewer high frequencies than sources closer to our ears. So to push a part back in the mix, just roll off some of its high-end. This can be useful with vocals, where high-end is rolled off harmonies so that they are located behind the lead.

Diagram 1: Sound can be described in many ways. Bass can be fat or wimpy, mids can be muddy or hollow and highs can be airy or dull. This diagram shows the frequency spectrum from 22kHz at the top (the highest frequencies humans can hear) to 20Hz at the bottom (the low limit for digital recording). The spectrum is split into five zones: highs, upper mids, lower mids, bass and sub bass, with various adjectives that are commonly used to describe the sound in each zone. 'Balanced' indicates the kind of sound you're aiming for. When a mix is unbalanced you end up with undesirable characteristics in specific or all zones. Use the chart as a problem solver to identify what is wrong with a mix and then take action to bring it back into balance. If the high end is too dull, for example, boost individual track levels and/or EQ in the 6–22kHz area to make it more airy and open.

When making EQ decisions it can be helpful to picture the tracks in your mix against a linear EQ line that goes from 20Hz to 22kHz. The aim of a solid mix is to fill the entire line. Each instrument, drum and vocal part should cover a different span of frequencies and peak at a different position. No single sound should overlap too much with its neighbours and no peaks should rise at the same place. Where parts do overlap use panning and spatial positioning to ease them apart.

Panning and stereo imagery
The pan control balances the volume of sound between the left and right speakers. Panning enables you to move sounds and spread them across the sound stage to create a sense of width.

	<< LESS	// BALANCED //	MORE >>
HIGH END			
22_khtz			
15_khtz	// DULL //	// SPARKLE // AIR // OPEN //	// SIZZLE // GLASSY // HISSY //
6_khtz	// MELLOW // LO-FI //	// CLARITY // BRILLIANCE // SHEEN //	// CRISPY // PIERCING //
UPPER MID RANGE			
3_khtz	// FLAT // MUTED // VAGUE //	// PRESENCE // ARTICULATE //	// SHARP // TINNY //
1.5_khtz	// SMOOTH // SOFT //	// DEFINITION // BITE //	// FORWARD // KLANGY //
MID RANGE			
800_htz	// HOLLOW //	// WARMTH // CRUNCHY //	// KNOCK // HONKEY//
400_htz	// THIN // BOXY //	// BODY // WOODEN //	// THICK // MUDDY //
BASS			
200_htz	// WIMPY //	// WARM // ROUND //	// MUFFLED//
100_htz	// LIGHT //	// FULL // SOLID //	// HEAVY //
SUB BASS			
50_htz	// LO FI //	// SUB // WEIGHT // THUMP	// RUMBLE // BOOMY //
20_htz		// CHEST // PRESSURE //	

Our ears are better able to distinguish the stereo placement of mid and high frequencies than they are bass ones. Keep the low frequencies central to retain punch and weight and prevent the mix from sounding hollow and airy.

The weight of sounds needs to be balanced evenly between left and right or a mix will start to sound lop-sided and disjointed. This is another reason to keep the most important elements – kick, snare, bass and lead vocal – anchored in the centre.

Short delays under a few ms can be used to offset the left and right channel, turning a mono sound into a stereo one. This works especially well on mid to high-range material to give it more character in the mix.

Depth and space

Using space is the third way to separate sounds in a mix.

In electronic music, depth and acoustic space is an illusion created using reverbs, delays and EQ. Short reverbs and delays are used to make sounds more lively and less flat, giving the impression that they are close to us, while longer reverbs and delays make sounds seem further away.

A classic trick is to load one short and one longer reverb onto different aux busses so that all tracks can be treated using either or both. Sending different sounds to the same unit helps pull them together and give the mix a unified sound. Where two tracks have similar timbres (like lead and harmony vocals) you can push one behind another in the mix by sending more of its signal to the same reverb.

Many producers – particularly in the minimal scene – use automation to move sounds between the front and back to create contrast, motion and excitement, changing the amount of a verb's wet signal as they go.

To get an accurate mix it is common to use two sets of monitors: one that highlights the mids and highs and a second to reveal what's happening in the bass and sub bass frequencies.

When using reverb and delays remember to filter the return signal to roll off highs and lows. This helps maintain clarity by not muddying either end of the spectrum unnecessarily.

Mix automation

Dance mixes are not static. Synth sounds evolve over time, vocal lines need to be ridden, filters turn on and off, and effects sends open and close. Automation lets you change the levels in a mix over the course of a track and is as important a part of the arrangement as anything else.

Automation can be useful for creative purposes as well as problem solving. It brings elements in and out of focus over time, keeping the listener engaged through the five or so minutes of a track.

Monitoring

To guarantee the best possible mix it is essential to be able to hear and judge all the sounds on a decent set of studio speakers, or monitors. Get the monitoring right and your mix will translate over to a full-frequency club system in all its glory. If the monitoring setup and studio acoustics are flawed, however, you will notice frequencies sticking out in all the wrong places when your tracks are played on other systems.

It is common practice to use two sets of speakers when mixing, regularly switching between medium monitors (5–6 inch drivers) to judge the mid and high range frequencies, and large (8–12 inch drivers) to judge the kick, bass and sub. The aim is to create a mix that works on both sets of speakers, and which will therefore translate well onto other systems.

Monitors need to be positioned correctly. Usually this is in a triangle formation with the speakers an equal distance apart and the mix engineer's head located at the triangle's third tip. The speakers should be set back a bit and aimed towards the listener. The optimum measurements here will depend on the monitors in question. Ask if you're unsure.

Monitoring all day at punishing volume levels leads to ear fatigue, and possibly tinnitus in the long-term too. Moderate volume levels are best for long sessions as your ears will continue to be sensitive to the entire frequency range. Regularly switch to low levels too: distortion, in particular, is often masked at higher listening volumes.

It's not just the speakers you use that impact on how you hear the mix. Problems with a studio room's acoustics will lead to bad judgements during mixdown. Reflections, echoes, fluttering and standing waves all colour the sound as it travels from the speakers to your ears and can leave you monitoring a highly coloured mix.

For this reason pro studios are treated with acoustic tiles, bass traps and panelling to make them sound more neutral and tight. A good room helps you make accurate judgements faster, which means higher quality and more mixes in the long run. In Sound on Sound magazine's long-running regular 'Studio SOS' column, trouble-shooters

/pro tips

the master bus

Some producers start the mix with a compressor or limiter on the master bus while others prefer to strap one on at the end or alternatively leave full-mix processing to the mastering stage.

Using a master bus compressor allows you to push the volume of all channels a little higher without risking clipping. It glues parts together and makes everything seem a little louder.

The classic choice for this treatment is the SSL Buss Compressor, which can sound natural when reducing as much as 5dBs worth of gain. Any more than that and the compression starts to sound aggressive – which can be useful for pumping electro and nu-rave tracks.

visit readers' studios to give insights into their mixes. In all but a handful of cases problems in mixes are explained by readers' poor listening environments.

Advanced mixing

Tip / Get direction from other producers' records. If you know a track translates will to a big club system use it as a reference when mixing. This can help you decide how loud the kick and bass should be and is useful as an A/B reference point throughout the mix.

Tip / Listen to the track at a range of different volumes, from bangin' loud to very soft. Many of the pros whack up the volume for a few minutes every hour to see how the track sounds loud. Different parts become clearer at different volumes.

Tip / Get the headphones out once in a while for a different perspective. Note that although headphones can reveal imperfections that you might never hear using monitors, they are also notoriously unreliable for monitoring so are best used sparingly.

Tip / Mix lacking warmth? Cut some highs and add gentle overdrive on parts that inhabit the low-mids. You're not looking for anything noticeable – just some additional harmonics.

Tip / When EQing always favour cuts over boosts. Cuts sound more natural and boosts can, when stacked, grate.

Tip / Keep EQ cuts and boosts small. Changes as small as .05dB will sound significant in a well balanced mix.

Tip / If a part is sitting low in the mix and not adding much to the track, try muting it. Every part eats all-important headroom.

Tip / When you're nearing the end of a mix, go and stand outside the studio door and listen to it. This can reveal level imbalances that weren't obvious when sat in front of the monitors.

Tip / Sleep on a mix, coming back to it with fresh airs the following morning to do any final tweaks. Rested ears make better decisions.

Tip / Test the track in mono. This can reveal phase problems and gives an indication of how well the mix will translate onto mono radio stations and club systems.

note to frequency chart

Every note on the keyboard has its own frequency. Knowing a note's frequency allows you to make informed decisions about how low to tune a bass and where to make EQ cuts and boosts (gentle EQ boosts on a note's fundamental frequency can sound great, particularly with bass sounds). Use this chart as a basis for decisions. C4 is middle C.

NOTE	FREQ (Hz)	NOTE	FREQ (Hz)	NOTE	FREQ (Hz)
C0	16.35	G2	98.00	D5	587.33
C#0/Db0	17.32	G#2/Ab2	103.83	D#5/Eb5	622.25
D0	18.35	A2	110.00	E5	659.26
D#0/Eb0	19.45	A#2/Bb2	116.54	F5	698.46
E0	20.60	B2	123.47	F#5/Gb5	739.99
F0	21.83	C3	130.81	G5	783.99
F#0/Gb0	23.12	C#3/Db3	138.59	G#5/Ab5	830.61
G0	24.50	D3	146.83	A5	880.00
G#0/Ab0	25.96	D#3/Eb3	155.56	A#5/Bb5	932.33
A0	27.50	E3	164.81	B5	987.77
A#0/Bb0	29.14	F3	174.61	C6	1046.50
B0	30.87	F#3/Gb3	185.00	C#6/Db6	1108.73
C1	32.70	G3	196.00	D6	1174.66
C#1/Db1	34.65	G#3/Ab3	207.65	D#6/Eb6	1244.51
D1	36.71	A3	220.00	E6	1318.51
D#1/Eb1	38.89	A#3/Bb3	233.08	F6	1396.91
E1	41.20	B3	246.94	F#6/Gb6	1479.98
F1	43.65	C4	261.63	G6	1567.98
F#1/Gb1	46.25	C#4/Db4	277.18	G#6/Ab6	1661.22
G1	49.00	D4	293.66	A6	1760.00
G#1/Ab1	51.91	D#4/Eb4	311.13	A#6/Bb6	1864.66
A1	55.00	E4	329.63	B6	1975.53
A#1/Bb1	58.27	F4	349.23	C7	2093.00
B1	61.74	F#4/Gb4	369.99	C#7/Db7	2217.46
C2	65.41	G4	392.00	D7	2349.32
C#2/Db2	69.30	G#4/Ab4	415.30	D#7/Eb7	2489.02
D2	73.42	A4	440.00	E7	2637.02
D#2/Eb2	77.78	A#4/Bb4	466.16	F7	2793.83
E2	82.41	B4	493.88	F#7/Gb7	2959.96
F2	87.31	C5	523.25	G7	3135.96
F#2/Gb2	92.50	C#5/Db5	554.37	G#7/Ab7	3322.44

/walkthrough
mixing a track in 32 parts

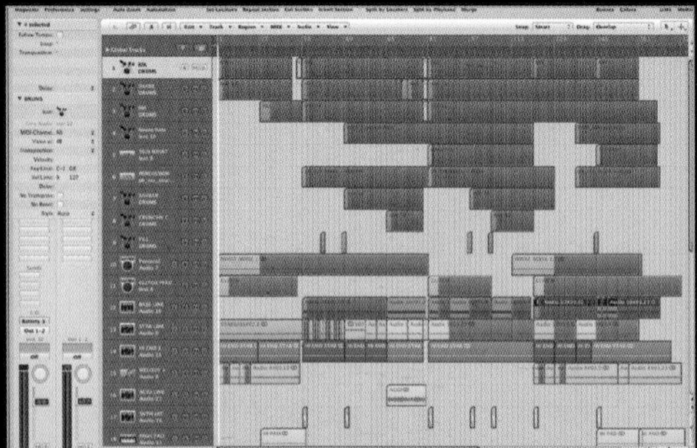

1 Get the arrange page in order, with parts coloured and instruments grouped, by following the steps outlined in 'Before you start', page 123. If you have them switch on your big set of studio speakers so that you can hear the whole spectrum accurately. Set them at a moderate volume level so you don't tire your ears within the first 30 minutes of mixing.

2 Start with the kick drum, the track anchor. Place loop points around a section that plays the bassline and most drum elements. Set the master output fader to 0dB (or unity gain) and solo the kick. It's important to leave plenty of headroom for the other elements, so set the fader on the kick so the volume peaks between -12dB and -9dB.

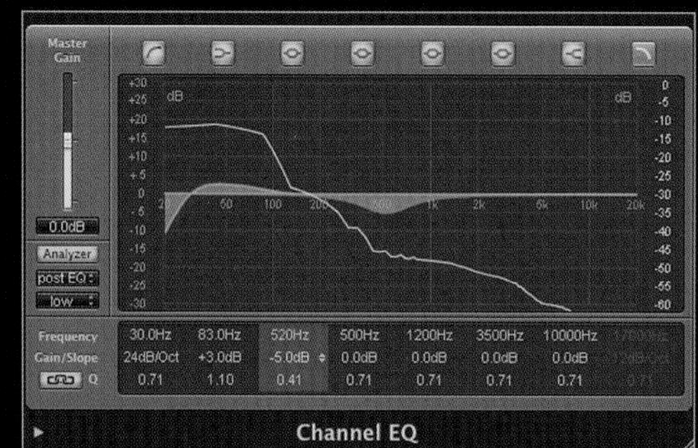

3 Treat the kick using EQ. This kick has too much ultra low-end and knocks too hard. A low-cut EQ rolls off the subs at 30Hz. The fundamental frequency is boosted at 70–80Hz and the knock tamed in the 400–800Hz area. Solo the kick and then play it with the other drums and bass to show you how any changes are impacting on the mix.

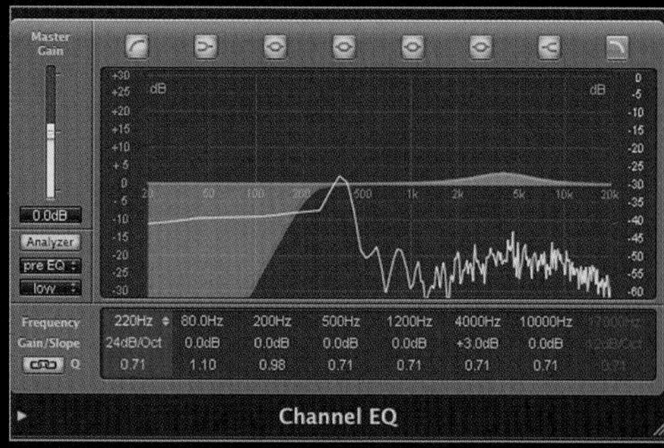

4 Start adding the snare/s, clap/s and hi-hat/s. This will fill out the mid and high frequencies, balancing the weight of the kick. Use a low-cut filter to roll off any unneeded low end from the snares and claps to stop them overlapping with the kick. Don't shave off too much unless you are aiming for a thin rhythm section.

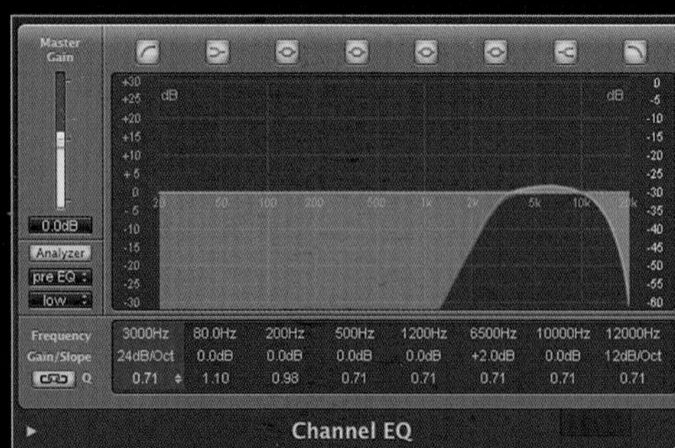

5 A typical house track contains two or more hi-hats. Most hi-hat EQ adjustments take place in the wide 1kHz–8kHz range, with some air above. Use a spectrum meter to check for rogue frequencies and sweep up with a high-pass filter to clean out low-end mud. You can often be fairly severe when rolling away hi-hat lows.

6 Give the different hi-hats their own space in the mix by using panning and stereo width plugins. Leave one steady hi-hat in the centre and use a plugin such as sample delay to create width and separation on a second one. A delay of up to a couple of milliseconds on one side will separate it sufficiently.

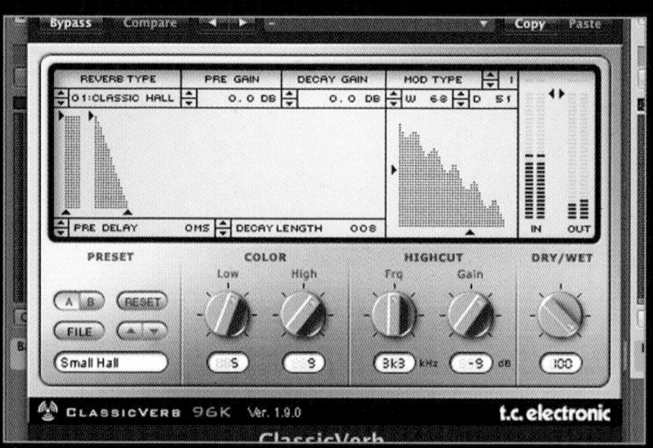

7 Give the drums more life by adding a reverb on an aux bus and routing each drum track, except the kick, to it individually. This helps bring them together in one space, adding depth and harmonics. Use a short decay time (under 1s) set to 100% wet. Check each sound in isolation and again in the context of the mix.

8 Group the drum sounds together by routing them to a single bus channel. This brings them all under one volume fader. Glue them into a solid unit using bus compression. Use a 2:1 ratio with fast attack and medium release. Lower the threshold until you see about 2–4dBs of gain reduction. This will get the drum track pumping nicely.

9 If the compressor has a wet/dry mix control you can introduce parallel compression (see page 111). This lets you smash the drums hard and mix the processed sound back in with the original dynamic signal. Use a high ratio of around 10:1 with minimum attack and fast to medium release. You can reduce as much as 25–30dB worth of gain.

10 It's time to bring the bass into the mix. Solo the main bassline and play it alongside the drum track. Slowly increase its volume so that drums and bass are in balance. If the rhythm track is overly busy solo the kick and bass together to start off with: sometimes it's easier to get the balance between these right first.

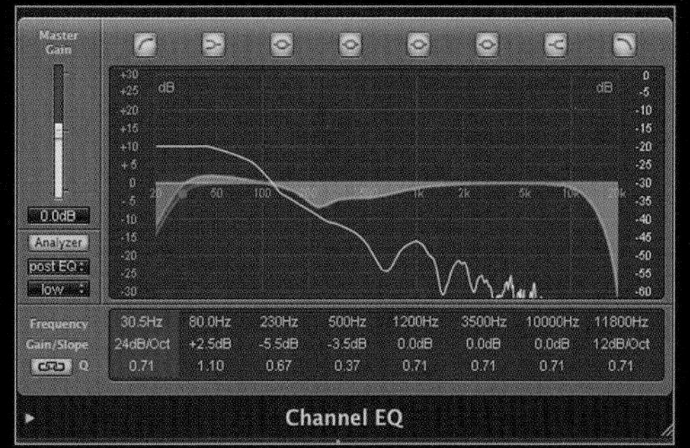

11 To improve the clarity of both kick and bass use EQ to clear overlapping frequencies. Insert a low-cut filter on the bass and sweep up from 20Hz. Roll off at around 40–50Hz. Warmer bass frequencies are located between 200–400Hz. Thickness is at 60–150Hz. When the bass sits tight you might need to tweak the kick EQ too.

12 Use sidechain compression on the bass to make it pump and bounce or to subtly lift it off the kick and make sonic room for both. If you haven't already done so, set up a specific sidechain track using a new kick drum and a steady four-on-the-floor Midi pattern to trigger it. See Sidechaining the bass walkthrough, page 37.

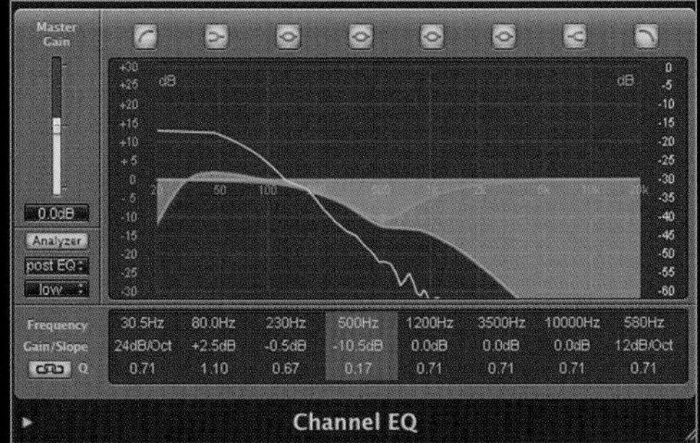

17 Percussion parts such as electronic blips, bongos and glitch noises can be panned across the stereo spectrum. Find two loops that work together rhythmically and pan them in opposite directions. Don't push them too far apart – complementary sounds should not lose stereo contact. Send both to the same bussed reverb.

18 If the snare/s, clap/s, kick or hi-hats need help cutting through the mix and you're reluctant to compress them then use a transient designer such as Logic's Enveloper. Increase the attack for more definition and increase release to add sustain and body. Use envelope plugins with caution and bypass regularly to check the effect on the mix.

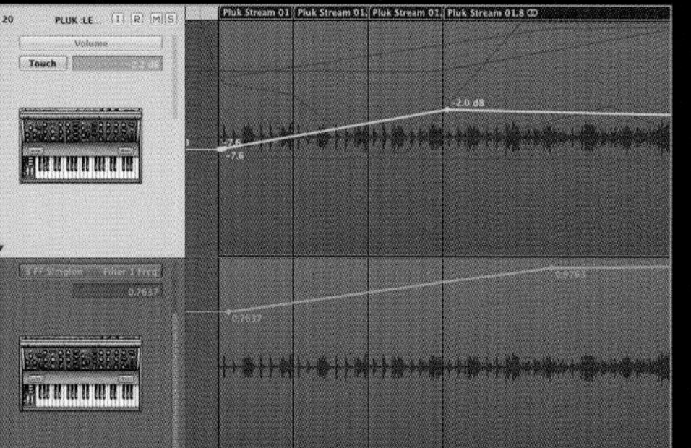

19 With drums, percussion and bass in place it's time to introduce the lead melody lines. Some leads are static. Others evolve during the track, changing in tone and timbre. These tracks will need to be automated so that their place in the mix doesn't change. Ride volumes manually, recording automation as you go and then fine-tuning.

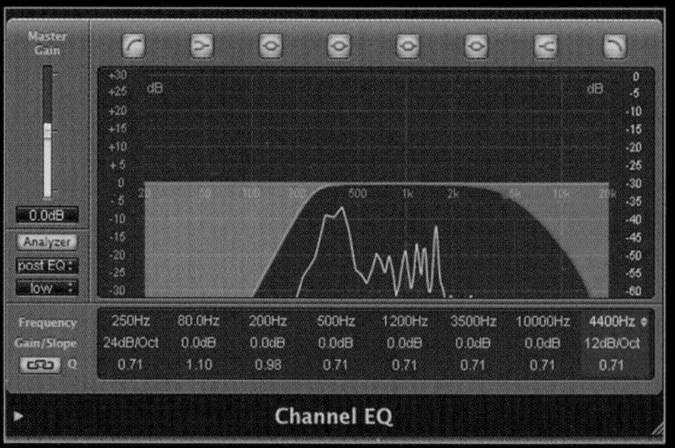

20 If the lead is made up of different layers they will need to be EQd to sit together. Reduce overlaps. Specifically beware of the 200–800Hz mid range (easily gets muddy) and the highs (too much content here is searing and irritating). Try reducing highs on sounds with warmer low ends: EQ cuts are better than boosts.

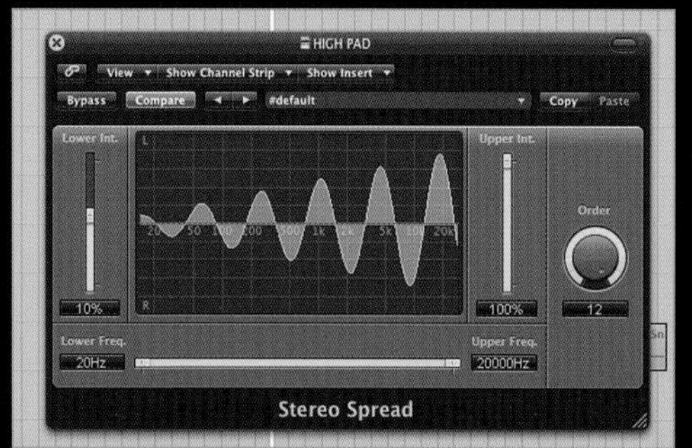

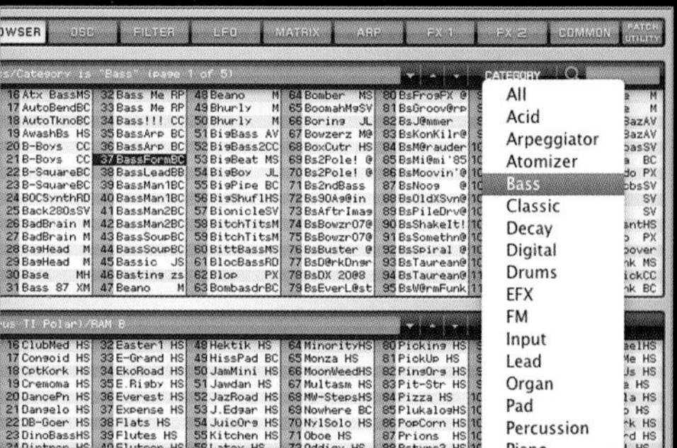

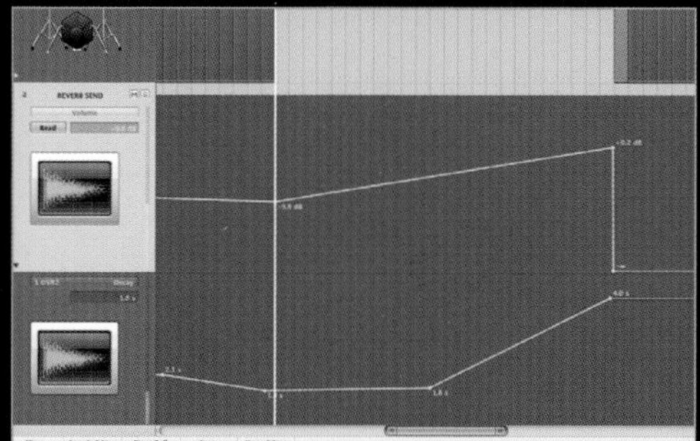

25 If breakdown effects use big reverbs and delays the tails will carry over into the drop. This quickly gets messy. There are several ways of silencing this spill. The easiest is to automate the volume of the FX channels down to 0 at the moment of the drop. Another way is to mute the FX channel as the track kicks back in.

26 If a sound is processed using a non-bpm-synced flanger or phaser then the sweep is likely to catch at different points – some better than others. To keep the sweeping consistent, bounce down the sound and then cut it up in the arrange page to get the best parts. Bouncing effects in this way helps you maximise control over them.

27 Place sound effects that need individual processing on different tracks. Effects should be levelled so that they augment the track but don't draw too much attention to themselves. Most of the time you only need to hear a small frequency range of an effect so be brutal with EQ. Remove as many sub, bass and lower-mid frequencies as possible.

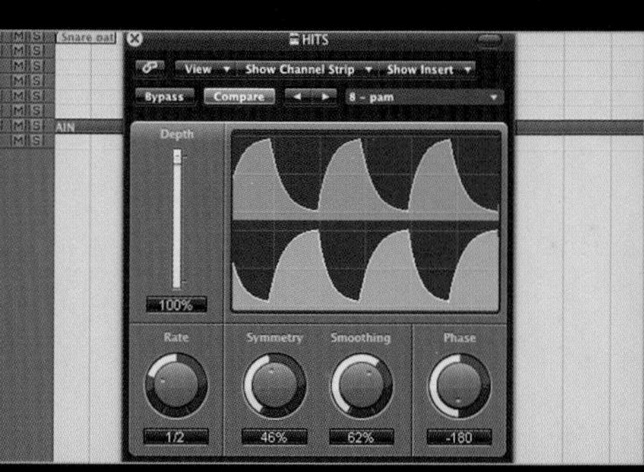

28 Use a tremolo or auto-panner on white noise sweeps and hits with long trailing echoes. Effects sound great panning from speaker to speaker because the ears can pick out the stereo movement of high frequency content easily. Use a sine wave LFO for smooth movement and a square wave for hard panning effects.

29 There are several points in the track where the bass frequencies of the kick drum are killed before a drop. For this classic 'DJ console' vibe use a high-pass filter with a cutoff point of 120Hz and switch it on and off by automating the bypass parameter. Take it one stage further by sweeping the cutoff up and down as well.

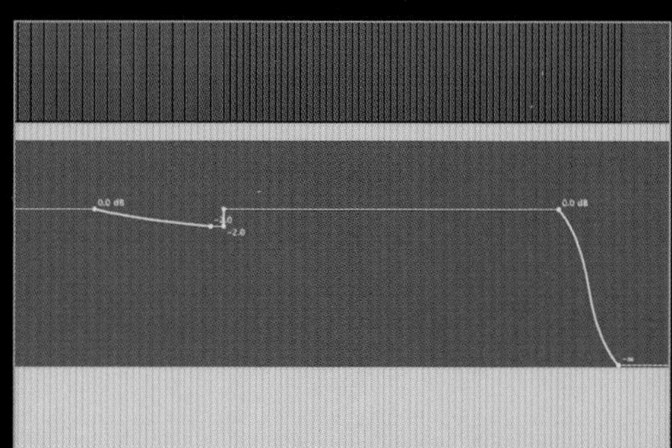

30 The volume level of the master output can be automated for several reasons. This could be to apply a simple fade out at the end of the track, or to gradually lower the volume during the breakdown before raising it back up for the drop so that it kicks in with more impact. See The pre-drop fade walkthrough, page 135.

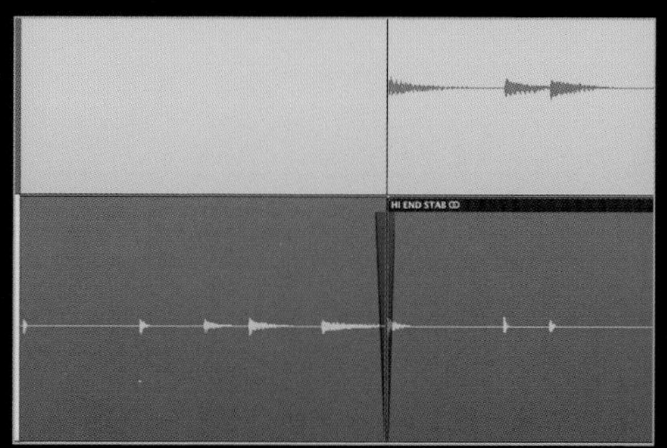

31 Before performing the final bounce have one last close listen through both sets of speakers and headphones to check for glitches, clicks and pops on audio files. Add fade ins/outs and cross fades to regions where necessary.

32 Bounce the mix down as a 24-bit stereo Aiff or Wav file. Label it 'unmastered'. Some producers like to do a quick self-mastering job so they can play the track out straight away. If so, add a limiter to the stereo master and aim for 2–4dBs of reduction. Now it's time to check the mix on different sound systems to see how it stacks up.

/mastering

often seen as a dark art at the end of the mixing process, mastering takes your mix and gives it a final polish.

To get a mix to properly shake the dance-floor, it will need to be mastered. The idea behind this last stage of the mixing process is to take the mix, fine-tune the EQ to get the best spectral balance, then use dynamic processers to make it louder, clearer, punchier and tighter than the original. It is crucial to do a proper mastering job before playing a track out on a club sound system or it won't match the power of mastered tunes and will sound weak in comparison.

Mastering plays a key role in album projects too. It helps continuity by matching relative volume levels between tracks. Without it you'd be reaching for the volume control with each new song. Mastering can also add gloss and a unique sonic character to an album.

The mastering chain

The essential processors in a mastering chain are EQ, compressor and limiter. The **EQ** comes first and is used to shape the overall balance of the frequencies. It is common practice to use a low-cut filter to taper off the bass. This maximises headroom and gives the master engineer space to make the track louder. A similar treatment occurs at the other end, with a high-cut / shelving band to round off any brittleness. Optimising the high-end also makes a track sound warmer. A shelving or parametric EQ is used to boost or cut the main bass region, followed by extra parametric bands for mid and high frequencies. In general it is best to use medium to wide Q settings for the parametric bands, especially when boosting. Narrow bands should only be used for cutting specific problem frequencies. Be careful not to make drastic cuts in the mid-range, as this can result in an unnaturally hollow sound.

If a mix already sounds good the mastering engineer will only need to make small EQ adjustments – no more than a couple of dBs here and there to reduce a honky frequency or add a little more presence.

Next in line is the **compressor**. Some engineers use several compressors in series, with each one doing a slightly different job – introducing different flavours to the mix. As with all processing units, each compressor has its individual strengths and weaknesses.

Although not particularly common, sometimes a very small amount of hall **reverb** will be applied to add a subtle sparkle when the mix is too dry. The effect level needs to be low enough to preserve transients and punch.

Although it can be tempting to reach for one, stereo width expanders are rarely used when mastering as they reduce the amount of punch at the centre of the mix.

Last in line is usually a **limiter**, used to give a final push of volume without distorting the signal. A good limiter can reduce peaks by several dBs while maintaining transparency.

When judging the quality of a mastering job, it is important to continually A/B between your original and the mastered version. It can be tempting to overdo the mastering process and mess up a perfectly good mix. Continual referencing back will remind you of the track's original strengths. When A/Bing ensure that the volume of both is the same. If not you're likely to favour the louder mastered version on the basis of volume alone.

/pro tips
loudness wars

Tracks have been getting progressively louder over the years to the point where some engineers believe music is being mastered overly loud. The problem with compressing music so hard is that while it might sound great for the first couple of minutes, aggressive limiting becomes fatiguing to listen to over an extended period.

Everyone wants their track to sound louder than the rest – especially in a club environment – but that shouldn't be at the expense of sound quality.

Overdoing compression or limiting suffocates the mix and leaves it sounding muddy and garbled. Spatial quality and depth also suffer, with reverb tails getting pushed awkwardly through gaps in the mix and more minor elements fighting to be heard.

Multi-band enhancement

Multi-band compression allows you to treat the bass, mid and treble regions of the frequency spectrum independently. The main objective is to capitalise on every available inch of headroom in the mix, but it can also be an invaluable tool when it come to rescuing a problem mix. Multi-band compression can improve transient detail in the mid or high range without compromising bass girth. This is especially useful when mastering vocal tracks that need a pumping bassline but not a pumping vocal.

There are many all-in-one mastering processors such as the Izotope Ozone (**right**). Alongside EQ and a limiter it has three stages of multi-band processing including dynamics, exciter and stereo imager. Although it gives you the power to radically alter a mix, it's important to exercise restraint when using it or you can end up with a final master where all three bands seem to operate independently, with no backbone holding the mix together.

What a mastering house wants

Even though there are a range of excellent plugins available at reasonable prices, mastering is one of the jobs that is often still best left to the pros. Not only will they have a great listening environment – allowing them to get a true feel for the mix – they will also have access to often prohibitively expensive high-end analogue kit and, most importantly, a pair of neutral and experienced ears that will be hearing your track for the first time rather than the five-hundredth.

The mastering engineer will do a better job when they have a 24-bit Wav or AIFF file with lots of headroom. It is good practise to make a pre-master without any compression or limiting on the master bus, although many producers mix using subtle compression on the bus to help gel their productions.

Whatever you do, leave at least 3–6dB of headroom and avoid normalising the file. Double check the mix for glitches and spills and listen carefully to the start and end of the track to ensure any reverb or delay tails are intact. Make a last examination of the waveform for signs of clipping. When you're happy, send the file to mastering.

If you can't attend the mastering session in person speak with the engineer and let them know what kind of result you are looking for. Send reference tracks so they can hear the kind of sound you're after. A good engineer will let you know if your mix has a problem that is best addressed back at the mix stage. In such cases take their advice and go back to tweak the mix.

Self mastering caution

However desirable it is to get a mastering engineer on the job, sometimes it's just not possible, especially if you've finished a song that you want to play out the same night.

If you take the DIY mastering route, don't rush the job. There is a point where you start to get diminishing returns by pushing the mix too hard. It's also common to overdo it when attempting to master a track after a long session as the ears are often already tired. For this reason always try to master tracks with fresh ears. Spending one more hour at this stage is well worth it: it is a shame to trash a mix you've spent weeks on with a few tired and rushed mastering decisions.

Cutting to vinyl

Mastering for vinyl requires a lot more skill and technical knowledge than for digital and should only be done by the pros. Cutting to vinyl can be problematic, with particular issues surrounding stereo imagery in the bass end and distortion caused by sibilant frequencies in the 5–10kHz range. After the master has been made, there is a lengthy process that involves metal plates being cut and the final copies getting pressed. Despite the extra work, a good vinyl master has an unmistakable quality that digital has yet to emulate and some die-hard vinyl producers have been known to master to vinyl and then re-record that for the digital release.

/how to find a mastering house

The best way to find a mastering engineer is word of mouth. If another producer you respect is getting great results with their mixes then it's a good chance the same engineer can work their magic on your mixes too.

The mastering room should offer excellent acoustics and equipment to help the engineer make judgements that are accurate and never left to chance.

Most engineers will let you know if the mix has a problem that cant be fixed at the mastering stage. In these cases, they will offer some feedback and advice about what to change to achieve a better master in the long run. Taking this one step further, it can be useful to take a laptop with the mix/arrangement running live to the session so that any final tweaks can be done in the mastering house as the mastering is being done. This is becoming more common and some engineers will even offer joint mixing/mastering services where you send them the track stems to allow them to tweak levels if necessary.

/walkthrough
mastering the mix

1 Import the pre-master. For best results ensure it has been bounced without compression or limiting. Set the channel fader to 0dB. Listen to the track and check the peak level to see how much headroom is available. Use gain reduction to take the volume down so there is 3–6dB of headroom from the highest peak.

2 Check each part of the signal through an analyser. A volume meter allows you to see how the mix is affected by each process. The peak value shows the highest volume level, while the RMS level represents the average. The aim of mastering is to bring the peak up to 0dB and increase the RMS as well.

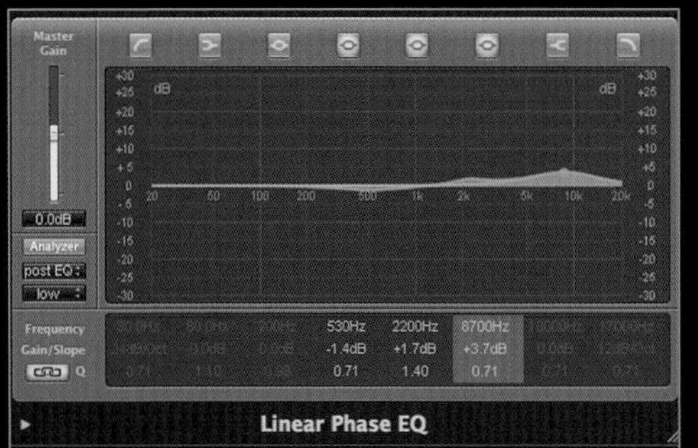

3 For most jobs a broad three-band EQ with high/low pass filters is fine. Tracks often benefit from gentle brightening in the 5–10kHz area to increase definition and clarity. If the 500Hz–3.5kHz mid-range needs attention tread softly, with no more than 2–3dBs cut or boost. Overdoing it can leave the mix sounding hollow or overly harsh.

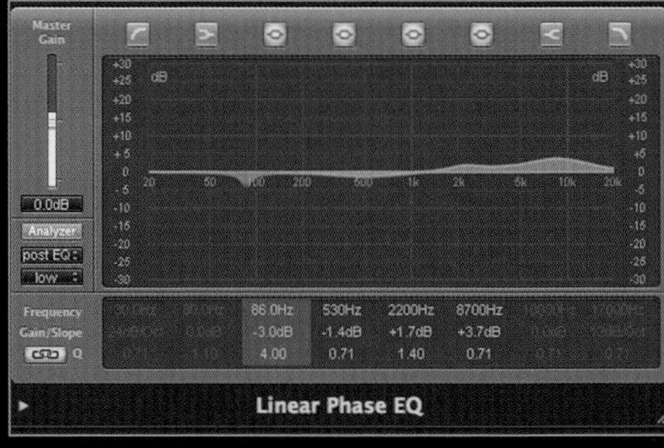

4 If there is muddiness in the kick and bass area perform a gentle cut using parametric EQ somewhere between 70Hz–110Hz. Then make a small boost where the bulk of the bassline energy is centred. You shouldn't need to use more than 2–3dBs. The exact frequency range will depend on the sounds used and the key of the track.

5 Open a compressor. This will help bring out the details in the mix and add punch. By lowering the threshold and increasing the ratio the background sounds will become easier to hear. Remember there's a point where too many sounds are brought to the fore at the expense of depth and space in the mix.

6 Brick-wall limiting is next, to prevent the volume from clipping. Lowering the threshold will increase the amount of effect and the volume of the track. The limiting process can be heard working even before any signs of gain reduction show in the meter. 2-4dBs of peak reduction should be enough to tighten up the mix.

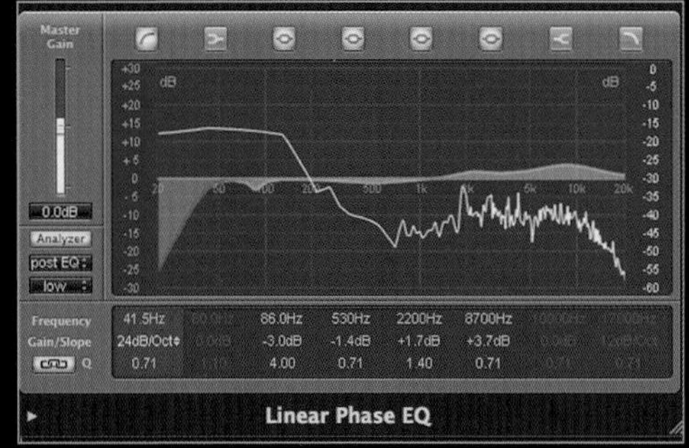

7 You can get an extra ounce of loudness if you're willing to sacrifice some sub bass. Use a 12 or 18dB/oct high-pass filter on the EQ. Start at 30Hz and work up slowly, keeping an ear open for any sudden drops in bass energy. Some engineers cut as high as 50–60Hz. The highest you can go will depend on the key of the track.

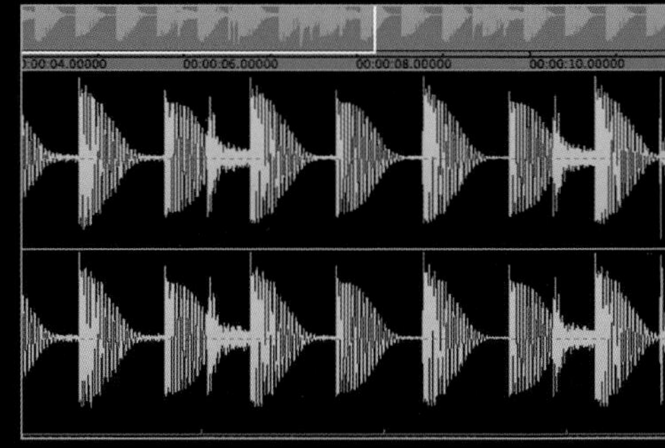

8 Bounce the mastered mix and open it in an editor. Note how the waveform is denser and the highest peaks are all squared off. Setting the output limit to -0.1dB means no peak should rise above that. The process has brought the track to maximum volume so there's no need to normalise it. Now it's time to see if it cuts it on the dancefloor.

/walkthrough edits to the master

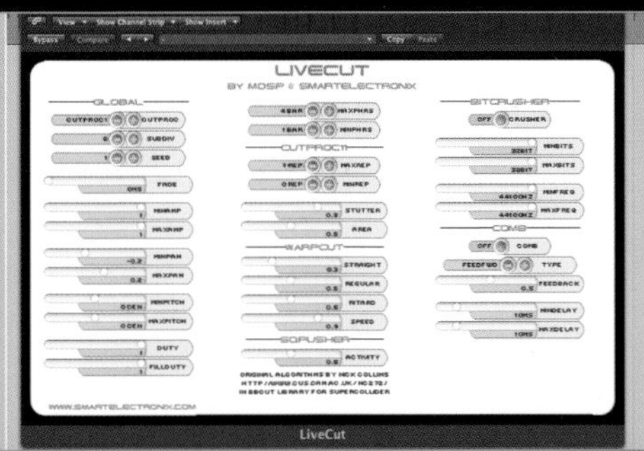

1 Once the master is done you can add edits and effects to take the track to the next level. Start by importing the stereo file into a new arrangement. Set the correct bpm so it's easier to chop chunks accurately to the beat and bar. We are going to run the whole track through an assortment of plugins to generate fills and edits.

2 Add a plugin such as MDSP's Livecut, dblue Glitch or Audio Damage's Replicant/Automaton as an insert and tweak the effect so that it produces a good balance between tight beat-synced choppiness and random chaos. Bounce the whole track, re-import it into the arrangement and place it on a new track.

3 Listen through the new bounce and chop out the most interesting parts to use as fills. If the tracks line up perfectly it will be easy to chop and mute sections from the original and replace them with the glitchy edits from the new bounce.

4 Another trick to spice up a fill is to create a sonic contrast between it and the main track. Find a fill section that needs some extra sonic candy, chop it out and stick it on a new channel. Add a filter or EQ and experiment by cutting the bass or using a beat-synced LFO to sweep it up or down in time.

/walkthrough the pre-drop fade

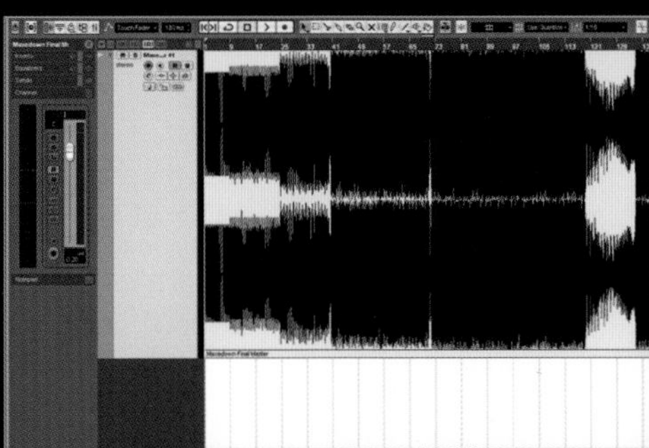

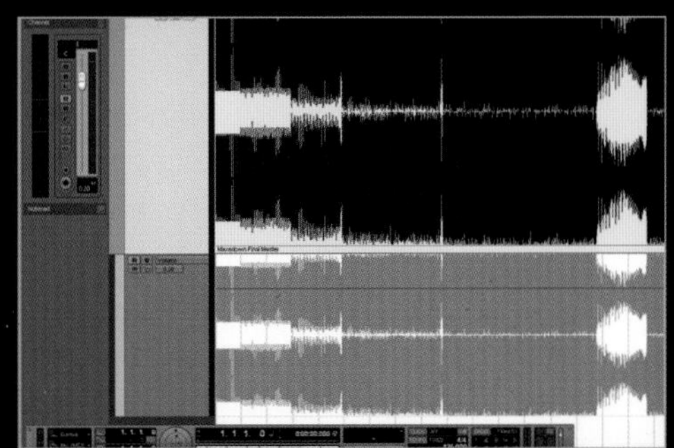

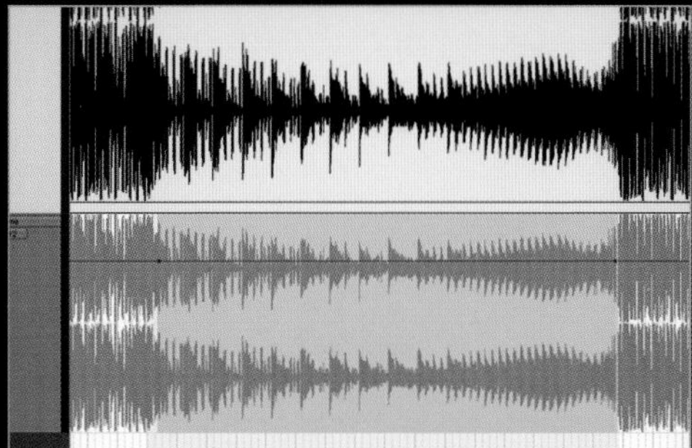

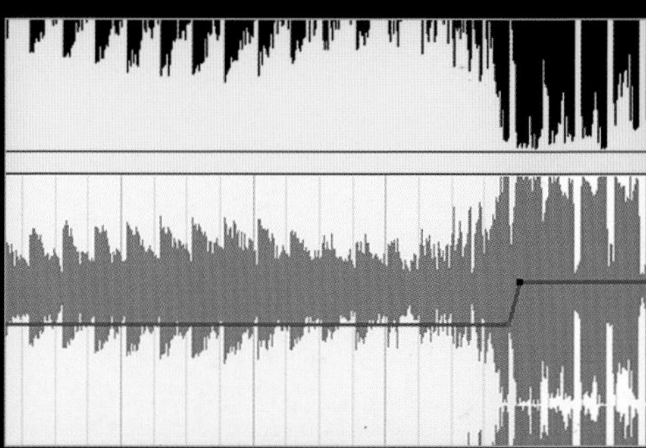

1 Good mastering makes everything louder. Because of this, the breakdown can get pumped up so that the drop doesn't have the impact it needs when it kicks back in. Fix this by introducing volume changes on the stereo master using automation. Firstly import the stereo mixdown into the arrangement page. Match the tempo to the track.

2 Open the automation track and select the volume parameter from the menu. Set it to unity gain or 0dB.

3 Locate the start of the breakdown and draw in an automation point at 0dB. This will anchor the volume at its peak. Draw in another 0dB point at the end of the break where the track drops back in.

4 Now the tricky bit: you need to get to a position where the volume immediately before the drop is between 2–4dBs lower than 0dB. But you need to do it so subtly that there is no obvious decrease in volume. That means programming the change over the full breakdown. As the drop hits, the volume should quickly return to 0dB again.

/remixing

when you're approached to remix someone else's track where should you start?

The remix has its roots in Jamaica. In the late 1960s producers like Lee Perry and King Tubby started releasing 'dub mixes' of tracks to occupy a single's B-side. These mixes would be different versions of the same song, featuring a heavy use of effects like spring reverb, tape delay and flange to get the characteristic 'dub mix'. As the tradition grew, parts were re-arranged to construct totally new takes of the original track. Nearly five decades on and remixing plays a major, and increasingly lucrative part, in the music business, with artists from Kylie through Britney to Moby all seeking the services of high-profile house remixers

Remixing allows you to change the style and feel of a track by re-arranging it, re-programming parts and adding additional elements. Although the remixer has a foundation of existing material to build on, there are no restraints on the direction you take it in: it's your chance to give a unique spin to a mix, introducing your own characteristic style to someone else's production.

There's one thing a remix isn't. It is not your chance to re-produce a track, keeping all the elements as they are but making a more professional sounding mix (in your opinion): the remix must, at least, be about change.

Take inspiration

Before you start the remix, get to know the original track. Listen out for the chief elements: particular sounds that inspire, the groove, the melody, the bassline and the flow of the arrangement. All of these can spark ideas and send you in specific remix directions. Make a note of the sounds you want to use then hunt them down from the stems.

Most of the time there will be an obvious hook, riff or sound that will carry the remix, but you could go the opposite way and use one of the more obscure sounds to build on. Try to combine this in a new way with one or two of the other elements to make it the centre point of the remix.

If you are musically inclined, make a note of the chord progression. This will make it easier to experiment with the tuning of new samples and loops.

Remix work can originate from all musical genres. You may be asked to remix a chillout track or a pop song. In such cases you will need to alter the stems so that they are at a different tempo or pitch. Using the best time-stretch algorithms you have at your disposal is important here. Remember that different settings are optimised for different types of material, like vocals and rhythmic parts. That's not to say you need to stick with the 'right' settings: abusing them by treating vocal parts with a drum time-stretch algorithm, for example, can yield interesting new effects.

Tip / Don't be shy of returning to the artist whose work you are remixing to ask for additional elements, like Midi files and original dry parts that have been sent to you effected (you might ask for the pre-vocoded vocal line, for example, so you can do your own thing with it).

Tip / Use your personal sample library to bring your signature sound to a remix.

Tip / There is a difference between a remix and a re-edit. A re-edit is not about changing the sounds, but the arrangement. You might, for example, extend a breakdown or add a 16-bar section to change the pace of a track. DJs frequently re-edit tracks so that they are easier to mix with. This frequently involves changing the lengths of sections such as the intro or outro.

Tip / Always bear in mind the function of a remix: to give a different spin to a mix and open a track to a different buying audience.

/pro tips
what you need

To prepare one of your own tracks for the remix treatment you need to create **stems** to give to the remixer. Stems are made by bouncing down the various tracks from the original mix into mono or stereo audio files, usually Wav or Aiff files. The stems should be bounced from the same starting point, usually the first beat of the track. The idea is that when the remixer receives them, they can import the stems into any DAW and lay out all tracks from the start.

Organise tracks into the main groups such as drums, percussion, lead, pads, bass and FX. If the track is simple there will probably only be around 8–12 tracks to bounce, but if it has loads of layers you will need to decide which sounds to separate onto their own stems and which to group together when bouncing. If the hook has several layers bounce them to one stem to preserve the relationship between them. Likewise with vocal arrangements: try to keep them on one track, or split between lead and backing.

It's up to you whether or not to bounce stems with automation, or if effects such as reverb and delay should be included with the parts. Generally, bouncing with effects helps to keep the original flavour, while leaving them out gives the remixer more creative freedom to take sounds in different directions. A good rule of thumb is to bounce parts down with any trademark effects if they define a track. If in doubt, bounce one wet and one dry version.

Kick-starting a remix: Four approaches

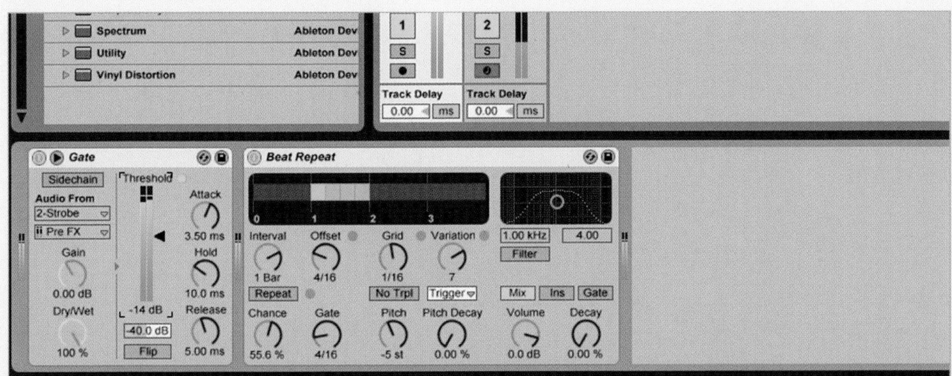

1: THE DRUM RE-GROOVE: If the track you're remixing revolves around a groove, use the rhythm stems as a starting point. Most producers use their own signature drum sounds for remixes, but there's nothing to stop you mashing up the original beat for background loops and fills. Import three or four drum parts into the DAW. Add beat-synced autofilters, beat repeaters and glitch plugins on different tracks to build new hooks from the original drum loops. If the new groove is messy insert a noise gate on the channel and trigger it using a new Midi pattern. This will chop up the beat and introduce space in which to build a new groove.

2: NEW VOCAL HOOKS: Chop up the vocal stems into individual words and re-trigger each word using a different sampler note or pad. This makes it easy to re-order the words and alter the tuning of the line to make whole new vocal hooks. Experiment with each sample's amp envelope parameters, especially the release. Add Midi effects like arpeggiators and randomisers to the pattern for instant inspiration. Use audio effects such as beat repeaters or Replicant to make crazy random stutters. Check out the **Minimal vocal walkthrough** on page 68 to see how to use a sampler to create new glitched vocals.

3: SWITCH OUT THE SYNTHS: If the track is based around a strong synth hook, try copying the pattern and replaying it using a new synth sound, preferably one of your own signature tones. If you need help working out the notes in a riff use a tuner plugin or Audio-to-Midi note convertor such as intelliscore, WIDI or Melodyne. There's plenty of room to build around the hook using elements from the original such as other synth layers, special FX and vocals. Change the drum sounds, especially the kick and snare, but make them play the same pattern as the original to keep some of the track's original feel.

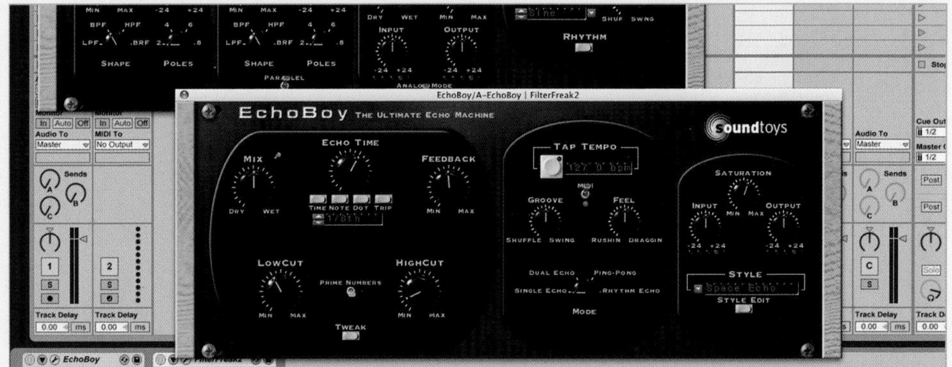

4: DUB IT OUT: For the classic dub remix build a groove using some of the original percussion elements and a new kick. On the aux busses, set up two reverbs (one short, one long) plus a nice tape echo/delay with plenty of filtered feedback. Choose a groove-laden lead from the original and filter it in and out hypnotically. Experiment with different reverbs, adding EQ, distortion, and sidechain compression to produce contrasting textures to feed the sounds through. Set up a Midi controller to control the effects live and record automation changes into the arrangement. Cut up these live automation tweaks and use the best in the remix arrangement.

/part eight

outro

We hope you've found this book useful. We've offered a range of insights into a wide range of genres.

We've heard from some of the producers who have conquered the house world.

And we've torn apart effects units, arrangements and synths to show how they do their job.

There are other books out there. Some go into scientific detail about effects; others are bibles of knowledge on music theory; others again dissect the dark art of lyric writing. There are many useful forums online, zounds of tutorial videos made by passionate producers and a world of blogs to help you take your music to the next level.

Loops is what we've done at Sample Magic for three years, winning awards along the way and growing a brand that is relied on and trusted worldwide. We've included hundreds of our best sounds for you on the bonus CD to use and abuse in the songs we hope this book inspires.

All that's left, aside from the boring (but occasionally useful) index is a short essay from our very own Sharooz.

This book was never about business, or about making cash from music. Maybe we'll cover that in a future title. The cash is important. But not as important as creating great tracks.

Have fun doing it.

/...a word on the biz

beatport chart regular, label owner, dj and sample magic co-founder sharooz offers a few tips on how to make money from your music.

Successful producers are often a mix of musician, publicist, marketing guru and manager – but you'll need all of these skills if you're serious about selling your music.

Rule 1: Remember you're a business

As obvious as it might sound, many of us forget that we are in fact self-contained businesses. Over the course of the past ten years the music business has shrunk from a huge money-spinning machine to something of a cottage industry, and many of today's talents have risen to the top through their own marketing efforts. It's also worth remembering that most of the industry's longest surviving stars have always maintained a firm grip on their own business affairs. Of course it's always more fun to spend time in the studio, but it does no harm to study the mechanisms which the industry runs on.

Do your research – read up on contracts, deal points, advances, publishing and so on. At the very least you'll be less likely to fall foul of a dodgy deal. Being proactive with your own marketing and promotion does no harm either – it's unlikely you'll be discovered if all you do is sit in your studio and wait for the big guns to come calling.

Keep your fingers in as many pies as possible

In today's climate it's getting increasingly difficult to make a living from 'record' sales alone. Remember that there are many other ways to maximise your income. Music publishing is a thriving industry, so start cataloguing your radio plays and public performance income and register with a performing rights society.

Look at alternative ways in which you can exploit your tracks. Get internet radio play, sell music to advertising agencies, write for video games and TV, create samples for sample packs. These are all good revenue streams which open new opportunities.

If you produce dance music, look for DJ or live performance options, perhaps at your own club nights, and look for compilation licensing opportunities (getting your tracks on commercially available mixes). All of this will keep you ticking over while you wait for that elusive hit.

Negotiation is key

If your music, production and marketing are all strong enough then chances are you'll soon attract the attentions of a record label. But what do you do when the contracts start arriving in your inbox?

First up, examine them until you can examine them no more. Then pass them onto someone with a keen legal eye. There are plenty of music law firms that specialise in helping newbies, and many that also offer a 'first half hour for free' consultation or similar – just call one and ask. In the UK the Musician's Union (www.musiciansunion.org.uk) offers a free contract consultancy service where specialist lawyers look over your contract and give you feedback on it.

Don't be scared to negotiate advances and royalty percentages upwards. Many record labels will have both an opening gambit and closing figure in mind when they approach you and usually a compromise will be reached somewhere in between.

At the same time keep a lid on outgoings. Keep all of your receipts for tax reasons – you can offset many legitimate business costs against your income. Also barter down the prices of services you buy in (mastering costs, studio hire, web design, etc), never forgetting that many of the companies or individuals you'll be dealing with are independent self-employed businesses just like yours.

Keep your costs down – maximise your profits

Once the money starts rolling in, what do you do with it? There's no sense in buying yourself a new car with your first royalty cheque. The music business is not geared towards long-term prosperity and there is no guarantee that just because you've had one success more will follow. That's why it pays to invest your money wisely and closely scrutinise every purchase you make. Also remember you'll need to pay tax on your earnings, so keep records of all your income.

Of course, we all want to enjoy the fruits of our labour – who doesn't? – but investing back into your business in the early days will lead to a brighter future. There's a good reason why big blue chip companies hold their cost cutters and finance heads in such regard.

Keep abreast of the now

If you're making music to earn cash then – for better or worse – you'll need to keep an eye on what is selling in the marketplace. If your product (that is, your music) sounds stagnant and dated, consumers, and label bosses who need to make a living too, won't queue to snap it up.

The industry is constantly evolving so ensure you're on top of what's current: read magazines and blogs, browse MySpace, Tweet, listen to radio stations, go clubbing and buy music regularly. This doesn't mean you have to sound like everyone else or keep up with the zeitgeist just for the sake of it – there's nothing worse than an artist who is constantly trying to keep up with cool – but keeping abreast of current trends will ensure that you don't get ignored, or left behind, by the masses when the scene moves on.

...and five day-to-day rules that will help lead to success...

1 **Don't be afraid to keep a part-time job.** You're not giving up on your dream or selling out to the 9–5 – you're just making it easier to facilitate your career by bringing in some income to pay the bills or buy new equipment.

2 **Stay grounded.** If fame and fortune does come thick and fast keep your feet on the ground. Everyone prefers to work with a nice guy. There's an old maxim that says: "All the people you meet on the way up you'll meet on the way back down". There's never been a truer word spoken. Leave your ego at the door and have a positive, friendy attitude and you'll never be short of people to work with.

3 **Don't fool yourself.** When making new tracks seek the opinions of others as often as you can. Form a circle of the 'trusted few' – friends and fellow producers who you think are qualified to comment on your music and who you can rely on for feedback when you need it. Online forums can be great for this, with supportive producers in the same boat willing to offer feedback. Listen to their advice: it's always hard to take criticism, but if you're your only fan you'll be your only buyer.

4 **Keep supply up.** In the old days, when music publishers signed musicians off the back of an impromptu on-the-spot audition (this actually did used to happen!), they would commission their new investment to write a certain number of songs each week. Not all of these songs were released of course, they just wanted to make sure that there was plenty of practise going into landing that golden egg of a best-seller. As a producer making tracks as often as you can means you'll be continually improving your writing and production skills, maximising your chances of making the ideal track.

5 **Stay motivated.** It's hard to stay focused at times and incredibly easy to lose your way. When you're working on a track learn to shut out external factors. This is not as easy as it sounds, of course – we all have personal lives and commitments – but studio sessions are rarely productive if all your time is spent thinking about things other than music. If you're getting distracted turn off the mobile and close down email. Write down your goals and your motivations and keep them close. When you're flagging and wondering why the hell you're wasting all your time in a windowless studio, look at the list of motivations and take strength from them.

Sharooz is a DJ/producer with a string of releases and remixes under his belt. He has worked with acts such as Moby, Robyn, Mylo, Kings of Leon, Craig David and Howard Jones, and released on leading dance labels such as Dim Mak and Sunday Best. His DJ schedule has taken him all over world. Sharooz is also co-founder of Sounds To Sample and the record label La Bombe.

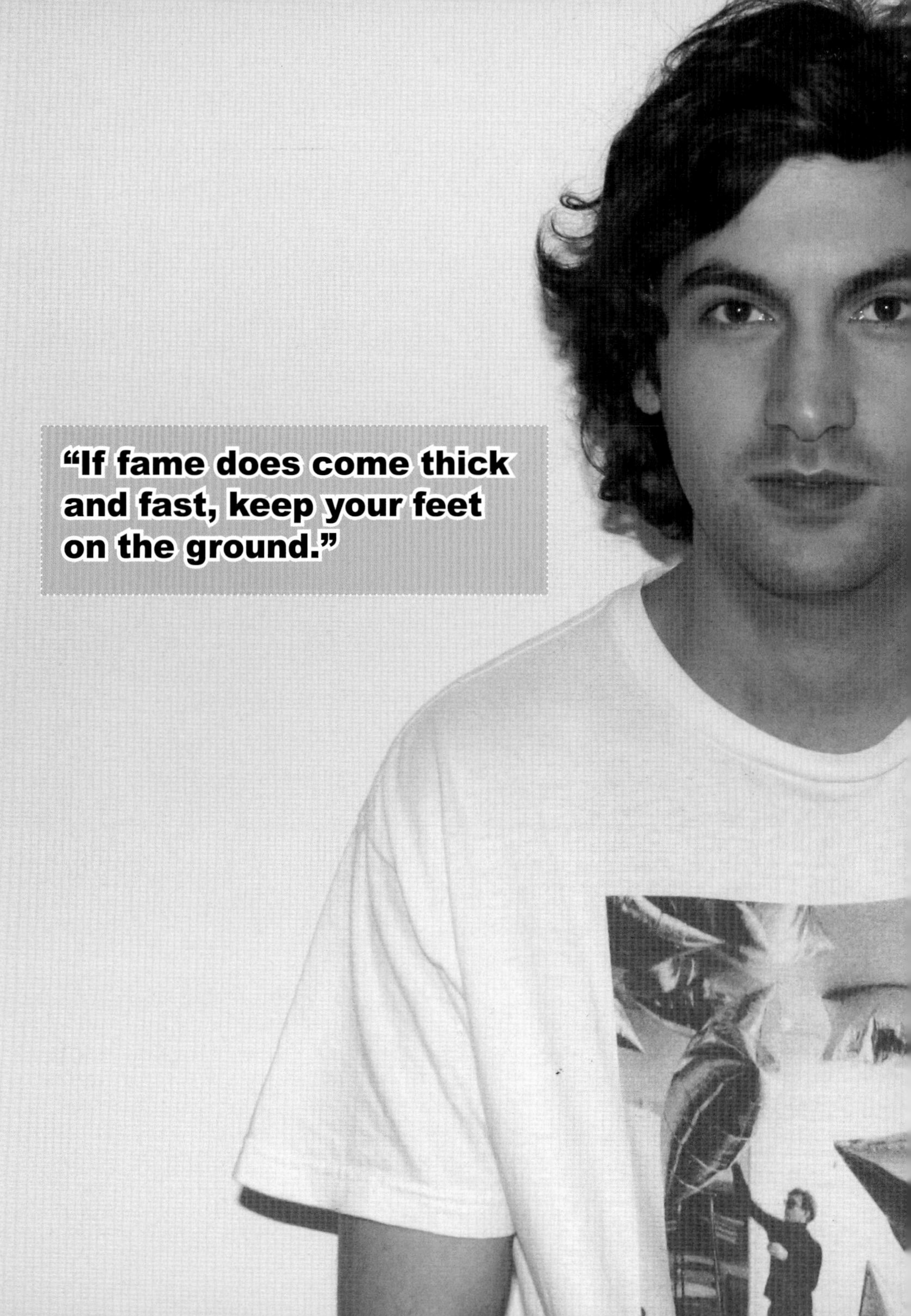

"If fame does come thick and fast, keep your feet on the ground."

/index

Ableton Live 15, 24, 26, 37, 40–43, 80, 89
Acid 86
Akai MPC60 19, 24
amp simulators see overdrive
Apple Loops / AIFFs 86, 90–91
Apple Loops Utility 90–91
arps (arpeggios) 80
arrangement see structure
automation 20, 63, 66, 67, 69, 70, 85, 94, 96, 101, 126, 135
auto-panner 118
Auto-Tune 56, 58, 67, 117
aux see bus

bass 32–45
compression 36, 38, 40, 41, 45, 111
effects 39
EQ 36, 39, 41, 43, 45, 124
overdrive 44
programming ideas 40–45
sub bass 32, 38–39, 76, 117
Battery 13, 18, 25
bit-crusher 19, 22, 44, 64, 66, 70, 71, 79, 113
breakdown 92, 100–107
breaths (vocal) 66, 67
build 199
bus (mixing) 65, 110, 114
business 140–141

chorus (effect) 39, 85, 94, 116
chorus (vocal) 55, 56, 58, 60, 64, 65, 66, 106–107
claps – see snares and claps
comping 54, 56, 57
compression 110–111
bass 36, 40, 41, 43, 45
kick drum 12
mastering 133, 134
multiband 62, 66, 111, 30
parallel 36, 111
recording 54
Rhodes 85
sidechaining 30, 36–37, 42, 111, 123
snares and claps 14
sub bass 38
vocals 62, 63, 65, 66, 70
crash cymbal 21, 94
Cubase 15, 37, 56

de-esser 19, 63, 64, 112
deep house 25, 34
delay 19, 63, 64, 65, 79, 85, 94, 95, 97, 115
disco 18, 21, 25, 34, 35
distortion see overdrive
DJ 100, 101
double tracking 55
Dr:Rex 27
drop 25, 92, 100–107
dynamics 123

echo see delay
effects (processors) 108–119
effects (SFX) 92–97
bomb 93
crash swell 95
dub siren 97
downshifter 94
elevator 96
full mix FX 97
minimal verb build 97
sweep 93
vocal FX 67–71
white noise crash 94
electro-house 22, 25, 29, 34, 35, 39, 43 , 70, 81, 100, 102–103, 112
ensemble 39, 63, 85, 116
EQ (equalisation) 110
bass 36, 39, 41, 43, 45
FX 71
hi-hats 19, 20
kick drum 12
mastering 132, 134
mixing 123–127
sub bass 38
synths 79
vocals 62, 63, 64, 65, 69
envelope 76
exciter 117
EXS24 18, 87

fidget see electro-house
fills 100, 101
filter (resonant) 77, 110
flanger 39, 94, 116
Flex (Logic) 87
FM synthesis 22, 23
funky house 18, 29, 34, 45, 84, 106–107

guitar 124
groove see swing
groove templates 24, 25, 26, 27, 89
Guru 18, 24

harmonies 57, 61
headphones 54, 127
headroom 38, 122–123, 130–131
hi-hats 18–20, 116–117
EQ 19, 20, 124
mute groups 18
shaping 19
white noise hats 20
high-pass filters see EQ
hook 46
humanising 85
insert 114
intro 101
inversions 82, 84

key tracking 77
keys (piano / Rhodes) 78, 84–85, 124
kick drum 10–13, 30, 124
Roland 909 kick 12
analogue kicks 11
compression 12, 111
EQ 12
layered kicks 13

layering sounds
kick drum 13
snares and claps 17
Lazer FX 23
LFO 77
limiter 66, 79, 93, 112, 132, 136
Linn Drum 15
lead sounds 30, 80–81, 111, 124, 137
Logic 18, 25, 26, 37, 39, 56, 68, 69, 70, 71
loops 21, 86, 100
low-pass filters see EQ
lyrics 51, 53, 55

master bus see mix bus
mastering 30, 46, 72, 132–135
major chords 78, 80, 84
Melodyne 53, 58–61
microphone 53, 54, 55
minimal house 18, 20, 21, 22, 29, 40, 67, 96, 100, 104–105
MiniMoog 35
minor chords 78, 80, 84
Midi 18, 21, 136
drum patterns 20, 28–29
sequencing 24

programming 25
mix bus 72, 111, 127
mixing 101, 120–131
monitoring 30, 38, 39, 46, 126–127
multi-band compression 30, 63, 132
mute groups 18
music business 138–139

New York compression see parallel compression
note-to-frequency chart 127
noise gate 82, 83, 112
nu-rave see electro-house

oscillator 76
outro / playout 100, 101
overdrive 38, 44, 64, 66, 67, 71, 113

Q see EQ

pads 82–83, 112, 124
panning 19, 60, 65, 66, 94, 122–124
parallel compression see compression
percussion 21, 124
bongo 21
claves 21
conga 21
loops 89
programming 23, 25
synthetic percussion 23–22
tom 21
phase cancellation 39
phaser 116
pitch correction 56, 117
pitch shifter 117
portamento 40, 77, 81
pre-delay see reverb
programming
arpeggios 80
basslines 40–45
drums 24–25, 28–29
lead synths 81
pads / gated pads 82
percussion 25
rave piano 78
soulful Rhodes 84–85
stabs 78
vocoder 69
progressive house 28, 34, 79, 81, 83, 100

quantise 24

reverb 114–115
convolution 114, 116
gated reverb 16
percussion 22
mastering 130
mixing 126
reverse reverb FX 71
SFX 93, 94, 96
snare drum 15, 115
vocals 63, 64, 65, 66, 115
Reason 24, 27
ReCycle 86, 88
remixing 136–137
Rex / Rex2 loops 86, 88
Rhodes 84
ride cymbal 21
ring modulation 22, 67, 118
Roland TB-303 35
Roland TR-808 15, 22, 24
Roland TR-909 12, 15, 22, 24
root (of chord) 80

saturation see overdrve
shuffle see swing
snares and claps 14–17
analogue snare 14
compression 14
EQ 15, 124
gated reverb 16
reverb 15, 115
stereo width 15
sibilance 66, 112
sidechain compression
see compresion
song-writing 51
song-share agreement 53
soulful house 84
speakers 30, 38, 39
step sequencing 24
stereo imagery 124
stereo widener 39, 65, 119
structure 51, 72, 98–107
studio (using a) 52, 53
sub bass see bass
swing 24, 26, 27, 28–29, 89
synth architecture 76–77, 92

talk box 67
tech-house 18, 28, 79, 81, 100, 104–105
time-stretching 86
tremolo 118
triplets 24, 25
transient shaper 11, 19
kick drum 12

Ultrabeat 11, 24, 67

vinyl 39, 133
vocals 48–71
adlibs 66
automation 63, 64, 66, 67, 69
compression 62, 65, 66, 70, 111
de-esser 112
delay 64, 65
EQ 62, 65, 124
FX 67–71
lead vocal 63
noise gate 112
remixing 137
reverb 63, 64, 65, 66, 115
stereo widener 65
structure 106–107
vocal transformer 70
vocoder 67, 69, 118

walk the dog 51
Wav loops see loops
white noise 20, 22, 95, 96